ARTWORKS

for Elementary Teachers

Developing Artistic and Perceptual Awareness

Eighth Edition

Donald Herberholz, Professor Emeritus
California State University, Sacramento

Barbara Herberholz
Art Consultant

Boston, Massachusetts Burr Ridge, Illinois Dubuque, Iowa
Madison, Wisconsin New York, New York San Francisco, California
St. Louis, Missouri

McGraw-Hill

*A Division of The **McGraw·Hill** Companies*

ARTWORKS FOR ELEMENTARY TEACHERS

 This book is printed on recycled paper containing 10% postconsumer waste.

1 2 3 4 5 6 7 8 9 0 QPD/QPD 9 0 9 8

ISBN 0–697–34424–X

Editorial Director: Phil Butcher
Sponsoring Editor: Cynthia Ward
Marketing Manager: Margaret Metz
Project Manager: Marilyn Rothenberger
Production Supervisor: Sandy Hahn
Designer: Kay Fulton Design
Cover art by Megan Grasty
Photo research coordinator: John Leland
Art Editor: Brenda Ernzen
Compositor: Shepherd, Inc.
Typeface: Times Roman
Printer: Quebecor, Dubuque

Library of Congress Cataloging-in-Publication Data

Herberholz, Donald W.
    Artworks for elementary teachers: developing artistic and
perceptual awareness / Donald Herberholz, Barbara Herberholz.
    –8th ed.
        p.   cm.
    Includes bibliographical references and index.
    ISBN 0–697–34424–X
    1. Art—Study and teaching (Elementary)   I. Herberholz, Barbara.
II. Title.
N350.H47   1997
372.5'044–dc21   97–15266
                                               CIP

www.mhhe.com

R Brucker
2/99

Contents

4
Understanding the Principles of Art:
Response and Production   72

Part III
Responding to Art   102

5
Art Criticism, Art History, and Aesthetics   102

Color Galleries

Introduction

Artworks for Elementary Teachers is a text for a one-semester college or university course for nonart majors who plan to teach art to children. It provides future classroom teachers with introductory experiences in both knowing how to create and respond to art. The focus is on those skills deemed most likely to be meaningful in developing students' understanding and production of artworks. In *The Schools We Need,* E. D. Hirsch proposed that an individual cannot teach children without teaching content, and that one cannot teach skills without the information—"the intellectual capital"—that gives the skills substance.[1] We believe that experiences described in this text will enable students to understand art through interaction, and through both response and production strategies.

Art in the elementary classroom is comprised of four areas of study:

1. **Aesthetics,** as it pertains to perception and the nature and meaning of art
2. **Art production,** in which students work with various art media to express their thoughts, feelings, and perceptions in creative ways
3. **Art criticism,** as students practice looking at artworks and putting into words their own descriptions, analyses, interpretations, and judgments
4. **Art history,** in which students develop an understanding of the importance of art throughout the ages and in diverse cultures

Text discussions usually focus on one of these areas at a time; however, it is through their integration that students reach a full understanding of art.

The four areas of art study are explained in *Quality Art Education, Goals for Schools: An Interpretation,* a booklet published by the National Art Education Association.[2]

Many state curriculum guides and frameworks for art have defined the content of art in similar ways. This agreement is also reflected at the local level in many counties and individual school districts throughout the United States. Both a special issue of the *Journal of Aesthetic Education,* entitled "Discipline-Based Art Education,"[3] and Elliot W. Eisner, in *The Role of Discipline-Based Art Education in America's Schools,*[4] also identify and define these same areas of study for art education.

To address the four areas of art study in a practical and concise manner, the text is divided into three parts:

Part I provides students with opportunities to investigate **how artists work,** what has inspired them, and how society views them. It also provides information on **how the elementary child grows artistically** and what types of experiences are helpful in maximizing each child's artistic potential.

Part II focuses on the **visual language of art—the elements and principles of art.** These chapters enable students to become fluent in the terminology and concepts related to the vocabulary of art that will help them both in responding to art and in producing it themselves. This language links visual literacy and verbal vocabulary, making it possible to delve into the mystery often associated with understanding the world of art so that students can enjoy its "magic." In these two chapters, students explore—through reading, looking, discussing, and producing art—the elements of art (color, value, line, shape/form, texture, and space) and how they combine to create the principles of art (balance, emphasis, proportion, movement, pattern, variety, and unity). These elements and principles of art are used in drawing, painting, printmaking, crafts, architecture, and graphic design to express ideas visually. Art reproductions in these chapters have brief descriptive notations that will help students in their understanding of each element and principle of art. A brief section after each art element relates ways in which children are capable of dealing with that element when they produce art.

The art production activities described in Part II are not designed to turn students into "instant artists." Rather, students (1) are introduced to ways of perceiving the world visually, (2) begin developing skills in using materials, (3) become actively aware of their choices in using the elements and principles of art, and (4) are motivated to express visually, with some measure of confidence, their own ideas and feelings with paint, paper, clay, and other art media.

Part III is devoted to **how we can respond to art.** Chapter 5 explores **aesthetics** and **response strategies in relation to art criticism and art history.** Aesthetics is a branch of philosophy that deals with the nature of art. As such, it asks questions that cause us to ponder and question art's meanings and purposes. Students initially tend to feel inadequate with regard to art criticism because "criticism" in many peoples' minds is usually associated with saying something negative or "bad." In contemporary art education, art criticism involves understanding an artwork through describing, analyzing, and interpreting it—that is, putting into words what we see and feel about it. When art criticism strategies are interwoven with art history, we also learn when, where, how, and why an artist in a specific culture created a particular artwork. After exposure to both art criticism and art history, students frequently evaluate what they initially considered esoteric or even repugnant artworks differently. Such thought processes also help students become more competent in evaluating their own artwork, as well as the artwork of elementary children.

Chapter 6 is a chronological or sequential **summary of the history of world art.** Students should use it as a reference—to learn where, when and in which historical context different artists lived so as to better understand their special or specific contributions. This information should help students understand some of the important developments and connecting links in global art. While more in-depth information about art periods, diverse cultures, and specific artists can be found in libraries, media centers, museums, and on the Internet, the condensed format of Chapter 6 gives students a starting point. Artists' birth and death dates are provided, as is a pronunciation guide for artists' names. Instructors may choose to use reproductions, slides, or tours of art museums (actual or virtual, via the Internet) to expand on aspects of this narrative time line. Students who develop an inquisitive attitude about art history will likely convey the excitement and joy of learning about art to their future elementary students.

When we reflect on what is best remembered as the highest attainments and achievements of each world

culture, we usually begin by referring to that culture's art. Students would do well to speculate on what future generations will remember of today's civilization.

The **Color Gallery** contains a variety of artworks to which students can refer to perceive visual information regarding an element or principle of art or perhaps, to seek works that represent one of the major styles of art (realism, abstraction, expressionism, and surrealism.) This eighth edition introduces a small collection of drawings and paintings by boys and girls in the **Children's Color Gallery.** These works represent different age groups, a variety of media, and numerous expressive ideas.

Students' participation and involvement in the Interactive Extensions at the end of each chapter will increase their understanding of text concepts. Finally, Resources for Art Education at the end of the book lists packaged art programs, catalogs, sources for reproductions, and children's books about art that will enable students to begin developing their own collections for classroom use.

ACKNOWLEDGMENTS

Suzanne Adan, Armando Alvarez, Phillip C. Dunn, Robert Else, Phil Evans, Emanuel Gale, Maureen Gilli, Mallory Grasty, Megan Grasty, Alec Herberholz, Daniel Herberholz, Maru Hoeber, Jorjana Holden, Oliver Lee Jackson, Michaela Le Compte, Frank La Pena, Judith Lowry, Harry and Severina Marsh, Jose Montoya, Malaquias Montoya, Ann Dobson Palmer, Lisa Reinertson, Ruth Rippon, Victoria Rivers, Emily Scherschligt, Stephanie Taylor, Yoshio Taylor, Wayne Thiebaud, Beth Tronbig, Roger Vail, Peter Vandenberge, Gerald Walburg, Susan Willoughby, Maria Winkler, and the students and teachers of Sacramento Country Day School.

LIST OF REVIEWERS

John M. Hicks
Drake University

David McCormick
Southeastern Community College

Randolph B. Miley
Northeast Louisiana University

Kristen Rauch
State University of New York (SUNY) at New Paltz

Bernard Schwartz
University of Alberta

Jean Sommer
Cleveland State University

Chapter

1

....

Artists and the Images They Make: Artworks in Diverse Cultures and Times

Art objects from every culture—both past and present—are artifacts that tell us of the society and individuals that produced them. An understanding of why these artworks were created leads to a better understanding of ourselves. These objects had their foundations in the thoughts, feelings, and ideas of a society or in an individual's beliefs, perceptions, priorities, values, customs, religion, tragedies, and triumphs.

Our view of art throughout the world must consider art's diverse functions—the purposes it has served and continues to serve in different cultures and in other times and places. Can you find examples of artworks in your community that were created for each of the following purposes?

1. **Art serves society.**

1 • Art tells **stories** about events in history, myths, religion, and literature.

2 Art may **convince, inform, inspire, criticize, persuade,** or **move people to action** in relation to **religious, political, national,** or **social** causes.

3 • Art objects are often used in **rituals,** and ceremonies that ask for protection and help in controlling natural forces.

4 • Art often serves as a **memorial** or **tribute** to honor a special person, place, or event. Vietnam Wall

2. **Art records images and expresses an artist's feelings and imagination.**

1 • Art has, over the years, shown us how people, places, and objects **have looked.**

Figure 1.1   Gerald Walburg, *Indo Arch,* 1977–79. Cor-Ten steel, 40 × 40 × 15 ft.
Courtesy of the City of Sacramento, CA.
Commissioned by the city of Sacramento, California, this installation serves as a landmark, connecting Old Sacramento with the newer town center.

2 • Art expresses the **way artists feel** about people, the land, nature, cities, the sea, and so on.

3 • Art expresses an **individual's creativity** and communicates an artist's innovative representation of an idea.

4 • Art can show us an artist's **dreams, fantasies,** and rich **imagination.**

1

Figure 1.2   Armando Alvarez, detail of *We the People*, 1994. Steel sculpture in Gallup, N.M., 300 ft. long wall with ninety-three life-size figures.
Courtesy, Armando Alvarez, artist, 1994.
This monument is unique; it does not copy other monuments. Unlike the figures on the Parthenon frieze, which are idealized expressions of the artist's melding of truth and beauty, the multiple shapes of *We the People* depict a slice of ordinary northwest New Mexico life—from flea market customers to the country club crowd. Alvarez's work celebrates ordinary people creating an extraordinary freedom.

- Art can reveal the **pure visual impact** of the organization of colors, shapes, lines, and textures.
- Art can delight our senses with its **embellishment** and **decoration** of objects in our environment.
- Art can be used as a **symbol** for an idea.

3.   Art serves our functional needs.

- Art can have **functional considerations,** such as architectural design, city planning, furnishings, containers, utensils, clothing, and jewelry.
- Art provides us with advertising, layout, logos, and other elements of **graphic design.**

■ ARTISTS IN SOCIETY: A BRIEF OVERVIEW

Artists as a class were not high on the social scale in ancient Greece and Rome, in spite of the high quality of their work. Throughout classical antiquity and the Middle Ages, artists were on the same plane as laborers, since they worked with their hands. The role of artists (those who made ritual and utilitarian objects) was clearly defined in church-centered medieval Europe: They had the same status as weavers, bakers, and other tradespeople. Artists joined guilds during the later Middle Ages. Painters belonged to the guild of physicians and apothecaries as late as the sixteenth century, probably because their work involved obtaining and using materials that were pulverized.

Michelangelo's father did not want his son to become a sculptor because he considered manual labor beneath the family's dignity.

Artists' status was elevated during the Renaissance when interest in artworks as aesthetic objects was renewed. Artists viewed imagination, learning, and inspiration as necessary components to creating art. The Church was the primary patron of artists in the Middle Ages and the Renaissance. Later, the courts of kings and nobles called upon artists to paint their likenesses and to otherwise embellish their courts. By the seventeenth century, court artists were given titles.

During the eighteenth century, sculpture and painting began to reflect the tastes of the upper classes. It no longer merely served utilitarian purposes but was being created to please the eye and elevate the spirit. By this time, male artists considered themselves on a higher social level and did their best to keep women from becoming artists. Nineteenth-century artists often appeared at odds with society, since the public and the critics deplored and refused to accept new ways of painting. These artists forged ahead but gained no fame or funds during their lifetimes.

In ancient Egypt, artists worked as a team of professional craftspeople: An outline scribe made the initial drawing, a second person chiseled the relief, and a third artist added paint. In a similar manner, teams of ten to fifteen artisans in India worked to create paintings and sculptures, with some workers painting only faces and others working on other parts. The works were usually anonymous, as dictated by tradition, and the artisans were required to work within rigid specifications as to poses and symbols. Before contact with Europe, all art in India was created for religious purposes.

Within African tribes, the artists usually had status, often serving as both smith and medicine man. They were apprenticed and selected on the basis of their talent. Many tribal sculptors were farmers, but rulers assembled court artists with outstanding skills to make objects that showed the wealth and power of their kingdoms. Individual carvers are remembered by name as masters with apprentices in some areas of Africa. The African sculptor spent years of apprenticeship learning how to use tools and materials to create artworks filled with symbolism that the village people would understand. Ram horns might symbolize aggression and strength; small triangles in circular layers could show a person's rank and prestige.

Folk artists master, practice, and teach the cultural arts of their communities, carrying on artistic traditions from generation to generation. They share a deep pride with the past and a desire to transmit skills and knowledge. While folk art stands on its own, an understanding of its symbols enriches our appreciation of the art objects as well as of the culture that produced them. While traditions may have ancient roots, works of folk art are often not replications of what was done before but creative interpretations of a

Figure 1.3   Ferdinand Cheval, detail of *Le Palais Idéal Hauterives,* 1836–1924.
Photo by Barbara Herberholz, 1995.
A French mail carrier, unschooled in art, spent years collecting rocks and shells in his after-work hours to create this monumental installation. He imitated world-famous works of architecture, taking his information from photographs.

culture's beliefs and thinking re-presented in more contemporary modes and often with present-day materials.

Folk art includes works of high craftsmanship and beauty that were created for both personal and community use, and with serous, religious, or even humorous intent. Folk art may include toys, adornments, masks, costumes, containers, figures, and other forms. We thrill to the carved santos in New Mexico, the handsome quilts of Hawaii, the embroidered baby shoes from China, and the papercuts from Poland, since they show us the diversity and universality of the creative impulse. But we also delight in seeing whimsical animals and figures made from bottle caps and plastic containers.

Studying the lives of artists and the images they make give us a better understanding of the place of art in our lives. Investigating how artists work, what inspires them, and the nature of their early art education can help us as elementary teachers to provide an environment for our students' maximum growth.

■ ARTISTS, CREATIVITY, AND SELF-EXPRESSION

Artistic creativity and self-expression is a rather recent concept. Indeed, individuality was not important until the

Oliver Jackson, a contemporary American artist: "Art changes you—it is a *form* that changes you. That is why there are so many cultures that don't have a word for art. . . . Early people were not playing around with "culture"—they weren't talking about what we are talking about—something on the wall! They were talking about those things that adjust the psyche in a way that helps you to be spiritually healthy. Those things they made were forceful and direct. One of the things that you talk about when you talk about primitive art is *clarity.*"
Photo by McHugh.

Figure 1.4   Stanley Marsh III, *Cadillac Ranch,* **1985.**
Photo by Barbara Herberholz.
Ten automobiles from the years 1949 to 1963 are imbedded in the flat plains along the highway on the outskirts of
Amarillo, Texas. Visitors are encouraged to use cans of spray paint to add their own vision to this site-specific
installation.

Renaissance, when most artists first began signing their work. Before then, some mural artists were paid by the square foot or by how many figures were included!

Western art since the Renaissance has been strongly based on the creativity and self-expression of individual artists—artists who earned their place among the "greats" by having a new idea, applying paint in an inventive way, selecting unique subject matter, seeing the world in special ways, or exploring new and different methods for handling color, line, and shape. Critics and the public often initially rejected these new images, but ultimately, these works inspired other artists and added another "rung" to the ladder of art. Artists who followed built on the inventiveness of earlier artists as they climbed this ladder and explored and created more new worlds.

Jackson Pollock achieved an important place in twentieth-century art for his action painting. Some scoff at Pollock's work and declare, "My child could do that—anyone could do it." The point, however, is that Pollock was the *first* to do action painting. No one else had the daring idea of dripping paint onto a canvas placed on the floor, with the artist becoming immersed in the action of the work as it progressed.

Since the Renaissance, Western artists have been far less tied to limitations imposed by tradition, and thus, individual artistic creativity has flourished. During the Renaissance, the imagination separated art from crafts and set the precedent of the artist being in a superior position to the craftsperson and being a creative intellectual. The concept of fine arts, as opposed to craft objects made for a particular function, emphasized an artwork's creative value and encouraged artistic individuality. Though individuality was admired, the people of that time generally believed that an artwork should be skillfully made, appropriate, and beautiful. However, independence and imagination in handling materials and technical problems, and also in demonstrating inventiveness and creativity began to take on new importance.

A brief overview of this period of time in art in the Western world is marked by creative artists and groups of artists who found new ideas to express and new ways to express them:

A major breakthrough in creativity occurred in the early fourteenth century when Florentine artist Giotto achieved a feeling of three-dimensional space in his frescoes by showing solid figures with a warm human quality placed in lifelike positions. Interestingly, however, while he used shading techniques to achieve round forms, he neglected to paint shadows that his figures cast on the ground. These new techniques were far more realistic than those of artists who had preceded Giotto—artists whose stiff, flat figures had an otherworldly quality and served as symbols. Giotto's creativity gave impetus to the Italian Renaissance as other artists emulated his ideas. The history of art in the Western world is filled with other examples of artists whose creativity inspired major changes in the ways other artists perceived the world and made art.

Later, viewers demanded that noble subject matter and elevated feelings be the proper content of art, with paintings and sculptures telling stories in a highly realistic and traditional way. They wanted subject matter that was ennobling or appealing, with a message that communicated courage, patriotism, or heroism. A different type of subject matter became prominent a bit later, with artists such as Fragonard painting wealthy aristocrats at play on their country estates, while artists such as the Le Nain brothers, Vermeer, Rembrandt, and Chardin began to paint peasants and ordinary people wearing plain clothing as they engaged in everyday tasks. High-minded critics dismissed as trivial these paintings that showed common folk engaged in ordinary activities.

The concept that art could be a means of self-expression first appeared during the romantic period in the early nineteenth century, with painters looking inward as well as outward. Romantic artists challenged the idea of having only noble and heroic subject matter, believing in the exaltation of *all* human feelings. Their subject matter was sometimes frightening, exotic, or mysterious. Romantic artists even gave landscapes a character that expressed deep feelings.

In the Western world, the power of tradition declined further during the nineteenth century as experimentation and personal creative expression became the mode—in spite of outcries from the public and critics who scoffed at and rejected artists' new ways of perceiving and producing paintings. Political, social, and economic factors were instrumental in changing pictorial modes. The Catholic Church, along with royal and aristocratic patronage in all areas of life, declined, and the conservative attitudes and needs of these agencies no longer restricted artists. Artists were now free to produce art for the fast-growing middle classes and to suit a wider range of individual tastes. Artists began to ask themselves: In what subjects would clients other than the church and royalty be interested? What styles could they develop as appropriate modes? Whose needs would they serve? Could an artist create in any way he or she chose?

By the mid-nineteenth century, a few artists had disregarded neoclassical and romantic art and recorded life as they saw it, painting ordinary landscapes in an unidealized and unromantic manner. These realist painters strove to paint the real world and real life, with artists such as Millet and Courbet choosing the peasants and working classes as subject matter. A bit later, Edouard Manet shattered academic tradition with his female nudes painted as ordinary people instead of goddesses. His loose brush techniques, hard edges, and black outlines outraged the public but inspired to the impressionist painters who followed him.

In the second half of the nineteenth century, the impressionists angered everyone with their dabs and daubs of unblended colors. They were endeavoring to show the sparkle of the atmosphere and the effect of light on subjects; the subject of the painting (often, beautiful people in lovely landscapes) had no message. Soon, people came to realize that a painting did not need to have dramatic or heroic subject matter and that this new way of applying paint was actually quite beautiful.

The creative ferment of the postimpressionists firmly rejected the lighthearted world of Renoir and Monet before long, however. Postimpressionist artists such as van Gogh, Paul Gauguin, and Toulouse-Lautrec painted in highly individualistic and expressive manners. Artists such as Paul Cézanne began to see the world as made up of cubes, cylinders, and spheres. He painted it in chunky, blocky brush strokes—a creative breakthrough that caused Picasso and Braque to invent cubism, the real "kickoff" for modern twentieth-century art. Where tradition had once given artists direction, artists now took a more creative view. They trusted what they were doing and believed in their own ideas. Van Gogh, for instance, courageously painted in a different manner than anyone else, in a way that was not accepted in his time. He persevered, however, and believed that his own ideas were good and true.

A nineteenth-century invention—the camera—had a great impact on creativity's role in the development of Western art. While some artists used photographs as inspirational and visual resources, many artists concluded that realism was not as important as it had been previously; for realism, there was the camera. These artists began to explore new ways to paint and express their intensely personal creativity. Taken together, these individual artists created the "modern art" of the twentieth century, in which uncensored creativity and self-expression are considered rights.

Although each individual artist's creative spirit is unique and personal, the culture in which he or she lives places special values on specific activities, providing the need, the format, and the materials for individuals to fashion art objects. In the many and varied cultures outside of the Western world, an artists's individual creativity and inventiveness are not emphasized or desired. The needs of the particular culture or tribe supersede the artist's creativity in that art objects must carry on highly structured, inherited traditions. A particularly effective artist may come along in this setting and make a contribution that changes the tradition somewhat and causes a gradual evolution in the tribe's tradition. Tribal and folk artists—for instance, the Native American artists along the northwest coast of North America, the Australian aborigines, and the San Blas Indians of Panama—must work with a high degree of skill within narrow parameters established by tribe or group traditions. The ceremonial and utilitarian art that is produced is highly valued and is an integral part of that particular tribe's culture.

Paul Beckman beside Peter Vandenberge's clay portrait. Paul Beckman posed six times for this ceramic portrait. Vandenberge first took photographs and then made ten drawings in charcoal from different angles. He then made two maquettes before deciding on a size. He used the coiling method with plastic sculpture clay to form the finished piece, which was then covered with white ceramic slip. After firing the sculpture, he applied ceramic stains, using them like watercolors. Over the stains he applied a clear glaze and fired the portrait a second time.
Photo by Donald Herberholz.

Figure 1.5   Maya Ying Lin, *Vietnam Veterans' Memorial,* **1982.**
Photo by Emanuel Gale.
Each granite wall is 250 ft. long and 10 ft. high. A twenty-one-year-old Chinese-American art student made the design for this monument as a class project at Yale. Names of the dead were engraved in the order in which they had been killed. Lin planned the design so that observers would see their own reflections in the polished stone.

Indeed, some cultures have no vocabulary for "art." The produced art—masks, containers, or other objects—is so integrated with function and ritual as to be inseparable from life.

■ ARTISTS ARE INSPIRED IN DIFFERENT WAYS

Artists have made many statements about what inspired their work. **They are often motivated by the observation and memories of their surroundings.** For example, Monet was inspired by light's changing effects on his garden and water-lily pond. Many artists can see the same object or place in many different and unique ways. This may inspire them to create a series of paintings of the same object or place because a single painting cannot express all that they see. At age seventy-one, Henri Matisse lay in bed ill, but he had a "library of images" in his mind, and he continued using his memory to create bright, colorful collages. Marc Chagall based many of his fanciful paintings on memories of his childhood in a Russian village. He was also inspired by imaginative Russian folktales. Grandma Moses did not begin painting until she was sixty, but her rich storehouse of childhood memories provided plenty of material for her artworks.

Contemporary Osage Native American artist Gina Gray has stated that motherhood and the arts have been the priorities of her life. She said:

I have always drawn from and incorporated my Osage traditions along with my contemporary lifestyle into my paintings. I do not consider myself a traditional Native American artist, however. During my younger years, my family, along with many other Osage families at the time, was encouraged to move to a more urban settlement to experience the mainstream of society. So, technically, my cultural upbringing was very

Maru Hoeber collects pine saplings to construct what is a recurring theme in her sculpture—a boat cast in bronze. *Photo by Barbara Herberholz.*

diverse. This was probably the origin of my strong usage of colors; the brilliance of the universe, the multiheritages of an urban collaboration, the personalities and the influences this multicultural lifestyle has had upon my people, however corrupt or divine.[1] *(See fig. 6.60)*

Let's examine how their immediate surroundings influenced the following artists:

1. As a child, Louise Nevelson collected wood pieces from various sources and her family owned lumberyards both in her native Russia and in the United States. These early childhood experiences probably influenced the art forms she produced in her adult life.

2. In his early work, David Smith collected cut pieces of metal from junkyards and welded them into sculpture. Smith was trained as a painter. To help support himself as an artist, he worked in an automotive assembly plant and welded parts together to make cars.

3. Another noted sculptor, Alexander Calder, made stabiles and mobiles out of large pieces of sheet metal. He was trained as a mechanical engineer at a time when furnace boilers and steel bridges were riveted together. Many of his stabiles are riveted together, since the art of welding came later.

4. Japanese-American artist-teacher Yoshio Taylor draws ideas for his work from a myriad of sources—his memories, common objects, and everyday occurrences. His work consists of narrative, figurative sculpture combined with geometric shapes—shapes that relate to his impressions from architectural forms and the landscapes of Japan and America. His work is usually an extension of himself in which he tries to capture and express emotions common to all of us. (See colorplate 25 in the Color Gallery.)

5. Artist-teacher Frank LaPena has said that his art is created to honor and show respect for those important in his life. Foremost are the elders and traditionalists—teachers who have shared with him the cultural richness and heritage of his Wintu-Nomtipom tribe, and who have helped to build cultural bridges between many Northern California Valley tribes. (See colorplate 24 in the Color Gallery.)

When children recall their own experiences, when they observe their world and its myriad sights and activities, and then use these sources for their artworks, they are working as artists. Teachers can guide students to explore these sources prior to an art activity by asking questions and making comments that activate students' thoughts, feelings, and perceptions.

The works of other artists have always been a source of inspiration for artists. Contemporary artists

Figure 1.6   Malaguias Montoya, *El Profe*, 1996.
Courtesy of Jose Montoya.
Computer portrait of Jose Montoya from a black-and-white
photograph by Art Luna. New technology provides opportunities
for the creative use of photographs.

have access to a wider range of artworks than was ever
available in the past. These are in the form of books with
fine color reproductions, slides, inexpensive posters and
large reproductions, videos, the Internet, CD-Roms, and exhibits in art museums, galleries, and the community at large.
These sources allow access to contemporary art as well as to
the art of previous centuries. Henry Moore was inspired by
sculpture from many different cultures and periods, especially the sculpture of Africa and Mexico.[2] Picasso and
Braque were inspired by African masks, and Mary Cassatt
and van Gogh were intrigued with Japanese prints.

Darren Vigil-Gray, Jicarilla Apache artist, was inspired
by seeing his two cousins, who had returned from studying
at the Institute of American Indian Arts in Santa Fe. He saw
"this transformation . . . that they were exposed to something else. . . . I saw a lot of important stuff happening.
So that influenced me."[3] His tribal upbringing resonates
through his work, with animal figures appearing frequently.
He loves birds of prey and includes half-human half-bird
figures in his paintings. His works show an ordered world
of natural harmony, with humans living in accordance, but
not dominating. He peers within the human psyche, his
paint strokes illuminating human emotions.

When Vigil-Gray visited Europe, he found the long-
established European art traditions to be equally inspiring:
"Looking at European art, you understand that these people
have been painting for thousands of years. They've got it
down."[4] He has also adopted ideas from contemporary
artists:

> *What I find interesting is, for example, the abstract expression-
> ists like Jackson Pollock, and even before him, Picasso, who
> looked toward indigenous peoples' art and found something
> that was so soulful, honest, and direct, and so simple that
> they had to use it. So why can't we do the opposite, why
> can't I use an element of Picasso or an element of Pollock or
> De Kooning."[5]*

Not following the mainstream, Vigil-Gray is inspiring
a new generation of artists to think beyond the regional
confines of Native American art. For him, the artist's job is
to "see the unseen."

Robert Bechtle, a photorealist painter, revealed in an
interview by Brian O'Odoherty in *American Artists on Art
from 1940 to 1980,*[6] that the inspiration to do new work
came to him from a number of sources and that he became
interested in figure painting because of his teacher, Richard
Diebenkorn. He also liked the American painters Thomas
Eakins, Winslow Homer, and Edward Hopper, and admired
Vermeer and Degas very much.

Artists study the artworks of other artists, both past and
present, and their work often reflects this historical knowledge. Jacob Lawrence spoke of who his favorite artists are,
and why, when he said:

> *Perhaps I can explain best [what influences I have experi-
> enced] by telling who I like, Orozco, Daumier, Goya. They're
> forceful. Simple. Human. In your own work, the human subject
> is the most important thing. Then I like Arthur Dove, I like to
> study the design, to see how the artist solves his problem, how
> he brings his subject to the public.*[7]

Artists today study the works of other artists and know
who their favorites are, and this visual information gives
them inspiration or a basis for their work. Most painters do
not start out to be abstract painters; in fact, most artists are
still trained today to draw from real objects, natural or of
human origin. Their training usually involves a long and intense search to find their subjects and their unique style of
expression.

Knowledge about artists and their artworks can inspire
elementary students. An introduction to the many different
kinds of artworks that have been created in diverse cultures
and in different times can provide elementary students not
only with knowledge about art but also with the attitude
that there is no one "right" or "wrong" way to make art,
even though the theme or subject matter may be the same.

**Artists sometimes use photographs and literary and
historical references as resources for making art.** Up
through the nineteenth century, artists' links with artists in

Maria Winkler's still-life themes are directly related to her own childhood—her memories and feelings and objects that she or her parents once collected and treasured. Working in watercolors or pastels, she focuses on antique toys and games, cacti, shells, water lilies, and koi fish. Winkler first arranges her still lifes and takes a number of slides. Then she uses the images to help her perceive lines, shapes, colors, reflections, and shadows as she creates her composition.

Photo by Barbara Herberholz.

Figure 1.7   Robert Else, *Portraits,* 1994. Acrylic on canvas, 36 × 36 in.
Courtesy of Robert Else.
Robert Else was inspired by a family photograph of his mother when he painted this portrait. The floral bouquet is a personal symbol for the artist: His father was a gardener.

other countries and the images made by those artists were limited. Some artists traveled long distances to other places to study the paintings and sculptures being produced there. Today, however, sophisticated twentieth-century technology brings cameras, videos, films, computers, and artwork reproductions to people everywhere. These visual influences have made artists aware of images and ideas of other artists from diverse cultures and often have an impact on artists' works.

The invention of photography in the nineteenth century inspired a number of artists. For instance, Edgar Degas often cropped his compositions in the manner of snapshots. Henri Rousseau photographed his friends in a horse-drawn cart and used the picture to make a painting. Contemporary painters Chuck Close, Maria Winkler (colorplate 38 in the Color Gallery), and Robert Else (see fig. 1.7) are among the many artists who have created extremely diverse artworks from visual imagery in photographs.

Historical and literary references also inspire artists. Jacques Louis David used the historic account of two Roman families who swore to a fight-to-the-death battle in *Oath of the Horatii.* George Caleb Bingham told the story of Daniel Boone's adventures in his painting of this frontiersman and his family as they headed westward toward Kentucky. Emmanuel Leutze's enormous painting of *Washington Crossing the Delaware* is a favorite of viewers in the National Gallery of Art in Washington, D.C. Judy Lowry's painting, *The Funeral of Frida Kahlo* (colorplate 36 in the Color Gallery), was based on a description she found in a biography of this remarkable Mexican artist.

When children compare and contrast an assortment of photographs related to a particular subject (for example, horses, flowers, figures-in-action, etc.), they can perceive the many different varieties of a subject; analyze the shapes, colors, lines, and textures; and observe angles and proportions. Increased perceptual input results in a richer outpouring of artistic expression.

Artists are collectors. Artists collect objects that excite their artistic visions. An object's uniqueness or any one of its aesthetic qualities may be attractive. For example,

Phil Evans creates figurative pieces and sculptural furniture using metal and rocks, often finding inspiration through collecting and handling smooth stones. Whether making abstract decorative pieces or functional works for interior or exterior use, Evans works from sketches and works on a number of pieces at one time.
Photo by Barbara Herberholz.

pop artist Andy Warhol collected a wide range of unusual objects. Fritz Scholder, a contemporary painter, has collected an extremely wide range of objects that attracted his fancy, even though he does not use them directly as inspiration for his paintings. Georges Braque surrounded himself with many different collected objects, which he kept in his studio for visual inspiration: a rug, a guitar, thistles, fine art reproductions, bones, African masks, pebbles, and so on. A number of artists—for example Henry Moore, Barbara Hepworth, and Georgia O'Keeffe—have collected animal bones for inspiration. Rembrandt spent large amounts of money purchasing exotic items from around the world, later using them as costumes and props in his paintings. Artists are usually highly selective in what they choose to view or in what might inspire them or influence their thinking. Marisol said that her art was influenced by pre-Columbian Mochica pottery jars, Mexican boxes with pictures painted inside, and early American folk art.[8]

Sculptor Louise Nevelson collected "found objects" from the streets of New York because they intrigued her vision, and she later incorporated some of them in her sculptures. She also collected rugs, a Paul Klee, Mexican santos, and African sculpture.[9]

Young Pablo Picasso ignored his toys and carefully collected items that appealed to him. It is said that once,

when he broke one of his seashells, he threw a temper tantrum and could not be consoled: He had discovered that each shell was unique. Children are natural collectors and need little or no encouragement to horde seashells, interesting stones, feathers, dry leaves, and other items.

Artists sometimes learn more about their works by reading or listening to an art critic's review. American artist Jasper Johns talked about how the art critic can help other people to see in a new way and can even influence the artist's future work:

There is a great deal of intention in painting; it's rather unavoidable. But when a work is let out by the artist and said to be complete, the intention loosens. Then it's subject to all kinds of use and misuse and pun. Occasionally, someone will see the work in a way that even changes its significance for the person who made it; the work is no longer "intention," but the thing being seen and someone responding to it. They will see it in a way that makes you think, that is a possible way of seeing it. Then you, as the artist, can enjoy it—that's possible—or you can lament it. If you like, you can try to express the intention more clearly in another work.[10]

The dialogue of the art critic, fellow artist, and/or the public stimulates the artist to change or extend an idea, and the dialogue is never-ending. Art teachers serve a similar function as art critics when they assist their students in

Figure 1.8   Donald W. Herberholz, *Egg Juana,* **1995.**
Photo by Barbara Herberholz.
A braised copper iguana stares at an encased ostrich egg while holding a bouquet of calla lilies, suggesting humor
and whimsy.

assessing their own artwork. A teacher's comments can focus specifically on positive aspects—what the student has done that has made the painting show balance, harmony, and unity; how the student has been especially creative or imaginative; or how the student has shown a special mood or feeling. Comments and questions can also help students to focus on how they might change the painting or how they would choose to do it next time.

■ ARTISTS WORK IN MANY DIFFERENT WAYS

When we study the lives of artists through the things they have said or written, or what has been written about them, we can better understand their work habits and how their thought processes evolved in creating art. When we increase our understanding of the meanings and functions of artists' work, we are better able to know how art can function in the lives of elementary students.

Artists focus on a particular theme, medium, or technique for their artworks over a period of time. The implication of this for us as art educators is that, in the elementary classroom, multiple experiences with the same theme, medium, or technique are preferable to one-time-only exposures.

On the other hand, **artists are challenged by variety or a change in media or themes.** For instance, after working intensely in oil paints over a period of time, an artist may find new inspiration and opportunities for solving aesthetic problems by switching to printmaking or, perhaps, a three-dimensional medium. Pablo Picasso, who produced

an enormous number of paintings during his long and productive life, combined scrap metal and children's toys to create fanciful sculptures.

Artists make sketches or drawings before they do their final artwork. Some artists make sketches or preparatory drawings on grid paper. This same grid drawing is then transferred to a canvas with a larger grid for the finished artwork. Artist Joan Miró, for example, used this grid system in planning his large paintings. A few artists, such as action painter Jackson Pollock, use a more spontaneous approach, but more often, artists mull over the idea or experience for a period of time and make sketches before they create the final artwork. Time to reflect is an important factor. Elementary students should be encouraged to make sketches and give thought to the preparation of an artwork.

Artists are totally engrossed in their work. As expressed in an old saying, inspiration comes to the prepared mind, and a lot of perspiration is involved in inspiration. To the layperson, a painting or piece of sculpture may appear to spring directly and immediately from the artist's hands and mind—a burst of genius. However, most artists develop ideas by making many sketches before beginning the final artwork. Their sketchbooks constantly freshen their vision and sharpen their skills, as well as help them select a viewpoint, frame their composition, observe nuances of light and shadow, and simplify and abstract the basic elements. They may draw the same object or pose again and again—changing, accenting, deleting, and distorting.

Degas kept a wooden horse in his studio after making numerous sketches at the racetrack. Thomas Eakins made a small boat from a cigar box, placed little rag figures inside, and then tried to get the true effect by putting the box and its occupants out in the sunlight. Sculptors such as Michelangelo and Rodin always made models of clay or wax first. Modern technology has given today's artists the camera, duplicating machines, computers, and other aids to help them plan their compositions.

Some artists do not make preliminary sketches, but they have a general idea of what they wish to make, and as they progress, the work itself gives them direction. American painter Robert Motherwell, when asked what one of his pictures meant, said, "I realized there were about ten thousand brush strokes in it and that each brush stroke is a decision."[11] The work in progress becomes the inspiration as each change occurs. Or, as Motherwell said, with the application of each new brush stroke, another decision is made. This is often the way younger children paint.

The medium may dictate the way the artist works. Artists think in terms of the medium while they make preparatory sketches because of numerous in-depth experiences with particular media. If artists are not familiar with a new material or technique, they often approach it in a free

and playful way until they can judge what they can and cannot do. Similarly, elementary students need multiple experiences with each art medium to gain knowledge of its expressive potential.

Some artists respond to their environment not only with sketches and drawings but with verbal descriptions as well. Vincent van Gogh was extremely articulate with both words and paintbrush. His letters to his brother Theo testified to this, for he frequently described in vivid and lush details his perceptions and feelings about how he was drawing and painting his surroundings and about the people who inspired his artworks. One of his letters described his painting *Night Cafe:*

I have tried to express the idea that the cafe is a place where one can ruin oneself, run mad, or commit a crime. I have tried to express the terrible passions of humanity by means of red and green. The room is blood-red and dark yellow, with a green billiard table in the middle; there are four lemon-yellow lamps with a glow of orange and green. Everywhere there is a clash and contrast of the most alien reds and greens in the figures of little sleeping hooligans in the empty dreary room, in violet and blue. The white coat of the patron, on vigil in a corner, turns lemon-yellow, or pale luminous green.[12]

Figure 1.9   Roger Vail, *Petrochemical Tanks and Tower,* **1980.**
Courtesy of Roger Vail.
Photographer-professor Vail captures gradations of light reflections and detail in nocturnal images. He uses time exposures of up to several hours and lens apertures small enough to get an infinite depth-of-field sharpness. His subjects include carnival rides, moonlight, the night sky, water and piers, boats in ports, oil refineries, landscapes, and structures.

■ ARTISTS BEGIN AS CHILDREN OR ADULTS: THEIR ART EDUCATION

The starting point in the education of artists is their sensory impressions as children. These first impressions are as diverse as the individual styles manifested in their mature artworks. Some artists use their perceptions to begin drawing and painting images at a very early age; others have parents who are artists and who provide early instruction.

The age at which artists first show their exceptional abilities and intense drives to make art varies considerably. If we examine the careers of some familiar artists, we find a wide disparity in the time of life when they began to pursue a career in art.

Charles Russell, the well-known artist of the American West, is said to have drawn pictures from characters that came to his mind as his mother read Bible stories. When he was four years old, he strayed from home and followed a man with a trained bear on a chain. That evening, he scraped the mud from his shoes and modeled a small figure of the bear, his first sculpture. At age twelve, he received a blue ribbon for one of his drawings at the St. Louis County Fair. From his earliest years, Russell loved the West, learning of the adventures and life on the frontier from relatives who had built a fort on the Arkansas River and had been fur traders on the Upper Missouri. After receiving a pony on his tenth birthday, he decided that one day he would go West and be a cowboy. Later in military school, where he had been sent by well-meaning parents, he filled his notebooks with sketches of cowboys and Indians and then spent most of his time walking guard duty as punishment for his inattention. One term there concluded Russell's formal education.

A famous artist named Cimabue discovered Giotto, the forerunner of the Italian Renaissance, one day when Giotto was a young boy and was drawing with a sharp stone on a flat rock. The French artist Toulouse-Lautrec, the Spanish artist Pablo Picasso, and American artists Edward Hopper, Thomas Hart Benton, John James Audubon, Winslow Homer, Georgia O'Keeffe, and Mary Cassatt are all artists whose talents and ambitions bloomed early in exceptional ways. French artist Maurice Utrillo was encouraged at age eighteen by his artist mother, who brought him paints and picture postcards when he was confined to a hospital for alcoholism. Southwestern artist Darren Vigil-Gray stated that he started painting as a teenager and always wanted to paint, that he never wanted to do anything else: "I didn't want to be a carpenter . . . electrician . . . plumber, I didn't want to be President."[13]

Russian artist Wassily Kandinsky began his artistic career later in life. He had obtained a law degree and was offered a professorship but left for Munich to study painting. French artist Henri Matisse was also trained to be a lawyer, but while recovering from an illness, he began to paint and soon gave up his law career. Vincent van Gogh decided to be an artist at the age of twenty-seven, after having failed at a number of other endeavors. French naive artist Henri Rousseau was a customs official until he retired at the age of forty to paint. The explosive artistic energies of Paul Gauguin caused him to give up family and a prosperous stock brokerage and leave behind the confines of city life. He fled to the French countryside, and later to the South Seas, to paint.

Perhaps you know a child who loves to draw and paint, who does it regularly with skill and creativity, and whose parents are supportive; this child may already be saying that he or she "wants to be an artist." Yani, a young Chinese girl, began showing her magnificent talent at the age of three. Her paintings have been widely exhibited in U.S. museums. At the other end of the age continuum, you may have a parent or grandparent who "took up painting" for the first time in an adult education class and found that he or she was able to achieve a lifelong goal. Americans Horace Pippin and Grandma Moses are typical examples of late bloomers.

The training of many artists in the past consisted of studying and copying great works of art. As youths, many artists trained as apprentices in studios of professional artists. But one thing all artists have in common, no matter what their age, is an inner drive to create art. Nothing else matters to them except the urge to produce art. It is an all-consuming passion that in most cases drastically changes their lives.

Today, in our highly technological world, most artists have formal art training. They often start their art careers at home under the guidance of an artist parent or in art classes for children. Public-supported schools provide training for the artist as well as for the doctor, lawyer, engineer, and elementary teacher. A number of outstanding contemporary artists teach at major universities.

There is no one way to train or educate an artist. Anyone who draws or paints probably has at some time or other copied from drawings, photographs, or paintings. Contemporary artist Grace Hurtigan copied the works of famous artists from history to try to understand where she really came from. She had to find her roots.

Studying to be an artist is like studying for any other profession: You study the content of the subject. Most artists have stated that they became artists because a strong inner feeling always told them that is what they wanted to be. As a nine-year-old, Louise Nevelson said when a librarian asked her what she wanted to be when she grew up, "I am going to be an artist. No. I want to be a sculptor, I don't want color to help me."[14] Nevelson did not become a world-famous artist by just wishing to be one. She received training, studied art, and enriched her understanding of herself to accomplish her goal.

In studying the lives of artists, the images they make, what inspires them, what they collect, and what they say about their artworks and their working processes, we begin to see the diversity of their individual approaches to each of these aspects of their lives. By examining their production techniques, we, as elementary teachers, can better plan studio activities for the students in our care. Through this study, we will be better able to relate this content to our students to assist them in producing and responding to their own artworks.

■ INTERACTIVE EXTENSIONS

1. Choose an artist mentioned in Chapter 6, and explore and list at least two references (books, videos, Internet, magazine articles, CD-Roms). Include the following in a brief outline, and then compare your artist with those researched by other class members:
    a. Artist's name, life span, nationality
    b. Artist's childhood experiences, early education and influences, parents' occupations
    c. Artist's working habits, sources for inspiration, items collected (if any)
    d. Artist's subjects and themes, style, prevalent medium, major contribution (why do we find this artist's contributions notable?)
    e. Events/people of the same period in which the artist lived that influenced his or her work
    f. Artist's degree of success in lifetime, and later
    g. Artist's influence on other artists or on society
    h. Quotation by artist
2. Keep a diary and/or a scrapbook about artists you read about in newspapers and magazines, see on television, and learn about on visits to art galleries.
3. Read a newspaper critic's review of an exhibition on display in a local gallery or museum. Then visit the exhibit, and compare your observations and reactions with those of the critic.
4. Read *The Artist* by Edmund Feldman (Englewood Cliffs, N.J.: Prentice Hall, 1982), and relate what he says about the artist's development in society with the chronological history of art in Chapter 6 of this book.
5. When you draw, paint, or work in three dimensions, what sources do you use for inspiration? Are they similar to or different from those of the artists described in this chapter? If you have taken any studio art classes, were you encouraged to use similar sources of inspiration?
6. What objects do you collect? Did you collect anything as a child? What relationship do these items have to any art you might create?
7. Read the epilogue "Solving the Puzzle of Art" in the book *Invented Worlds* by Ellen Winner (Cambridge, Mass.: Harvard University Press, 1982), and describe what insight you gained in your understanding of how, what, and why artists create.
8. How have recent technology and new inventions provided avenues for artists to use in creating new kinds of artworks?
9. To explore some of the different purposes that artworks have served in different cultures, refer to one or more art history books, and select an artwork from your own culture and an artwork from each of two other cultures. Write the name of each of the three different cultures in the blanks at the top of the chart "Establishing Cultural Connections through Art." Complete the chart with information that explains how each artwork was made and how it was used in fulfilling a particular purpose in its culture. Make photocopies of the artworks, and discuss your choices in class with other students.
10. Review three children's books on
    a. Individual artists
    b. Themes, periods, or styles of art
    c. Preparing children for a museum visit
    d. Identifying lines, shapes, colors, and so on, in nature and art (See Resources for Art Education on p. 185.)

Establishing Cultural Connections through Art			
Purposes	My Culture:	Other Culture:	Other Culture:
Inspiring or instructing for religious purposes			
Ceremonial, controlling natural forces			
Recording a likeness			
Telling history, myths, legends			
Propaganda, political, social comment			
Personal expression			
Utilitarian			
Decorate, embellish			
Other			

Chapter

2

When Children Make Art Inseparable Companions: Art Production and Art Appreciation

Children come into this world with the desire to draw, or we might say that they have the impulse for art in their genetic fuel. Children are intrinsically motivated in kindergarten through the third grade and their continual searching, experimenting, and questioning are striking evidence of this fact.[1] We have all seen the results of art that young children make without instruction. They begin by making marks and proceed to drawing graphic symbols (geometric schemas). Some continue on to artistic representation (realism). For most children, this natural progression in graphic expression is sequential. The questions, then, are: How do we as teachers and parents instruct children in art to enhance and deepen their artistic growth? What is the content of art that children can learn through instruction? In the past, giving children materials and telling them to create was thought to be sufficient. Art educators today believe that instruction in both art production and art appreciation is important.

This position was expressed by Tom Anderson, who stated:

> *That expression in art and appreciation of art should be taught in close relation to each other is fundamentally sound; more insights will be gained in both areas when one is interrelated to the other. In addition, seizing opportunities to have one activity lead organically into another creates a sense of connectedness in the minds of students between making and perceiving art.*[2]

Anderson further stated that he is referring to two different types of art talk. One is "largely for instruction to

Students respond to artworks by describing, analyzing, interpreting, and judging. *Courtesy of the Sacramento Country Day School.*

further students' artistic development," and the other is discussion of the formal qualities and thematic content of the larger realm of art appreciation. As students learn through study and instruction in art, they grasp the expressive and formal content of artworks as well as grow in their own art expression. The development of students' creativity in general by encouraging creativity in art denigrates the importance of art, since each art discipline—art production, aesthetic judgment, art criticism, and art history—possesses a unique content and body of knowledge. Yet, one art discipline should not take precedence over another. They should be intermingled in the instructional period so that students learn to produce and understand art simultaneously.

A seven-year-old student draws plates of food at Stoneman Elementary School, Pittsburg, California.
Photo by Harry Marsh.

Howard Gardner, director of Harvard's Project Zero, took a similar position on the value and importance of art production when he said that "making art is central to artistic learning and . . . perception and reflection activities must be linked directly to student production of art." Gardner sees school as a place that should develop different components of the mind, and he believes that "artistic thinking—thinking in artistic symbols—is a distinctive way of using the mind." He said that all the arts represent separate sets of cognitive skills and that "if we omit those areas from the curriculum, we are, in effect, shortchanging the mind." He strongly believes that art production should remain central in the teaching of art to young children: "That is, we think artistic learning should grow from kids doing things: not just imitating, but actually drawing, dancing, performing, singing on their own." Production is "central to our approach—and it's very different from just learning traditions from the past or just talking about art." He emphasizes that "production should be linked intrinsically to perception and reflection. Perception means learning to see better, to hear better, to make finer discriminations, to see connections between things. Reflection means to be able to step back from both your production and your perceptions. . . ." He urges using questioning strategies that require the student to ask "what, why, and how well am I doing this."[3]

Art production should be central to the art program because it provides, as Gardner said, a "distinctive way of using the mind." Perception and reflection in both art production and art appreciation must be intermingled in art lessons to offer the greatest opportunity for the child's artistic growth.

■ BLUEPRINT FOR ARTISTIC GROWTH

Jean Piaget's theories of cognitive development have had a lasting impact on understanding child development.[4] His studies dealt with perception (how we take in information) and conception (how we form ideas, use symbols, and understand abstract relationships), and revealed that a child's cognitive development occurs in stages. Art educators, most notably Viktor Lowenfeld, have identified and described a child's art production in stages of creative and mental growth as these stages manifest themselves, beginning at about two years of age.[5]

To effectively teach elementary art, a teacher needs to know how children develop in their art production. All of us have seen the marks that one- to two-year-old children make. Author Desmond Morris said that the child is intrigued by the fact that something comes out of the end of the pencil.[6] It is an unexpected bonus connected with the child's arm movement. Children will repeat the experiment

Chelsea, age eight, works on a contour line drawing at Murwood Elementary School in Walnut Creek, California.
Photo by Harry Marsh.

Alden, age six, combines media in making a puppet figure at Murwood Elementary School.
Photo by Harry Marsh.

until they tire of the activity or until the surface on which they are marking is covered.

Around age three, children start to clarify their marks and begin to make distinct shapes. The line closes upon itself and becomes an outline for a shape. Experiments with crayons and pencils continue, and circles, squares, triangles, and crosses are made at random or for the satisfaction of being able to repeat a shape. The child at this time is involved in the artistic process out of pure intuition and kinetic energy and, without any help or direction, frequently produces compositions pleasing to the eye.

The next stage of graphic discovery occurs when, as Morris stated, "a few lines or spots are placed inside of the circle and then, as if by magic, a face stares back at the infant painter."[7] Once the symbol for the face is realized, the child attempts to enrich it by adding details—eyes, ears, hair, arms, and legs. Soon, the child creates other images— the sun, flowers, houses, and so on. These beginning symbols gradually become more detailed until, as Morris stated, "accurate representation is achieved, and precise copies of the outside world can be trapped and preserved on paper."[8]

At age six to eight, children become less exploratory in their art, focusing more on communicating important ideas and feelings. At this time, children use lines and mostly geometric shapes to form their symbols. At age eight or nine, symbols give way to more realistic representations of figures, objects, and space as children become more visually perceptive of how objects really look.

Let's take a close-up view of each of the sequential stages of a child's artistic growth.

Making Marks: Two to Four Years of Age

The toddler's earliest mark-making is often referred to as "scribbling." Dictionaries tend to define scribbling as meaningless marks and lines; hence, the term has negative connotations that belittle the importance of this activity in the child's development: "Lori is just scribbling." This stage is an action time when the child enjoys movement and the arranging, cutting, and manipulating of art materials. Children at this point in their development are not attempting to make realistic images. They begin by making marks on the table, wall, or paper, using any available instrument—crayon, pencil, chalk, or pen.

Children are delighted to discover how to make lines on any surface. If they have an opportunity to practice making marks, children will develop greater control over the direction of the lines and the kinds of shapes that they are making.

Generally speaking, children make lines and marks between the ages of two and four, but some will start earlier, and some will start later. In the beginning, they make these marks in what appears to be an uncontrolled fashion. Soon, they gain enough control to make straight lines or curved lines whenever they wish. After children have worked in a

Controlled circular marks by Mallory, a two-and-a-half-year-old, show vigor and confidence.

controlled fashion for a period of time, they will begin to tell stories about their marks.

When children name their marks, they are retaining a mental image and thinking about concrete objects and events during the act of drawing. If children's visual attention is directed to observing detailed aspects of the environment, they become more visually perceptive and aware. They should touch, smell, taste, and listen, as well as look at objects and things in their world. According to Kamii and Radin:

Only after thorough sensory-motor acquaintance with real things does the child become able to reproduce actions in the absence of objects. Children need to internalize sensory-motor perception through art production so that they can form their own private images before they can be related and then constructed into their own world of private visual symbols."[9]

In summary, the child's artistic growth in the earliest years has four recognizable stages:

1. There is no control and no deliberate repetition.
2. Line is controlled and can be repeated.
3. Shapes are made and can be repeated.
4. The child names the mark or shape, sometimes before it is made and sometimes afterward.

Parents and other adults should remember that children develop at different rates. Some children are slower in both

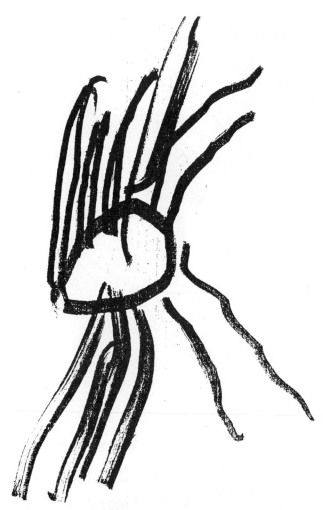

A repetition of lines radiates from an enclosed shape by Mallory, a two-and-a-half-year-old.

Figure 2.1   Alec, *Boxers*.
This work by Alec, age four, shows exaggerated arm lengths and strong stances.

Figure 2.2   Emily, *I Am Picking Flowers*.
Five-year-old Emily shows flexible use of schema.

their physical and mental development. Others have had many opportunities to manipulate art materials and have been encouraged in their art activity. Such children will demonstrate this in more sophisticated art production and in talking about their artworks.

Making Symbols: Four to Eight Years of Age

In children four to eight years of age, the naming of marks unfolds into forming simple, recognizable images called symbols, often nothing more complicated that a head-feet figure. Producing a recognizable symbol with a meaning is now a deliberate and controlled act. The symbols produced tell us what events, people, or objects impressed the child at a particular moment. Children develop a variety of symbols for objects in their environments, such as dogs, houses, flowers, and toys, but they most frequently draw people. Their first figures usually are of themselves and their parents, siblings, and friends. These first images often do not

relate to other images in the same drawing. Children are intent on drawing one symbol at a time, and only later do they relate symbols within the same drawing. This act usually necessitates a baseline or ground line on which objects and figures are placed.

Children have a certain logic in the way they depict and relate their symbols. The first symbols of figures in a drawing may all look alike, except the child may use different colors to signify different individuals. The most important

Daniel - 5 years old

Figure 2.3   Daniel, *Train.*
Five-year-old Daniel completed this work after he had used wood
scraps and glue to make a small model train.

Figure 2.4   Dorothy, *Playing in the Snow.*
Six-year-old Dorothy combines cut paper shapes and tempera
paint in this work.

Figure 2.5   Megan, *Dinnertime.*
Six-year-old Megan solves a spatial problem by using mixed plane and elevation to show the tabletop and table legs.

figure is often larger than the others. The baseline with objects placed on it represents the child's first attempts to depict space. The sky is at the top of the page, the grass or ground is at the bottom of the page, and air is between. As children develop and advance their spatial concepts, they solve spatial problems in various ways, including making curved baselines, elevated baselines, X-ray (see through) views, and mixed plane and elevation drawings. These logical but not visual interpretations of space are based on what the child knows, rather than on what the child sees. Colorplates 1, 2, 3, 9 and 10 in the Color Gallery are examples of children's art from the symbol stage.

At the beginning of the symbol stage, color is not yet related to objects. Later in the symbol stage, the first color relationships are established, usually blue for sky, yellow for sun, and green or brown for grass or ground. By the end

of the symbol stage, visual realism begins to dominate, and children begin to draw more of what they see, rather than what they know. The geometric lines that they have been using to make their symbols gradually give way to more realistic lines that depict their concept of the actual object they are drawing. For example, students are no longer satisfied with depicting a symbol for an eye—a circle and a dot—and attempt to draw the eye as they see it. A flat, green line no longer stands for grass, clouds are no longer colored white in a blue sky, objects in the distance are now higher up on the page, and the figure is no longer the largest object on the page. At this critical point, students begin to be aware of how things look in the real world and to sense a discrepancy between what they see and the representative symbols they have been using. The stage of realism begins.

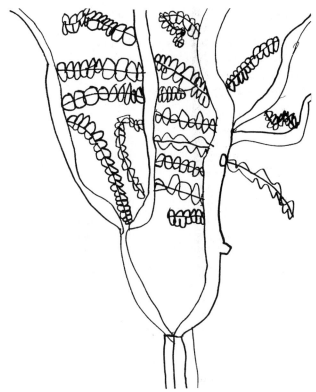

Figure 2.6   Jacob, *Tree.*
Seven-year-old Jacob used a viewfinder to define the detailed
portion of a tree that he observed on the playground.

Jesse, age ten, uses his observation skills and concentrates on
feather patterns as he draws his turkey at Murwood Elementary
School.
Photo by Harry Marsh.

Realism: Eight to Twelve Years of Age

The realism stage is generally considered the last outpost
for pictures composed of symbols. A newfound realistic approach to making pictures begins at about eight or nine
years of age. Students may still retain the remnants of the
uncritical blissfulness of childhood fantasy, but their thinking about what they see and how they make their art
changes dramatically. The geometric symbols that satisfied
them in their earlier artworks no longer suffice. Children
begin to show in their drawings that they perceive that the
sky meets the horizon and that objects can overlap and create new spatial effects.

Students in the realism stage want to draw more realistic figures with a greater sense of visual proportion and
less exaggeration of body parts. They give attention to the
hair and clothing of the figures they draw and also show
figures in action. Correct colors are seen on objects and
people. More perceptive children attempt to shade objects,
to draw shadows, and to make distant objects smaller with
less detail. Students begin to be aware of visual space and
perspective. Figures are drawn smaller than previously in

relation to the size of the paper. Students often show objects overlapping and extending off the page.

During the realism stage, as in other levels, a single
artwork may exhibit a mixture of stages. Most children of
this age benefit from close observation of the objects they
wish to draw. They can gain the visual information that
they need not only from actual objects, models, and landscapes, but also from photographs. A study of artworks can
help students understand how artists have perceived and depicted similar subjects, moods, and themes, as well as how
artists have used media and solved aesthetic problems dealing with space, shading, and color changes. If children of
this age are to continue in their artwork, they need to learn
realistic drawing skills, or in frustration, they may stop
drawing altogether. Colorplates 4, 5, 6, 7, and 8 in the
Color Gallery are examples of children's art from the realism stage.

In Japan, the different stages of artistic development
are considered in the preparation of a national curriculum

to meet students' developmental needs. One hundred minutes per week are spent on art. Each child has an art textbook, since the Japanese have a century-old tradition of using art textbooks for a standardized, nationally adopted curriculum. The books are completely changed every ten years and revised every third year. The books show three categories for art lessons: Drawing Activities or Making Pictures, Making and Constructing Activities, and Making Functional Objects. The third-grade through sixth-grade books include historical knowledge of world art, and the first-grade and second-grade books include an additional category of Playing Together and Making Friends.

In Grade 1, Japanese children drawing a figure in a posed action position. In Grade 2, they draw the figure in profile. In later grades, they continue drawing the figure, along with animals, flowers, and landscapes. By Grade 6, they are dealing with foreshortening and drawing groups of figures. Each student completes a large woodblock print self-portrait during Grade 6.

The sequences in the Japanese texts show that skills learned in the lower grades are prerequisites for skills introduced in the upper grades. In Japan, the concept that effort equals success contrasts with the thinking in the United States that success is determined by ability, according to Mary Sue Foster. The Japanese, Foster stated, emphasize "grasping with intuition, having premonitions, inspiration for fast realization of what is needed for a task. The values of diligence, endurance, choosing to do the hard thing, whole-hearted dedication, and cooperativeness are stressed."[10]

■ MOTIVATING FOR ARTISTIC GROWTH

Motivations are the basic means teachers have of evoking artistic responses in elementary students. A motivation is composed of a dialogue in the classroom prior to art production, a dialogue that is usually enriched with visual images for analysis—for example, actual objects, posed models, photographs, or computer images. Some motivations may include stories and poems that stimulate the child to imagine and fantasize before making a drawing or painting.

Motivations in which children are actively and enthusiastically engaged provide a focus—a structure within which students are free to express their thoughts, feelings, and perceptions and thus grow artistically as well as creatively. Regularly and sequentially presented motivations allow children to repeat and sharpen their skills with each art material through repeated use and provide an environment that nurtures each child's artistic potential. Repeated art experiences give children the opportunity to create images based on their perceptions, the life experiences of their culture, and the events and objects of importance in their world.

To produce and respond to artworks, students need guidance in how to see and select with finer discrimination. The sequential growth of manipulative skills requires time and instruction. If media are changed too often, students will never master the world of tools and materials. Understanding the nature and degree of assistance that each student needs requires teacher observation of individual children. Keeping a portfolio of each student's work to assess progress over the school year is helpful. In this way, the teacher can note if developmental stages—for example, with regard to depictions of figures, houses, and space—are in general alignment with those expected at that age level. For instance, a child who draws rather realistic figures running and throwing a football, but who persists in drawing the sky as a strip across the top of the paper, may be helped by the teacher to see clouds moving along behind the treetops.

Motivations need to be ongoing while children are drawing. A teacher may notice that a child continues to draw very small objects even though the paper is quite large. This usually signals a lack of confidence and/or knowledge about, and perceptual experience with, the subject. The teacher can help such students to realize how much more they actually know or feel about the subject in a technique called **accretion,** which means extending, expanding, or adding onto the original tiny figure, house, or animal that the child has drawn.[11] Questioning strategies can direct the child's attention, memory, and/or perception: "What a fine rabbit! Do you remember what Alice did when she saw the rabbit? How tall was Alice? How big was the rabbit? Where was the hole she fell through? What happened next?" and so on. Or "You made the lion look like he's roaring. Good for you! When we went to the zoo, do you remember what the lion's cage looked like? How big was it? Was there a tree in the cage? Was there another lion? How large was he? What animals were to the left and to the right of the cage? Where did you walk next? What else did you see?" and so on.

Children have the inborn capacity to transform their primary means of knowing—that is, their experiences of feeling, thinking, and perceiving—into unique art forms. Motivations may have one or more emphases, which culminate in the child's art product. Motivations may underscore (1) viewing an object in detail; (2) recalling past experiences; (3) having empathy; (4) becoming involved with the formal aspects of the elements and principles of art; (5) delving into one's art heritage; (6) exploring feelings, fantasy, and the imagination; or (7) being inventive and experimental with art materials.

A strong self-motivation can transform perceptions, feelings, and thoughts into an art form; however, the teacher usually needs to provide motivation for the students and to help them order their impressions and concepts.

In responding to a motivation, students are challenged to reflect, to observe, to imagine, and to form ideas. They are encouraged to be inventive, imaginative, and original. They are guided in exercising judgment and self-discipline as they choose and arrange their visual images.

Motivations to encourage elementary students' artistic growth, then, are both intrinsic and extrinsic. Two kinds of motivations with different emphases are found in two well-known art textbooks for elementary students. *Art in Action,* Grade 1, Lesson 29 focuses on lines and shapes and asks the six-year-old student to combine letters of the alphabet into a design after looking at an abstract artwork by Stuart Davis.[12] *Discover Art,* Grade 2, Lesson 41 requires second-grade students to point out and identify the various shapes and patterns that they see in a photograph of a house, and then to create a real or imaginary fancy house.[13]

A motivation that calls on students to remember, imagine, and observe what they see—as well as to give visual form to their observations and feelings about objects, figures, and places—may include the following:

1. A **theme** or **subject** that is clear to the students at the outset.
2. An open-ended discussion with students that activates **thoughts and feelings** that they already have about the subject and also provides them with new information. This interaction encourages children's imaginative responses, helping them reflect on thoughts and feelings before they create their artwork.
3. An open-ended discussion on **perception** can direct students to observe what they see—perceiving differences and similarities of shapes, colors, lines, proportions, angles, and so on. Teachers will find it helpful to use **real objects, posed models,** or **a variety of photographs** that relate to the motivation. Visual information is essential when children make art; therefore, students need to perceive the many different colors, shapes, sizes, and patterns seen in nature. Photographic images can provide a vast wealth of information to assist children with their visual thinking about:
   a. The **many varieties of a single subject** (houses, animals, trees, birds, flowers, etc.) for **comparing shapes, sizes, colors, and patterns**
   b. Details, via **closeups,** that could be perceived no other way
   c. The subject engaged in a **variety of activities**— horses, for instance, grazing in a field, racing, or pulling a wagon

      Students may also surf the Internet to seek out visual information for the subject or theme they are analyzing.
4. Thought-provoking questions, comments, and observations can help students formulate plans for what they will select from what they see and feel, and how they will arrange their compositions. Each student individualizes information gathered from visual research— whether the research involved a posed model, an object, or a photographic file—as he or she chooses, changes, combines, and deletes shapes, sizes, colors, lines, and textures in creating a personal and unique solution to the motivational challenge.
5. **Reproductions** of artworks that relate to the subject, theme, medium, or technique can involve students in description, analysis, and interpretation. They also introduce students to the concept that artists from diverse cultures have many ways to make art that focuses on similar themes.

The models that follow suggest a variety of motivational approaches. They contain guided dialogues that teachers can use to stimulate students to reflect and think visually.

■ K–6 INTERACTIVE MOTIVATIONS

K–3—Cobbler Clooney Needs Help!

This is a fantasy story by Maureen Gilli, an art teacher at Sacramento Country Day School, Sacramento, California. Children were given tall pieces of paper for their figures and colored markers.

Focus: Students make a drawing of themselves wearing an imaginative pair of shoes after listening to the following story:

Mr. Clooney, the Cobbler of Crockerville, made all kinds of shoes for all kinds of people. He was a tall, thin man with a moustache that twitched when he talked, and he wore glasses that sat on the middle of his nose. His leather apron had pockets of all sizes and shapes that were filled with tools he used for making shoes. He made shoes with strings and straps, laces and cuffs, buckles and flaps. He made shoes with eyes and tongues, and heels and soles, shoes that were high and shoes that were low, and even shoes that were open-toed.

Cobbler Clooney made shoes for everyone in Crockerville—boots for hiking, slippers for dancing, and shoes for running. But Cobbler Clooney was tired of making the same kind of shoes. He wanted some new ideas. One day as he walked past the schoolyard, the children stopped playing to call hello to their friend. That's when Cobbler Clooney was struck with an idea! He told the children of his dilemma—that he needed new ideas for making shoes. All the children started to speak at once.

"I want shoes with bright blue feathers." "I want shoes of pink and green leather." "I want shoes with zebra stripes." "I want shoes that will help me dance all night." "I want shoes that will make me jump." "I want shoes like an elephant's." "I want shoes that sparkle and glitter." "I want shoes that are long and slithery." "I want shoes that will match my hat." "I

want boots for a rainy day." "I want purple polka-dot shoes just for play." "I want shoes with pockets and secret places, shoes with wings to take me places." "I want slippers with precious jewels." "I want shoes of rainbow hues." "I want shoes to store a snack." "I want shoes with matching socks." "I want slippers that are warm and fuzzy." "I want shoes that tell the time." "I want shoes that help me climb."

Cobbler Clooney laughed and said, "I can't remember all these wonderful ideas." So he told the children to draw themselves wearing the pair of shoes that they dreamed of owning.

Reproductions: *Feathers in Bloom,* Marc Chagall; *Tar Beach,* Faith Ringgold; *Head of a Man,* Paul Klee; or similar artworks.

Look how these artists used their imagination. It is fun to pretend. The children in Ringgold's quilt-painting are on a rooftop on a hot summer night. See how the little girl imagines herself flying above the bridge. Chagall combined things in *Feathers in Bloom* that don't really exist: blossoms for a rooster's tail and human feet on a blue donkey. Paul Klee's *Portrait of a Man* looks more like a balloon because of its shapes and warm bright color.

K–3—Jumping Rope

Focus: Students draw themselves and/or their friends jumping rope after acting it out, observing, and remembering the movements and actions involved.

Thinking and feeling: Do you like to run and play games on the school grounds with your friends? Or do you sometimes play by yourself? Jumping rope is something that we can do alone or with friends. It has been a favorite of children for many years. People once believed that the higher they could jump rope, the higher their crops would grow, so every year in the spring, they had a jumping contest. Most children know singsong rhymes that they chant as they jump rope. Do you know any? Who can show us how to jump rope alone by turning the rope over your head? Can you jump rope as you run around the playground, or do you stand in one place? Can you jump on one foot? How many times have you jumped without missing? Did you ever cross your arms while you were jumping? Do you get out of breath? Can you feel your heart beat faster?

Perceiving (line, proportion, shape): Let's draw a picture about jumping rope and try to show the figures in action. *While a child is demonstrating, ask the following:* Where are his arms when the rope goes up? Where are his arms when the rope goes down? How high are the arms held? Are his elbows bent? How does he hold the rope handles? Does he bend his knees? Does he jump high? How is he dressed? Let's say a jingle with him and feel the rhythm. *While two children are swinging the rope and another child is jumping, ask the following:* Are they swinging the rope

with one of their arms or both? See how high their arms must go to make the rope go all around. How do they place their feet? Now look at the jumper. Is she bending her knees or jumping straight up and down? Is she jumping on one foot or two? How does she hold her arms? Does her hair fly up when she jumps? How are the children dressed?

Reproductions: *Sunny Side of the Street,* Philip Evergood; *Snap the Whip,* Winslow Homer; *Dancing at the Louvre,* Faith Ringgold; *The East River,* Maurice Prendergast; or similar artworks.

In Evergood's painting: Where are these youngsters playing? Have you ever played hockey? They are using those white sticks to hit the puck. We can also see lines drawn on the street that remind us of another game—hopscotch. How do we know that the boys in this painting are running and moving? (*They have bent knees, are kneeling, have slanted bodies, etc.*) The man and the other figures that are closest to us are the largest. They are in the foreground. Can you find them? How can you tell which ones are farthest away? (*They are the smallest and highest up.*) The yellow and orange colors make us feel as if the boys are having a lot of fun. Describe how the figures show movement in the other paintings.

Grades 4–6—A King or Queen

Focus: Students observe a costumed model, make a contour drawing, and apply color.

Thinking and feeling: How would it feel to be a member of a royal family? You would have both privileges and responsibilities. There aren't very many kings and queens in this day and age. Hundreds of years ago, kings and queens spent quite a long time posing while having their portraits painted. They did this often because royalty and other rich people wanted to have a record of how they looked, and cameras hadn't been invented yet. Perhaps you remember about some kings and queens in storybooks. Have you read about good kings and queens, dignified ones, strong ones, selfish and mean ones?

Perceiving (shape, color, pattern, texture): *Students observe posed models. Have two students model as a king and queen. They may stand or sit. They may wear improvised costumes—robe, paper crown, beads and jewelry, perhaps hold a flower or a scepter, and so on. Have all the students close enough to one of the models to make good observations. Students may use a viewfinder to help them focus on a viewpoint and format. Use colored paper as background.*

Look carefully at the model closest to you, and think about how you will place your drawing on the paper. You may choose to draw the figure from the waist up, or you may want to draw the entire figure. Some of you will be drawing a frontal view, while others will be drawing a profile or three-quarter view. A vertical format is probably the best. Image the model on your paper; that is, try to decide where you will place the figure so that most of the space on the paper is filled. Block in the big, important shapes of the figure first. Look at the top of the crown, and make a mark with a piece of chalk near the top of your paper. Make more marks where you want the shoulders, the waistline, the arms, and so on to be. Then draw in more edges and details, using contour drawing. Keep looking at the model, trying to see one part in relation to another part. You may want to exaggerate and distort some parts to create a special effect. You may want to make your king or queen look very powerful and strong or very rich and magnificent. When you have finished drawing your figure, use tempera paint or oil pastels for color. Look for the different colors that the model is wearing. Look for small shapes that can be repeated to make a decorative pattern. You can paint beads and jewels with a tiny brush or a Q-tip. (*If you have some gold and silver tempera, make it available to students.*)

Reproductions: *Queen Elizabeth I,* Nicholas Hilliard; *She-Ba,* Romare Bearden; *Old King,* George Rouault; *Edward VI as Child,* Hans Holbein; or similar artworks.

Nicholas Hilliard painted this portrait of Queen Elizabeth I of England more than three hundred years ago. She is wearing a very elaborate dress that is covered with jewels. She is wearing a number of necklaces, too. She even has jewels in her hair. Look at her collar. Her hand is bare of jewels. What is she holding in her hand? This red rose is a symbol of her family—the Tudors—and this means that as the queen she is protecting the land. Look at the wonderful way the artist painted the different textures. We can almost touch the different pieces of jewelry. We see her in three-quarter view; that is, we see both eyes and only one ear. The artist painted the background very flat and dark so that our attention would be totally on the queen and her magnificent clothing. Does her face seem almost masklike? Does she look friendly, or aloof and royal?

Describe the ways the individuals in the other portraits are dressed. Can you find elaborate clothing and jewelry? What are they holding in their hands? What might these objects symbolize? Which portraits are front view, three-quarter view, profile? Which look very real? Which look dignified?

Grades 4–6—Designing a Postage Stamp

Focus: Students make a creative connection with social studies by basing their designs for commemorative postage stamps on events or persons in U.S. history.

Thinking and feeling (social studies connection): What events do you think are very important in U.S. history?

Which discoveries do you think are the most significant? What people do you think should be remembered and honored for their contributions in some field—science, inventions, explorations, sports, art, theater, the military, music, government, and so on? You will need to use some reference books to get the right facts and visual information. If you collect postage stamps, bring some to class to show how artists have designed them as commemoratives. Look at them, and you'll see how words and images are usually combined in their designs.

Perceiving (line, shape, texture, value, balance): Let's each design a postage stamp about someone or some event important in American history. We'll use a special kind of paper called Scratch-art (*available in art supply catalogs*). It is black on the surface, but when we scratch lines on it, a bright color comes through. You will want to include the words *U.S. Postage* and the monetary value in the design. You may also want to include a brief phrase or title, or the person's name. You can frame your design with a repeated motif that reminds us of perforations.

First, make some rough sketches of your idea on a 4¼-by-5½-inch piece of white bond paper or tracing paper. Try arranging the images and words in different ways until you have made a pleasing and balanced design. Make your lettering neat and easy to read. Study examples of lettering in magazines. Then choose your best sketch, and transfer it to the Scratch-art paper that has been cut to the same size. To do this, turn your design over, and go over the lines with white chalk. Then tape your design to the Scratch-art paper, and go over the lines with a sharp pencil. White will transfer to the black surface. Now use a toothpick to scratch off the black to reveal the color underneath. Try to make different textures and patterns and to have a balance of dark and light areas. Use hatching, cross-hatching, and stippling to create different textures and values.

Reproductions: *George Washington,* Gilbert Stuart; *Daniel Boone in the Cumberland Gap,* George Caleb Bingham; *Washington Crossing the Delaware,* Emmanuel Leutze; or similar artworks.

Here we see a portrait that the artist Gilbert Stuart painted when George Washington was sixty-four years old and president of the United States. He has a look of authority, a serious gaze in his eyes, and a thin, unsmiling mouth. Washington was so tired of having his picture painted that Stuart had to tell amusing stories. The uncomfortable look around Washington's mouth was probably caused by his new false teeth. He is staring straight at us. In fact, his eyes seem to follow us around the room. The dark background and clothing as well as the white ascot at his neck emphasize the textures of Washington's skin and hair. Stuart often left the background unfinished because he lost interest once the face was finished. He sometimes even left parts of the bare canvas exposed. Once when Martha Washington commissioned Stuart to make a painting of George, he prolonged giving it to her so he could make copies to sell to other people. He once made more than seventy replicas of an "unfinished" work, selling them for $100 each and calling them his "hundred-dollar bills." He painted more than a thousand portraits during his lifetime, including six presidents. If you look on a dollar bill, you will see another portrait of Washington by Stuart. Postage stamps have also carried the image of President Washington.

Grades 4–6—Skies: Weather and Mood

Focus: Students view photographs of various kinds of skies—stormy, pleasant, with sunsets, and so on—and observe diminishing sizes and placement of distant clouds, and how dark/light values determine cloud forms, show weather, and create a mood.

Visual resources (photographs of skies): Have you noticed the beautiful colors in a sunset recently? Do you remember seeing the sky before a storm and how threatening the clouds and lightning looked? Look at a variety of photographs, and find ones with clouds that are streaked and tinged with strong colors. Find clouds that are white and puffy. Look closely to see where the cloud shapes are darkest and where they are the lightest in value. Notice that the clouds that are nearest the horizon are the smallest. This is because they are the farthest away. Clouds that are seen as closer are near the top of the picture. Some clouds are light against a dark sky, and some are dark against a light sky. You may wish to let the color of your paper show as background.

If you draw a line across the lower portion of a piece of colored paper, it can be your horizon line. Then use white or colored chalk pastels to draw some cloud shapes. Color your shapes by blending in another color or two and rubbing the colors with your finger until they are smooth. You may wish to add a flock of birds, a hot-air balloon, a kite, a flash of lightning, the moon, fireworks, and so on to your sky. Then add some details to suggest the land or sea at the bottom of your picture. You could add fences, fields, cattle, a road, a lake, or trees.

Reproductions: *Buffalo Trail,* Albert Bierstadt; *Blindman's Bluff,* Jean Fragonard; *Fox Island,* Marsden Hartley; *Starry Night,* Vincent van Gogh; *Thatched Cottages,* Maurice de Vlaminck; or similar artwork.

In Bierstadt's work, the enormous, dark, blue-black clouds tell us a storm is coming. The rays of sun shining through show us some details in the foreground. The light white patches in the sky create an intensely dramatic picture. Compare the mood of Bierstadt's clouds to the puffy sunlit clouds and brilliant blue sky in Fragonard's painting.

Then compare Hartley's bold cloud shapes with the swirling brush strokes in van Gogh's *Starry Night* and the bold slashes of color in Vlaminck's stormy sky.

Grades 4–6—Abstraction: A Still Life

Focus: Students look for the essential shapes within a still-life arrangement and use them for creating an abstract design of colored paper.

Thinking and feeling: Let's choose some objects and set up a still-life arrangement. We'll choose something tall and something low. We'll choose something small and several round or oblong items. We'll have some objects in front of others. Think about selecting and arranging a variety of colors and shapes.

Perceiving (shape, space, emphasis, balance): Let's make an abstract still-life composition with colored paper. You will be concentrating on the shapes of the objects rather than trying to make the objects look rounded and solid. Try not to draw the objects first; cut directly into the paper, concentrating on the essential shape of each object and making your cutouts large. When you finish cutting out one shape, try another, using another color of paper. Cut out some shadow shapes, too. You can exaggerate, distort, and change the shapes you cut so that your design will fit together in a balanced way. When you have cut out all the shapes you need, place them on a piece of paper, 9 by 12 inches. Decide on a focal point. Let some pieces overlap; let some pieces extend off the edges of the paper. Try to make all the positive and negative shapes fit together like the pieces of a jigsaw puzzle. When you are satisfied with your arrangement, paste the pieces to the background paper. You may want to add some lines with a black marking pen.

Reproductions: *Guitar, Glass, Fruit Dish,* Pablo Picasso; *Le Jour,* George Braque; *Interior with Eggplants,* Henri Matisse; or similar artworks.

Look at the variety of shapes in this abstract still life by Picasso. The negative and positive shapes fit together so neatly that we could put a piece of tracing paper over the reproduction and trace each shape to make a jigsaw puzzle. What positive shapes do you see? There is a guitar shape, a glass shape, and a fruit-dish shape. What else? What is the focal point? Can you find the shape of the tabletop? Do you think Picasso was more interested in suggesting the shapes of these objects or in painting them exactly as he saw them, as rounded, three-dimensional forms? How did Picasso balance this abstract design? Can you see any shadows that are important shapes? Picasso has used flat, dark colors for the shapes that represent shadows. They are important parts of the composition because of the way they fit together in Picasso's design. Compare Picasso's abstraction with those by Braque and Matisse.

■ ASSESSING THE ARTWORKS OF ELEMENTARY STUDENTS

In responding to and evaluating students' artistic growth over time, elementary teachers should consider the following four areas:

1. **The degree of technical skill seen in the artwork.** This is the extent to which the student has demonstrated increasing mastery in handling and controlling a given material. For example, do artworks have puddles of excessive paint? Do cut-paper collages show evidence of messy glue handling? Artworks should be evaluated on the basis of increasing skills over time. Very young children are not expected to be highly developed in controlling materials, but an improvement in this area, along with a desire to develop more control, are suitable areas to evaluate.

2. **The manner in which the student has organized the artwork.** This has to do with artistic considerations related to the elements and principles of design. When variety and unity are seen in an artwork, the colors, lines, shapes, and so on give us a feeling of completeness. The different parts are organized so that the work offers a feeling of wholeness, balance, and harmony.

3. **The extent to which the student has shown feelings and emotional qualities in the artwork.** This has to do with the expressive qualities of showing happiness, sadness, anger, and so on in an artwork. It is governed not only by color choices and the expressive use of lines and shapes but by the subject matter as well.

4. **The degree of creative imagination and ingenuity that the student has shown.** This is seen when a student makes unusual connections, relating two ordinarily unrelated ideas, or when a student depicts an original theme, worked in a humorous or insightful way, or finds a fresh new way to express an idea, solve a visual problem, or use a material.

Comparing the artworks of several children in a negative manner is inappropriate, but teachers can use questioning strategies when students complete a project to help each student understand not only what is pleasing and good about his or her product but also what important things happened during the process of making the artwork. Teachers will find that some of the questions that follow are helpful after an art activity. Select questions from this list that apply to the focus of the art lesson. First, guide students to reflect on the process they have undergone in making their art. Then ask them to talk about the successful aspects of their art products and to evaluate those aspects that could be improved.

■ HELPING STUDENTS TO PERCEIVE AND REFLECT ON THEIR ARTWORK

Process

Did you take a careful look at the object (horse, tree, figure, flower) that you were drawing and observe its contours (edges), darks and lights, colors, textures, proportions, big and little shapes?

Did you think about how you would place it on the paper before you started? Did you play around with your idea, maybe making a sketch before you started?

Did you discover any new ways to work with this art material?

Did you try to improve your skill in handling this medium?

Did you work longer at your artwork than you usually do? Would you like to repeat this activity?

Did you "take a critical look" now and then while you were working?

Can you think of a different way you would draw this subject another time?

Do you know about an artist who painted this same theme or used this medium?

Product

Did you keep the format of your paper in mind? Did you fill spaces and allow some lines and shapes to touch the sides of the paper?

Are your negative spaces interesting?

Would this picture fit better on tall paper, larger paper, smaller paper?

Did you make the figures or important shapes large enough for your idea?

Could you make the ground, sky, or background more interesting?

Did you include enough details to tell what you had in mind?

Did you make a center of interest? How?

Did the colors you used give your picture the feeling you wanted? Would you use the same colors next time?

Did you show variety in any way—in sizes, shapes, colors, line thicknesses, patterns, and so on?

Does your composition feel balanced?

How did you show contrast—texture, color, value, shape?

Would some exaggeration or distortion have helped to create a stronger emotion?

How did you show deep space? Are distant objects higher up and smaller?

Did you make any of the parts of your picture in a new or different way?

Tom Sullivan and Bryan Hamby work with Audra Holcome to import digitized images they have recently scanned into their computers.
Photo by Phillip Dunn.

If you could make this picture again, what would you change?

Would your picture have been more effective if you had used a different medium?

■ INTERACTIVE TECHNOLOGY AND ELEMENTARY ART EDUCATION
Contributed by Phillip C. Dunn, University of South Carolina

Like it or not, over the past thirty years, technology has assumed an increasingly crucial role in almost every aspect of our existence. As teachers, we have become accustomed to Xerox copiers replacing mimeograph machines, VCRs and laser disks supplanting 16-millimeter movie projectors, and fax machines being used instead of first-class mail.

Perhaps the most important technological development, however, has been the continuing refinement of the personal computer. As each bundle of improvements has been unveiled, personal computing costs have come down rather than gone up. Computer power is now eight thousands times less expensive than it was thirty years ago.[14] The downside of the rapid pace of this progress is that many individuals find it daunting to keep up with each new generation of software and hardware. Many teachers labor

under the impression that they must become experts to even begin to use technology for anything more than word processing. Funding for technology in education has continued to be an issue, and schools remain far behind business and industry in incorporating computer technology into the curriculum[15]. As we shall soon see, however, incorporating technology into the school art program offers elementary teachers an interesting and valuable means to: (1) integrate components of the elementary school curriculum, (2) access and nurture higher-order thinking skills, (3) provide opportunities for cooperative learning, and (4) develop individual creativity and problem-solving abilities.

An Instrument for Making Art

Incorporating computer technology into elementary school art programs means that the computer can be an instrument or tool for making art. This line of thought should begin with one caveat: Technology cannot and should not completely replace interaction with traditional art forms and art media in elementary art programs. Just as we learn things by making art that cannot be learned by studying art, we learn things by interacting with traditional art materials and processes that cannot be learned by using a computer. However, incorporating computer technology in the form of any of a host of computer-assisted drawing, painting, design, three-dimensional modeling, and image manipulation programs can provide new and stimulating avenues for children to explore as they seek to create artworks that communicate their preferences, convictions, and feelings. Among the most popular and teacher-friendly programs for using the computer as an art-making tool are those from Fractal Design.

Fractal Design Dabbler 2 is perfect for elementary art programs. It features an intuitive interface that contains icons for each of the mark-making or painting tools available. Users open a drawer, select the tools with which they wish to draw or paint, and then create by clicking and moving the mouse. Fractal Design Poser offers human mannequins that can be posed and then incorporated into a drawing or painting. Fractal Design Painter, a much more sophisticated art-making program, has many additional creative features but is still easy for both elementary schoolchildren and adults to learn. These programs contain excellent animated tutorials that teachers who feel artistically challenged can use with students to teach techniques and processes. The programs can also be used in concert with photo-manipulation software like Adobe Photoshop so that students can combine photographic images with images they have created completely inside the computer.

The basic equipment necessary for using computers as an art-making tool is little more than what many classroom teachers already possess—namely, art-making software. If you wish to pursue more advanced art-making features, then additional hardware, such as graphics tablets, digital cameras and/or flatbed scanners, and color ink-jet printers may be desirable. All four of these pieces of hardware can be purchased for just over a thousand dollars. Many elementary schools purchase these items and share them among classroom teachers.

The inclusion of this technology in school art programs can actually make teaching art and creating art easier. For classroom teachers who feel less than comfortable manipulating traditional art media and for students who are not gifted with high levels of manual dexterity in the manipulation of materials, the computer offers an almost infinite number of advantages. Students who have a difficult time drawing and painting may excel when provided opportunities to digitize images in a scanner and to manipulate, synthesize, or combine these images with other scanned or computer-generated images to create an artwork.

Perhaps the greatest advantage of including computer-assisted imaging technology in an elementary art program is that it encourages children to create multiple versions of artworks until they settle on a "best" or "most satisfactory" answer to the problem they have been attempting to solve.[16] If we think of art experiences as visual problem solving, then any technology that promotes seriation of this

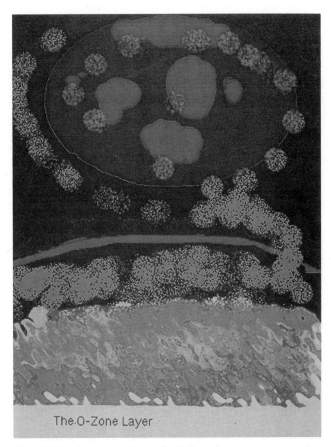

The.O-Zone Layer

Figure 2.7   Ross Steppling, *The O-Zone Layer.*
Ross Steppling created this work in the computer graphics class at the Young Artists Workshop sponsored by the University of South Carolina.

nature helps to demonstrate children's cognitive processes when they use technology to express themselves visually.

This kind of problem solving also helps students learn to delay coming to closure when confronted with problems. Too often in school, learning is a race to come up with the "correct" answer. Little hands begin to rise even before the teacher finishes posing the question. This may work for lower-order cognitive activities like simple recall, but the kinds of higher-order thinking we really wish to instill in our pupils can only occur when children take time to synthesize, analyze, hypothesize, and experiment with potential answers until they arrive at a solution that demonstrates the application of relevant rules and principles in their individual problem-solving efforts. All of life's really important problems seem to have more than one potential answer. Unfortunately in school, most of the problems we give to students only have one correct response. Elementary art is one of the few places in the curriculum where children are encouraged to engage in the kind of divergent cognitive activity that can help them become highly skilled thinkers, and technology certainly can play an important role in encouraging the development of such skills. Regardless of whether or not art students dedicate their lives to making art, the technical training they receive in an art class affords them opportunities to use computer-assisted drawing and design programs as creative learning tools that can be applied to other problems in work and in life.

An Instrument for Studying, Criticizing, and Philosophizing about Art

Computer technology offers additional art education applications in the form of integrated interactive programs. Integrated interactive media, or hypermedia, are computer applications that utilize various combinations of text, graphics, images, sound, voice, animation and video to create a seamless, multifaceted presentation. *Hypertext* is a term used to describe programs that permit the storing and linking of text in a variety of ways so that users can access information in ways that make sense to them.[17] Hypermedia programs are strong learning tools because they can support a child-centered approach by shifting a significant amount of control over the learning process from the teacher to the learner. Rather than being bound by some sequence that the teacher has designed, the student has freedom of choice within the confines of the hypermedia program in use.[18] This inherent flexibility in the sequence in which information is presented allows students of either gender or from various ethnic backgrounds to access information in ways that make sense to them. Cognitive psychologist and intelligence theorist Howard Gardner stated that technologies such as this can maximize the chances that students will learn and then display what they have learned in ways that are comfortable to them.[19] When this happens—that is, when technology is used to provide freedom of choice, to give the user control over the order in which new information is presented, and to make information instantly available—then schooling becomes exciting because it is more meaningful and more personally relevant to the student.

Hypermedia programs are potent instruments for learning about art, analyzing and critiquing art, and placing art from a variety of sources into a personal or cultural context. Thousands of works from major museums have been uploaded to the Internet or are available on compact disk (CD) or videodisk for reasonable cost.[20] The Art Institute of Chicago's CD With Open Eyes or the Microsoft Art Gallery CD, a collection of works taken from the National Gallery of Art, London, are excellent interactive resources that can be used as learning centers for individuals or small groups, or as presentation tools for entire classes.

Electronic discussion groups provide a means to ponder, discuss, analyze, and research everything from the most obscure artist to major developments in art criticism, art history, and aesthetics. Virtual student art galleries allow students to display their works and view the works of fellow students from around the world.

Hypermedia authoring programs make it possible for students to create everything from works of art to sophisticated multimedia presentations. Such programs allow students to research, collect, organize, and present information in ways that have never before been possible. Therefore, the question is not, "Is computer technology appropriate for school art programs?" but rather, "How can we use computer technology to reach more students and teach them more efficiently?

An Instrument for Developing Curriculum in Art

Classroom teachers who teach art are often at a disadvantage because curricular resources are few. Interactive technology makes it possible for teachers to share their ideas with each other. The Curriculum Navigator for Art: Elementary School is an example of hypermedia specifically designed for this purpose.[21] The Curriculum Navigator consists of a series of planning templates that allow teachers to share goals, themes, concepts, study units, and all the accompanying lessons with just a few clicks of the mouse. Whenever possible, the goals, themes, concepts, and cultures suggested for each grade in the Curriculum Navigator have been integrated with those being covered in language arts, social studies, science, geography, and math. Therefore, the Curriculum Navigator automatically begins the process of integrating the entire elementary school curriculum.

Software Programs for Elementary Children

DRAWING AND PAINTING SOFTWARE
Deneba Artworks
Fractal Design Dabbler 2
Fractal Design Painter
Fractal Design Poser
Kid Pix
Superpaint
*IMAGE MANIPULATION AND ANIMATION
     SOFTWARE*
Adobe Photoshop
Morph
Ofoto
Ray Dream Studio
*INTERACTIVE HYPERMEDIA AUTHORING
     SOFTWARE*
Authorware
HyperCard
HyperStudio
SuperCard
Macromedia Director

List of Software Programs for Elementary Teachers

CURRICULUM DEVELOPMENT AND STUDENT ASSESSMENT SOFTWARE
Curriculum Navigator for Art: Elementary School
INfolio: An Interactive Assessment Tool
The Print Shop
CURRICULUM RESOURCES
Microsoft Art Gallery
With Open Eyes
The Art Historian
Le Louvre
Survey of Western Art
Passion for Art
Paul Cézanne
History through Art
Great Paintings (Renaissance/Impressionism)
Painters Painting
The National Gallery of Art Videodisk

Glossary of Basic Technology Terms

Bit: Short for binary digit. A single digital piece of information, generally represented by the numeral 0 or 1. The smallest piece of information that a computer deals with.

Byte: (bite) Eight bits. See *bit.* The basic "word" of digital signals. Frequently written as an eight-digit binary number. One letter of the alphabet in ASCII code takes one byte.

Central processing unit (CPU): The "brains of the computer," consisting of a microprocessor (computer chip) that can process thousands upon thousands of computations per second.

Compact disk (CD-Rom): A system of storing digital information that can then be accessed (read) by the computer.

Desktop: An analogy for using the computer is to think of the monitor screen as your desktop. Clicking on any window that is open on the desktop brings it to the top of the pile.

Digital camera: A camera that substitutes a magnetic disk for film. Exposures are digitized rather than "developed." Images become visible when downloaded into a computer and opened up in an image manipulation program like Photoshop.

Digitize: The term used to denote binary coding of text, images, or even sounds. Computers save and retrieve information by reducing it to a string of numbers (ones and/or zeroes).

Flatbed scanner: Similar to a copier but instead of printing out a copy of the original, this machine reduces the data to digital information that the computer can then store and retrieve.

Graphics tablet: Similar to a mouse except that the user uses a pressure-sensitive pen to "draw" or "paint." A graphics tablet more closely approximates traditional artistic drawing and painting processes than a mouse.

Graphic user interface (GUI): The visual interface that the user employs to interact with the computer. A GUI employs a mouse in conjunction with graphic icons rather than keystroke commands.

Icon: A small, graphic representation of a program, folder, file, or other item. Double-clicking on the icon tells the computer to activate the program or process that it represents.

Integrated interactive media (hypermedia): Software programs that utilize various combinations of text, graphics, images, sound, voice, animation, and video to create a seamless, multifaceted presentation.

Laser disk: A system for storing analog information (images, text, sounds, etc.) that the computer can then access.

Memory (random access memory—RAM): The capacity of a computer to operate one or more programs simultaneously. RAM is electronic, which means that if electrical power is interrupted, anything that has not been saved (transferred to storage) will be lost.

Monitor: The television screen or display. Information on this screen is said to be on the "desktop."

Mouse: A small handheld piece of hardware that controls the positioning of the computer cursor. Clicking the mouse once sensitizes an icon; clicking it twice tells the icon to perform its function.

QuickTime Movies: Short video clips that can be inserted into interactive programs.

Storage: The capacity of a computer to store information. Storage is usually notated by the capacity of the hard drive and is measured in megabytes or even gigabytes. Storage is magnetic rather than electric and is not affected by losing power or shutting down the machine. Floppy disks, CD-Roms, and zip disks are also examples of magnetic storage.

Virtual reality (QTVR): A variation of Quicktime movies in which the user can pan from left to right, right to left, look up or down, and advance of move back within a video clip.

Window: A portion of the monitor display. A window can be thought of as a piece of paper on the desktop.

Selected Home Pages of Interest to Elementary Art Teachers

ArtsEdge (http://artsedge.kennedy-center.org): The mission of ArtsEdge is to help artists, teachers, and students gain access to and/or share information, resources, and ideas that support the arts as a core subject area in the K–12 curriculum.

ArtsEdNet (http://www.artsednet.getty.edu/): The Getty Center for Education in the Arts sponsors this home page to facilitate the exchange of ideas on K–12 art education.

The Asian Art Museum of San Francisco (http://sfasian.apple.com/): This Web site presents the latest in Web-surfing technology in its virtual reality (VR) gallery.

The Civilized Explorer—Art on the Internet (http://www.crl.com/~philip/Arthome.html): This is a jumping-off point for locating art from many cultures and countries.

Electronic Media Interest Group (EMIG) (http://www.cedarnet.org/ans/arted.html): This is an on-line resource for those who use technology to teach art in schools. EMIG sponsors a lively exchange of information, ideas, and opportunities for making technology an integral part of art education.

Index of On-Line Art Resources (http://www.msstate.edu/Fineart_Online/art-resources/): This directory is a resource and starting point for people interested in art and in the possible relationships between art and technology. Hundreds of art resources that can be accessed via the Internet are indexed. Web sites, gophers, ftp sites, mailing lists, and other types of resources are included.

InSITE: Art Education Resources (http://curry.edschool.virginia.edu/insite/content/art/artrs.html): This lists good resources for those interested in arts advocacy and in collecting ideas for teaching art.

Leonardo da Vinci (http://www.leonardo.net/museum/main.html): This is a virtual museum displaying images by da Vinci.

Metropolitan Museum of Art (http://www.metmuseum.org/): The Metropolitan Museum of Art collections include more than 2 million works of art—several hundred thousand of which are on view at any given time—spanning more than five thousand years of world culture, from prehistory to the present. This Web site gives visitors an overview of the collections on display in the museum's galleries.

The Smithsonian (http://www.si.edu/): This Web site links each of the various components making up the Smithsonian, such as the National Museum of African Art (http://drum.ncsc.org/~kmw/nat-mus-afr-art.html), whose permanent collection introduces the art of Africa south of the Sahara.

The Webmuseum Network (http://mistral.enst.fr:80/): This is a worldwide network of museums that share images and information on art.

Women Artists Archive (http://www.sonoma.edu/Library/special/waa/): This site exhibits a collection of medieval through contemporary works by over one thousand female artists.

■ INTERACTIVE EXTENSIONS

1. Observe two- to four-year-old children as they make marks. Then collect three or four of their artworks. Talk with the children about their drawings after they have finished. Does this information add to your understanding of how children of this age are developing in their artistic expression? If so, how?

2. Make a collection of drawings by children in the symbol stage, and look for differences and similarities in how they use color, figures, and space.

3. Collect three or four artworks by children ages six to eight. Describe how the children use color, line, and shape. Then collect three or four artworks by children ages nine to twelve, and compare their use of color, line, and shape. (See sections in Chapter 3 on how children use the elements of art.)

4. Collect three children's artworks from each of the three stages of artistic growth, and compare how the children have each used the art elements in emotional or expressive manners.

5. Do some research on safety in relation to the use of art materials. For example, review the health hazards in such books as *Safety in the Artroom* by Charles A. Qualley (Worcester, Mass.: Davis Publications, 1986) or check state requirements regarding health standards in relation to art materials.

6. Write an art motivation for Grades 1–3, stressing the emotional involvement of the individual in a personal experience. Before you write your motivation, review the ones in this chapter. Then look at the questions in the pamphlet *Quality Art Education* (National Art Education Association, 1916 Association Drive, Reston, Va. 22091) that children must be confronted with in making an artwork. In most motivations, children need guided visual analysis of the figures and objects with which they are dealing in the proposed artwork. In addition, many motivations are enriched by the incorporation of a study of one or more famous artworks that are related to the activity either by theme, subject matter, style, or media.

7. Read at least three "Instructional Resources" in *Art Education* magazine. Then select an artwork and follow the same format in writing a lesson plan. For example,

see "The Farmer's Coat," *Art Education* 49 (November 1996):31. This is both a response and production lesson. It also introduces a cross-cultural approach by using clothing as artworks.

8. Volunteer in an elementary school to assist several teachers in arranging a display of children's artwork. Consider how the works should be matted or mounted, what labels and/or brief explanations should appear to explain the goals of the various lessons, and what learning was achieved.

9. Read one of the following children's books on an artist, and report on it briefly to the rest of the class: *Starting Home: The Story of Horace Pippin, Painter* by Mary E. Lyons (New York: Charles Scribner's Sons, 1993); *First Impressions: Mary Cassatt* by Susan E. Meyer (New York: Harry N. Abrams, 1990); *A Weekend with Winslow Homer* by Ann Kay Beneduce (New York: Rizzoli, 1996). (See Resources for Art Education on page 185 for additional listings of children's books on art and artists.)

10. Select two of the books from the following list, and report on the chapters on artistic growth to your class:

Chapman, Laura H., *Approaches to Art in Education* (New York: Harcourt Brace Jovanovich, 1978).

Day, Michael, and Al Hurwitz, *Children and Their Art* 6th ed. (New York: Harcourt Brace Jovanovich, 1995).

Eisner, Elliot W., *Educating Artistic Vision* (New York: Macmillan, 1972).

Gardner, Howard, *Artful Scribbles, The Significance of Children's Drawings* (New York: Basic Books, 1980).

Herberholz, Barbara, and Lee Hanson, *Early Childhood Art* 5th ed. (Dubuque, Iowa: Brown and Benchmark, 1995).

Herberholz, Donald W., and Earl Linderman, *Developing Artistic and Perceptual Awareness,* 4th ed. (Dubuque, Iowa: Wm. C. Brown, 1979).

Lowenfeld, Viktor, and W. Lambert Brittian, *Creative and Mental Growth,* 8th ed. (New York: Macmillan, 1987).

11. Select one reference from the following list and report to your class:

Ambron, S., "New Visions of Reality: Multimedia and Education," in *Interactive Multimedia: Visions of Multimedia for Developers, Educators, and Information Providers,* eds., Sueann Ambron and Kristina Hooper (Redmond, Wash.: Microsoft Press, 1988).

Dunn, P.C., *The Curriculum Navigator for Art: Elementary School* (interactive computer program) (Palo Alto, Calif.: Addison Wesley/Dale Seymour Publications, 1995).

Dunn, P.C., "Interactive Technology and Art Education," *Translations from Theory to Practice* 6 (Summer 1996)1:2.

Dunn, P.C., "More Power: Integrated Interactive Technology and Art Education," *Art Education* 49, no. 6 (1996):6–12.

Freedman, K., "Possibilities of Interactive Computer Graphics for Art Instruction: A Summary of Research," *Art Education* 44, no. 3 (1991):41–48.

Gardner, H., *Frames of Mind: The Theory of Multiple Intelligences* (New York: Basic Books, 1993).

Gregory, D.C., "Art Education Reform and Interactive Integrated Media," *Art Education* 48, no. 3 (1995): 8–17.

Keens, W., "Future Tense/Future Perfect," *Art Education* 44, no. 5 (1991):22–25.

McCown, E., and Malnig, A., "Collectors Editions," *ComputerLife,* October 1995, 113–121.

Naisbitt, J., *Global Paradox: The Bigger the World Economy, The More Powerful Its Smallest Players* (New York: William Morrow, 1994).

Thornburg, D., "Campfires in Cyberspace. Primordial Metaphors for Learning in the 21st Century," in *Keynote Addresses* (Reston, Va.: National Art Education Association, 1995).

Chapter

Understanding the Elements of Art: Response and Production

*I*nstead of using words, as authors do when they write poems or stories, artists use a visual language called **elements of art** when they create artworks. The elements of art are the basic ingredients, the building blocks of art. They are: **line, color, shape/form, texture, space,** and **value.**

This chapter highlights one element of art at a time, even though, ordinarily, such isolation or separation in artworks is neither possible nor desirable. We will identify and examine each element of art, defining and describing its characteristics and properties to see how artists use it in making art. Then we will apply what we have learned to producing our own artworks.

Chapter 4 focuses on the individual **principles of art.** There, we will explore the guidelines that help us analyze an artwork and understand how it is organized and composed. We will endeavor to unravel how an artwork gives us a feeling of informal balance, or how different kinds of lines lead our eyes to a focal point. We will come to understand how shapes can create a pattern, or how variety and unity must be closely allied.

The elements and principles of art are universal in concept, but artists in different cultures may use them in different ways. How a particular group of people uses color or pattern, for instance, may help us identify works from that culture.

A German school of design called the Bauhaus (pronounced *Bough house*), which Walter Gropius founded in 1919, emphasized understanding and working with the elements and principles of art. Great masters in many fields of

art and crafts taught there, all of them emphasizing the basic elements and principles of design.

The first step in understanding and responding to artworks, as well as in producing artworks, is to applaud each "performer" (each element and principle of art) individually as each one "takes a bow." Just as each actor, lighting technician, and stagehand has an important part in making a dramatic production a "hit," so does each element and principle of art have an important part in making an artwork a "masterpiece." Our thoughtful analysis and reflection, as well as our hands-on involvement with each art element and art principle, will start us on our way to becoming enthusiastic and interested viewers of artworks, as well as confident, eager artwork producers.

■ UNDERSTANDING ARTWORKS

Learning about Line

Ten to fifteen thousand years ago, when the Ice Age was ending and huge glaciers were receding, people lived in caves and used primitive weapons as they hunted the large animals on which they depended for food and clothing. This was the Stone Age, and from it came our earliest known artworks.

If you had lived then, perhaps you would have looked at the ceilings and walls of your domicile one day and in the undulating bulges and rounded forms of their surfaces seen what might have suggested to you the powerful forms of bison, horses, and other animals with which you were

Figure 3.1   Rembrandt Van Rijn, *Self-Portrait*, ca. 1637. Red chalk, 5⅛ × 4¾ in.
Rosenwald Collection, © 1997 Board of Trustees, National Gallery of Art, Washington.
The artist has used a variety of lines in this expressive sketch. Contour lines define the forms, others suggest texture, while others are combined in hatching effects to create volume. The drawing tool and paper surface contribute to linear quality.

Figure 3.2   Edvard Munch, *The Scream*, 1895. Lithograph, 19 × 15¼ in.
Rosenwald Collection, © 1997 Board of Trustees, National Gallery of Art, Washington.
Curving and straight lines contrast to create repeated patterns that intensify and clarify the mood and given emotional impact to the subject matter in this powerful and intense print. A strong diagonal line leads the eye to the central figure and creates a dynamic tension between it and the two figures in the background.

familiar. Do you think you might have been tempted to trace your finger around the edges of what you imagined you saw?

Perhaps you would have had the desire, as well as the ingenuity, to fashion a tool of some sort from bones and plant fibers or animal fur. You would have dipped this tool into a coloring agent made by mixing animal fat with charcoal or powders from ground rocks. You might have discovered that placing your hand on a cave wall and blowing around it with dry, powdery pigment through a hollow bone or reed created the outline of your hand. That was your "signature" and, incidentally, the first stencil. You might have marveled so much at your accomplishment that you repeated and perfected your line drawings on the cave walls in an effort to have some control over the enormous and often frightening creatures upon whom your existence depended. Your ability to make good likenesses of these creatures with your lines probably meant that you were held in high esteem by other tribe members, who thought you had special powers.

Since these early times, artists have used lines in many ways and have made many different kinds of this important element of art. Today, we certainly have many more sophisticated drawing implements than the early cave artists did.

Line may be defined as the mark left by a dot or point moving continuously through space or over a surface. It starts someplace and stops someplace, and leaves a path as it is drawn across the paper or other surface.

Probably the most common use for the element of line is to show the edges—that is, the **contours**—of an object. The line marks the place where the object stops and the air or space around the object begins. In a contour line drawing, we draw both the inner and outer contours of the person or object, or else we would only be drawing a flat shape with no details. This is usually thought of as a **silhouette**. In a line drawing, contour lines inside the object

Figure 3.3   Vincent van Gogh, *Grove of Cypresses*, 1889. Reed pen and ink over pencil on paper, 62.5 × 46.4 cm.
Gift of Robert Allerton (1927.543). Photograph © The Art Institute of Chicago. All rights reserved.
Van Gogh's characteristic swirling, curving strokes are repeated again and again to create restless trees in this landscape. The artist was skilled in achieving the utmost effect from a flexible pen.

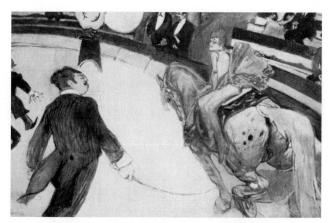

Figure 3.4   Henri de Toulouse-Lautrec, *In the Circus Fernando: The Ringmaster*, 1888. Oil on canvas, 100.3 × 161.3 cm.
Joseph Winterbotham Collection (1925.523). Overall view. Copyright © 1966 The Art Institute of Chicago. All rights reserved.
Lautrec takes a bird's-eye view and guides our eyes throughout this dynamic composition with directional lines, making optimal use of curving diagonals and contours.

give it a three-dimensional quality. Strong, black outlines and hard edges add clarity and interest, and sharply define the shapes in an artwork. They also make items stand out and add a decorative accent. Many painters do not use contour lines at all. They show the contour of an object by separate colors or textures. Turn to the Color Gallery, and identify three artworks in which the artist used lines to show edges; then locate three artworks in which different colors, rather than outlines, separate the edges of shape.

The **drawing tool** with which a line is made relates to the line's character. The thin, neat sharpness of a pen-and-ink line looks very different from the fuzzy, blurry one made with a crayon. The fluid, undulating line made with a soft, sable brush is very different from a crisp, constant pencil line. Of considerable importance also is the **drawing surface** upon which a line is made. An absorbent, coarse

paper responds to the same drawing tool in a different way than paper with a hard, smooth surface.

Line has a number of characteristics. It has **direction:** horizontal, vertical, and diagonal. *Vertical lines* suggest strength, stability, and dignity, and remind us of lofty or quiet things. They lead our eyes upward. Think of tall pine trees in a forest or a row of columns in Greek or Roman architecture. *Horizontal lines* give us a restful feeling and suggest calm, peaceful things. Think of floating on your back on the smooth surface of a lake. *Diagonal lines,* on the other hand, tend to create tension, movement, and uneasy feelings. They suggest motion and lead our eyes in a slanting upward, downward, or forward direction. Think of waves tossing on a stormy sea or a skier on a steep slope. These lines draw our eyes up, across, or down. Note how Wayne Thiebaud used strong diagonal lines in *Dark Green River* (colorplate 35 in the Color Gallery) and how Frank La Pena relied on dominant vertical lines to lend strength to the central form and on repeated diagonal lines to direct our attention to the figure's head in *Flower Dance Spirit* (colorplate 24 in the Color Gallery).

Our eyes follow the paths made by curving, angular, or diagonal lines, or by lines that meander and intertwine. For examples of this, turn to the Color Gallery. How are Picasso's *Girl Before a Mirror* (colorplate 29), Kandinsky's *Painting No. 198* (colorplate 26), and Franz Marc's *Yellow Cow* (colorplate 21) alike in the use of line? How are they different?

Lines that have been repeated in a rhythmic or random manner also lead our eyes in a certain direction. Lines that

Figure 3.5   Utagawa Hiroshige I, *The Mie River near Yokkaichi,* **Japanese, Ukiyoye School, Print, 37.9 × 25.2 cm. 1797–1858.**
© *The Cleveland Museum of Art. From the collection of Dr. T. Wingate Todd (1948.307).*
Movement and action are seen in the masterful use of line in this wood block print. Thick lines mark the posts on the dock. Delicate lines give a feeling of gesture in the windblown grasses and leafy tree branches. Can you find horizontal lines and diagonal lines that direct your eyes to the focal point?

capture a fleeting movement or the posture of a subject are called **gesture lines.** These lines are usually scribbled, free-flowing, and made with a quick and continuous hand movement. An **implied line** also can "take our eyes for a walk" in a composition. This means that a series of unlinked lines suggests a directional path or contour that our eyes tend to connect. Because we expect a line to be continuous, our eyes follow it even beyond the format of the picture.

Line has other characteristics as well. Lines have **length** and **width;** they may be short or long, thick or thin. They may be **dark** or **light** in value, either **blurred and uneven,** or **sharp** and **clear-edged.** They may change from thick to thin and be called a **gradated line.** They may be **continuous** or **broken.**

Artists have various intentions when they utilize the element of line. They may use line **realistically,** or they may use it **expressively** to show distorted and exaggerated objects. A line is **decorative** when it is used to embellish surfaces. In this capacity, it is often repeated in an orderly arrangement to create a **linear pattern.** An **abstract** use of line focuses on the line quality itself, rather than the object the artist is depicting.

Artists generally use line to make drawings and etchings. Line drawings may exist as ends in themselves and be regarded as artworks, or they may be preparatory plans for paintings, pieces of sculpture, crafts, or architecture. A line drawing requires coordinating the eye, the hand, and the mind, a process that requires practice. Instruction in making contour lines can help students learn to see lines in the natural environment and to develop the necessary skills to make drawings that are personally and individually expressive.

■ CHILDREN USE LINE

Very young children embark on their first adventures with art by making lines. At about two years of age, they begin to enjoy the kinesthetic pleasure of moving their hand and arm around while holding a crayon or marking pen. Thus begins the first stage in the child's artistic development. Soon, young children realize that they can control the lines they are making, and they proceed to make a variety of repeated movements. These are generally referred to as **circular** and **longitudinal marks.** A fascinating metaphorical connection was made by Rudolf Arnheim, who noticed that these circular patterns are similar to the manner in which particles of matter in outer space are organized into wheel-like shapes of spiral nebulae.[1]

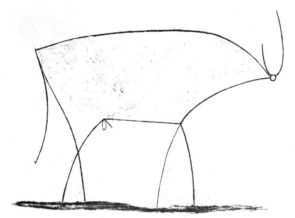

Figure 3.6 Pablo Picasso, *The Bull (Le taureau),* **1973 (second state [*top*], fourth state [*center*], eleventh state [*bottom*]).** *Lithograph on Arches paper.*
Alisa Mellon Bruce Fund, © *1997 Board of Trustees, National Gallery of Art, Washington.*
© *1997 Estate of Pablo Picasso/Artists Rights Society (ARS), New York.*
Picasso uses a favorite theme of his, that of a bull, to create a series of drawings that begin with a representational image and end with a simplified, abstract linear design.

At about age three or four, the young children discover that, when the arm moves in a circular motion and then stops, they have made circular shapes. They discover that they can make repeated lines, some short and some long, and that putting these circles and lines together stirs their imagination into seeing in front of them something they recognize and call "mommy," "daddy," or "me." Soon, they are making all sorts of linear symbols and calling them "houses," "my dog," "the school bus," and so on. Naming their marks means that they have established a connection between the lines they are making and the surrounding world. They are now set to explore the world through the use of line, making marks that will show their degree of perception, their intense involvement with an experience, and their emotional responses to what they have seen, thought, and felt.

During the **symbolic** or **schematic stage** that follows, children will develop their line- and shape-making skills, as well as their muscular coordination in handling drawing tools. If encouraged and motivated appropriately, they maintain a flexible, fluent, and original approach to the creation of images of things that are important to them.

At about age eight, children begin to be more critical of their artwork and usually become dissatisfied with the rather simple linear symbols they have been using. They are ready for direct instruction in how to draw more **realistically.** Teachers should provide experiences that develop the children's perceptual skills. They should also introduce media techniques that enable the children to create artworks that are acceptable to their maturing, critical eyes.

Children can identify, describe, and evaluate how they have used line in their artwork, as well as discover how artists have done so. For instance, they can compare the ways that Renault's lines in *Christ Mocked by Soldiers* (fig. 3.7) differ from Rembrandt's in his *Self-Portrait* (fig. 3.22). They can compare van Gogh's *Grove of Cypresses* (see fig. 3.3) and Hiroshige's *The Mie River near Yokkaichi* (see fig. 3.5) to discover similarities and differences, as well as to see how the drawing implement used has some degree of control on the line quality. They can describe the emotional feelings portrayed in these two artworks through line. In other artworks, they can search for places where line creates a variety of textures and patterns. In still other artworks, children can find ways in which line expresses strength and dignity, gesture and movement, or a decorative appeal.

■ PRODUCING ARTWORKS

Drawing Contour Lines

Contour drawing is an art skill that transcends the stage of drawing the symbols associated with early childhood to achieve the more realistic drawing associated with adulthood. This is often referred to as utilizing the resources of the right hemisphere of the brain instead of those of the left.[2]

Contour drawing is an excellent way to establish contact with our visual powers of observation. It is the fastest way to establish our belief in our ability to draw. It is a way to help students start drawing and to affirm that they really can draw what they see in front of them. The success of this technique may simply be that, due to intense visual concentration, we arrive at a state of heightened perception. When this occurs, time seems to stand still, and after a while, the drawing is accomplished with little effort. Great artists seem to take this leap naturally, with little or no outside help. Many of them do not realize that "seeing like an artist" is not something that everyone can do without instruction. The great artist Matisse was once asked if he saw a tomato the way everyone else did. He replied that if he was going to eat it, yes; if he was going to draw it, he "saw it like an artist."

Betty Edwards described an unusual technique that helps students understand this phenomenon and convinces them that they really can draw what they see in front of them.[3] A line drawing by an artist—for example, Picasso or Matisse—is placed *upside down* on the table in front of a student. The student is less able to see the rather complex arrangement of in-and-out lines, curving and angular lines, intersecting lines such as fingers, arms, hair, and such. The student does not name the parts of the picture and tries to eliminate words from his or her thought pattern. Then the student intently focuses on one line at a time—copying it and connecting it with another line. Gradually, the drawing is accomplished, and when turned right side up, bears a striking resemblance to the original drawing by Picasso or Matisse. Although we cannot turn landscapes, objects, and people upside down to draw them, the intense perceptual experience of observing contours in an unaccustomed manner (upside down) can be transferred to other situations, such as when the student is drawing items as a flower, cowboy boot, or eggbeater.

Our left brain is thought to label and categorize things through the use of words. Claude Monet, the great impressionist painter, said that, to see, we have to forget the name of the thing we are observing. As young children, we tend to think mostly in pictures, not in words; however, by age eight or nine, children seem to stop visualizing things freely and start putting word labels on them instead. Too often, the school's stress on verbal and digital skills rules out visualizing things to the extent that students no longer see anything with clarity and sensitivity and only recognize things by their labels.

To demonstrate how artists perceive contours, place a large sheet of clear vinyl over a large print by a great master, such as van Gogh, Gauguin, or da Vinci. Using a water-based black marking pen, slowly draw a continuous line around the outside edges of the figure or face; then draw the inside contour lines. Now place the vinyl on a white surface, and you will see a contour drawing. (The pen marks may be removed with a damp paper towel and the vinyl used again.)

Edwards stated that it is the left half of the brain that tells us that we cannot draw, insists on a hurried symbolic representation, and gives names to things.[4] The right side, on the other hand, is nonverbal and is fascinated with how a contour line, or edge of something, curves in here, juts out a little farther down, meets another edge at another place, and so on. Whether our right, left, or whole brain is involved, the drawing technique that follows works with adults and older children who feel that they cannot draw.

Simply stated, **contour drawing is using a continuous line to draw the outer as well as inner edges of an object while intensely looking at the object.** You will need some white paper, masking tape, and a soft lead pencil or fine-tipped nylon pen. (Using a pen is preferable in that the student is discouraged from stopping to erase.) Here are a few suggestions to help you make contour drawings:

1. Find several objects for practicing this technique—a leafy twig, a flower, a doll, car keys, a pair of pliers, a rubber glove, a turkey feather, your shoe, and so on.
2. Tape a piece of white paper on the table in front of you so it will not move. Your concentration needs to focus on what you are observing, not on keeping your paper from moving.
3. To break the old habit of looking at your paper rather than at the object you are drawing, your first few drawings will be **blind contour drawings.** To prepare to do this, poke the point of a pencil through the middle of a 4-by-6-inch piece of paper. Hold the pencil with your hand under the paper so that you cannot see your hand or the pencil point as they move on the drawing paper. This protective shield will force you to keep your eyes on the object you are drawing and not on your paper. Plan on making your drawing at least as large as the actual object.
4. Sit comfortably and relax. Listen to soft, relaxing instrumental music (no words!) if you wish. Plan to spend about ten minutes with each of your first contour drawings.
5. Place the object you are going to draw in front of you. Pick a point on the object and a corresponding point on your paper. Convince yourself that your pencil and eye are simultaneously following the object's outer contours. Better still, convince yourself that your pencil is actually *touching* the object and moving along its edges, rather than touching and moving on the surface of the paper.
6. *Draw slowly!* The line you make will be *continuous* and will follow every little in-and-out curve, bump, wrinkle, indentation, or angle that you see. To break any old habit you may have of drawing in a rapid, sketchy manner, pretend that a very sleepy little ant is crawling along the edge of the object and that your pencil is right behind it, pushing it along. Do not lift your pencil while you are drawing a particular contour line. When you reach a stopping point and need to

reposition your pencil to draw another contour line, stop drawing, peek under the protective shield, lift your pencil, find a new starting point, and continue drawing another contour. But do not start drawing again until your eyes are on the object.

7. *Draw inside contour lines* also. Keep adding as many linear details as you can find. Remember that a contour is where the edge of one thing stops and something else begins. Inner contours add realism and give your artwork three-dimensional form.

8. After you have made several blind contour drawings, remove the protective shield and begin making **modified contour drawings.** While you do this, your eyes should focus on the object about 90 percent of the time and on the paper the remaining 10 percent of the time. Try to look at the paper only enough to keep your lines meeting in the appropriate places. A slowly drawn, sensitive line is the result of careful observation.

9. Find someplace where you can practice drawing without interruption for about twenty minutes a day. Try making a contour drawing of a landscape, a person's face (your own in a mirror or a friend's), a mounted bird, a butterfly. You can use contour drawing skills while working with photographs as well as with real objects.

Lines That Are Curving and Straight: Drawing with Glue

Students draw by squeezing a bottle of glue onto black paper, leaving a trail of curving and straight lines. When the glue dries, the lines show up as black because of the dried glue's transparency. Chalks are then applied to the black paper to add color. If a spoonful of india ink is added to the glue and thoroughly mixed, the student can use this mixture on white or colored paper to create black lines. Color can be added with chalks, oil pastels, or watercolors (if the paper is white).

1. Make a contour drawing with a pencil on a piece of 12-by-18-inch black construction paper. Use pictures, scale models of dinosaurs, mounted butterflies, photos of birds or flowers, and so on as your sources of visual information. Carefully observe the outer and inner edges of your subject matter. Look for curving, straight, angular, and wavy lines. Make your object large, and include some background. Use lines to enclose shapes and to make repeated patterns. Have some of the lines extend off the edges of the paper.

2. Go over your pencil lines by squeezing a trail of glue from the bottle. You can make thick and thin lines, gradated lines, broken lines, and small dots. Let the glue dry several hours or overnight.

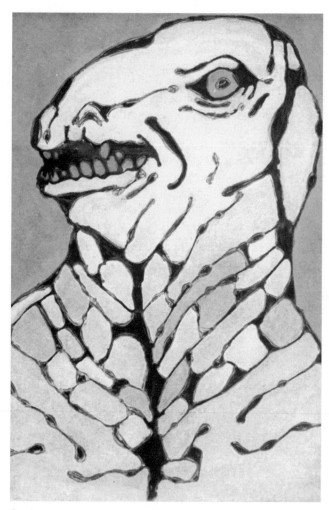

Student work: Drawing with glue.

3. Use chalk to color the shapes your lines created on the black paper. Blend colors with your fingertips. Limit your color selection, and endeavor to create a contrast between the subject and background.

Thick Black Lines: Painting with Tempera

Students use a photo as a visual resource and paint thick, black lines to enclose shapes that will then be painted with mixtures of color in the manner of the artist Georges Rouault.

1. Use L-frames and a photograph of something that interests you—a butterfly, an insect, an animal, a face, and so on. Look at the basic lines and shapes that you see, and simplify them as you make a large drawing of the object with a piece of chalk on a piece of white drawing paper. Enclose the various shapes and parts of the object you have drawn with strong contour lines.

Figure 3.7   Georges Rouault, *Christ Mocked by Soldiers,* 1932. Oil on canvas, 36¼ × 28½ in.
The Museum of Modern Art, New York. Given anonymously. Photograph © 1997 The Museum of Modern Art, New York. © 1997 Artists Rights Society (ARS), New York/ADAGP, Paris.
Bold, black outlines enclose shapes that are filled with thick paint applied with strong, thick brush strokes. Colors appear jewel-like in their stained-glass type of enclosures.

Divide the background area with horizontal, vertical, or diagonal lines that go to the edges of the paper. Think of stained glass and how strips of lead enclose each separate piece of glass.
2. Use some black tempera and a flat or round stiff-bristle brush, and paint over your chalk marks, making bold, black lines. Let the paint dry.
3. Choose two colors, or one color and white (or black). Try using two primary colors together, or two colors that are next to each other on the color wheel, or a pair of complementary colors. Brush the first color inside one of the enclosed areas, and add the second color to it. Do not mix the paint on a palette. Brush until the surface of the paper inside the enclosed space is covered. Try not to brush until all the colors are smoothly mixed. Let your brush strokes show in the manner that

Student work: Bold, black lines painted with tempera.

the artist Rouault did. (This manner of applying thick, opaque paint is called *impasto,* in that textural features of the paint and brushwork show on the painting's surface.) Choose two more colors, and continue painting inside each of the enclosed areas until the entire surface of your paper is covered.
4. Let your painting dry. Flatten it with an iron on the reverse side before mounting or matting.

Repeated Lines: Relief Prints

Students make a relief print by making indented lines in a soft sheet of Scratch-Foam.

1. Choose a newspaper photograph, and use L-frames to help you select the part you want to use as visual information for your print.
2. Cut a half-sheet of Scratch-Foam. Prepare a preliminary line drawing the same size as your Scratch-Foam half-sheet. Plan areas where you will repeat long or broken lines, crosshatched lines, or dots to create a pattern. Plan where you will have thick and thin lines, and where you will have white areas. Plan where you will have a center of interest. To create interest, make some of the lines extend off the sides of the composition. Remember: Everything that is *up* will print black; everything that is pressed *down* will print white.
3. Place your prepared sketch on top of the Scratch-Foam sheet, and go over the lines firmly with a pencil to imprint the lines on the Scratch-Foam surface. Remove the paper, and go over the lines again to be sure the

L-Frames

Cut on solid lines to create two L-shaped pieces of paper.

Use your pair of L-Frames to help you select a portion of a photograph or an artwork.

L-frames.

Student work: Making lines in foam prints.

imprints are deep enough. If they are not, they will fill with ink and not show on the print.

4. Put about a teaspoon of water-soluble printing ink on a small tray, and roll a brayer lightly over it in two directions to obtain an even coating of ink on the brayer. The brayer should *roll* over the surface of the tray, not slide.

5. Place the sheet of Scratch-Foam on a piece of newspaper, and roll the ink-coated brayer over the Scratch-Foam in two directions.

6. Place the Scratch-Foam in the center of a sheet of white ditto paper or a colored sheet of Fadeless, Astrobright, or Brighthue paper. (Colored construction paper has a rough, porous surface and does not make a sharp print.) Turn the paper and the Scratch-Foam over, and rub the backside of the paper. Remove the paper from the Scratch-Foam, and let the print dry.

7. Reink the Scratch-Foam for each print you make. Try using colored and white printing inks, instead of black, for a variety of effects.

Decorative Lines: Paper Batik

Students use a resist technique known as **batik** to create a linear design. Batik is an ancient process of decorating fabrics. Traditionally, melted wax is applied to fabric to cause the fabric to resist the colored dyes that are applied later to the unprotected areas. In this simplified version of batik, Dippity-Dye paper (available in art supply catalogs) is used instead of fabric. Batiks can also be created by applying melted wax (candle wax or paraffin) to the surface of the paper with a brush or a special batik tool called a **tjanting** (available in art supply stores and catalogs). This tool has a wooden handle with a tiny funnel at one end. When dipped in hot wax and trailed over the surface of the paper, a tjanting creates a flowing, fluid line.

1. As a visual resource, use photographs of tropical fish, birds, flowers, and so on, or adapt a motif from Japanese family crests or from symbols used by Aztecs, Mayas, or Southwestern Native Americans, and create a linear design with a pencil on a piece of white,

12-by-18-inch butcher paper. Then place a piece of same-size Dippity Dye paper on your design, and trace over your lines with a thick, black, *water-soluble* marking pen. You will be able to see your lines through the Dippity Dye paper. (Permanent markers will *not* work with this process.)

2. To melt wax safely, do not use an open flame, an exposed heating element, or boiling water. Instead, melt a small amount of candle wax or paraffin in a deep-fat fryer or electric skillet. You may wish to line the skillet with foil and place in it a small, low can of wax. Dip a natural-bristle brush (synthetic bristles may melt in the hot wax) of medium size into the melted wax, and carefully brush over all of your black lines. Let the wax extend on both sides of the lines. This creates a decorative white border on the sides of the lines in the finished product. Be sure to protect all the black lines with wax, or they will dissolve later when the color washes are applied to the paper.

3. Make a food-coloring solution by mixing about one-fourth cup of water with about one-fourth teaspoon of the highly concentrated food colorings found in cake-decorating stores. Use large brushes or the inexpensive sponge brushes found in paint and hardware stores. Brush these colors over the different parts of your design.

4. Let the Dippity Dye paper dry. Apply more wax over the dyed areas of the paper. This will assure an even surface on the finished product after it is ironed.

5. Place the Dippity Dye paper (and the butcher paper beneath it) between newspapers and iron it. Lift the Dippity Dye paper off the butcher paper while they are both hot.

6. Display your paper batik with a white backing paper, or hang it in a window, since the final product is translucent.

■ UNDERSTANDING ARTWORKS

Learning about Color

Painters, poets, writers, actors, and scientists of all sorts respond and react to the wonderful world of color. Indeed, think for a moment of living in a black, white, and gray world. Color appeals to our sense of beauty, whether we recognize and respond to it in natural objects or in works of human origin. We cannot help but be absorbed in watching the changing moods of a beautiful sunset. We delight in the incredible range of colors in flower petals, tropical fish, and butterfly wings—and in the wonderful colors of a fine impressionist painting.

Throughout history, people have used color for many purposes, one of the earliest being that of **personal decoration.** For centuries, individuals have decorated their bodies

for special occasions or tribal ceremonies. This practice continues today in the use of cosmetics, in clown faces, and in theaters where actors and dancers have specific ways to reveal character through facial design and color. In selecting a dress or shirt, all of us probably know which colors look best on us.

Color plays an important part in **our surroundings.** We have color preferences in the way we furnish our homes and the color of car we purchase. And most chefs and home cooks know to plan a pleasing variety of color in the foods they arrange on a dinner plate. A dinner of halibut, mashed potatoes, cottage cheese, white bread, and vanilla ice cream would not be visually appetizing!

Besides being decorative, color has long been associated with a **universal** or **cultural symbolism.** Certain colors are associated with each holiday; for example, red for Valentine's, orange and black for Halloween. We think of light colors for spring and warm reds, oranges, and browns for fall. Red, white, and blue are patriotic colors for Americans. We tend to associate blue with truth "true-blue," green with hope and everlasting life, black with sorrow and death, and purple with royalty. Perhaps the latter symbolism began in Egypt many centuries ago when the sun god Ra was assigned that color because of its rarity and the difficulty people had in obtaining it. Since then, purple has symbolized kings. In American culture, white is often associated with purity and weddings, but brides in India wear red, and in Israel, yellow. Especially in artworks made hundreds of years ago, particular colors stand for certain ideas and have special meanings.

While **emotions** are often linked symbolically to colors (we speak of being "green with envy," and "good as gold," and of feeling "blue"), many individuals have expressed unique and personal reactions to different colors. In her book *Hailstones and Halibut Bones* (New York: Doubleday, 1989), Mary O'Neill wrote poems that connected colors to feelings and also to the senses. She associated green with the smell of a country breeze and blue with the sound of the wind over water. In another poem, she said that gray is sleepiness and bad news. White is the sound of a foot walking lightly, as well as the part we cannot remember in a dream. Russian artist Wassily Kandinsky, who worked in the early part of the twentieth century, felt that each color had a **corresponding musical note.** He searched for a visual system in which he could express his conviction of an "inner mystical structure of the world." His splendid and often abstract canvases exploded with color as he divorced himself from the necessity of using any subject matter at all. Color took on a symbolic function with Vincent van Gogh because he used colors not locally true from a realistic point of view, but colors that spoke strongly of the emotions of his intense personality. For him, yellow was the color of love, warmth, and friendship, and we see it frequently, especially in his sunflower paintings. It is especially dominant in the painting he made of his own bedroom in the little house in Arles.

Color often serves **functional purposes,** too—those of **categorization** and **identification.** When a number of related objects are "color-keyed," it simplifies sorting them out and grouping them by certain colors. Football players wear uniforms showing team colors. The colors of different pages of a catalog may denote different categories of items. Long ago, kings assigned **heraldic colors** to knights for their brave deeds, and thereafter, the assigned colors of armor and shields identified the knights, since visors covered their faces.

Both artists and scientists keenly observe **colors in nature,** each for different purposes. Natural colors inspire artists and designers to suggest blends and combinations to be matched and used to represent the things they see, or to enhance and decorate a given surface. For instance, sharp observation shows us how nature uses color to conceal, mislead, hide, attract, and warn other creatures. Flowers use their vivid colors to attract insects to help in pollination. The Gila monster warns of its venom with its colored, beady scales. The chameleon changes its color from green to brown to gray, according to its surroundings. Male birds that must seek food among flowers and leaves have more vivid colors than their duller-colored mates that remain concealed on nests made of dried grasses. Tigers and zebras, with their highly contrasting patterns of stripes, appear almost invisible against a shadowy background. Indeed, armies have hired persons trained in art to study nature's camouflages and to help design concealing devices for machines and soldiers in wartime.

Artists may choose to use color in one of several ways. A **representational** use shows the actual or real colors of the depicted object. This is sometimes referred to as the **local color.** Or artists may choose to use colors **decoratively** to ornament or enhance a composition. Then again, they may choose to use color **arbitrarily,** if they wish to express a strong emotional feeling. And sometimes, they use color **symbolically** to express an idea.

People have always been in awe of the glowing, pure colors seen in the enormous arch of a **rainbow.** Hindus in India tell stories of the god Indra, who threw thunderbolts during storms and used a rainbow to shoot his lightning arrows. Polynesians believed that a rainbow was a ladder for heroes to climb to reach heaven. Some North American tribes thought that the rainbow was the beautiful bride of their rain god. Pit River Native Americans of California believed that the rainbow was a "rain-clear sign" sent by Old-Man-Above, who shaped the rainbow like the coyote's tail and colored it with the blue of the bluebird, the red of the rising sun, the yellow of the coyote's fur, and the green of the grass. The Old Testament says that the rainbow is a covenant that God made with Noah after the Flood.

The rainbow's beautiful colors can, of course, be explained scientifically. Rainbows are curtains of large raindrops in front of us when the sunshine is behind us. They appear in the west in the morning and in the east late in the afternoon. When the sun strikes the rain, each drop acts like a tiny prism, separating white light into colors. The red arc is on the outside, and the purple arc is on the inside. A second rainbow is sometimes above the first. It is pale, and the colors are reversed.

Both rainbows and color wheels have orderly arrangements of colors. The **color wheel** is a useful tool for learning the mechanics of color and for helping us select different combinations of colors, or **color schemes.** The **hues** (another name for colors) appear on the color wheel in the same order as they do on the rainbow. Think first of an equilateral triangle placed on top of the color wheel, and then think of placing one of the three **primary colors**—red, yellow, and blue—at each corner of the triangle. These colors are called primary because they are basic and cannot be made by mixing any other colors together. Mixing any two of the primary colors together makes another color. Doing this three times with a different pair of primary colors each time gives us the three **secondary colors**—orange, green, and purple (violet). (Red and blue make purple; yellow and blue make green; red and yellow make orange.) Each secondary color is positioned on the color wheel midway between the pair of primary colors used to make it. Mixing a secondary color with the primary color that is next to it makes one of the six **intermediate colors:** yellow-orange, red-orange, red-purple, blue-purple, yellow-green, and blue-green. This can be carried one step farther by changing the proportions of the two colors being mixed and making another complete set of colors. You then not only have yellow-orange but also orange-yellow, with the first being more yellow than orange and the second being more orange than yellow.

Analogous colors are several colors that are adjacent to each other on the color wheel. They are often called a "family" of colors in that they all tend to resemble each other. They share one color in common and can mix with each other without becoming dull or gray.

Two colors that are opposite each other on the color wheel are called **complementary colors.** If these two colors are placed at their full **intensity** (concentration) close together in a design, they quickly attract attention because they contrast strongly, often almost seeming to vibrate. If we mix a little of one color of paint with its complement, we find that the first paint's intensity is **dulled,** or grayed. The more of a color's complement that we mix with it, the duller the color becomes. Mixing two complementary colors in equal amounts results in a mousey or gray-brown color. Artists can mix a great variety of hues by using this dulling property of complementary colors. For instance, if a landscape has many different green tones—fields, trees, foliage—we can mix a great number of dull greens by adding differing amounts of red to the pure green. And, of course, we can make lighter tones or darker ones by adding either white or black to the blended color.

An interesting phenomenon occurs when our eyes become saturated by staring for a few seconds at one color. Place a small square of red paper in the center of a large piece of white paper. Stare at it for 30 seconds, and then remove the red square and look at the white paper. You will see a "ghost" square that is green, red's complement. Try this with other colors. What colors do you think you would see on a white surface after staring at the American flag?

When we plan a particular visual effect, whether we are making a painting, decorating a room, selecting clothing, or choosing a color for our car, we often think of colors as **warm** or **cool.** This is because we associate them with either warm or cool places or things in our environment. Water, lakes, ice, and snow are cool, and so we think of green, blue, and purple as cool colors. Conversely, fire and heat are associated with warm colors—red, yellow, and orange.

A color's **value** has to do with its lightness or darkness. We add white to a color to create a **tint.** We add black to create a **shade.** We can mix a **graded scale** of the tints and shades of one color. If we make a design or a composition with the tints, shades, and different intensities of one color, we call our artwork **monochromatic** (*mono* means "one"; *chroma* means "color").

Although we do not find black, white, and gray on the color wheel, we usually need them in creating artworks. They, along with tan and brown, are called **neutrals** and can be mixed with and used harmoniously with any color or set of colors on the color wheel.

Refer to the colorplates in the Color Gallery while you read the statements that follow regarding the ways the artists used color. Then choose three more artworks in the Color Gallery, and write short statements that describe how each artist used color and what emotions and feelings the colors invoke. Use the vocabulary and terminology you have just learned about color in the preceding discussion.

Colorplate 12: Seurat, *Sunday Afternoon on the Island of La Grande Jatte*
In a technique that he developed called *pointillism,* Seurat applied a myriad of tiny dots of pure color on this enormous canvas, relying on the viewer's eye to mix the colors from a distance. The numerous dots of paint create a grainy surface.

Colorplate 21: Marc, *Yellow Cow*
The artist's choice of bright, unrealistic colors creates a happy, lyrical artwork. Our eyes glide and sweep from one primary or secondary color to another.

Colorplate 26: Kandinsky, *Painting No. 198*
Primary and secondary colors fairly explode over the surface of this painting. The artist was the first to express feelings through the use of color alone, not relying on subject matter for his artworks.

Colorplate 28: Renoir, *A Girl with a Watering Can*
Renoir's love of bright colors and beautiful people is seen in this Impressionist artwork. A web of brilliantly colored tiny brush strokes merges at a distance to show us a realistic image of a child, roses, a garden path, and grass. The red ribbon in the child's hair attracts our attention to her face.

Colorplate 33: Chagall, *Green Violinist*
Neutral tones of gray accent and emphasize the secondary colors of green, orange, and purple in this highly imaginative painting. The orange violin accentuates the unrealistic green of the face and hand. A variety of purple shapes make up the coat and hat.

■ CHILDREN USE COLOR

Children of three and four years of age find visual pleasure in the colors they see around them. They sometimes select a particular color as their favorite. When they first begin drawing symbolic representations of people, trees, houses, and such, they usually do not relate the color they are using to the actual color of the object. A figure may have green faces and purple hair. Adults can point out particular colors in the environment in the course of normal conversations with these children, rather than correcting the choices that the children have made in their drawings: "I like your red sweater, Elaine." "Jim has made a fine painting of a dog that is chocolaty brown." "Thank you for the pretty bouquet of pink and yellow roses." Children can take "color discovery walks," identifying colors and making lists when they return of everything they saw that was a particular color.

To increase children's perceptual and cognitive awareness of color, the teacher can ask them to describe the colors they see in an artwork, whether it is their own or one by a great artist. For instance, we could ask the children to point out all the places where Franz Marc used green or blue in the painting *Yellow Cow.* They could decide which color they see first when they look at the painting and which color is used most. They could find a dark blue and a light blue. When they also notice the areas of green, yellow, red, and violet colors, they could then be told that the artist mostly used the primary and secondary colors for his composition and that he was careful to balance the colors. Children need to have a number of occasions to observe artworks and to describe the colors they see. Before long, they will be confidently identifying the colors they perceive and beginning to use more realistic and/or expressive colors in their symbolic representations of things that are important to them in their artwork.

When children arrive at the realism stage, at age eight or nine, they are rather insistent about using representational colors. The teacher can direct their attention to and discuss the variety of colors seen in landscapes, posed models, and still lifes. The children can profit from a familiarity with the color wheel and from learning the nuances of mixing light and dark hues, dulled colors, and blends of analogous colors to match the colors the children see in trees, houses, streets, animals, and such. The children may decide, however, to make an expressive rather than a realistic use of color and choose colors that communicate a particular emotion or a dramatic or fantasy event. Once again, a study of several artworks in which artists use expressive colors can help the children grasp the concept that different modes of expression call for personalized color choices. In describing Chagall's *Green Violinist,* for example, we might ask the children to find where the artist used unrealistic colors. We then might ask the children to imagine how the sad feeling of the picture would be changed had Picasso used realistic colors.

■ PRODUCING ARTWORKS

Daubs of Color: Impressionism

Students create a small tempera painting in the manner of the Impressionist artists, who painted their canvases with tiny daubs of color placed closely together to show how shimmering light was reflected from the surfaces of the things they saw. Impressionists did not combine and blend colors on their palettes in the traditional manner but instead depended on the viewer's eyes to mix the colors.

1. Find a color photograph of a landscape. Then use L-frames to identify a pleasing detail of the landscape. With a pencil, lightly sketch in the major shapes and parts of the composition you have selected on a 6–9-inch piece of white paper.
2. Dip the tip of a small, round-bristle brush or a Q-tip in thick tempera and **daub** it on the paper to enlarge the detail you have framed. Do not stroke or blend the colors with your brush or Q-tip. Let several colors pile up on top of each other and be close to each other. Let each color dry before you apply another color on top of it.
3. Cover the paper in the manner described. If you seek to portray a light green, apply green and then white and perhaps some yellow or blue. If you wish to show a dull color, daub in a pair of complementary colors; if you wish to show a dark color, daub in purple or blue.

Wild Colors: Fauvism

Students paint a person, using "wild colors" in the rather flat manner of the Fauves, a group of artists associated with Matisse around 1905 to 1907, who were dubbed "Wild Beasts" for their bold, startling, and unrealistic use of

colors. Students observe a posed model as the basis for the artwork.

1. Make a contour drawing (see p. 40) of a friend's face. Divide it with lines into different parts. Feel free to exaggerate and distort the shapes of the features. You may wish to draw the face with a thick, black marking pen.
2. Choose bright and unrealistic colors of tempera or acrylic paints to paint the face in a flat manner. Be sure to paint the background, too.

A Composite Painting: A Group Project

Students make enlarged drawings of small squares cut from a reproduction of an artwork by a great master. Then students look closely at the colors in the small squares and blend paint to match for the larger squares. When all the enlarged squares are completed and adhered to a background, the composite painting shows the famous artwork.

1. Make a color photocopy of a reproduction of a painting by a great master, and mark it off in approximately the same number of squares as there are students in the class. On the reverse side, number each square in sequential order. Then cut the squares apart on the paper trimmer, and attach each square to a small piece of paper with clear tape. Be sure each square is numbered properly and marked as to which side is the top.
2. Give each student a 5-inch-square piece of heavy, white drawing paper or mat board and one of the small squares from the cut-up artwork.
3. Each student should use a ruler to draw a vertical line and a horizontal line across the 5-inch square of white paper. Then students should lightly draw similar lines across the small detail of the reproduction, vertically and horizontally. They have now divided the small detail of the reproduction and the larger piece of white paper into fourths. Using pencils, students then enlarge the small squares on the white paper, matching what they see, part by part.
4. Students should use liquid tempera (or tempera cakes, acrylics, or watercolors) and practice matching the color blends and brush strokes that they see in the great master's work. They will need to decide if a color is a greenish blue with some white added, or if it is a dulled green that can be matched by mixing some red with it. They should paint their squares carefully, trying to obtain the same color values and intensities that the great master used.
5. When everyone finishes, paste the large squares in numerical order on a large poster board or piece of paper that has been ruled off in the matching number of 5-inch squares.

Student work: Students observe color blends, tints, and shades and endeavor to match them on small squares of white paper or mat board to make a Picasso composite.

6. Students can now identify the painting and evaluate how successfully they mixed and blended the colors they saw before them.

■ UNDERSTANDING ARTWORKS

Learning about Shape and Form

Do you remember as a child standing motionless between a strong light and a blank sheet of paper while someone carefully drew the shadow that your profile cast? The shape was a **silhouette.** It was a fairly good likeness of you after it was cut from black paper and mounted. It could even be identified as yours when all the silhouettes of your classmates were finished, even though it had no distinguishing details within its shape. We are often able to recognize an object by its shape alone. Etienne de Silhouette, who lived in the eighteenth century and served as the French controller-general, introduced economic reforms that made him the object of ridicule and hostility from the nobles, who thereafter used his name to apply to a "mere outline profile drawing."

When a line moves around and comes back and meets itself, it makes a **shape.** You can draw the shape of an

Figure 3.8   Ann Dobson Palmer, *Sonoma*, 1995. Pieced silkscreen, cotton fiber.
By permission of Ann Dobson Palmer.
Sharply defined edges contrast with soft, blurry ones to create horizontal shapes in this landscape, adding to the quiet mood and feeling.

apple with a line, or you can use a paintbrush to paint an apple with no outlines at all. In an artwork, a shape is a two-dimensional area. Its length and width are defined in some way, either by an outline or boundary around it, or by being a different color or texture from the space around it.

Whether we are describing an artwork or creating one, the element of shape requires careful consideration. Shapes have **size;** they can be large or small. Artists can create shapes that have sharp, clearly defined **hard edges** or **soft, blurry contours** that blend into surrounding shapes. If the shapes contain no interior details and are the same color or value, they are called **flat shapes.** In composing an artwork, artists know that shapes can be repeated to create a regular or irregular **pattern.** If they place shapes close together in an artwork, the shapes create a feeling of unity and compactness. When shapes overlap, they tend to give a feeling of depth; the one in front is seen as being close to the viewer. If an artist places similar shapes throughout a composition, our eyes tend to follow the path from shape to shape.

Artists frequently use **realistic shapes** in a two-dimensional artwork to represent three-dimensional objects (or forms) that they see in the natural world. Sometimes, artists simplify or change the shapes they see, **abstracting** the important parts and planes to serve an **expressive purpose,** or letting the shapes stand for symbols, ideas, or concepts. Artists are more interested in the form of an object than they are in the subject matter itself. Look at Picasso's *Girl Before a Mirror* (colorplate 29 in the Color Gallery), and observe how the artist simplified shapes for heads, breasts, and abdomens as he showed a young girl confronting the image of herself as she will be as an old woman. Look at the variety of open and closed shapes in Kandinsky's *Painting No. 198* (colorplate 26 in the Color Gallery). Kandinsky often created shapes in his artworks that had little or no relation to things in the natural world.

Figure 3.9 El Greco, *St. Martin and the Beggar,* **1597/1599. Oil on canvas, 76⅛ × 40½ in.**
Widener Collection, © 1997 Board of Trustees, National Gallery of Art, Washington.
The elongated shapes of the horse, rider, and standing figure contribute to the intensely religious feeling of this artwork done in the Mannerist tradition.

Figure 3.10 **Michaele LeCompte,** *Parterre,* **1990.**
Photo by Nikki Pahl, courtesy of Michael LeCompte.
Flat, abstract shapes cut from thick metal were arranged to create a colorful outdoor screen.

Gothic (colorplate 18) and Marisol's *Women and Dog* (colorplate 17), both artworks featuring figures. A regionalist author who focused on life in mid-America during the Great Depression, Wood shows us a sober, stern, thoughtful couple. The repeated shape of the pitchfork and the rather elongated shapes in the figures' faces contribute to the mood of the painting. On the other hand, Marisol sought to make a different kind of visual statement, so she chose abstracted forms for the bodies of her people and showed us a group of individuals, along with a dog on a leash, anxiously watching for traffic as they go on yet another shopping trip.

When you wish to make a realistic drawing, the technique of **blocking in the shapes** can help you perceive the configuration of the object. First, look at the total, overall shape of an object or a creature—a photograph or live version of, perhaps, a hen or a squirrel. Then look for the primary smaller shapes that make up the creature's total shape. For example, the hen's body is oval—somewhat like a large egg. The tail feathers form a triangular shape. The neck is a short, tapered rectangle with a round head attached. These individual shapes could all be lightly blocked in with a pencil or charcoal and then the details of feathers, beaks, eyes, and feet added to complete the sketch. Try this technique with a squirrel, a cluster of trees, the human figure, or any object. Perceiving the small shapes that make up the big shape and then blocking them in on your paper can enhance your drawing skills. The shapes you see depend, of course, on your **point of view,**—that is, the angle from which you see an object. Although the top of a table may be rectangular, the shape you draw will depend on where you are sitting while drawing it.

Form in art has to do with objects that have three dimensions—length, width, and depth. Generally, we speak

He was more interested in using shapes and colors to express particular feelings and emotional qualities than he was in depicting natural objects. He stated that objects got in the way of his paintings. We refer to this sort of shape as being **nonobjective.** Can you think how you might draw an ominous shape, a restful shape, or an exultant one?

The kinds of shapes that artists choose to use are determined by the message or visual statement they wish to convey. In the Color Gallery, we see Grant Wood's *American*

Figure 3.11   Jorjana Holden, *Reunion, 1986,* **1986. Bronze, 15 × 17 × 12 in.**
Courtesy of Jorjana Holden.
The artist first modeled this cast metal bronze sculpture in wax. The sculpture incorporates eye-leading movement with its diagonal forms in a composition that is pleasing when viewed from any angle or side.

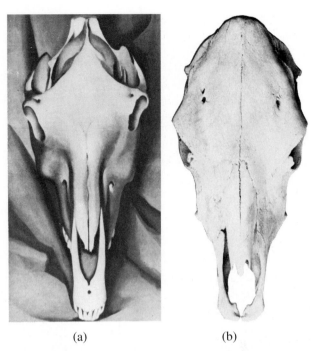

(a)   (b)

Figure 3.12(a)   Georgia O'Keeffe, *Horse's Skull on Blue,* **1930. Oil on canvas, 30 × 16 in.**
Arizona State University Art Museum, Tempe. Gift of Oliver B. James. © 1997 The Georgia O'Keeffe Foundation/Artists Rights Society (ARS), New York.
O'Keeffe collected objects that she treasured and later used as subjects for her paintings—bleached bones, smooth stones, antlers, and shells. Rather than seeing death in the clean, severe form of a horse's skull, O'Keeffe was fascinated with the positive shapes and negative spaces and painted the skull in a realistic manner. **(b)   Horse skull.**
Collection of the authors.

of form in relation to sculpture, architecture, and the various craft areas, such as ceramics. Such artworks take up and enclose space.

We also refer to form in two-dimensional artworks when an artist depicts solid objects on a flat surface. In the latter part of the nineteenth century, French artist Paul Cézanne rebelled against the emphasis on the surface quality of light striking objects that was the impassioned work of the impressionists; he insisted instead that everything in nature has basic forms: cylinders, cones, spheres, and cubes. His pioneering work in this field led to explorations with cubism by Picasso and Braque. Hence, Cézanne is called the "father of modern art."

When artists make sculptures, they work in either the **additive** or **subtractive process.** In the first, the form is built up by adding bits and pieces of clay, soft wax, or other pliable material. The final product is often cast in metal when it is finished. In subtractive works, the artist carves or takes away wood or stone from a large mass to form a figure or object.

Both shapes and forms can be classified as either **geometric** or **free-form. Geometric shapes** are two-dimensional

and remind us of mathematics—circles, squares, and triangles, as well as variations and combinations of these, such as ovals, crescents, semicircles, rectangles, hexagons, and so on. **Geometric forms** are three-dimensional and are reminiscent of cubes, cylinders, spheres, dodecahedrons, and such. Geometric shapes and forms are often used for decoration and make up more highly organized and structured artworks. They often seem less emotional than free forms and give viewers a feeling of perfection and intellectualism.

Free-form shapes and forms are irregular, uneven, and unmeasured, and they remind us of objects in nature. Many artists delight in the beauty of the natural forms of smooth, weathered driftwood, bleached bones, well-worn river rocks, and delicate seashells, and incorporate the characteristics of these natural forms into their own artworks. British sculptor Henry Moore had a studio filled with a lifetime's collection of such forms, and his massive works show evidences of the inspiration that the forms provided

Elementary students at Mission Avenue Open Elementary School in Sacramento, California, experience three-dimensional form by connecting rolled-up sheets of newspapers to create a monumental and dynamic piece of sculpture.
Photo by C. J. Hackett-Croom.

him The curving forms and carefully designed positive shapes and negative areas of Moore's artworks bring to mind stones, rolling hills, mountain ranges, and the monumental forms at Stonehenge.

Both Moore and Georgia O'Keeffe—the former creating three-dimensional artworks and the latter, two-dimensional—were cognizant of another important facet of working with shapes and forms, that of relating them to the **negative spaces** within and around the **positive shapes.** The positive shapes and forms in a composition are the objects themselves, while the negative spaces around the positive shapes contribute immensely to the unity, variety, and balance of an artwork.

■ CHILDREN USE SHAPE AND FORM

When children are about age four or five, they begin drawing symbols that stand for faces, figures, and objects in their environment. They rely heavily on geometric shapes, rather than on realistic or free-form shapes. They often make a round shape and add an oval or triangle for a body, and perhaps two long rectangles for legs and two more for arms. A hand is often a circle, with lines or loops symbolizing fingers. Houses are squares and rectangles topped with a triangular roof and a square chimney, balanced precariously, perpendicular to the roofline. In a young child's artwork, a tree is often seen as a long rectangle topped with a

circle—a "lollipop tree." Children tend to repeat this symbol in a stereotyped manner if they are not motivated as they mature to remember specific experiences with trees and assisted in making more detailed sensory observations.

The geometric shapes that very young children use to depict figures and objects are not adequate for their own critical eyes when they reach age eight or nine and want their drawings to "look right." At this time, children need motivational experiences, including discussions to help them remember and opportunities to act out their experiences. For example, to draw more realistic trees, children need to remember and experience climbing a tree's branches, playing on a swing or in a tree house, observing a ladder against a tree in an orchard, picking fruit, seeing a bird's or squirrel's nest, observing a tree bending and swaying in the wind, and catching a kite in a tree's branches. They need to be directed in observing a tree's seasonal changes in color, in feeling its rough bark, and in seeing the shapes of the tree's trunk, branches, mass of foliage, and individual leaves.

An emphasis on careful observation of the different shapes of things seen in the environment can help children make the transition from drawing geometric symbols in their early childhood years to drawing more realistic free-form shapes as they reach the realism stage. The more realistic free-form shapes will be more satisfying and acceptable to the children's own increasingly critical eyes.

■ PRODUCING ARTWORKS

The Shapes of Fruits and Vegetables

Students differentiate with cut-paper shapes the distinguishing and basic characteristics of the shapes of fruits and vegetables. Multiple cuts of several different shapes are arranged in an overlapping and pleasing composition.

1. Collect an assortment of fresh fruit and vegetables or photographs of them. Compare and contrast the different shapes. How would you describe the shapes of radishes, carrots, celery, pineapples, and green beans? How are the sizes alike or different? How is a green bean like a pea pod? How are the shapes of pears and eggplants different? Compare an apple with a slice of watermelon. Describe the shape of broccoli. Discuss how the grocer arranges the different bins in the produce section of the market. Are some vegetables and fruits stacked, overlapping, in rows, in baskets?

2. Using an assortment of colored paper, cut out the shape of one vegetable or fruit. Then make multiple cuts of the shape by cutting three or four pieces of paper at once. Think of how produce is arranged in the market.

3. Place your fruit or vegetable shapes on a piece of white or colored paper, overlapping and clustering the shapes in a pleasing arrangement. Do the same with several other different fruits and vegetables. Make your composition fit your paper. Paste the shapes down, and then use a black marking pen to outline and distinguish the separate shapes.

Student work: Tagboard print. Geometric shapes were cut out and glued to the background before the student made the print.

Combining Shapes for a Tagboard Print

Students cut geometric and free-form shapes for a composition that is pasted to a background and forms the design for a relief print.

1. Make sketches or collect several photographs of Victorian houses, trucks, birds, landscapes, and so on. Observe your selection closely to see all the different shapes that make up the whole.

2. Cut the shapes you see out of tagboard. Simplify, distort, exaggerate, repeat, delete, and change the shapes to suit your purposes and intent.

3. Arrange the shapes on a piece of 6-by-9-inch tagboard, overlapping some of them. Paste them down securely. This is called your **printing plate.** Be sure the glue is dry before you print.

4. Place a spoonful of black, water-soluble printing ink on a printing tray. Roll a printing **brayer** back and forth in the tray to cover the brayer evenly with ink. Place your printing plate on a piece of newspaper, and roll the brayer over it. The cut shapes will have a white "shadow" around them. This will accent the different shapes when you make your print.

5. Place your inked printing plate facedown on a piece of white ditto, Fadeless, Astrobright, or Brighthue paper. The colored papers are less absorbent than colored construction paper and will produce a sharper printed image when using water-soluble printing ink.

6. Turn the printing plate and paper over, and rub the backside of the paper with your fingers to ensure an even printing. Then remove the paper from your printing plate to dry. You can make several prints by reinking the printing plate each time.

Creating a Three-Dimensional Form: Modeling the Figure

Students model a seated, kneeling, or reclining figure from a cylinder of clay. Six or seven students work together, and each student models a small figure that will be displayed as part of a group. Fired objects may be glazed or painted with acrylics, or stained by brushing them with white or dark tempera before scrubbing off the excess paint. Students can refer to books showing ceramic models of small figures, such as *The Spirit of Folk Art* (Santa Fe, NM: International Museum of Folk Art, 1989). Suggested themes include:

> A musical group or small street band
> Playing ball at the beach
> A picnic in the park
> A funeral procession
> Telling stories to children
> A wedding party
> Acrobats, clowns and circus performers
> At the dinner table
> The crowd around an ice-cream cart
> People dancing
> Football or baseball players
> Playing marbles
> Cops and robbers
> Stranded on an island
> At the market
> Trick-or-treating

1. Work on a canvas mat so that you can rotate your artwork as you progress and observe it from all sides. The mat also helps keep the surface of the table clean. Form a piece of clay about the size of an orange into a 6- or 7-inch-long cylinder that is about 1½ inches thick.
2. With a tongue depressor, make a vertical cut at one end of the cylinder to form the legs of the figure. Squeeze the other end of the cylinder to form a neck and head.
3. Roll a coil from another small piece of clay, and cut the coil in half to make the arms. Score the shoulders and the ends of the cylinders that will be attached for arms, and then apply a little bit of slip. **Slip** is a creamy, thick mixture of clay and water. Attach the arms to the body, and use the end of the tongue depressor and your fingers to smooth the joined area.
4. You have created the basic figure and are now ready to bend the knees, elbows, waist, and neck into a seated, kneeling, or reclining position. Be sure to give consideration to the negative spaces.
5. Smooth the surface of the form, or give it a textural quality. The emphasis in producing this artwork is on the form and not on face or clothing details.

Constructing Forms with Clay Slabs: Castles

Students combine a variety of clay slabs to create an imaginary miniature castle (or other type of building).

1. Analyze photographs of different kinds of castles to distinguish and identify the battlements, parapets, baileys, buttresses, turrets, towers, drawbridges, and so

on. Then use your imagination to create a miniature castle (or a cathedral, temple, Indian pueblo, Victorian house, etc.).

2. Roll clay out on your canvas or vinyl mat with a rolling pin. Make a base for your construction that is no larger than 6 inches in any direction. It may be geometric or free-form. It need not be level.
3. Using a potter's needle, a plastic knife, or a tongue depressor, cut out slabs from rolled-out pieces of clay to make the walls, towers, and such. Try not to have any slabs thinner than one-fourth inch. Score any parts to be joined, and apply slip. You may need to roll out a tiny coil of clay and apply it to the places where two pieces of clay form a right angle to ensure that no cracks appear when the piece is dry.
4. You may add roofs, but be sure to cut out windows or doors so air can escape when the finished castle is fired in the kiln. To make a cone-shaped roof, cut out a pie-shaped section from a circle of clay, and form it into a cone.
5. Create textures by imprinting objects in the soft surface of the clay, by adding bits and pieces of clay, or by dragging a tool over the clay's surface.
6. Remember to keep looking at the form you are creating from all sides to ensure a balanced and unified design.
7. When the clay castle dries, it is called **greenware** and should be fired in a kiln. This is called the **bisque** stage. You can apply **ceramic glaze** to your castle and fire it again. Or you may choose to rinse your castle in water, apply white or colored tempera, and then wash the tempera off under running water. This creates a **stained** effect, with the tempera remaining in the low areas and the color of the bisque in the higher areas. You can then brush on a clear coating of Joli glaze, or you may choose to paint your castle with **acrylic paints.**

Creating a Three-Dimensional Form: Making Box Sculpture

Students design a piece of additive sculpture by collecting small cardboard boxes, adhering them, and decorating them in the manner of the artist Marisol (see *Women and Dog*, colorplate 17 in the Color Gallery). Marisol imaginatively assembled a variety of materials—wood, fabric, and plaster—to create boxy sculptures that made visual comments on contemporary life.

1. Collect boxes of various sizes. You may work on a small scale with film boxes, cereal boxes, and such, or you may choose to work on a large scale and use corrugated cardboard cartons.
2. Stack and assemble the boxes to create a figure, a group of figures, or an abstract arrangement. Attach them with masking tape.

Colorplate 1   Megan, *My Sister.*
Portrait made from observation of a posed model by a six-year-old child using a
black pen to draw the face and features. Crayon used on a warming tray was added
for color.

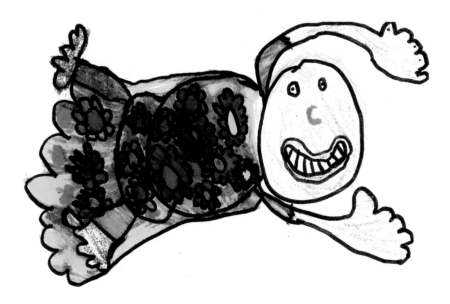

Colorplate 2   Emily, *When I Was a Baby.*
Six-year-old Emily drew herself as a baby
wearing a flower-patterned dress of her
favorite color, yellow.

Colorplate 3 Megan, *Indian Princess*.
A potato-print face was the starting point for this drawing in which a six-year-old child added a variety of colors, decorative patterns, and details with changeable markers.

Colorplate 4 Max, *Still Life*.
This painting by an eleven-year-old child shows careful and close observation of objects as well as the skillful use of tempera paint. Black lines were added with marking pen after the paint dried.

Colorplate 5 Ka Sandra, *Parade.*
A nine-year-old drew this marching band with oil pastels when she remembered a colorful, noisy parade on a downtown street.

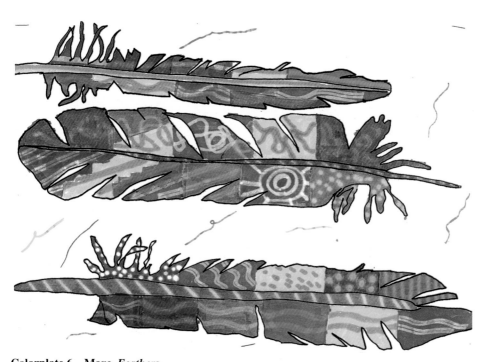

Colorplate 6 Marc, *Feathers.*
A twelve-year-old-student began with a contour drawing of turkey feathers and then used changeable markers to focus on the decorative and imaginative arrangement of colors, lines, shapes, and patterns.

Colorplate 7   Pam, *From Above, Looking Down.*
An eight-year-old student imagined herself in a hot air balloon to view the shapes, colors, and patterns and to create a tempera painting of the landscape below.

Colorplate 8   Jonathan, *Queen.*
Eight-year-old Jonathan used a posed model for visual information for this tempera painting.

Colorplate 9   Spenser, *Monkey.*
Seven-year-old Spenser cut legs, tail, head, and body
separately from colored paper before combining
them to create this nocturnal jungle scene.

Colorplate 10   Nicole, *Clown.*
Six-year-old Nicole used a glue line to
enclose the shapes. When the glue dried as
transparent lines on the black paper, she
added color with chalk pastels.

Colorplate 11   Vincent van Gogh, *The Starry Night*, 1889. Oil on canvas, 29 × 36¼ in.
The Museum of Modern Art, New York. Acquired through the Lillie P. Bliss Bequest.
Photograph © 1997 The Museum of Modern Art, New York.

Colorplate 12   Georges Seurat, *Sunday Afternoon on the Island of La Grande Jatte*, 1884–86. Oil
on canvas, 207.6 × 308.0 cm.
Helen Birch Bartlett Memorial Collection (1926.224). Photograph © The Art Institute of Chicago.
All rights reserved.

Colorplate 13 Paul Cézanne, *Le Château Noir,*
ca. 1904. Oil on canvas, 29 × 37 in.
Gift of Eugene and Agnes Meyer.
© 1997 Board of Trustees, National Gallery of Art,
Washington.

Colorplate 14 Li An-zhong, *Shrike and Bamboo,*
Sung dynasty, ca. 1110. Colors and ink on silk, ht.
10 in.
National Palace Museum, Taipei, Taiwan, Republic
of China.

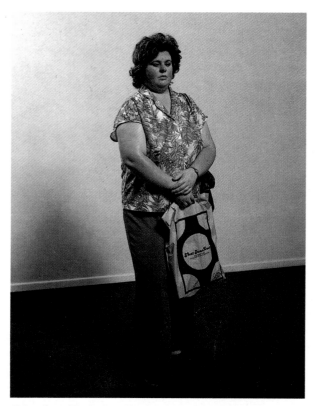

Colorplate 15   Duane Hanson, *Bus Stop Lady,* 1983.
Polyester and fiberglass polychrome in oil. Life-size.
© *Duane Hanson.*

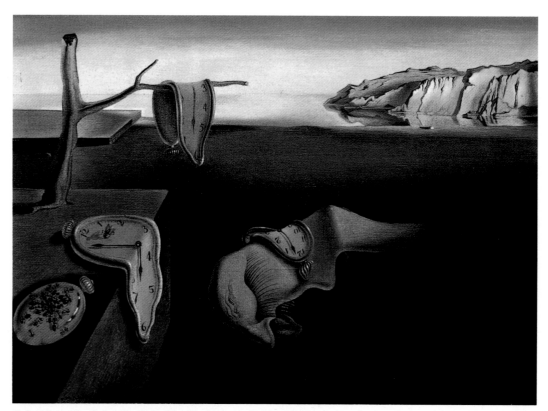

Colorplate 16   Salvador Dali, *The Persistence of Memory (Persistence de la mémoire),* 1931. Oil on
canvas, 9½ × 13 in.
*The Museum of Modern Art, New York. Given anonymously. Photograph © 1997 The Museum of Modern
Art, New York. © Demart ProArte ®, Geneva/Artists Rights Society ARS, New York.*

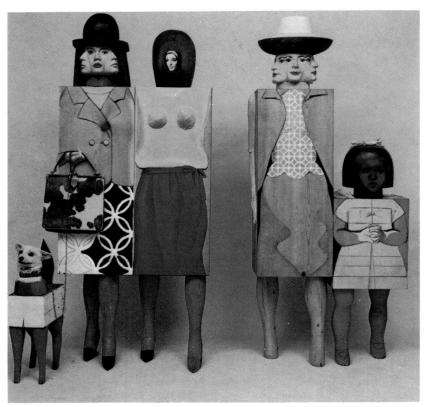

Colorplate 17   Marisol, *Women and Dog,* 1964. Wood, plaster, synthetic polymer, and miscellaneous items, 72 × 82 × 16 in.
Collection of the Whitney Museum of American Art. Purchased with funds from the Friends of the Whitney Museum of American Art (64.17). © Marisol/V.A.G.A., New York, 1994.

Colorplate 18   Grant Wood, *American Gothic,* 1930. Oil on beaver board, 76 × 63.3 cm.
Friends of American Art Collection (1930.934). Photograph © The Art Institute of Chicago. All rights reserved.

Colorplate 19 Fukaye Roshu, *The Ivy Land (Tsuta-no-hosomichi)*, Edo period, 1699–1755, Japanese. Sixfold screen; opaque color on gold ground, 133 × 271.8 cm.
© *The Cleveland Museum of Art, 1997. John L. Severance Fund 1954.127.*

Colorplate 20 Khemkaran, *Prince Riding an Elephant*, period of Akbar, 1556–1605, Mughal. Leaf from an album, gouache on paper. Signed.
The Metropolitan Museum of Art, Rogers Fund, 1925. (25.68.4). © 1988 By The Metropolitan Museum of Art.

Colorplate 21 Franz Marc, *Yellow Cow,* 1911. Oil on canvas, 55⅜ × 74¼ in.
Solomon R. Guggenheim Museum, New York. Photo by David Heald. © Solomon R. Guggenheim Foundation,
New York (49.1210).

Colorplate 22 Albert Bierstadt, *The Rocky Mountains,* 1863. Oil on canvas, 73¼ × 120¾ in.
The Metropolitan Museum of Art, Rogers Fund, 1907 (07.123). © 1979 By The Metropolitan Museum of Art.

Colorplate 23 Diego Rivera, detail of *Fresco in the Fountain Hall of the Detroit Institute of Arts*, 1932.
© 1997 *The Detroit Institute of Arts. Gift Edsel B. Ford.*

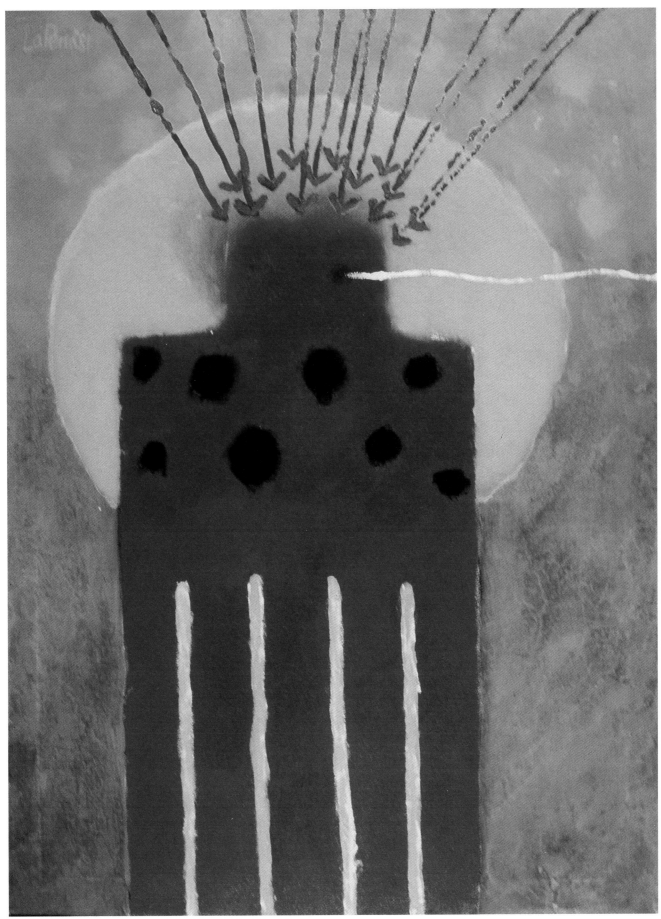

Colorplate 24 Frank La Pena, *Flower Dance Spirit*, 1981.
Courtesy Patty and Chris Gibson.

Colorplate 25   Yoshio Taylor, *Sanzo,* **1991. Clay sculpture, 73 × 27 × 17 in.**
Photo © Bill Santos.

Colorplate 26   Vassily Kandinsky, *Painting No. 198,* 1914. Oil on canvas, 64 × 36¼ in.
The Museum of Modern Art, New York. Mrs. Simon Guggenheim Fund. Photograph © 1997 The Museum of Modern Art, New York.

Colorplate 27 Leonardo da Vinci, *Ginevra de' Benci* (obverse), ca. 1474. Oil on panel, 15¼ × 14½ in.
Ailsa Mellon Bruce Fund, © 1997 Board of Trustees, National Gallery of Art, Washington.

Colorplate 28 Renoir, *A Girl with a Watering Can*, 1876. Oil on canvas, 39½ × 28¾ in.
Chester Dale Collection, © 1997 Board of Trustees, National Gallery of Art, Washington.

Colorplate 29 Pablo Picasso, *Girl Before a Mirror*, 1932. Oil on canvas, 64 × 51¼ in.
The Museum of Modern Art, New York. Gift of Mrs. Simon Guggenheim. Photograph © 1997 The
Museum of Modern Art, New York. © 1997 Estate of Pabalo Picasso/Artists Rights Society (ARS),
New York.

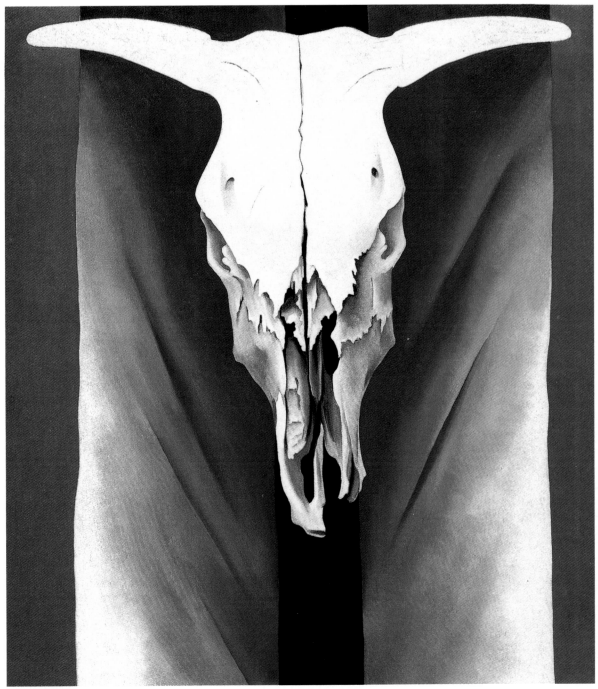

Colorplate 30   Georgia O'Keeffe, *Cow's Skull: Red, White, and Blue,* **1931. Oil on canvas, 39⅞ × 35⅞ in.**
The Metropolitan Museum of Art, The Alfred Stieglitz Collection, 1949. (52.203). © 1991 By The Metropolitan Museum of
Art. © 1997 The Georgia O'Keeffe Foundation/Artists Rights Society (ARS), New York.

Colorplate 31 Jacob Lawrence, *Vaudeville*, 1951. Tempera on fiberboard with pencil, 29⅞ × 19⁵⁄₁₆ in.
Hirshhorn Museum and Sculpture Garden, Smithsonian Institution. Gift of Joseph H. Hirshhorn, 1966. © Jacob Lawrence.

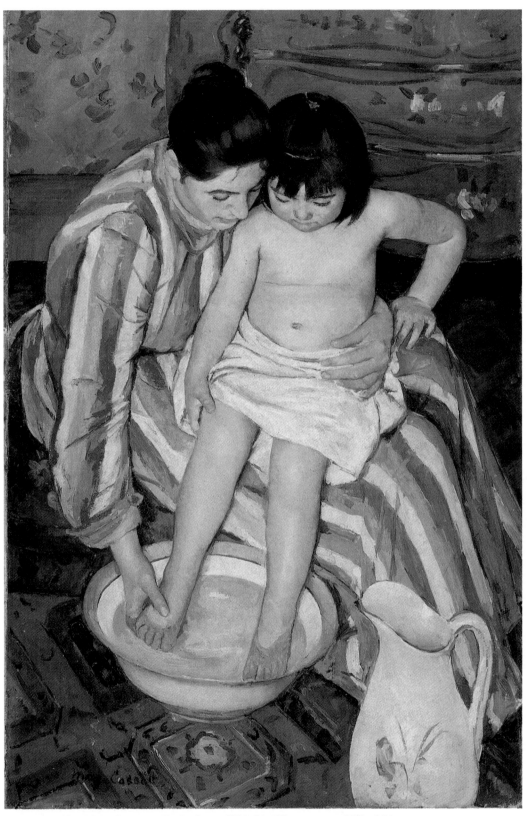

Colorplate 32   Mary Cassatt, *The Bath,* **ca. 1891–92. Oil on canvas, 39½ × 26 in.**
The Art Institute of Chicago. Robert A. Waller Fund (1910.2). © *The Art Institute of Chicago. All rights reserved.*

Colorplate 33 Marc Chagall, *Green Violinist*, 1923–24. Oil on canvas, 78 × 42¾ in.

Solomon R. Guggenheim Museum, New York. Guggenheim Museum, New York. Photo by David Heald. © Solomon R. Guggenheim Foundation, New York (FN 37.446). © 1997 Artists Rights Society (ARS), New York/ADAGP, Paris.

Colorplate 34   Armando Alvarez, *We the People*, 1994. Steel sculpture, 300 ft. wall with ninety-three figures. Gallup, N.M.

Colorplate 35   Wayne Thiebaud, *Dark Green River*, 1996. Oil on board, 11 × 14 in.
Courtesy of the artist.

Colorplate 36   Judith A. Lowry, *The Funeral of Frida Kahlo*, 1996. Acrylic on canvas, 68 × 94 in.

**Colorplate 37   Jose Montoya, *Court Appearance*,
1976. Oil, 28 × 36 in.**
From the Ricardo Favela Collection.

**Colorplate 38   Maria Winkler, *Marbles Spill III*,
1996. Chalk pastel, 22 × 33 in.**
From the collection of the artist.

**Colorplate 39   Cham Thor, detail of *Mona,
Hmong Daily Life*, 1994. Stitchery, 30 × 30 in.**
*From collection at University of California, Davis,
Medical Center.*

3. Cover the boxes with paper-toweling strips or brown paper bag strips dipped in wheat paste mixture.

4. Let your box sculpture dry. Then paint it, and glue on bits of fabric, photographs, and patterned paper as finishing touches.

■ UNDERSTANDING ARTWORKS

Learning about Texture

Young children are very curious. They learn through their senses, and they especially have a strong urge to explore and discover through their sense of touch. Adults often move breakable or potentially harmful objects out of reach or admonish children, "Don't touch!"

But not only the very young find the impulse to touch natural objects irresistible. How many of us love to stroke the soft fur of a kitten or puppy? The silky, lustrous quality of satin against our skin feels better than the scratchy roughness of burlap. We learn through experience about the texture of sandpaper or cactus, and usually prefer not to touch them. Through previous association, people sometimes find the texture of a toad or snakeskin repugnant.

The **tactile quality** of things appeals to our sense of touch, and this surface quality, whether we are describing natural objects or artworks, is referred to as **texture.** We use such words as *rough, smooth, hard, soft, slick, bumpy, fluffy,* and so on to describe texture.

Our senses respond to texture in artworks as well as in nature. The smooth surface of a piece of ceramics, the rich and wooly fibers that weavers use, and the polished sheen of a pewter bowl appeal to our tactile senses. Works of sculpture in museums are often so inviting to our sense of touch that signs and even guards must be posted to ensure that museum visitors keep "hands off." Our senses are attracted to a smooth marble surface, the warm glow of polished wood, or the burnished surface of a bronze statue. But even if we are not allowed to touch these surfaces, we know how they feel because we remember having touched similar objects.

We like **variety** in texture, too, and we plan our clothing as well as our interior furnishings to have different surfaces. An architect chooses several textured building materials in designing a structure—perhaps glass, stone, and wood—to achieve a pleasing effect and to create unity. Having too great a variety of textures, however, creates a chaotic effect. We enjoy variety in the textures of the foods we eat; steak and potatoes in toothpastelike tubes were abandoned when astronauts complained about the sameness of texture.

Artists are aware of tactile appeal and use texture to express a particular emotion or feeling, or to enhance their artwork in some way. They may want to use soft, fluffy textures to create a feeling of warmth, comfort, and

Figure 3.13   Vincent van Gogh, *La Maoumé,* **1888. Oil on canvas, 28⅞ × 23¾ in.**
Chester Dale Collection, © 1997 Board of Trustees, National Gallery of Art, Washington.
The texture created by van Gogh's brush strokes contributes to the strong appeal of his works. Often intent on getting a large amount of paint on his canvas, he would squeeze colors directly from the tube, sometimes using a palette knife or even his fingers to spread the paint and achieve the rich, textural impasto.

welcome, knowing that hard, slick surfaces seem cool and less inviting. They may also choose to depict a person's character through texture, showing the rugged, wrinkled face of a sea captain or, as Renoir did, the porcelain-smooth skin of beautiful young girls and women.

In responding to and in creating artworks, we refer to two kinds of texture:

1. **Actual texture** is the real surface of something, one that we could feel with our eyes closed. We most often associate actual texture with three-dimensional art—sculpture, architecture, and crafts. The appeal of Navajo weaving is not only in its symmetrical, stylized arrangement of shapes; its actual rough, woolen texture appeals to our sense of touch. A painting may also have actual texture if the artist applied paint thickly. Sometimes, artists use palette knives as well as brushes

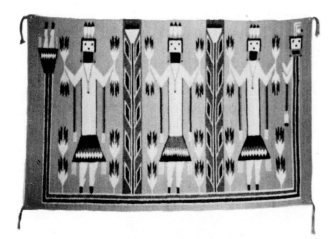

Figure 3.14   Navajo rug.
Collection of authors.
The wooly texture of the fibers used to weave this decorative artwork contributes to the rug's appeal.

and build up several layers of paint to create a real textural quality. This is called the **impasto** technique. Van Gogh sometimes created his thick, swirling brush strokes by squeezing the paint directly from the tube onto his canvas. Occasionally, this intense artist even painted with his fingers! Jackson Pollock created actual texture on his artworks by dripping and flinging paint on the canvas as it lay on the floor. It is, of course, easier to see this sort of actual texture when looking at an original painting rather than a reproduction. Collages, which may incorporate real pieces of burlap, string, and such, are examples of other two-dimensional artworks that can have actual texture.

2. Artists sometimes create **visual texture (or simulated texture)** in two-dimensional artworks to give the **illusion** of real texture. A finely detailed texture in an artwork appears closer to us; blurred, indistinct textures appear farther away. Our eye is attracted to texture, so an artist may use an appealing texture or a richly textured area to focus our attention on a particular area in an artwork. Texture provides **visual interest** for our eyes and gives more life to a painting, drawing, or print. Such texture appeals to our tactile sense, but we do not need to touch the surfaces represented to know how they feel because we have touched the real equivalents in nature. George Catlin worked closely from direct observation to achieve the texture of the fluffy fur of a white wolf around White Cloud's shoulders, as well as the texture of the spiky, eagle-quill headdress (see fig. 3.15). Artists who can create a variety of realistic textures are technically skilled.

Figure 3.15   George Catlin, *The White Cloud, Head Chief of the Iowas,* ca. 1845. canvas, 28 × 22⅞ in.
Paul Mellon Collection, © 1997 Board of Trustees, National Gallery of Art, Washington.
The spiky, sharp eagle quills in the headdress and the grizzly bear claws strung around White Cloud's neck accentuate the soft texture of the white, furry wolf skin that hangs from the chief's shoulders. Catlin devoted his life to making realistic images of members of various Native American tribes.

The French term **trompe l'oeil,** which means "to deceive the eye," describes the illusionistic skill in paintings that depicts the textures and colors of objects so realistically that we are "tricked" into thinking that the actual objects—perhaps a fly, bit of yarn, nails, pieces of wood, and such—are actually on the painting's surface Two nineteenth-century painters often associated with still lifes in the trompe l'oeil manner are William Harnett and John Frederick Peto.

We often use the terms *texture* and *pattern* together in describing an artwork, since they are related but not the same thing. A pattern is usually made by repeating a line or shape many times and spacing it evenly over an area. The effect may give the illusion of texture. Repeated lines and shapes may exist as a pattern alone, however, and not refer to a surface texture at all.

Figure 3.16   John Frederick Peto, *The Old Violin*, ca. 1890. Oil on canvas, 30⅜ × 22⅞ in.
Gift of Avalon Foundation, © 1997 Board of Trustees, National Gallery of Art, Washington.
A passion for portraying objects exactly as the artist saw them resulted in a form of visual realism called *trompe l'oeil*. The eye is tricked into perceiving actual objects rather than paint on a canvas. The textural qualities of wood (both painted and varnished), metallic hinges, a key, and torn sheet music attract and fascinate our eyes.

■ CHILDREN USE TEXTURE

Children explore texture in a variety of ways. They may cut and paste a variety of papers and fabrics, yarn, and so on to make an abstract collage design. Bits of textured materials may be "idea starters" for young children, since the concept appeals to their sense of touch. In this activity, children choose a scrap of textured material and ponder about what it suggests to them or of what it reminds them. For instance, a scrap of sandpaper may remind them of the beach or a sandbox, and after they paste it onto a piece of paper, they can use crayons, pens, pencils, or oil pastels to make the rest of their picture. A bit of foil might be the beginning

of a drawing about spaceships. A scrap of flat sponge, a feather, or a bit of ribbon can trigger all sorts of inventive ideas and increase fluent responses simply because of the tactile imagery evoked.

Another avenue for children to pursue with texture is that of making a variety of crayon rubbings of different textures found in and around home and school. Students can then cut and paste the found textures into pictures and designs.

Older children enjoy creating simulated textures in their drawings and paintings, and with instruction can develop a certain amount of skill in showing the visual surface qualities of their subjects.

■ PRODUCING ARTWORKS

Creating Actual Texture in Relief Sculpture

Students create a variety of textures on a clay slab to make a relief sculpture of a flat building, a figure, or an animal, either by **imprinting** the clay with a variety of objects repeatedly, by **dragging** an implement across the clay, or by **adding** bits and pieces of clay on top of the slab.

1. Decide on a theme for your textured slab project. You may wish to use visual reference materials, such as sketches you have made of Victorian houses, or you may find pictures of them in reference books. As a group, you may wish to create a "Frontier town," with each student making a different storefront for Main Street. Or you may wish to make a figure or animal. Keep each clay slab 6–8 inches high. Make a paper pattern of your object's shape.
2. With a rolling pin, roll out a **slab** of wedged clay on a piece of canvas or on the fabric side of a piece of vinyl. Place the chunk of clay between two thin sticks of wood to ensure that the slab will be of an even thickness. The sticks of wood should be about three-eighths inch thick.
3. Place your paper pattern on the clay slab, and cut it out with a needle cutter or a plastic knife. Remove excess clay.
4. Imprint with different gadgets and tools to create a variety of textures on your house, storefront, figure, or animal. Try dragging a tool across the clay. Try adding tiny bits and pieces of clay to the surface; be sure to brush some slip over the surface first.
5. When you are finished, let your textured slab dry. After it is fired, you may glaze it and fire it again. Or you may paint it with acrylics or tempera. Or you may dip it quickly in and out of water and apply thinned tempera—white or a color; then hold it under water and brush off excess paint to reveal a stained,

"antique" effect. When your slab is dry, brush on Joli glaze.

Actual and Simulated Textures

Students use oil pastel, and several differently textured fabrics and papers to create a collage with actual and simulated textures.

1. Collect a variety of textured materials, both fabric and paper, such as velvet, felt, corrugated paper, sandpaper, glossy paper, corduroy, velour, ribbon, sponges, and so on.
2. Select a theme for your artwork, such as fishing in the river, walking in the rain, robots on parade, dancers on the stage, birds in a tree, and so on. Decide on several different textured materials, and cut from them some of the objects you will include in your composition. These will be the **actual textures** in your artwork. Try placing them on a piece of 9-by-12-inch background paper, white or colored, and think about how you will relate them to the environment and other objects in the composition. Set them aside.
3. Place your background paper on several sheets of newspaper, which provide a cushioned surface to make working with oil pastels easier. Use the oil pastels to create **simulated textures** for the other items in your composition. You may want to use a sharp tool and scratch some of the areas where you have applied a thick layer of oil pastels. Blend several colors of oil pastels by rubbing them with your fingertip. Try adding black, white, or another color on top of a color.
4. When you have finished with the oil pastels, glue the objects you made in Step 2 in place.

Creating Actual Texture: Weaving

Students use a variety of different-textured yarns to weave a small tapestry on a flat cardboard loom. Small chipboard looms (6½ by 13 inches) with slits already cut across the top and bottom can be purchased from art supply catalogs. Or you can make your own loom by cutting a small rectangle from chipboard, mat board, or corrugated cardboard, and then making short slits, about one-fourth inch apart, across the top and bottom. The appropriate needles and a variety of weaving yarns are also available from art supply catalogs.

1. To **warp** the loom, wrap the warping fiber around and around the loom through the slits at the top and bottom. Use pearl cotton, string, or other nonstretch fiber for warps. Tie the beginning of the warp to the end of the warp on the backside of the loom.
2. Select a variety of yarns with different textures (nubby, rough, smooth, shiny, fuzzy, etc.) for your **wefts.** Limit

your selection of colors to achieve unity. Try a monochromatic color scheme. Or try using two or three neutral colors and one or two brighter colors.

3. Cut a piece of yarn about a yard long, and thread your needle. Needles should be blunt-pointed and have a large eye for the yarn to pass through. Begin weaving across the warp strings, going over and under in alternate rows. This process is called **tabby weaving.** To speed up the process, you may wish to use a **pickup stick** to lift the warps. To do this, use a flat stick such as a ruler and weave it across the warp fibers, going over and under each string. When you turn the stick on its side, it lifts alternate warps, enabling you to send your needle across the loom more rapidly. However, you will have to weave manually back across the loom, as the pickup stick only allows use in one direction. Pack your rows of wefts tightly and neatly together with a plastic comb, a fork, or your fingers.
4. Start or end a piece of yarn near the center of the loom, rather than at the sides. The 2–3 inches of extra yarn will then fall on the backside of the woven piece instead of projecting from the sides. These loose ends can be woven into the back of the tapestry later, or they can be glued in place.
5. You can weave the weft in curves rather than in straight rows across the loom. You can weave only partway across, leaving a slit or interlocking the wefts. You may choose to include some natural found objects—bark, lichen, twigs, and such—in your weaving.
6. When you are finished, cut the warps in the middle on the backside of the loom, and tie the first warp string to the one next to it, and so on, across the top of the loom. Tie knots in the same manner at the bottom of your woven piece.
7. Cut lengths of yarn for fringes across the bottom. Double each yarn length over, thread the loop into your needle, insert the needle through the bottom of the tapestry, and slip the yarn through and loop. Repeat across the bottom edge to add a decorative effect to your tapestry.

■ UNDERSTANDING ARTWORKS

Learning about Space

Raise your arms above your head. Stretch them out in front of you. Take two steps forward. You have moved in **three-dimensional space**—not the "outer space" frequented by spaceships, astronauts, and little green beings, but the kind that we deal with in looking at artworks and the kind that sometimes presents head-scratching problems for us in creating art, especially two-dimensional art. Natural objects—as well as those forms created by sculptors, architects, and

Figure 3.17   M. C. Escher, Belvedere, 1958. Lithograph, 46 × 29.5 cm.
Courtesy of Vorpal Gallery, Soho, New York. Photo by D. James Dee. © M. C. Escher Heirs/Cordon Art-Baarn-Holland. All rights reserved.
Famous for his innovative and unusual use of space, Escher created a world of wonder with his sharply delineated perspective.

craftspersons—exist in space. They are defined by the space around and within them. Three-dimensional space is the emptiness or areas around, above, below, and between objects, as well as the space inside hollow objects.

Architecture is concerned with enclosing **actual space** in a functional and unified manner. Landscape architects and people involved in city planning design spaces where people will live, work, and play. They are skilled in making practical and beautiful use of environmental spaces, and this involves how they combine forms, colors, and textures. **Sculpture** is also an art form that takes up actual space. It is freestanding, and viewers must move through the space and around it to view all its sides. **Relief sculpture** is somewhat different in that it projects outward from

a flat surface and is seen from only one point of view—the front side.

One kind of actual space that we deal with in responding to artworks and in creating our own is the **flat surface of the picture plane.** This is the space determined by the length and width of the canvas or paper upon which the artwork is created. Artists plan carefully to achieve a feeling of balance and unity throughout a composition, leaving no spaces that do not function in harmony with the rest of the artwork. Piet Mondrian had a keen desire to order space in his stark compositions. His later works are devoid of any aspect of volume or three-dimensional form. He extracted the essence on several themes, moving from relatively naturalistic drawing, through vividly unnaturalistic and expressive color, to a linear simplification that shows a two-dimensional space divided in perfect relationships of squares and rectangles painted with black, white, and the primary colors. Mondrian lived in Holland, where the horizon is as flat and sharp as if drawn with a ruler, and the space in his work is similarly flat, sharp, and in perfect balance.

The difference between, and the close relationship of, **positive shapes** and **negative spaces** in the two-dimensional space contained within the format of the picture plane are important. The figures or objects themselves are the positive shapes, and the empty spaces between and around them are the negative spaces. In painting, we frequently refer to this as **figure-ground.** An artist creating a two-dimensional composition strives to intermingle and relate the positive shapes and negative spaces so as to achieve harmony. Placing tracing paper over a composition such as Rubens's *Lion* and drawing around all the negative spaces readily shows how, when finished, we have inadvertently drawn the positive shape of the animal.

This knowledge about the relationship of positive shapes and negative spaces can help us draw an object that otherwise might seem perplexing and complicated. Hold a viewfinder very steadily in front of you. Keep one eye closed, and focus on a section of a bare-branched tree. You will see branches and the trunk creating negative spaces between each other as they extend off the four sides of the viewfinder. With a pencil, concentrate on drawing these negative spaces on a 9-by-12-inch piece of paper exactly as you see them through your viewfinder. When you finish, you will have drawn the section of the tree. The positive and negative spaces fit together like the pieces of a jigsaw puzzle. Focusing on negative spaces, rather than on the more complicated positive shapes of what you are observing, can help you solve some drawing dilemmas.

Many sculptors include negative spaces within their artworks, planning carefully to strike a pleasing balance between positive and negative areas and to create a variety of interesting open areas. In 1929, British sculptor Henry

Figure 3.18 Edward Hicks, *The Cornell Farm,* **1848. Canvas, 36¾ × 49 in.**
Gift of Edgar William and Bernice Chrysler Gabisch, © 1997
Board of Trustees, National Gallery of Art, Washington.
The Quaker preacher who painted this pastoral scene in 1848 had no formal art training, yet he knew how to create the illusion of great spatial depth with diminishing sizes, elevated placement of objects, and lighter tones and fewer details in the background.

Figure 3.19 Victoria Z. Rivers, *Bali Moon,* **1989. Mixed media on fabric, including stitching and beads.**
Courtesy of Victoria Z. Rivers, Collection of Susan Matthews.
Diminishing sizes, elevated placement, and parallel lines going toward a vanishing point make for a depiction of deep space in this night landscape.

Moore pierced his first opening through a solid mass in a piece of sculpture and began exploring the many ways in which negative spaces can be integral parts of three-dimensional artwork.

Creating the **illusion of actual space** and giving a feeling of depth to a two-dimensional artwork have long been challenges that have perplexed and fascinated artists, especially those in the Western world. While this photographic realism has been readily accepted in the West, Asian artists at one time might well have questioned this concept of "realism." (Do people and objects *really get smaller* in nature when they are farther away?) Objects in space have three dimensions—height, width, and depth—yet the flat surface of a piece of paper, a wall or ceiling, a wood panel, or a canvas has only two dimensions—height and width. During the Renaissance, artists began studying nature much more closely to determine just how to accomplish an illusion of actual space more accurately and realistically. German artist Albrecht Dürer contrived a gridded frame through which he could look at an object directly in front of him and then copy, and even foreshorten, what he was seeing on his gridded drawing paper. Some artists puzzled over the use of converging lines and vanishing points. Others found that shading a face or arm from light to dark made the object look rounded rather than flat. These early artists attempted and succeeded in using the picture plane or surface to create a painting that made viewers feel that they were looking through a window to the real world.

Let's try this window-to-the-world idea. Look out a window, and locate which objects are nearest you. If you were making a painting of this scene, these objects would be in the **foreground.** The part that is farthest away is the **background,** and the space in between is the **middle ground.** To draw or paint this window scene, you would need to create the illusion of space on your paper and would find some of the techniques that follow helpful. Sometimes, artists choose to use only a few of these techniques. Sometimes, they use all of them, depending on whether they wish to create a realistic and representational view; whether they wish to express some emotion or feeling about what they see by exaggerating, omitting, or distorting the images; and whether they are more interested in the shapes, lines, and colors of what they see than they are in the actual depiction of what is in front of them.

1. **Overlapping** occurs when one opaque object covers part of a second object. The one in front seems closer. If only a few shapes in a composition overlap, and if that is the only way the artist uses to show depth, we say the composition has **shallow** or **flat** space.
2. **Size** plays a large part in depicting three-dimensional space on a flat surface. Picture two ballplayers on a field. One is several feet away from you. The other one is far away; you could raise your hand and block from your view his entire figure. In a two-dimensional artwork, large objects appear to be closer than small objects. A very small object appears to be farther away in the distance. This is often referred to as **diminishing**

sizes. If our eyes are led far back in the picture plane, we say the composition has **deep** space.

3. **Placement** of figures and objects also plays an important part in the illusion of creating space on a flat surface. Figures and objects that are placed on the ground and lowest in the picture plane appear to be closer to the viewer than those placed higher up. Those that are farthest away are highest from the bottom of the picture, and they are found near or on the eye-level line or horizon line. Now picture what happens to this rule when we regard the sky, which is, of course, above the horizon line. The largest clouds (or balloons, helicopters, or birds) are those that are closest to us, and they are at the top of the picture. The most distant clouds (or other objects) are smaller and are seen lower and toward the horizon. Next time you drive down a highway, notice the size and placement of the clouds that you see through your windshield. Notice how the boats on the horizon line lead your eye back into the distance in Winslow Homer's *Breezing Up* (fig. 5.1). If you shield these small boats with your hand, you immediately see how the picture changes and no longer suggests deep space.

Try placing a sheet of clear vinyl over an artwork such as Georges Seurat's *Sunday Afternoon on the Island of La Grande Jatte* (colorplate 12 in the Color Gallery). Use a water-soluble black marker to trace around the largest figure and then several smaller figures that are elevated from the bottom of the composition. Remove the vinyl, and observe the size and placement of the figures. Clean the vinyl with a damp paper towel. Try tracing over photographs of figures, trees, and such to see how smaller objects are higher up to show distance.

4. **Details, colors,** and **textures** of the figures and objects closest to the viewer are clearest and brightest, and have the sharpest edges and the most visible details of texture. Objects farther away lack textural detail and have hazy or blurred outlines and indistinct patterns. Lighter, less brightly colored objects seem farther away. Have you ever observed several layers of mountain ranges and noticed that the one closest to you is the darkest and that each succeeding one becomes a lighter blue? This is often called **atmospheric** or **aerial perspective.** Notice the dramatic grandeur of aerial perspective that the artist Albert Bierstadt achieved in his rendering of an American landscape in *The Rocky Mountains* (colorplate 22 in the Color Gallery).

5. **Directional light** gives **modeled form** to three-dimensional objects. When a light shines on a figure or object, the side closest to the light is shown as lighter; the side away from the light is darker. Think of a white circle on a red background. It is flat. Now think of a

Figure 3.20   Frederic Bazille, *Negro Girl with Peonies,* **1870. Oil on canvas. 23¾ × 29¾ in.**
Collection of Mr. and Mrs. Paul Mellon, © 1997 Board of Trustees, National Gallery of Art, Washington.
The light shining from the right on the girl's face and body gives her three-dimensional form and creates a highly realistic illusion of depth.

white sphere. What makes it appear to have three-dimensional form? A gradual change from light to dark gives the illusion of depth and form. This concept was introduced during the Italian Renaissance by such masters as Leonardo da Vinci and Raphael. (Turn to colorplate 27 in the Color Gallery for an example: *Ginevra dé Benci* by da Vinci).

6. **Converging lines** lead our eye back into the deep space of the picture. The ways these lines seem to converge and where they seem to meet are somewhat rule-governed if an artist seeks to make a realistic or representational picture. But, as in all rules for creating artworks, we can distort, exaggerate, omit, or change the rules to create a desired expressive effect. At any rate, perspective with converging lines simply means that you, the artist, establish an **eye-level line.** This is usually an imaginary horizontal line that you project in front of you, somewhat like a horizon line. As you start to draw, notice all the vertical lines, such as the upright sides of buildings, fence posts, table legs, and so on. Draw them straight up and down, parallel to the right and left sides of the paper. Draw the corner of the building, the table leg, or the fence post that is closest to you first. But all the lines that are horizontally parallel to each other that move away from you in space will seem to converge and meet at a place on the eye-level line called the **vanishing point.** Different sets of parallel lines meet at different vanishing points. These vanishing points are often off the paper; that is, the

Figure 3.21   Maurice Utrillo, *Rue à Sannois*, ca. 1911. Oil on canvas, 21½ × 29¼ in.
Virginia Museum of Fine Arts, Richmond, Va. Collection of Mr. and Mrs. Paul Mellon. © 1997 Virginia Museum of Fine Arts. © 1997 Artists Rights Society (ARS), New York/SPADEM, Paris.
Utrillo frequently painted street scenes, in which he defined three-dimensional depth with sharp use of one- or two-point perspective. Here, the sides of the street converge at a vanishing point on the eye-level line. Buildings are smaller but placed higher above the bottom of the picture as they recede into space.

eye-level line is extended beyond the sides of the paper.

Try placing a sheet of tracing paper over a reproduction, such as Utrillo's *Rue à Sannois* (fig. 3.21), or over a photograph of a street scene. With a ruler and pencil, trace the converging lines. Then remove the tracing paper to see how horizontal lines that are parallel to each other meet at a vanishing point on the eye-level line.

A special kind of perspective called **foreshortening** refers to the drawing or depiction of an object that appears to be projecting directly toward the viewer.

Artists in ancient Egypt were not usually concerned with aspects of visual realism as presented by perspective. Medieval art took a somewhat similar position and placed theological over physical truth. One-point perspective was common in mid-fifteenth-century artworks but was gradually replaced by two- and three-point perspectives. Systems of perspective were developed during the Renaissance in both Italy and northern Europe, and artists since then have been free to use perspective in ways of their own choosing. Some twentieth-century painters argue that perspective is a deception and deny its use on a two-dimensional canvas.

In addition to knowing these perspective rules, artists oftentimes use a **sighting** technique to help them draw objects in space. To do this, they hold a pencil in front of them, at arm's length, and with one eye closed, they measure objects' comparative lengths and widths. They also use sighting and the vertical and horizontal directions of the pencil to determine the angle at which lines are converging. They then draw the angles they see on paper, using the vertical and horizontal sides of the paper to guide them.

■ CHILDREN USE SPACE

Young children go through several stages in their explorations of space. Scribblers soon begin to identify heads in the tangled web of their circular scribbles and, with exaltation, add two eyes and a mouth and tell us, "This is me!"

This usually occurs around age three or four. Then one day they discover that they can add two long lines to a circular shape and make what for them is a satisfying figure, one that has often been referred to as the "head-feet" or "tadpole figure." At this time, they are content to fill the paper with variations of head-feet people, letting them randomly float on the picture plane with little or no relationship in space or even to one another. Young children like to name what they are depicting: "There is Mommy. There is my dog. There is my house," and so on.

Sometime during their fourth or fifth year, children begin to connect objects in space in their drawings, and they begin to tell and show us what they know about spatial relationships in artworks with such themes as taking the dog for a walk and how a clown sits on a swing. They begin to organize objects and to show more relationships and connections between objects in space.

When children are about six years old, they make a significant spatial discovery: They put several objects on a line that symbolizes the ground. This line is often referred to as the **baseline,** and it is used repeatedly as children deal with the problem of telling about their experiences with things in the environment. The baseline represents the child's ability to relate objects to one another in space—by placing them on a line that symbolizes the ground.

Six-year-olds typically see the sky as a line or band across the top of the picture plane, with the space between the baseline and the sky thought of as "air." At this time in their development, children are drawing what they logically know about space, rather than what they are visually aware of perceiving.

Since the baseline concept of six- and seven-year-olds is based more on nonvisual and expressive uses of space than on realistic representations, their thinking must be kept flexible and fluent. The adult can help sharpen and strengthen children's awareness of how objects exist in the three-dimensional world. If children are limited in their depictions of space to a rigid, straight line drawn across the bottom of the paper to represent the ground and another line drawn across the top for the sky, they will be restricted in solving a number of spatial problems in their artwork. To encourage and stimulate their growth in regard to the nonvisual and expressive uses of space, the following themes or topics are suggested as motivations:

1. "We are climbing a mountain (or going skiing)." This calls for the baseline to be *bent* in a curve or placed on a diagonal. ("Did you ever climb a mountain? Was the trail flat or steep? Did you get tired and out of breath as you climbed higher and higher? How tall were the trees? Did you see any rocks, rabbits, or squirrels? Was there a waterfall? How were you dressed?")
2. "Picking fruit in an orchard." This topic needs *several baselines* to have the space to place different objects on each one. ("Did you ever pick apples or cherries in an orchard? Do you remember how the trees grew in long, straight rows? You could walk up and down between the rows of trees. Did you climb a ladder to pick the fruit, or could you reach it standing on the ground?")
3. "Under the sea; inside a mine; ants under the ground." An *elevated* baseline is required to show the subject matter that is below the surface, it being more important than what is actually on the surface. ("If you could be a deep-sea diver and explore underneath the ocean, what do you think you would see? Probably a lot of different kinds of fish, shell creatures, and plants. You could leave your boat on the surface of the water and descend downward and see all kinds of sea life. What shapes would they be? How would you be dressed?")
4. "We are having a picnic at the beach (or we are playing checkers on the table)." The child frequently *mixes plane and elevation;* that is, the top of the picnic table (or table and checkerboard) is drawn as if we are looking down at it, while other objects are drawn on eye level. ("Taking a picnic to the beach is a lot of fun. We can spread a cloth on the sand or put it on a table and then put our food on it and sit around it to eat. What kind of food would you take on your picnic? Would you take your family and a friend or two? Would you set up near the water and maybe take along an umbrella to protect you from the hot sun? Would you play ball after you ate?")

In some similar conceptualizations of space, the child mixes plane and elevation in such a manner that, if the sides of the paper were folded upright, the picture would be quite realistic three-dimensionally. For instance, the child may solve the spatial dilemma when drawing a topic such as "floating down the river on rafts" or "a parade on Main Street" by mixing the plane and elevation and showing the river or street lying flat in the middle of the composition, with the objects on each side drawn perpendicular to it. If the sides of the paper are *folded up,* the buildings and trees on the sides of the river or street appear as they do in the natural world. ("Did you ever go with your family on a raft and float down the river on a hot summer day? You wore a life jacket and your bathing suit, and you probably used a paddle to make the raft move. As you floated down the river, what did you see when you looked to the left of the raft? Houses, docks, trees? What was on the right side?")

At age eight or nine, children generally arrive at the **stage of realism** and strongly desire to make their artwork more representational. They tend to abandon the symbolic way of depicting space, as detailed in the aforementioned baseline deviations, and are looking for more realistic ways of depicting three-dimensional space on a flat surface. Instruction that incorporates direct observation of people, animals, objects, and landscapes can assist in spatial explorations. Students can begin to use viewfinders and L-frames to help them select and focus on what they see. Sighting can help them to measure the relative sizes of objects and to perceive how angles in the natural world are related to the sides of the paper. Instruction in the basic tenets of perspective and shading also help children achieve their goals of drawing in a more realistic way.

■ PRODUCING ARTWORKS

Three Figures in Space—Diminishing Size and Placement

Students make an artwork that places three figures of diminishing sizes on different elevations of the picture plane to give an illusion of depth and distance.

1. Choose a theme such as one of the following: scarecrows, dancers, sailors, cowboys, robots, mermaids, mountain climbers, surfers, skiers, kings, queens, clowns, knights, farmers, and so on. Cut three figures of different sizes from colored paper. Make the largest figure 5–6 inches tall, make the medium-sized figure several inches shorter, and make the smallest figure about 1 inch high. You can cut out the different parts for the figures separately and then paste each figure together.
2. Arrange your figures on a piece of paper. Place the largest figure low on the paper. This is the foreground. Place the medium-sized figure a little farther up. This is the middle ground. Place the smallest figure farther up on the paper, in the background.
3. Cut out environmental details from other pieces of colored paper, or use oil pastels or crayons to complete your picture. If the latter, wait to paste your figures in place until you have finished using the oil pastels or crayons.

Floating Boxes: Two-Point Perspective

Students follow step-by-step guidelines for two-point perspective to draw a series of boxes that are viewed above, on, and below the eye-level line.

Look at photographs of streets and buildings, or take a few pictures of streets and buildings with your camera. Place tracing paper over several of the photographs, and use a pencil and ruler to draw the vertical and converging lines that you see. This will help you understand how horizontal lines that are parallel to each other in nature appear to converge at the same point on the eye-level line when you draw them. Vertical lines in nature are vertical when we draw them and should be drawn parallel to the sides of the paper. When you make a perspective drawing, the eye-level line is a horizontal line straight ahead of your eyes. If you are drawing objects that are below your eye level, you will see the tops of the objects. If you are drawing objects that are above your eye level, you will see the bottoms of the objects. Use a ruler or any straightedge and a pencil for this exercise. You will be drawing nine lines to complete each box. You will see three sides of the finished box.

1. Fold a 12-by-18-inch piece of white drawing paper horizontally a little below the middle. The fold line is the eye-level line. At both ends of the line, mark "VP" for "vanishing point."
2. Somewhere above the eye-level line, draw a vertical 1½-inch line. This is the closest corner of a floating box that you will be drawing. It will be above the eye-level line.
3. Use your ruler and pencil to connect the bottom and top ends of this short line to the vanishing point on the left side of the paper.
4. Then connect the top and bottom ends of this short line to the vanishing point on the right side of the paper.
5. Draw two vertical lines, one on each side of the first vertical line. These two lines will be somewhere in between the long lines you drew toward the vanishing points. They will mark the two corners of your box that are the farthest away.
6. Connect the base of the vertical line that you just drew on the right with the vanishing point on the left.
7. Connect the base of the vertical line that you just drew on the left with the vanishing point on the right. This line will intersect the last line that you drew. You have completed drawing a box. Erase the lines that go beyond the box.
8. Draw more floating boxes in the space above your eye-level line. Make one box overlap another. Draw a long, narrow box piercing a large box. Try adding windows, doors, wings, and words, using the guideline of drawing the nearest vertical first and connecting its top and bottom to the vanishing points.
9. Turn your paper upside down, and your floating boxes seem to be on the ground. You can draw boxes below eye level in a similar manner as just described.
10. To draw boxes on the eye-level line, make a vertical line that intersects the eye-level line. This is the corner of the box that is nearest you. Draw lines from its top and bottom to the vanishing points. Then draw the two verticals to determine the box's dimensions. You will not see either the top or bottom of this box, just the two sides. Use your knowledge of two-point perspective to observe and draw a picture of a building.
11. Make a drawing that combines floating boxes to create a mechanical dinosaur, robot, or space city.

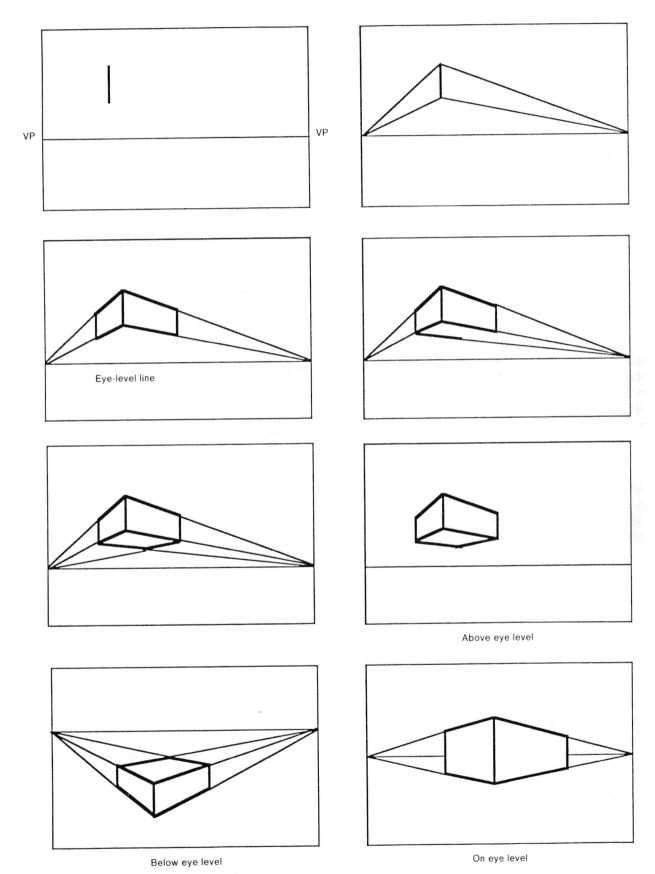

VP   VP

Eye-level line

Above eye level

Below eye level   On eye level

Floating boxes: Diagram for two-point perspective.

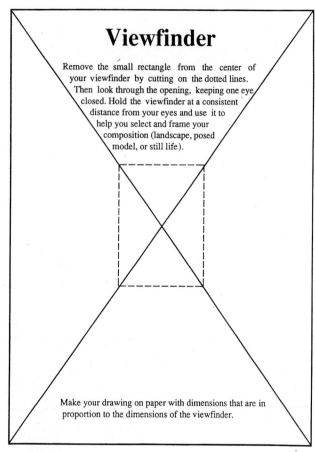

Viewfinder

Remove the small rectangle from the center of your viewfinder by cutting on the dotted lines. Then look through the opening, keeping one eye closed. Hold the viewfinder at a consistent distance from your eyes and use it to help you select and frame your composition (landscape, posed model, or still life).

Make your drawing on paper with dimensions that are in proportion to the dimensions of the viewfinder.

Viewfinder.

Drawing Negative Spaces

Students look through a viewfinder and concentrate on drawing the negative spaces, one by one, rather than on drawing the more complicated positive shapes of the selected subject. The positive shapes and negative spaces in a picture fit together like the pieces of a jigsaw puzzle. By drawing the more easily perceived negative spaces, students inadvertently draw the object itself. To make a viewfinder, cut a small 1½-by-2-inch rectangle in the center of an 8½-by-11-inch piece of tagboard. Hold the tagboard steadily at arm's length, with one eye closed.

1. A viewfinder is like a small camera. Look through it, and adjust your view until the subject is so framed that parts of it are touching three or four sides of the viewfinder. This creates negative spaces for you to draw. Your drawing paper should be proportional to the small rectangle cut in your viewfinder—for example, 8 by 11 inches.
2. For your subject matter, use a bicycle, a chair, a piece of machinery, a potted plant, a portion of the trunk and branches of a tree, or some other object with clearly defined parts. Sit near it, and look through your viewfinder, keeping one eye closed. Hold the viewfinder steady and always at the same distance from your eye so that the negative areas do not shift and change.
3. As you look through the viewfinder, concentrate on seeing each negative shape. Try not to see the object itself. Then, on your paper, make a contour drawing of each negative shape, with the lines extending to the edges of your paper in the same places that they touch the edges of the viewfinder. After you have drawn all the negative spaces, you will have drawn the object.
4. Use a black marking pen or a brush and india ink to fill in the negative spaces, leaving the object itself white.

■ UNDERSTANDING ARTWORKS

Learning about Value

The term *value* refers to the element of lightness and darkness in an artwork. A color's value may show a range of tints and shades—that is, white may have been mixed with a pure hue to make a gradated scale of tints, and black may have been mixed with the same pure hues for a scale of shades. An artwork that uses only variations of one color has a monochromatic color scheme. Notice the range of light and dark values of color in Albert Bierstadt's *The Rocky Mountains* (colorplate 22 in the Color Gallery). Within an artwork that utilizes a number of colors, an artist may use a great variety of tints and shades of one hue. See, for example, the many tints and shades of purple in the man's coat in Marc Chagall's *Green Violinist* (colorplate 33 in the Color Gallery).

But value does not always depend on a color's lightness and darkness. Many artworks that have no color at all depend on value to communicate their message. These include pen-and-ink, charcoal, and pencil drawings; etchings; block prints; and black-and-white photographs. A piece of sculpture may be all one color, or black, white, or gray; by its three-dimensional form, it catches the light in such a way as to present the viewer with an impressive range of darks and lights.

Artists use value in their artworks in several ways. In drawings, paintings, and prints, artists can create the **illusion of the form of a natural object** by changes in value. This technique is called shading or modeling. It was first introduced and developed during the Renaissance, when the arrangement of light and shadow was called **chiaroscuro,** an Italian word derived from *chiaro,* meaning "bright," and *oscuro,* meaning "dark." Artworks before that time tended to be flat because they lacked light and dark modeling to show three-dimensional forms. Many artworks since then

Figure 3.22   Rembrandt van Rijn, *Self-Portrait,* **1659. Oil on canvas, 33¼ × 26 in.**
Andrew W. Mellon Collection, © 1997 Board of Trustees, National Gallery of Art, Washington.
Deep sorrow and the troubling events in his life are reflected in this expressive portrait that the artist made of himself several years before his death. Rembrandt understood the dramatic effect of contrasting dark against light values in an artwork. He was extremely skilled in blending colors to create shading and to show form.

Figure 3.23   *Utah House.*
Photo by Barbara Herberholz.
Sharp changes in value seen in the dark and light shapes define the architectural dimensions in this old house, giving it a feeling of isolation similar to paintings of houses by the American artist Edward Hopper.

Figure 3.24   Georgio De Chirico, *The Delights of the Poet,* **1913. Oil, 27⅜ × 34 in.**
Collection of Helen and Leonard C. Yaseen, © 1997 Foundation Giorgio de Cirico/Licensed by VAGA, New York, N.Y.
Strange and dreamlike, this haunting composition of a broad landscape with a bright light sharply defining the shadows makes a highly dramatic use of dark, medium, and light values.

have continued to use differences in value to show modeled form, but many artists show little change in value within shape, depicting forms as flat areas of color.

The angular surfaces of buildings or boxes call for the artist to make **sharp changes** in value from one side of the structure to the next. This helps us to see the buildings or boxes as three-dimensional. On the other hand, the curving, rounded surface of any cylindrical or spherical form must be handled differently. Think of an apple sitting on a table. The side of the apple closest to the light source is the lightest because that is where rays of light hit most directly. The other side of the apple is the darkest, with the change from light to dark very gradual. Therefore, depicting the curving, rounded surface of any cylindrical or spherical form requires a **gradual change** in value.

Darker values of a color are seen as being closer to us, while lighter tones are viewed as being farther away. Notice how in *The Rocky Mountains* (colorplate 22 in the Color Gallery) Albert Bierstadt used this device to create **near and far.** Also note the emphasis he created with light tones against dark in the middle ground, where a waterfall plummets into a lake.

Figure 3.26   Suzanne Adan, detail of *Horse Sense* (Side A), 1990. Clay glaze, 4 × 8 ft. Natoma Station, Folsom, Calif. *Courtesy of Suzanne Adan.*
In this tile mural, the artist dramatically contrasts dark and light shapes.

Figure 3.25   Albrecht Dürer, *Melancholiah 1*, 1514. *Philadelphia Museum of Art: The Lisa Norris Elkins Fund.*
In this etching, Dürer creates a variety of dark, medium, and light values by skillfully repeating fine lines. Straight line hatching shows the flat planes of geometric forms; curving lines give the illusion of rounded forms.

Refer to back page of geo shapes

Four shading techniques help us create different values to show the illusion of three-dimensional form on a flat surface:

1. **Hatching** involves making a series of fine parallel lines of the same or different lengths. Hatching is best accomplished with pens or pencils since they make sharp, clean lines. The closer together the lines are, the denser and darker the value appears. When the lines are spaced farther apart, the effect is a lighter value. Several printmaking techniques, such as woodcuts and etchings, also incorporate hatching.

2. **Cross-hatching** involves making two or more intersecting sets of parallel lines. The farther apart that both hatched and crosshatched lines are, the lighter the value; the closer together they are, the darker the value. Squinting your eyes sometimes helps you to see the darks and lights and the differences and changes in value, and thus to perceive the three-dimensional

illusion of the form. To effectively create the illusion of form, both hatched and crosshatched lines should follow the contours—that is, the curves of cylindrical or spherical objects. To show the flat surface of a building or box, the lines should run parallel to one edge of the surface.

3. **Stippling** is making many repeated dots with the tip of the drawing instrument. If the dots are very close together, even touching each other, they present a dark value. If the dots are more widely spaced, the effect is a lighter value.

4. **Blending** consists of a gradual, smooth change from dark to light value. Lead pencils that range in their degree of softness may be used and the blending accomplished with the fingertips or a small piece of tissue. Charcoal is frequently used in black-and-white studies to create blended values. Chalks and pastels are also easily rubbed and blended. Oil paints, watercolors, acrylics, and even crayons and oil pastels also present blending possibilities.

In addition to showing the three-dimensional qualities of modeled forms, value can elicit **expressive** responses because of the **dramatic** qualities of strong darks and lights. The variety of contrasting dark and light areas often grabs our attention and provokes intense feelings. Artists can create **emphasis** by using the direction of light to show a strong contrast of light and dark shadows. Rembrandt's portraits, whether they were of himself or others, reveal character because of his heavy reliance on light sources from one direction. Notice how the dark background accents the highlighted sadness of features in his *Self-Portrait* (fig. 3.22).

■ CHILDREN USE VALUE

When children reach the realism stage at age eight or nine, they begin to want their drawings to "look right"; that is, they want to represent people and objects in a more realistic manner. Instruction in shading techniques, as well as in directed observation of angular and rounded objects and how to represent their dark and light areas, can assist these students in their art production. They can also observe how artists—both painters and graphic artists—have used the four shading techniques to show three-dimensional form. Good examples of hatching/stippling techniques are found in newspaper and magazine illustrations and political cartoons. Reproductions of paintings and original works of art seen in museums can help children see how blended paint can create the illusion of form on a flat surface.

■ PRODUCING ARTWORKS

Lights and Darks: A Monochromatic Design

Students paint a monochromatic design that has concentric bands of one color that become either increasingly lighter or darker as they encircle the shape of an alphabet letter in the center of the paper.

1. Make a **value scale** of one color. Cut a 2-by-12-inch strip from a piece of white drawing paper, and mark it by inches along its length. Paint the first inch-wide strip across one end with white tempera. Then mix a tiny bit of one color with white. Brush this **tint** next to the white on the long strip. Then add a bit more color to the white, and paint another inch-wide strip next to the last one. Continue until you reach the middle of the strip, where you paint a strip of the pure hue. Then add a tiny bit of black to the pure color to make a **shade,** and paint it next to the pure hue. Continue adding a little more black to the blend until you reach the last section of the strip, which you paint pure black.

2. Draw a letter of the alphabet with pencil or chalk in the center of a 12-by-12-inch piece of white drawing paper. Make the letter about 6 inches high and an inch or so thick. Draw five or six concentric bands encircling the letter. The bands may vary in width, and as they reach the sides of the paper, they may form an incomplete or broken encirclement.

3. Pour a small amount of one color of tempera, as well as some black and white, on a small paper plate. Use a small- or medium-sized flat-bristle brush to mix tints and shades of the color. Be sure to wipe your brush clean on a paper towel or damp sponge before you mix a new tone.

4. Either paint the letter the pure color you have chosen, or mix a tint or shade of the color. Then begin painting the bands around the letter, lightening or darkening each

Value Scale

Use a pen or soft lead pencil for hatching, cross=hatching and stippling. Use a soft lead pencil for blending.

Light——————————— to ——————————— Dark

Hatching

Cross=hatching

Stippling

Blending

Value scale.

concentric band to make a gradated arrangement of colors around the alphabet letter. Fill the paper with paint.

Showing Three-Dimensional Form with Gradated Values

After completing four value scales, students use a variety of hatched, crosshatched, stippled, and blended values to shade a small contour drawing of a leafy twig or several overlapping feathers.

To make value scales, use a ruler and a soft lead pencil to draw four 1-by-6-inch rectangles. In the first rectangle, use hatching to show a gradation from light to dark. In the second rectangle, use cross-hatching to show such a gradation. In the third, use stippling, and in the fourth, use blending. Hold your pencil on its side rather than in the writing position when blending so you are not making lines. Rub the surface with your fingertip or a tissue to smoothly blend from dark to light.

1. Place a large sheet of black paper close to you on the tabletop. Then place two or three overlapping turkey feathers (these may be ordered from art supply

Student work: Showing a three-dimensional form with hatching, cross-hatching, and stippling.

catalogs) or a leafy twig on the black paper. Close one eye, and hold a viewfinder in front of you in such a way that part of the feathers or leaves extends off the four sides, thus creating negative spaces. Make a modified contour drawing, as explained on page 42, on a 5-by-7-inch piece of white paper. The parts of the leaves or feathers that touch the edges of your viewfinder as you look through it will be what you draw on your rectangular drawing paper. Drawing the contours of the negative spaces rather than the shape of the object itself sometimes helps you draw the object. Complete your composition by drawing inner and outer contour lines on the feathers or leaves.

2. Shade your drawing by creating gradated values. Endeavor to show the curving forms of the feathers or leaves by gradually changing from light to dark. Use all four techniques—hatching, cross-hatching, blending, and stippling—in your feather or leaf drawing. Squint your eyes at the feathers or leaves to see the darkest areas. Refer to your value scales to help you decide where to show the darkest, lightest (or white areas), and in-between values. You may need to use an eraser to keep the white areas clean. Plan on shading in the negative spaces rather than leaving them white.

Creating Value with Hatching

Students form a figure such as a scarecrow by making small patches of different densities of hatches to create different gradations of dark and light values. No outlines are used.

1. With a ballpoint pen, make a variety of practice hatches—some in which the lines are far apart and others in which the lines are close together. Make cross-hatches with several layers of lines going in different directions. Squint at them. Which is the darkest? Which is the lightest? Cut them out, and arrange them in a progression from lightest to darkest value.

2. Look at real scarecrows, remember ones you have seen, or find photographs of them. Then imagine being a scarecrow, arms outstretched. Try standing in this position. Would you stand straight or be slightly tipped to one side? How would it feel to stand this way in the sun, wind, and rain day after day? Would you be lonely? Would birds be afraid of you? Or would you welcome a few friendly crows on your outstretched arms? Would you be wearing shabby clothes? What would be on your head? What would be near you—tall cornstalks? a fence? a barn? Could you see the sun and the moon?

3. Lightly draw a tall vertical axis and a crossbar for outstretched arms on a piece of 8½-by-11-inch or 9-by-12-inch white paper. Begin making hatches and crosshatches of various densities to build the form for your figure. Vary them in size, shape, and value. They may overlap. Let the hatches and crosshatches suggest details—a tattered garment, hat, scarf, hair, eyes, and so on. As hatching is added, the scarecrow grows. Do not use any outlines.

4. Make another hatched drawing. For example, create a rocky landscape, a cluster of flowers, a group of trees, a mermaid, a magician, a witch, a sports figure, a dancer, and so on.

▓ INTERACTIVE EXTENSIONS

1. To provide you with visual information for producing artworks, collect photographs from magazines, calendars, and such for a photo file. Look for specific categories: buildings, trees, flowers and plants, birds, fish, animals, insects, people at work, people at play, faces, machines, transportation, landscapes, seascapes, clouds, and skies. Trim the photos, and attach them to tagboard or railroad board cut to 8½-by-11-inches. Keep your collection in expandable legal folders, large envelopes, or file folders.

2. Use several different techniques or media to portray a theme or a particular subject matter. Reflect on how the technique or medium affected your interpretation of the subject matter. List the art elements you used and the effects of each on the outcome.

3. Explain how emulating an artist's style increases your understanding of the artist's technique and of your use of specific aspects in your own work.

4. Investigate how the elements of art are used in teaching art to children by reviewing the lessons in the grade-level text and accompanying teacher's manual for one of the following student textbooks: *Art in*

Action and *Discover Art* (see Resources for Art Education, p. 185). Select one element and follow its sequencing in Grades 1–6. Note how many different approaches and media are suggested, and how the student skills become more sophisticated with each lesson.

5. Select a fine-art example from each of the elements of art described in the chapter. First emulate the style of the artist; then create an artwork that uses the same style but different subject matter. For instance, draw a house or bird, using van Gogh's pen-and-ink style in *Grove of Cypresses* (fig. 3.3).

6. Make a small poster about color. Clip photographs from magazines, travel folders, calendars, and such that illustrate warm colors, cool colors, primary colors, analogous colors, complementary colors, neutral colors, and so on. Also include postcard reproductions of famous artworks that demonstrate some aspect of color.

7. Make small posters about each of the other art elements, using photographs from the natural world and the world of art. Label and use these to teach students about line, shape/form, texture, value, and space.

8. On a piece of white drawing paper, use a ruler and pencil to make ten 2-inch squares. Use three or four lines within each box to convey five different emotions: explosive, dignified, aggressive, excited, calm. Then use shapes to convey the same feelings in the remaining five boxes.

Chapter

4

Understanding the Principles of Art: Response and Production

*I*f you have ever made a casserole or a cake, you measured, chopped, mixed, sautéed, or baked according to some directions. First, you read the list of the ingredients and then how much of each one, whether you had to slice or sift, in what order to combine the ingredients, and how long the dish or dessert had to bake before it was ready to eat.

When we make an artwork, our "ingredients" are the *elements of art* discussed in Chapter 3: *color, line, shape/form, texture, value,* and *space.* Some individuals organize and carefully plan their artworks; others, such as naive or primitive artists and young children, work more intuitively, achieving an aesthetic result almost unconsciously. Similarly, some cooks take "a pinch of this and a cup or so of that," while others read the recipe and measure each item carefully.

Whether we work intuitively or consciously, we plan, use, and control the **principles of art** when we create an artwork. We can improve our artworks by learning to recognize each principle. We can gain a richer understanding of the artworks of the great masters by analyzing how they handled the principles of art and achieved harmony in their artworks.

The principles of art are basic guidelines for producing certain effects in whoever is looking at, and responding to, artwork. Whether we wish to understand an artwork or improve our own art production, analyzing and using appropriate language to describe how the principles of art work are important. The principles of art are: **balance; emphasis; proportion; movement; rhythm, repetition, and pattern;** and **variety and unity.**

■ UNDERSTANDING ARTWORKS

Learning about Balance

In artworks, balance is more a **visual feeling of weight** than an actual quality of being heavy or light. Our eyes seem to seek things that "feel balanced." Have you ever walked into a room in which a picture was crooked and felt a compelling urge to set it straight? Have you ever made an arrangement of flowers, then stepped back to check your work and thought, "Somehow it doesn't feel balanced yet," and then added a few more zinnias to the left side? An artwork with a feeling of imbalance creates the uneasy response in viewers that something is "wrong." The imbalance might even distract us from seeing the subject matter of a painting or the artist's finely detailed textures. What causes this feeling of balance or imbalance? Balance is achieved when no one portion of an artwork seems too heavy visually or overpowers any other part of the artwork.

Artworks can have two kinds of balance. The first is called **formal** (or **symmetrical**) **balance,** and the second is called **informal** (or **asymmetrical**) **balance.** In the first, a real or an imaginary median line runs through the center of the composition. The parts, details, shapes, colors, and lines on one side are an exact duplicate or mirror image of the other side. A butterfly with its wings flattened is an example of formal balance. Our own bodies, seen from the front, show formal balance. Formal balance is the simplest kind of balance and usually produces less visual interest than does informal balance. Many pieces of traditional architecture appropriately show formal balance. Can you find

Figure 4.1   St. Francis Cathedral, Santa Fe.
Photo by Barbara Herberholz.
A clear example of formal balance, this type of architectural symmetry lends itself well to a feeling of dignity, stability, and enduring values. Radial symmetry is seen in the round stained-glass window in the center area.

Figure 4.2   Papercut.
Formal balance on a vertical axis is evident in this delicately cut design from Mexico. Paper is folded in half and then cut to create perfect symmetry before being mounted on bark paper.

examples of formal balance in buildings in your community—perhaps public buildings such as courthouses, office buildings, museums, churches, temples, and capitol buildings? Do they elicit in you a feeling that the work or worship that goes on there is dignified, stable, and enduring? Finding paintings and sculptures that show formal balance is more difficult, perhaps because artists generally strive to hold our attention by presenting less predictable parts in their compositions. The monotony of perfect balance can be offset or relieved by a variation called **approximate symmetry.** Here, the artist arranges the objects on either side of a central axis in an almost formal manner with just enough variation to hold our attention.

Another kind of formal balance, in addition to approximate symmetry, is **radial balance.** Radial balance occurs when lines, shapes, and colors radiate outward from a central point and form a circular design. Radial balance is often used for decorative purposes in architecture, textile design, jewelry, stained glass, and other crafts. Nature has many examples of radial balance—the petals of a flower, the cross section of an orange. Can you think of others? If you have ever been fascinated with the ever-changing designs in a kaleidoscope, marveled at the six-pointed symmetry of an enlarged photograph of a snowflake, or stood in awe as light streamed in through a stained-glass rose window in a cathedral, you understand the basic concept of radial balance. The city of Paris was planned as a radial design. In oriental art and religion, the **mandala** is a round design that symbolizes the universe. Some barns in Pennsylvania have large hex signs painted on them to bring good luck to the owners. They, too, are radial configurations.

Informal balance gives us a comfortable visual feeling of weight, even though both sides of the artwork are dissimilar. In this type of balance, the elements work to offset each other to make a harmonious whole. When artists use informal balance, they strive to achieve a comfortable, even casual, feeling in the way they arrange the elements. Though informal balance may seem to take less planning, it can be complicated and difficult to achieve. Can you describe how Picasso achieved a comfortable feeling of balance in *Girl Before a Mirror* (colorplate 29 in the Color Gallery)? Though the post of the mirror frame divides the composition in half, both halves are different and are connected by the arm reaching toward the reflection in the mirror. What differences in size, shape, pattern, and line can you find on either side? How does the manner in which the artist achieved balance contribute to the mood of the artwork?

Figure 4.3   Henri Rousseau, *The Football Players*, 1908. *Solomon R. Guggenheim Museum, New York. Photo by David Heald.*
© Solomon R. Guggenheim Foundation, New York (FN 60.1583).
Rollicking ball players seem to dance politely and gracefully between nearly identical rows of trees in this carefully arranged composition. Would you call its balance formal, approximately formal, or informal?

Figure 4.4   Berthe Morisot, *The Artist's Sister at a Window*, **1869. Canvas, 21⅝ × 18¼ in.**
Ailsa Mellon Bruce Collection, © 1997 Board of Trustees, National Gallery of Art, Washington.
A clear example of asymmetrical balance, this painting places a dark shape on the left with a similar one on the right to give our eyes a feeling of comfortable weight. Try "erasing" any one shape in the composition to see how the informal balances change.

Check your understanding of the two different kinds of balance by tossing a handful of paper clips, erasers, car keys, and such onto a piece of paper. First move them into a formally balanced arrangement and then into an informally balanced arrangement.

How are artists able to arrange the elements of art in an informal way and still elicit a comfortable feeling of balance in the viewer? First, we know that our eyes are drawn to bright colors more than low-intensity colors. Therefore, an artist can achieve a feeling of balance by using a **small area of bright color to balance a larger area of duller color.** Also, **warm colors appear heavier to our eyes than cool colors.** Therefore, an artist would probably choose to use a lesser amount of red and orange than blue and green.

Second, a strong contrast in value between an object and its background has more visual weight than does an object that is closer in value to its background. A **dark value of a color seems heavier than a light value of a color,** so in making a composition, we tend to use less of a shade than a tint to achieve balance.

Third, our eyes are attracted to the more interesting textures in a composition—those that are rough or bumpy rather than those that are smooth and even. Therefore, we can balance a **small, rough-textured area with a large, smooth one.**

Fourth, shapes need to be positioned in a two-dimensional space so that large ones near the center or dominant area of a composition are balanced by smaller objects placed farther away. A **large shape seems heavier than a small one,** so several small shapes may be needed to balance a large one. Notice in Seurat's *Sunday Afternoon on the Island of La Grande Jatte* (colorplate 12 in the Color Gallery) how the two large figures on the far right balance the groups of smaller figures on the left. Can you find other ways in which the artist has shown informal balance in this pointillistic artwork? In a similar manner, shapes that are **more complicated** tend to catch our eye first and to appear heavier than those with simpler contours. Knowing this, we would probably choose to balance a large, simple shape with a small, complex one.

Turn to the Color Gallery, and analyze how artists of several artworks achieved balance through one or more of the elements of art. Record your analysis of each artwork in a chart similar to the following:

	Color	Line	Shape/form	Texture	Space	Value
Balance						

■ PRODUCING ARTWORKS

Formal Balance: Fold-and-Blot Designs

Students use a fold-and-blot technique with paint and paper to create a formally balanced design based on visual observation of things in nature.

1. Fold a piece of white drawing paper in half and then unfold it. Apply watercolors or tempera paint to the paper on one side of the fold. Quickly fold the paper along the crease, and blot the painted area onto the opposite side of the paper. Think of things you have seen that show formal balance, and continue applying paint, folding, and blotting. You may wish to paint a face or mask, a butterfly, an insect or spider, a frog, reflections of trees in a lake, a full frontal figure, an alligator, and so on.

2. When the paint is dry, use a black marking pen or a small brush and black ink to add flourishes and linear details.

Informal Balance: A Cut-Paper Mural

A group of students work together to design and complete a cut-paper mural in which the figures, animals, and objects are arranged in a harmonious, unified, asymmetrical manner. Themes for cut-paper murals can be taken from literary sources, social studies, and the sciences, as well as from other areas of the curriculum.

1. A suggested theme is "The Circus." Use books, videos, and photographs about the circus as motivational materials and for visual information about costumes, action poses, and so on. List items to include on the chalkboard so that students can choose the items they wish to make from cut paper: clowns, thin person, fat person, trapeze artists, strong person, fire-eater, person shot from cannon, animals in cages, high-wire act, bear act, tattooed person, contortionist, sword swallower, lion tamer with flaming hoop, balloon seller, popcorn and cotton candy seller, elephant act, seals balancing balls, circus wagon, ringmaster, band, and so on.

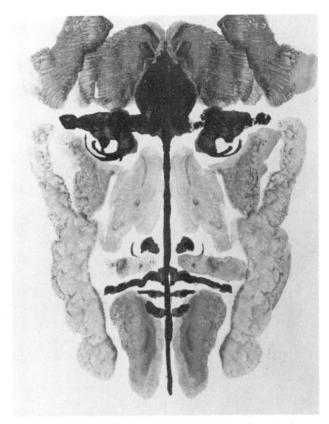

Student work: Formal balance is created by applying paint in a controlled manner before folding and blotting.

University students made this colorful cut-paper mural based on a circus theme. Cut-paper words formed the frame. No objects were pasted to the background until all the students finished, enabling animals and figures to be rearranged to create an informal balance.

Decide upon a scale; usually, agreeing that most objects will be about the size of one's hand establishes a good proportional relationship.

2. Students select from a variety of small, cut-up pieces of paper of various colors and surfaces. From these, they will cut and assemble the different parts for their figures and animals. A symmetrical shape can be cut from folded paper. If repeated shapes are needed, students can cut the shape from several thicknesses of paper. Students should endeavor to show the action, color, and excitement of the circus. Each student should also make one or more small head-and-shoulders of cut paper to be placed row on row for the audience.

3. Paste the circus rings and a large shape for the circus tent to a large piece of colored banner or butcher paper for the background. Place the background paper flat on a tabletop for assembling the individual items.

4. As students finish their figures and animals, they may place them temporarily on the background until all of the items for the mural are complete. Then, by shifting, moving, and overlapping the objects, the students should strive to achieve a comfortable feeling of informal balance in the arrangement—for example, a group of small dogs on one side could balance a large elephant on the other side. Give consideration to having one or more centers of interest, overlapping objects, and repeating shapes to create a feeling of movement, rhythm, and unity. Remember to place objects so that the viewer's eye is led around the composition. Place all the head-and-shoulders close together to represent the audience. Paste items securely in place, and hang the mural on the wall. Narrow strips of black railroad board can frame the composition.

■ UNDERSTANDING ARTWORKS

Learning about Emphasis

What catches your eye when you first look at an artwork? **Emphasis** is the principle of art that directs and centers our attention on one significant part of an artwork. This **focal point** or **center of attention** is the one object or area that is **dominant** over the others. Secondary areas of emphasis are subordinate to the main center of interest. Artists usually try to avoid creating too many focal points in an artwork, since this tends to be confusing. On the other hand, an artwork may not need a center of attention; for instance, fabrics, with their patterned motifs, present a repetitive, allover design with no designated focal point.

Normally, our eyes are drawn immediately to the center of a picture, so anything placed **near the center** will most likely be noticed first. However, most artists do not place their focal point in the exact middle of their

Figure 4.5   Frederic Remington, *The Apache*, 1890. *Rockwell Gallery, Corning, New York.*
What do you see first in this scene from the American West? The Apache sits astride his horse, resting his rifle on the diagonal line of rock, a slanted line that moves toward the covered wagon in the distance. The reins of the bridle are draped over his arm, creating lines that move our eyes upward to his face. He points his rifle directly at a covered wagon. Even the lines of the cactus point to the unsuspecting settlers.

Figure 4.6   Judith Leyster, *Self-Portrait*, ca. 1630. Oil on canvas, 29⅜ × 25⅝ in.
Gift of Mr. and Mrs. Robert Woods Bliss, © 1997 Board of Trustees, National Gallery of Art, Washington.
Her pleasant face, off to the left, gazes at us across the centuries. Framed by her coif and bit of dark hair, we almost wait for her to speak to us. The horizontal line of her assuredly placed arm takes our eye to the diagonal of her paintbrush and upward to the secondary emphasis, the figure on the canvas that she is painting.

Figure 4.7   Hughie Lee-Smith, *Boy with a Tire*, 1952.
© 1997 The Detroit Institute of Arts. Gift of Dr. S. B. Milton, Dr. James A. Owen, Dr. B. F. Seabrooks, and Dr. A. E. Thomas Jr.
© 1997 Hughie-Lee Smith/Licensed by VAGA, New York, N.Y.
With his hand on a tire, the tall, isolated figure stares intently at us and rivets our attention. The light area of concrete where he stands is framed and defined by the fence on the left and the dark shadow on the right. Notice how the sharp, pointed shape of the shadow of a utility pole on the right points to the secondary focal point, the unoccupied shabby building in the background.

artwork, since the static and less interesting qualities of formal balance make for a boring composition. Most artists create emphasis by **placing to the right or left of center** the object or area they wish to use as a focal point. Notice that the child's face in Renoir's *A Girl with a Watering Can* (colorplate 28 in the Color Gallery) is above center. In *Le Château Noir* (colorplate 13 in the Color Gallery), Cézanne has placed the building in the center of his composition; in addition, he has made it the lightest area and aimed the branches of several trees in its direction.

Artists create emphasis in several other ways. The **subject matter** of the artwork sometimes draws our attention automatically. We are naturally drawn to artworks with **figures and faces** in them, since as human beings, we respond to images of other human beings. Infants learn very early to focus on the faces of the people around them. The face is often the center of attention in an artwork, since we are already accustomed to looking at someone's face during a conversation, and we respond in the same manner when we look at a portrait. The eyes, often claimed to be "mirrors of the soul," especially rivet our attention. Portraits by Grant Wood and Leonardo da Vinci (see colorplates 18 and 27 in the Color Gallery) gaze directly outward. They hold our attention in a compelling way, almost as if the personages they represent are looking at us.

Our attention is also drawn to faces presented in an **unusual** way, since we are accustomed to a more natural

Figure 4.8   Philip Evergood, *Sunny Side of the Street*, 1950.
Oil on canvas, 50 × 36¼.
In the Collection of The Corcoran Gallery of Art, Washington, D.C. Museum Purchase, Anna E. Clark Fund.
Converging lines of one-point perspective meet in the distance to focus our attention on the busy activities of this city street. Within the triangular shape they create, the white lines for children's games on the concrete, the blind man's white cane, the white figure on the left, and the white hockey sticks provide focal points that create a lively, active scene.

visage. For instance, the human face, even in a mask form, is normally symmetrical. Therefore, when we see a cubist portrait that shows both frontal and side views of the face all at once, such as Picasso's *Girl before a Mirror* (colorplate 29 in the Color Gallery), or when we look at an Iroquois face mask with its twisted, lopsided features, we do a double take. When we look at Marisol's *Women and Dog* (colorplate 17 in the Color Gallery), we cannot help but be intrigued by the triple-faced images on two of the figures. If the subject matter of an artwork is itself surprising and presents an unusual combination of factors, or if it contains shocking material, such as the figure of Feida Kahlo being cremated (colorplate 36 in the Color Gallery), our attention

Figure 4.9 Mary Cassatt, *The Boating Party*, 1893/1894. Oil on canvas, 35⁷⁄₁₆ × 46⅛ in.
Chester Dale Collection, © 1997 Board of Trustees, National Gallery of Art, Washington.
The artist carefully created a focal point in this painting by using the massive curving lines of the boat to sweep our eyes upward to the woman and the child she is holding. The triangular bit of sail on the left is tied to the boat by a rope that points to her sleeve. The oar in the man's hand also directs our eye to them. The dark, clearly defined shapes of the water and the man tend to contrast and frame the lighter shapes of the woman and child.

is caught. Dali grabs our attention and interest with his limp watches, one of which is covered with black ants, in *The Persistence of Memory* (colorplate 16 in the Color Gallery).

Another way that artists create emphasis is through **lighting.** Just as theatrical directors throw a spotlight on the stage to direct our attention, some artworks also use this same device. The Dutch artists Rembrandt, Leyster, and Vermeer often had light from outside the composition directed at their models.

Artists also direct our attention to a focal point through the use of **pointers.** Did you ever notice someone standing on a street and looking up at the sky? Did you then direct your gaze upward to see what had caught that person's attention? The same thing occurs if the eyes of a person in a picture are looking in a certain direction; we feel compelled to look there also. When you wish to direct someone's attention to something, do you ever point your finger? Sometimes in artworks, the subjects themselves are pointing at something or holding an object, perhaps a hockey stick or a sword, that directs our attention to the center of interest. The arrangement of these pointers may be subtle, or it may be obvious, with the lines "framing" the focal point. Look at Lawrence's *Vaudeville* (colorplate 31 in the Color Gallery), and decide how this artist used pointers. Then

observe Homer's *Breezing Up* (fig. 5.1), and see if you can find any pointers.

The **converging lines** of perspective, as seen on a winding road or city street, often encourage our eyes to "take a walk" to a primary or secondary focal point. The converging lines of radial configurations may direct our attention to the center of a circular arrangement.

Our eyes also are drawn to an object that is **isolated** or **set apart from** other shapes in a composition.

Artists also create emphasis by using **contrast**—of shape, color, line, value, or texture. Think how one large rock stands out from a lot of pebbles or how one person with black hair stands out in a room of red-haired people. The ways to create such contrast in an artwork are innumerable.

Long used by artists as a basis for pictorial compositions, the **triangle**—with its base at the bottom of the canvas and its apex directing us to the focal point—emphasizes an important face or figure that becomes the center of attention.

Turn to the Color Gallery, and analyze how artists of several artworks achieved emphasis through one or more of the elements of art. Record your analysis of each artwork in a chart similar to the following:

	Color	Line	Shape/ form	Texture	Space	Value
Emphasis						

■ PRODUCING ARTWORKS

Creating a Center of Interest: A Watercolor Landscape

Students create a pleasing composition either by (1) using L-frames and a colored photograph of a landscape, (2) using a viewfinder and an actual landscape, or (3) projecting a slide of a landscape onto a screen and using a viewfinder to select a portion of the landscape that clearly has a focal point. The student makes a contour drawing of the main lines in the selected portion and then applies watercolor washes.

1. Move L-frames (a 9-by-12-inch piece of paper from which two corners in L-shapes are cut) over the surface of a landscape photograph until you focus on a small portion of the scene. Or use a viewfinder to frame a portion of an actual landscape or one seen on a projected colored slide. Choose either a vertical or horizontal format. Frame your composition in such a way that a definite focal point is the center of attention and dominates the other parts of the composition.

Student work: A watercolor landscape is created by applying washes over a contour pen drawing.

2. Use a permanent black pen and a piece of 9-by-12-inch white watercolor paper or heavy white drawing paper to make a contour drawing of the part you selected. If you use a water-soluble pen, the black lines will blur when watercolor washes touch them.

3. Put a few drops of water on each color in the watercolor tray to soften the pigments. Look for the dark and light areas in the section of the photograph or scene so that you can paint light and dark areas on your paper. Apply watercolor washes on your contour drawing in a loose, free manner. Paint the large background areas first. When the paper dries, details such as fence posts, windows, tree branches, and so on can be added with a smaller brush. Use soft sable brushes, both round and flat. With watercolors, work for a fresh, clean, spontaneous effect, leaving some white paper showing to create contrast and sparkle. Be sure to try the following watercolor techniques:

Wet on wet: The wet-on-wet technique makes the edges of objects look soft and blurred, which is why it is recommended for backgrounds, skies, and water. First, cover an area of your paper with clean water, back and front, to make it stick to the tabletop. Place a little water in the lid of your watercolor box, and add pigment to make a wash. A lighter color requires more water; darker washes need more pigment. Then smoothly stroke the wash onto the wet paper with your brush. You may flow another color in while the first color is still wet, but try not to scrub and overwork the colors. To make a gradated wash from dark to light, add more water as you work down on the paper. While the paper is still wet, you can blot it with a sponge or a wad of paper towel for a special effect or sprinkle it with salt to create tiny, dark specks of color.

Wet on dry: The edges of objects done with the wet-on-dry technique will look clear and precise. Mix your washes in the lid of your watercolor box, and apply them to dry paper with a wet brush. Apply light colors first, and let them dry before adding darker layers on top. Do not scrub or brush back and forth, or the colors will become muddy and overworked.

Showing Emphasis: A Wash-Away Painting

Students use tempera and india ink to design a composition that places the subject matter either to the right or left of center, that uses pointers to direct the viewer's attention to the dominant object, or that uses contrast to make one object stand out from the rest. After a final application of ink is washed off, the overall effect is that of having created a focal point.

1. On watercolor paper, use a pencil to make a simple line drawing of your subject. Use a photo (or actual model or object) as a visual resource. Simplify, distort, exaggerate, omit, enhance, combine. Try to make enclosed shapes.
2. Draw over your pencil lines with a black marking pen.
3. Mix tints and blends from a variety of different colors of tempera, and apply them to your composition. In mixing tints, be sure to add the color to the white paint, rather than adding white to the color. Just before you apply the paint to one of the shapes in the drawing, mix in a few drops of white glue. Try not to paint over the black pen lines. After a layer of paint dries, you can apply a second layer of color in some areas if you wish. Any areas of white paper left exposed will be black in your finished composition.
4. After the paint is thoroughly dry, brush india ink over the paper's entire surface. Let it dry thoroughly.
5. Place the paper on a cookie sheet or other flat surface, and hold it under running water. Rub gently to remove the black ink.
6. Let the paper dry. Press it with a warm iron on the backside before matting or mounting.

■ UNDERSTANDING ARTWORKS

Learning about Proportion

Proportion has to do with relationships—with the relationship of one part to the whole or of one part to another part. Have you ever used the phrase "out of proportion" or commented on the lines of a car as having "good proportions"? Proportion does not only have to do with size. Other elements, such as texture and color, may be used in pleasing proportions to achieve harmony, balance, variety, and unity.

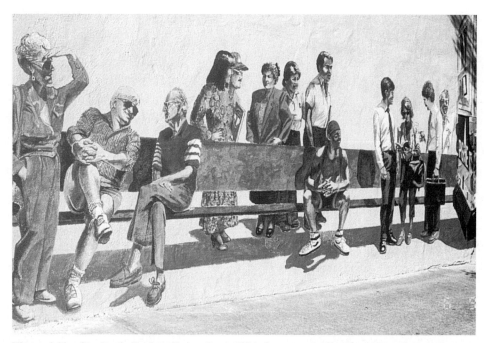

Figure 4.10   Stephanie Taylor, *Generations*. 1994. Sacramento Regional Transit mural.
Realistic and accurate proportions in these *trompe l'oeil* figures painted on an exterior wall "trick the eye" into believing the figures are real.
Generations *mural, artist, Stephanie Taylor. Clinet Sacramento Regional Transit and PG & E.*

In ancient Greece, when people were striving for the perfect body, the perfect mind, and perfect artworks, they began seeking an ideal for harmony and beauty that could be applied to their architecture and sculpture. They wanted a mathematical ratio of size comparisons that could be used to ensure the uniformly perfect results that they desired. In the sixth century B.C., Pythagoras found that he could apply mathematical equations to both geometric shapes and music. Then in the third century B.C., Euclid found that he could divide a line in two parts so that the smaller line is to the larger as the larger is to the sum of the two, a ratio of 1 to 1.6. When the ancient Greeks used this ratio, called the **Golden Section,** they felt they had found the perfect proportion for sculpture and architecture. Centuries later, Renaissance artists rediscovered this proportion and began consciously using it as the basis for their compositions. In the succeeding years, many artists continued to use the Golden Section, some consciously and others unconsciously, because it made things "look right." But, of course, the Golden Section's ratio is not the only arrangement of parts that presents us with harmonious relationships. Most artists do not believe in only one rule for "correct" proportions.

An artwork shows **realistic proportions** when we see the same relationships of parts that we see in a person, a place, or a thing. One of the best ways to perceive realistic proportions is called "sighting." This easily learned technique involves holding a pencil at arm's length with one eye

Figure 4.11   Elisabeth Vigée-Lebrun, *Portrait of a Lady*, 1789. Oil on wood, 42⅛ × 32¾ in.
Samuel H. Kress Collection, © 1997 Board of Trustees, National Gallery of Art, Washington.
This seventeenth-century artist used realistic proportions in both figure and face to show the subject to best advantage.

Figure 4.12   Amedeo Modigliani, *Head of a Woman,* **1910/11. Limestone, 25¾ × 7½ × 9¾ in.**
Chester Dale Collection, © 1997 Board of Trustees, National Gallery of Art, Washington.
Inspired by African masks and sculptures, this artist boldly distorted the shapes and proportions on this sculptured head.

Figure 4.13   African face mask, nineteenth to twentieth century, Zairian. Wood and paint, ht. 17½ in.
The Metropolitan Museum of Art, The Michael C. Rockefeller Memorial Collection of Primitive Art. Bequest of Nelson A. Rockefeller, 1979 (1979.206.83).
This example of tribal art, with its unrealistic and distorted placement of the features and decorative linear patterns, is an emphatic presence.

closed while measuring the relative proportions of whatever it is we wish to draw. Try observing a chair from a distance of 10–12 feet. Hold a pencil vertically as described, and use your thumb to measure the chair's overall height. Now measure the height of one of the chair legs in the same way. You can use these relative measurements when drawing the chair.

Artists do not always choose to use such realistic proportions, however. When they exaggerate, distort, or deviate from what we consider normal proportions, the effect can be powerfully expressive or quite decorative. Moods and feelings are more readily shown through elongated faces, and grace and movement through curving or spiraling forms.

Young children's artworks often have emotional proportions that reflect the intensity of an emotional or physi-

cal experience the child has undergone. For example, a child will draw a huge foot to demonstrate how it felt when he stubbed his toe. A child may draw a sister or brother disproportionately large if that sibling is bossy and dominant over her. Similarly, ancient Egyptians painted the pharaoh much larger than the less important servants. When children reach the stage of realism at about age eight or nine, they want things to "look right," and they need experiences in observing and using realistic proportions.

Whether we choose to use realistic proportions or whether we want to achieve a special effect by exaggerating and distorting, we need to know the normal proportions of the human figure, since so much of the art in the world deals with depicting the human form and so much of what students do is related to the human figure.

The average adult is about 7½ heads high. Children, especially infants, have larger heads in relationship to their bodies than adults. A child is 5–6 heads tall, and an infant is 3 heads long. By establishing the height of a figure's head, we have a unit of measurement for completing the rest of the figure.

Turn to the Color Gallery, and analyze how artists of several artworks dealt with proportion through one or more of the elements of art. Record your analysis of each artwork in a chart similar to the following:

	Color	Line	Shape/form	Texture	Space	Value
Proportion						

■ PRODUCING ARTWORKS

Proportions of the Figure: Crayon Rubbings

Students cut sixteen rectangular pieces of paper that approximate the relationships of the different body parts. By arranging the pieces on a paper, students create a figure in action and make a crayon rubbing.

1. From a piece of lightweight tagboard or a piece of construction paper, cut an oval about 1 inch high, and place it on a piece of lightweight white paper (ditto or typing paper). This it the head. Then cut a strip that is about twice as wide as the head. This is the torso. Cut the torso in two parts: The upper torso is about 1½ heads high, and the lower torso is about 1 head high. (If you wish to make a profile figure, cut the torso in half vertically.) Round the corners on all the pieces. Taper the sides of the upper torso from the shoulders to the waist. Taper the lower torso toward the waist also. Place the two pieces beneath the oval shape of the head. Try letting the torso bend at the waist to achieve a feeling of gesture and movement.

2. Now let your own arms drop to your side, and feel where your elbow touches your body. The upper arms are about the same length as the upper torso. So cut another strip, quite a bit narrower than the strip you cut for the torso, and cut two pieces from it that are the same length as the upper torso. Place them on the shoulders. Cut two pieces for the lower arms that are the same length as the upper arms, and place them at the elbow joint. You can overlap these different pieces. Taper the rectangles from the top of the upper arm to the elbow, and from the elbow to the wrist.

Student work: Crayon rubbings of a sixteen-piece figure. In this front view of the figure, the student adjusted the paper upon which the rubbing was being made several times to achieve a feeling of movement.

Student work: Crayon rubbing of a sixteen-piece figure. By cutting the torso in half vertically, the student made a profile view of the figure. Note the overlapping upper arms and upper legs.

Student work: After a crayon rubbing is completed, the student places white drawing paper over the rubbing and makes a pencil drawing of the figure, adding clothing and environment, and then completes the artwork with oil pastels, crayons, markers, or tempera paint.

3. The thighs are also about 1½ heads high but are thicker than the upper arms, so cut another strip of paper, and make the upper legs. The calves are thinner but are about the same length as the thighs. Taper these rectangles from the top of the thigh to the knee, and from the knee to the ankle. A narrower strip will serve for the hands and feet. Try measuring your hand in relation to your head, and you will find that your hand is the same length as the face from chin to hairline. Your foot is 1 head long. Cut a small piece for the neck of your figure. Now you have a sixteen-piece figure that can bend at the joints and perform almost any action.

4. When you are satisfied with the proportions of your figure and with its action pose, use a tiny amount of paste or glue to attach the sixteen pieces to the white paper background. (Large blobs of paste or glue will show through later on the crayon rubbing and be distracting.) Then place the paper on a thick pad of newspapers, and place another piece of lightweight paper on top of it. (White drawing paper is too heavy.) Avoid

making a crayon rubbing on the hard surface of a tabletop. Use the side of a thick, black crayon with the paper removed, and make a crayon rubbing. (To remove the paper from a crayon quickly, soak the crayon for a while in warm water.) Hold the crayon on its side, and make a number of short, firm strokes to bring out the sharply cut edges of the figure. Make the figure's silhouette stand out from the background.

5. Practice with several more pieces of paper until you are able to make a crisp rubbing with strong contrasts of dark and light. Try moving the paper over a bit and making a second and then a third rubbing on the same paper to give a feeling of motion. Try brushing a watercolor wash or a food-coloring solution over the figure or the background. Combine your figure with those of several of your classmates on a larger sheet of paper. For such a group project, place a length of white butcher paper on a table, and have students bring their cut-paper figures to it to make rubbings.

6. To make a clothed and detailed figure, place a sheet of lightweight paper over your crayon rubbing, and hold them both on a window so you can see through the top paper. Draw your figure, and then add clothing, facial details, and environment. You can use crayons, felt pens, oil pastels, pencils, and so on.

Proportions of the Face: Crayon Rubbings

Students experience the actual proportions of the face and then make a crayon rubbing of a portrait.

As preparation, stand still in front of a mirror, and close one eye. Draw around the contour of your head on the mirror with a marking pen or crayon, starting at the top of the head. Then make a line across the center where you see your eyes in the mirror. Now step back. The eyeline is in the middle of your head. Step back to the mirror, and reposition your head in the oval shape that you drew. Mark the tip of your nose, and then make a line between your lips. This divides the bottom half of your face approximately into thirds.

To further experience the relationships between and the placement of the facial features, place your thumb on the bridge of your nose, and stretch your third finger up to the very top of your head. Hold your hand in this caliper-like position, and measure from the bridge of your nose to your chin. Once again, you will perceive that your eyes are halfway down from the top of your head. You might try measuring a photograph of a face in a magazine or in a realistic portrait by a great master.

Other facial proportions are also important. Use your fingers as calipers again, and measure the width of one eye, as well as the distance between your eyes. You will find both measurements to be about the same. Now place your

Student work: In creating his self-portrait, this university student used several colors of paper for skin tones.

finger directly below the center of one eye, and move the finger downward. You will find the corner of your mouth directly below the center of your eye. Now place a thumb and forefinger on the top and bottom of your nose, and then carefully move this finger measurement to one side of your head, and measure your ear. You will find that your ears are about the length of your nose and are level with it. Your neck is not as wide as your head, and it extends downward from the side of your ears that is closer to your head.

1. To make a crayon rubbing of the front view of a realistic portrait, fold a 9-by-12-inch piece of tagboard or construction paper in half, and draw a half-oval shape about 7 inches high on the folded side. Cut it out, unfold it, and then fold it in half horizontally. The larger end of the oval will be the top of the head and the lower, the chin. Cut a neck and shoulders separately,

and place the head on the neck, either straight or tipped to one side. Place them both on a lightweight piece of typing or ditto paper. Now look in a mirror or at a friend's face, and cut out two pieces of paper in the shape of the eye. Be sure to observe how the lid covers a portion of the round circle of the iris. Keep looking in the mirror or at a friend's face, and cut out shapes for the eyebrows, nose, lips, and ears. Cut out some shapes or perhaps some fringed strips for hair. Remember that the tip of the nose and the line between the lips divide the lower half of the face into thirds. Let the cut shapes overlap, and attach them in place with a minimal amount of paste. Proceed to make a crayon rubbing as described for the sixteen-piece figure in the previous exercise. Try making a group portrait of an entire class of students by arranging the cut-paper portraits beneath a long strip of butcher paper and then making the crayon rubbings.

2. You may wish to apply a light food-coloring or water-color wash over all, or parts of, your finished rubbing.

■ UNDERSTANDING ARTWORKS

Learning about Movement

Without movement, there is no life. Each tiny organism is in motion. The heart pumps in a regular beat and keeps us alive. Thanks to stop-frame photography, we can see the rosebud open to a full blossom in a few seconds or the butterfly emerge from the cocoon. Our eyes are attracted to moving things: The infant gazes attentively at the fluttering mobile suspended above its bed. We follow the antics of a frolicsome kitten. The beauty of a vapor trail streaking across the sky in the wake of a speeding plane compels our eyes to follow its moving line. We watch with delight the ballet dancer's graceful and rhythmic movements.

Primitive cave painters made the first artworks. Their dynamic depictions show the running motion of deer, horses, and bison. Throughout the history of art, artists have endeavored to catch and simulate motion, and to create the **illusion of movement** in their artworks. This has not always been easy. To draw the legs of a galloping horse realistically, you need to freeze or arrest the horse in one split second of its galloping movement because the motion is quicker than our eyes can follow. In 1878, which was some years before motion picture cameras could show a whole sequence of multiple images and thus stop action in a single frame, California governor Leland Stanford made a $25,000 bet with a friend that a galloping horse sometimes has all four hoofs off the ground. He hired photographer Eadweard Muybridge to set up twelve still cameras, each one connected to a thread stretched across the racetrack. As the horse ran down the track, the threads clicked the camera shutters and enabled Stanford to win his

Figure 4.14   Marcel Duchamp, *Nude Descending a Staircase*, 1912.
Philadelphia Museum of Art: Louise and Walter Arensberg Collection. © 1997 Artists Rights Society (ARS), New York/ADAGP, Paris/Estate of Marcel Duchamp.
The cinema was in its infancy when Duchamp discarded completely the naturalistic appearance of a figure, keeping only the abstract shapes of some twenty different static positions in showing the successive action of descending stairs. This artwork was the hit of the Armory Show and was interpreted by thousands of Americans as the manifestation of futurism, an art movement emphasizing mechanical processes.

bet. While the high-speed lenses of today's cameras can clearly show split-second arrested motion, photographers sometimes deliberately move the camera to make details indistinct and to enhance the feeling of great speed and energy. Perhaps you have seen other pieces of art whose streaking blurs conveyed a vibrant sense of the illusion of movement.

Figure 4.15   Rosa Bonheur, *The Horse Fair*, 1853. Oil on canvas, 96¼ × 199½ in.
Metropolitan Museum of Art. Gift of Cornelius Vanderbilt, 1887 (87.25).
This enormous canvas is alive with the illusion of motion. The artist, who lived in the nineteenth century, was once called "the world's greatest animal painter." She was the first woman artist to receive the Cross of the Legion of Honor. Concerned with anatomical accuracy in her art, she visited slaughterhouses, attended cattle markets and horse fairs, and even dissected animal parts obtained form butcher shops.

Figure 4.17   W. H. Brown, *Bareback Riders*, 1886. Oil on cardboard mounted on wood, 18½ × 24½ in.
Gift of Edgar William and Bernice Chrysler Garbisch, National Gallery of Art, Washington.
This charming circus painting by an American naive or primitive artist portrays a rather stiff and static illusion of movement. How does it differ from Bonheur's *The Horse Fair*?

Figure 4.16   Lisa Reinertson, *MLK*, 1989. Bronze sculpture.
Photo by Scott McCue.
Arrested movement has been caught in the forward stride and flowing garment of Martin Luther King Jr.

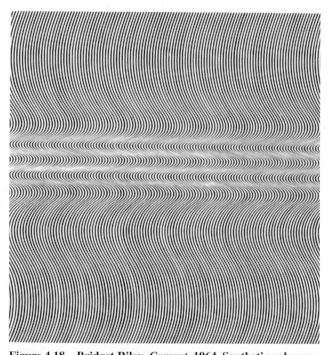

Figure 4.18   Bridget Riley, *Current*, 1964. Synthetic polymer paint on composition board, 58⅜ × 58⅞ in.
The Museum of Modern Art, New York. Philip Johnson Fund. Photograph © 1997 The Museum of Modern Art, New York.
This British artist chose to explore the possibilities of optical movement inherent in curving lines. She thus created a new mode of perceiving and experiencing motion.

Figure 4.19   Alexander Calder, *Mobile,* **1978.**
National Gallery of Art, Washington, D.C.
Photo: Barbara Herberholz.
On display in the central courtyard of the East Building of the
National Gallery in Washington, D.C., is Alexander Calder's giant
red mobile, which actually moves, constantly changing the
relationships of its parts.

The **futurists** were a group of Italian artists led by
Umberto Boccioni who, beginning in 1909, were obsessed
with speed and the sensation of motion. Boccioni endeavored to show that living things go through constant change
and growth. He liked to show everything happening at
once. To do this, he created paintings and sculptures with
circular forms that roll like waves, colliding and reacting
with each other.

Other artists have investigated ways of making colors
and shapes seem to move backward and forward. Victor
Vasarely, known as the "father of op art," has been a leader
in painting **optical illusions.** He and other **op artists** took
advantage of the way our eyes see things to make paintings
that seem to move. After looking at one of Vasarely's
paintings for a few minutes, you see colors and patterns
that begin to bulge, buckle, swell, and retreat. Nothing is

stable; everything moves; colors change. Bridget Riley creates movement by making her paintings undulate, push out,
whirl, and push back. She achieves a sense of depth that
moves up and down the painting's surface. She places dots,
lines, or circles with a mathematical regularity that makes
her paintings appear to dance and move. She takes advantage of the optical effect called the *afterimage.*

Some artists plan their artworks with more than the *illusion* of actual movement in mind: Their artworks actually
move. Alexander Calder's **mobiles** were inventive and pioneering in their explorations of movement. The artists most
concerned with actual movement in the two-dimensional area
are probably involved in making films and video productions.

In addition to creating illusions of movement, artists
use combinations of the different art elements to cause the
viewer's eyes to move or sweep over a composition in a
particular manner. Our eyes are directed to a focal point, or
they sweep along an important visual channel that includes
all areas of the picture plane and leaves no dead or void
spots. To do this, the artist exploits the direction of a line or
utilizes the compelling force of a path made by repeated
shapes or colors.

In Van Gogh's *The Starry Night* (colorplate 11 in the
Color Gallery), the triangular shape of the tall, dark cypress
tree on the left echoes the tiny, centrally placed church
spire, thereby stabilizing the spirally, rolling movement in
the night sky. Let your eyes move along the curves, following Van Gogh's definitive and characteristic brush strokes,
starting on the left and moving in a dizzying roll to the
horizon on the far right. Then follow the gentle diagonal
movement of the hills downward to the left and back to the
cypress tree and thence upward again to the starry sky.

Turn to the Color Gallery, and analyze how artists of
several artworks created movement through one or more of
the elements of art. Record your analysis of each artwork in
a chart similar to the following:

	Color	Line	Shape/ form	Texture	Space	Value
Movement						

■ PRODUCING ARTWORKS

Varying a Cut-Paper Shape to Show Movement

Students create a pleasing shape as the basis for a cut-paper
composition, and vary its size, placement, and color to
show movement.

1. For practice in cutting shapes, use a scissors and a
   6-by-9-inch piece of paper. Place the paper deep into

Figure 4.20   Henri Matisse, *Dance* (first version), 1909. Oil on canvas, 8 ft. 6½ in. × 12 ft. 9½ in. *The Museum of Modern Art, New York. Gift of Nelson A. Rockefeller in honor of Alfred H. Barr, Jr. © 1997 The Museum of Modern Art, New York. © 1997 Succession H. Matisse, Paris/Artists Rights Society (ARS), New York.*
Matisse simplified the human form, leaving out distracting details, to create an alternative, rhythmic motion of graceful, curving figures and darker negative spaces for our eyes to follow.

the V-shape of the scissors blades, and turn the paper, not the scissors, as you cut. First, make straight, angular cuts, entering the piece of paper at one side and making continuous short and long cuts until you have explored and exited the paper at its opposite side. Then take another piece of paper and make only curving cuts, entering and exiting the paper in the same manner.

2. Now practice cutting out geometric shapes of various kinds. Cut freely; do not draw the shapes first. Next, make some free-form shapes. Then make a shape that is a free-form/geometric combination. Keep your shapes fairly simple.

3. Select the shape that you like best. Using three different colors of paper, make several more of the same shape, varying either the shape's color or its size. Make some of the shapes small, some medium, and some large.

4. Place the shapes on a 9-by-12-inch piece of black or colored paper. Let some of the shapes overlap. Group some of them closely together to show movement. Try to place a series of small shapes so that they move your eye around the composition. When you are satisfied that your arrangement creates a feeling of movement, paste the shapes down on the background paper.

Figures Showing Movement

Students make a drawing of a moving figure or animal from a newspaper photograph, determining action lines and rendering the drawing with a series of elongated ovals.

1. Select several newspaper photographs that show figures in action: athletes, dancers, racehorses, and so on. Use a soft lead pencil, conte crayon, charcoal, or marking pens on newsprint or manila paper. Look at the photograph, and identify the action lines—the long, sweeping main line that usually begins with the head and extends through the torso and to one foot. Also look for the directional lines that the arms and legs make.

2. Draw these action lines roughly and quickly. They will serve as guides and should give the feeling of running, jumping, throwing, reaching, and so on.

3. Let each part of the body be represented by an elongated oval. Make a large oval for the upper torso (or chest) and a smaller one for the lower torso (or hips). Make two long ovals for each thigh and two more about the same length for the lower legs. Now make two long ovals for the upper arms and two for the lower arms. Make two small ovals for the hands and two more about the length of the head for the two feet.

4. Skip around from one part of your figure to another as you progress, so that the different parts fit together better. Then make an outline, giving a little attention to details or clothing.
5. Try several more action drawings of people and animals.

■ UNDERSTANDING ARTWORKS

Learning about Rhythm, Repetition, and Pattern

Repetition in the world of nature and in artworks forms rhythms and patterns. From our early years, we respond to rhythm as well as create it. Small children clap their hands to the beat of music and quickly learn the words of singsong rhymes. Who can resist the toe-tapping rhythm of a polka or the strong beat of a marching band! Our lives are governed and surrounded by tempos, beats, and rhythms of all kinds—the rising and setting sun, our heartbeats, and flashing neon lights. We see visual rhythms in the natural world as well as in artworks—on pineapples and cacti, on turtles, fish scales, and seashells. **Rhythm is a regular or harmonious pattern that repetition of lines, shapes, and colors creates.** Rhythm can create an exciting visual beat for our eyes to follow. Just as in music, rhythm and repetition in art can be smooth and flowing, or they can be sharp and staccato. It depends on the effect the artist is trying to create.

Artists use **pattern** that results from visual repetition of lines, colors, and shapes in many ways. In certain artworks, the repetition of a unit called a **motif** creates a **decorative effect** that often results in wallpaper, tile floor, fabric, and other patterns. The motif can be a line or shape, or a combination of lines and shapes. Pattern can **visually enhance** both two- and three-dimensional artworks, as well as provide **visual interest** and focus. Sometimes, painters use a patterned area to **simulate texture** or to **reveal the form** of an object or figure. Notice how the pattern of stripes on the woman's robe shows the contours of her body in the warm and unified artwork *The Bath* by Mary Cassatt (colorplate 32 in the Color Gallery).

Pattern can also be a vital part of an object's **actual physical structure** in that the material and its structure create the pattern. Woven tapestries, baskets, and the brickwork of a building are all examples of pattern integrating decorative elements within a structural function.

Repetition and pattern can be simple or complex. The simple repetition of a regular motif or element creates a **regular pattern** that is often used to embellish the surface of an object. In this kind of pattern, the repeated motifs, as well as the spaces between them, remain the same. In regular allover patterns, the even distribution of the motif usually follows one of several basic invisible grids or networks. Some of these networks are based on a square, a checkerboard, bricks, or a staggered grid; others may

Figure 4.21   Henri Rousseau, *The Equatorial Jungle*, 1909. Oil on canvas, 55¼ × 51 in.
Chester Dale Collection, © 1997 Board of Trustees, National Gallery of Art, Washington.
The primitive or unschooled artist usually has an innate and intuitive sense of the decorative beauty of repeated patterns. Notice the variety of leaf motifs that overlap and intrigue the viewer in this almost dreamlike jungle scene. Note how repeated fine lines in the foreground simulate the texture of fine grasses.

Figure 4.22   Pedro Ramirez Arrazola, *Painted Dog*, 1987.
Collection of the authors.
This folk artist's innate love for, and understanding of, decorative pattern is evident in this hand-carved and delicately painted wooden dog form Oaxaca, Mexico.

Figure 4.23   Grant Wood, *Stone City, Iowa,* **1930.**
Joselyn Art Museum, Omaha, Nebraska. © 1997 Estate of Grant
Wood/Licensed by VAGA, New York, N.Y.
The artist, remembering that "cornfields in spring look like black
comforters tied in green yarn," painted the sprouting stalks in a
graded or progressive pattern that leads our eyes deep into the
spatial depth of this landscape. Look for other motifs that the artist
repeated. He developed and relied on keen observational skills,
researching old maps, atlases, Currier and Ives prints, family
photos, and line drawings in Sears catalogs.

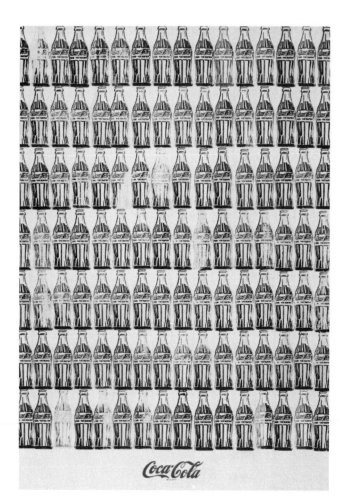

Figure 4.24   Andy Warhol, *Green Coca-Cola Bottles,* **1962.**
Whitney Museum of American Art, New York. Purchased with
funds from the Friends of the Whitney Museum of American
Art (Acq. #68.25).
Monotonous, regular repetition of a single motif purposely makes
a statement about consumerism and contemporary life in this
artwork classified as "pop art."

follow a half-drop or diamond arrangement. Sometimes,
these networks are visible, and are an important element of
the finished pattern (checks, stripes, lattice, and so on).
Spaces between the network lines usually interlock or connect endlessly in any direction. This sort of allover repetition is called a **tessellation.** Artist M. C. Escher visited the
Alhambra in Spain early in his career and became fascinated with walls and floors that were covered with repeated
tile motifs. He subsequently used the tessellation concept in
designing numerous artworks that create illusions with their
intriguing, flowing patterns.

We can achieve variety and complexity within a pattern by changing the colors, positions, shapes, and directions, or by changing the intervals or spaces. This **irregular**
or **alternating pattern** is usually more interesting than a
regular one, since two or more motifs may be used instead
of just one. Artists know that the visual excitement of the
unexpected adds suspense and surprise to an artwork.

Still another kind of repeated pattern shows an orderly,
step-by-step **progression** or **gradation** of the motif, perhaps in size or in color intensity. For example, the same
motif may be steadily repeated but gradually become
smaller, lighter in color, or closer together.

However, not all visual rhythms that we see and make
in our artworks are created by a regular arrangement of the
motif and its intervals. A **random pattern** has no obvious

order, either of the motif or the intervening spaces. We see
random patterns in wildflowers on hillsides, cloud puffs in
the sky, and horses grazing in a pasture.

A **flowing pattern** consists of lines and shapes that are
repeated in waving or curving arrangements. Our eyes tend
to rhythmically glide along a flowing pattern as the direction it takes makes smooth and gradual changes, or perhaps
abrupt and forceful ones. Leonardo da Vinci was fascinated
with the patterns that waves and moving water make and
sketched his observations of them carefully. If we look at
the curly ringlets that frame the face of *Ginevra dé Benci*
(colorplate 27 in the Color Gallery), we see how da Vinci
made a visual connection between moving currents of
water and the repeated pattern he used to simulate the texture of his subject's hair.

Figure 4.25   Li-Ting, Hollow-legged tripod, China, reportedly from Hsi An, ca. 950–900 B.C., Zhou dynasty. Bronze, ht. 22.9 cm.
© *The Cleveland Museum of Art, 1997. Gift from various donors by exchange and the John L. Sevrance Fund 1961.203.*
Flowing, decorative design enhances the surface of this bronze container, repeating endlessly and leading our eye in an intriguing, rhythmical pattern around the tripod's contours.

Both two- and three-dimensional artworks use the decorative principles of rhythm, repetition, and pattern. Patchwork quilts, baskets, pottery and sculpture, jewelry, masks, and many other pieces of traditional tribal and ethnic arts are often richly embellished with surface patterns. Architects plan for a variety of pattern when they design a building. How will they arrange multiple units of windows and doors? How will brick and tile patterns interact and relate with other structural surfaces? Landscape architects plan different groupings of trees, walkways, ground cover, and rocks to create harmonious patterns of shapes, textures, and colors. City planners strive for unity, order, and balance in their arrangements of houses and streets in irregular and regular patterns.

The artwork of young children often shows their innate love for, and understanding of, repetition and pattern. They may take delight in the rhythmic repetition of dots and lines to create a decorative border around the outside edges of their painting. They may use repetition and pattern to show realistic or symbolic details of the objects they are depicting. On a more structured and conscious level, they can study the relationships of patterning in math and art

Figure 4.26   *Icon of the Virgin.* Egypt, Byzantine period, sixth century. Tapestry weave, wool, 178 × 110 cm.
© *The Cleveland Museum of Art, 1997. Leonard C. Hanna Jr., Bequest 1967.144.*
Intricate and varied shapes create a storytelling pattern to form a border on this ancient tapestry.

through weaving and through simple printmaking activities using potatoes, erasers, or gadgets.

Turn to the Color Gallery, and analyze how artists of several artworks created repetition, rhythm, and pattern through one or more of the elements of art. Record your analysis of each artwork in a chart similar to the following:

	Color	Line	Shape/ form	Texture	Space	Value
Repetition, rhythm, and pattern						

Figure 4.27   City buildings.
Photo by Barbara Herberholz.
Direct observation of city buildings or collecting photographs of
city skylines provides stimulus for making artwork that
emphasizes repeated patterns.

■ PRODUCING ARTWORKS

Designing a Cityscape with Varied Patterns

Students use direct observation and photographs of buildings to create an imaginary city. The overlapping, flat,
frontal arrangement of tall buildings is drawn with a black
marking pen on white paper, embellished with a variety of
different repeated patterns, and then painted with watercolor washes.

1. Notice the different shapes of tall and short city buildings. Observe their rooflines. Notice how closer buildings overlap those behind them. Look for repeated
   shapes in windows, balconies, doors, and fire escapes,
   as well as different patterns that bricks, tiles, and shin-
   gles make.
2. Use a black marking pen, a ruler, and assorted templates (jar lids, small blocks of wood, tongue depres-
   sors, plastic templates from art supply stores, etc.), and

Figure 4.28   *The Flooded City.*
A child's watercolor painting of his city after a winter storm shows a flooded street and flyaway umbrellas, as well as repeated patterns
of windows and raindrops.

draw on white paper. Draw a large rectangle to serve as the front of the building nearest the viewer. Then draw other buildings behind and beside it, varying the rooflines. Fill most of the paper with your cityscape. Then cover the surface of each building with a different repeated pattern of windows, bricks, and so on.

3. Mix watercolor washes, and add color to your cityscape. Wet washes on wet paper are recommended for the blurry effect of skies; wet washes on dry paper create sharp edges of buildings. Let some of the white paper show to add sparkle and freshness. If you used a water-soluble black marking pen, the black lines will run when water touches them. This can add to the effect you wish to create. Permanent marking pens are unaffected by watercolor washes. (Crayons, chalk, oil pastels, or colored markers can be used to add color to your cityscape design.)

Allover Patterns: Carving a Rubber Stamp

Students carve a design in an eraser, ink it on an office stamp pad, and print it as a repeated allover pattern.[1] (Safety-cut, found in art supply catalogs is available in sheets that can be cut in small squares and used instead of erasers.)

1. Use a small white or pink eraser that you purchase in an office-, school-, or art-supply store. These come in square and rectangular shapes. Draw around the eraser on tracing paper, and fit a design into the shape. Try a simple geometric design, or find a design idea in books that show leaf and flower motifs, Japanese family crests, heraldic symbols, southwestern Native American pottery, Celtic art, snowflakes, M. C. Escher's tessellations, the Bayeux tapestry, or Mexican or Egyptian designs. You may wish to base your design

on your astrological symbol, a business logo, or your initials.

2. Think in terms of raised (black) and cutout (white) areas. Go over the lines of your design with a soft lead pencil. Turn the paper over, and attach it to the eraser with tape. Go over the lines with a sharp pencil to transfer your design to the eraser. The design should be in reverse on the eraser. Hold it up to a mirror to see how the printed image will appear. Words and numbers must be carved in reverse.

3. Now go over the fuzzy pencil lines on the eraser with a black-tipped pen. Use denatured alcohol on a tissue to rub off the pencil smudges. This makes the carving much easier, since the black lines of the pen will remain. Use V- or U-shaped linocutters to carve your design.

4. Make a test print by pressing the eraser onto a well-inked office stamp pad and then pressing it onto paper. Add stamp-pad ink, if necessary. If you are not satisfied, you may wish to carve away more areas.

5. Create an allover pattern by printing your rubber stamp design on a large piece of paper many times. You may choose to make a regular pattern first and then experiment with a brick grid, checkerboard grid, and so on, on additional paper. Use your stamped paper for book covers or for wrapping paper. Try other variations with your stamp, and create borders, notepaper, posters, labels, and so on.

Pattern by Repetition: From Above, Looking Down

Taking a bird's-eye point of view, students design a landscape composition that shows what is seen from above, looking down, dividing the paper into areas that are then painted with repeated patterns.

1. Imagine yourself floating in a hot-air balloon and looking down. You might see and include some of the following in your composition: fields with crops in rows; orchards; fence posts; cars on highways; cars in a parking lot; boats on a river; bridges; ships in a harbor; horses, cows, and lambs in fields; scarecrows; windmills; telephone poles; a family of crocodiles or turtles; and so on. Photographs in *National Geographic* may trigger other ideas. Lightly sketch the main spaces and shapes with chalk.

2. Pour small amounts of tempera on a paper plate. Use another plate to mix your colors. Paint the large areas first, and let the paint dry. Then add details and patterns in the different areas, using a small brush or a Q-tip and contrasting colors. Plan a center of interest. Try to include a variety of regular patterns, irregular patterns, and gradated patterns.

Student work: The eraser print of the angel motif is repeated in a bricklike grid.

Figure 4.29   Ruth Rippon, *The Lollies,* 1978. Pavillions, Sacramento, Calif.
Photo: Barbara Herberholz. Courtesy of Ruth Rippon.
These two ceramic women pause to chat while shopping. Variety in the position of the feet and hands, the tip of the heads, and dress color and pattern is evident. Unity is achieved through similar forms, related textures, and like colors.

■ UNDERSTANDING ARTWORKS

Learning about Variety and Unity

Would you like to live in a room in which the walls, floor, furniture, and window coverings were all covered with red polka dots of the same size? Would you like to eat the same food for every meal, seven days a week, month after month? Would you enjoy hearing the same music played over and over again without interruption or any change to another selection? Our eyes, taste buds, and ears like variety and seek it out. For example, we may choose a solid blue carpet, a floral-patterned sofa, and tan-colored walls. We consider the different textures in the same room, striving for a harmonious blending of woods and fibers. In planning our meals, we select from a variety of vegetables and fruits, and we like to try new foods and restaurants to relieve sameness and monotony. As any good cook knows, different sauces on the same vegetables can entice and intrigue the taste buds.

Variety is the art principle that is concerned with differences. The old saying, "Variety is the spice of life" also applies to art, since differences and contrasting elements enliven artworks. Sameness throughout a composition bores us, and our attention wanders elsewhere.

Artists know that even if the same shape is repeated in a composition, variety can be achieved by using **different sizes** of shapes or by varying the shapes' **colors, surface textures,** or **patterns.** Thick, bold lines provide striking **contrast** with spidery, brittle lines. Within the confines of one color, variety can consist of tints in one area, shades in another, and dulled tones in yet another. Different kinds of textures draw our attention to various areas of emphasis.

In artworks, excess variety tends to create a feel of haphazardness and even chaos, while lack of variety invites boredom. Somewhere between these two extremes is a harmonious balance that contributes to a feeling of unity. In *Girl before a Mirror* (colorplate 29 in the Color Gallery), Picasso achieved unity and harmony through controlled and limited variety. He used a limited selection of bright colors and explored differences through changes in the sizes and placements of circular shapes. A variety of patterned areas is tightly balanced against flat, plain spaces.

Unity is the way we feel when we look at a completed artwork—our own or that of a great artist—and know that nothing should be changed, added, or taken away. **Unity** is the art principle that makes all the separate elements of an artwork look like they belong together. The elements blend harmoniously. The different parts and art elements are

The richly patterned designs on this butterfly were made with changeable markers by an elementary school student after careful observation of nature.

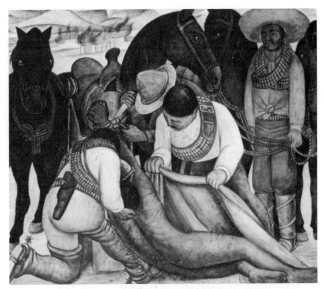

Figure 4.31   Diego Rivera, *The Liberation of the Peon,* **1923.** *The Philadelphia Museum of Art. Given by Mr. and Mrs. Herbert Cameron Morris.*

Closely grouped horses and figures give a feeling of unity in this artwork that was created to evoke solidarity and cooperation in the fight for agricultural and land reform in Mexico. Rounded, full forms relate to one another to add to the unified effect.

Figure 4.30   Narcisco Abeyta (Ha-So-De) Navajo, *Running Horses,* **1948.**
Collection of the authors.

Horses show unity through their overlapping, clustered arrangement and variety through their different positions and colors. Delicately painted plants provide fine details that harmonize with the grace and movement of the horses.

arranged so that they each contribute to the overall effect. Nothing seems to distract our eyes or to bother us as not being quite "right." We can concentrate on the entire artwork because no one part demands our attention. The different elements help and complement each other. Nothing "interrupts" our conversation with the artwork. The various

parts are in harmony and in accord with each other. The colors match the feeling; the shapes interact with the mood. We are led around and through the composition by any one of several devices—colors, lines, or shapes—that connect various elements. For centuries, the triangle has been an underlying structure that relates and unifies the figures or other elements in an artwork.

Several techniques contribute to a feeling of unity. First, we can place different shapes and objects close together, **clustering** and **overlapping** them and **surrounding them with an area of negative space,** while at the same time minimizing the spaces between the shapes. Contrast the appearance of a large pile of rocks with the same number of rocks scattered randomly over a large area.

Second, **limiting the variety** of colors, shapes, lines, or patterns within an artwork also contributes to unity. Too many different elements can lead to a feeling of chaos. Notice how Vincent van Gogh achieved unity in *The Starry Night* (colorplate 11 in the Color Gallery) through consistent and overall sameness of brush strokes. The limiting factor of using only two colors—blue and yellow—also tends to create a feeling of completeness and wholeness, and thus, unity.

Now look at *The Bath* by Mary Cassatt (colorplate 32 in the Color Gallery). The artist has achieved a feeling of unity in several ways. First, the overall effect of light and limited colors matches the happy and relaxed mood. The colors have been repeated in a number of places. The

Figure 4.32   Jacob Lawrence, *Daybreak—A Time to Rest*, 1967. Tempera on hardboard, 30 × 24 in.
Anonymous gift, © 1997 Board of Trustees, National Gallery of Art, Washington, 1967. © Jacob Lawrence.
The curvilinear plant forms that tend to frame the abstracted, foreshortened figure offer variety. Several stalks are resting places for insects in the foreground. Contrast is made between the dark, sleeping figure and other tones in the composition.

pattern of stripes on the mother's robe lends unity, while variety is seen in the direction of the lines. The mother gazes downward, as does the child. Notice how the repeated circular shapes (heads, abdomen of child, washbowl) add to the consistent unity.

Turn to the Color Gallery, and analyze how artists of several artworks achieved variety and unity through one or more of the elements of art. Record your analysis of each artwork in a chart similar to the following:

	Color	Line	Shape/ form	Texture	Space	Value
Variety and unity						

Figure 4.33   Louise Moillon, *Still Life with Cherries, Strawberries, and Gooseberries*, 1630.
The Norton Simon Foundation, Pasadena, Calif.
This fresh and delectable still life shows a variety of different plump and rounded shapes. Against a dark background, the patterned bowls and basket contain a pleasing variety of textures, color gradations and blends, and sizes. The tiny sprig of gooseberries and droplets of water in the lower center give contrast. Cherry stems and contours of leaves create an interesting linear note, and the horizontal edge of the table accents the rounded shapes of the containers.

■ PRODUCING ARTWORKS

Stitchery: Limiting Variety to Achieve Unity

Students make a variety of stitches with different colors and textures of yarn to create a unified artwork on burlap or other loosely woven fabric.

1. Use a 12-by-15-inch piece of plain or colored burlap, or any loosely woven fabric, through which a large needle easily pulls yarn. Place masking tape around the edges to prevent the fabric from raveling.
2. Select a theme, such as fireworks; earth strata; a spider's web; a volcano; things that grow, above and below; jungle flowers; and so on. Sketch your idea on paper before you begin working on your fabric. Then sketch the main parts of your design on the fabric with a piece of chalk.
3. Choose appropriate colors and textures of yarns to match your theme. Limit the variety to a maximum of five. This will help give your stitchery unity.
4. Limit your stitches to an inventive use of the following: **running stitch, cross-stitch, blanket stitch, couching, fly stitch, backstitch, chain stitch, satin stitch,** and **French knots** (see the diagram on p. 97). You can achieve variety by changing the length, size, direction, color, and placement of the stitches. Repeating them will add to the unity of your artwork. Let stitches overlap.

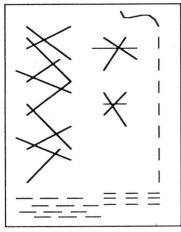

Running stitch and variations

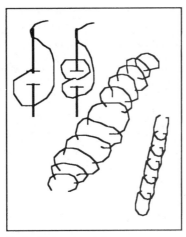

Chain stitch and variations

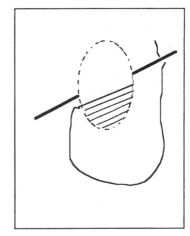

Satin stitch

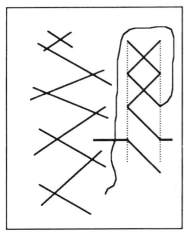

Cross-stitch and variations

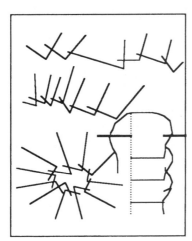

Blanket stitch and variations

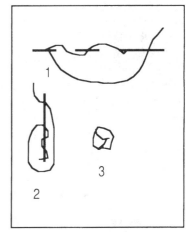

French knot

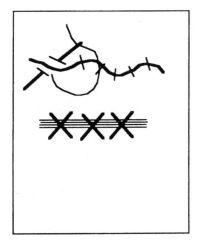

Couching variations

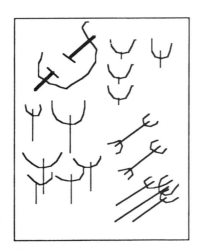

Fly stitch and variations

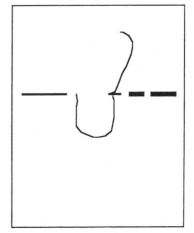

Backstitch

Basic stitches commonly used with yarn and loosely woven fabric.

5. Place the stitches so that one area is emphasized, thereby creating a center of interest or focus for your composition.

Weaving with Paper Strips

Students weave a two-dimensional design, using a variety of widths, colors, and textures of paper strips, to create a unified artwork.

1. Collect a variety of papers—colored, foil, shiny, velour—as well as patterned wrapping paper, ribbons, brown paper bags, sandpaper, magazine pages, wallpaper, and so on.
2. Cut 9- and 12-inch strips of varying width.
3. Spread a half-inch strip of paste along one of the 9-inch sides of a 9-by-12-inch piece of construction paper. Then attach the 12-inch strips (called the **warps**) to the pasted area, side by side, so they can be lifted up as you weave the 9-inch strips across. Select a pleasing variety of widths, textures, and colors of paper strips.
4. Begin weaving over and under the warp strips with the 9-inch strips. These are called **wefts.** Push the weft strips up to the top of the warp strips. You can weave in a random or regular pattern, but try to create a composition that shows unity.
5. Fill the warps from top to bottom. Then paste the warp and weft ends to the construction paper.

Showing Variety and Unity with Chalk Dipped in Tempera

Students dip the tip of colored chalk repeatedly in thick, white tempera and make short marks on black paper to create a design that shows both variety and unity. Photographs are used for visual information.

1. Use colored chalk that is designated for use on paper, not chalkboards. Break pieces in half.
2. Dip the tip of a piece of chalk in white tempera, and make a variety of short marks—curving, straight, zigzag, circular, dots, and so on—on a piece of black construction paper. Marks may overlap. Keep dipping the tip of the chalk. Work to make a mark that shows the bright color of the chalk edged with the white tempera.
3. Decide on your subject matter (fish, birds, fireworks, a warm or cool sun using either warm or cool colors of chalk). Dip the tip of the chalk repeatedly in the white tempera, and make marks on a sheet of black paper until your composition is finished. The marks you make and the black background give your artwork a unified effect.

■ SETTING UP FOR DIRECT OBSERVATION: STILL LIFES, COSTUMED MODELS, AND LANDSCAPES

1. **Sit comfortably close to the subject matter** to perceive its details and relationships. Try moving your chair until you have an interesting point of view.
2. **Use a viewfinder** to (see p. 66) help you frame your composition This will help you select your subject and place it within the format of your paper. The positive shapes bump the sides of the viewfinder, creating negative spaces that you can draw on your paper. Viewfinders eliminate distracting, irrelevant, and confusing elements in the environment.
3. **Have the supplies you will need** conveniently at hand.
4. **Take time for a visual analysis** of the subject matter:

   Look at the **proportions** and the relationships of **sizes** of various parts: larger than, smaller than, twice as tall as, wider than, the same as, and so on.
   Look at the **relationship of the locations of parts:** halfway up, to the left of, below, in the upper right, in front of, behind, overlapping, and so on.
   Look for inner and outer contour **lines** and **angles.**
   Look for significant basic **shapes** of the principal objects and then of smaller parts of those objects: cones, circles, squares, rectangles, cylinders, and so on.
   Look for different **colors** and different **values** of each color: Where is the red darker? Where is the lightest area?
   Look for different **patterns:** repeated shapes and lines, regular or irregular repeats.
   Look for **cast shadows.**

5. **Decide if you will make a highly realistic artwork,** interpreting what you see in a personal way. For instance, if you apply paint with little overlapping daubs to create a feeling of sparkling sunlight, you will be painting as the impressionists did. If you apply your paint with tiny dots, placing several colors so close together that your eyes blend the colors, you will be painting as the pointillists did. You may create a **fantasy,** painting in a realistic manner but creating an unlikely relationship or environment, as **surrealists** do. You may choose to work like an expressionist, emphasizing the **mood and emotion** of your subject matter. Or you may focus on creating a more abstract artwork, emphasizing the **formal aspects** of color, line, shape, texture, and so on. If you break up what you see into planes and cubes, creating a new structure from several viewpoints, you will be working as the cubists do.
6. You may exaggerate and distort. You may change and delete and repeat what you see. You, the artist, will make decisions as you compose your artwork—

selecting, refining, combining, eliminating, and repeating the elements you need to give meaning to your artwork and to create balance, pattern, direction, emphasis, and movement.

7. **Make several different drawings or paintings** of the subject matter, changing your viewpoint and trying to see it in a different way each time.

Still Lifes

Still lifes are drawings or paintings of objects that do not move—books, candles, pitchers, musical instruments, baskets, containers, toys, fruit, vegetables, flowers, and such—usually arranged on a tabletop. Still lifes have been a popular subject for artists for many years. An old legend tells of a Greek painter in the fifth century B.C. who painted a bunch of grapes that looked so real that birds tried to peck them.

The expression "still life" appeared about 1650 in Holland, where artists loved to use vivid accuracy. Citizens in seventeenth-century Holland delighted in decorating their homes with beautiful still-life paintings that reflected their possessions. These still-life objects were often selected for their symbolic value, reminding the viewer not only to remember death and the passage of time, but also to celebrate life. A number of still lifes of this time made symbolic references to the five senses. A later group of artists used still lifes to "trick the eye" and make the viewer believe that the objects in the composition were actually there and not painted.

In the nineteenth century, Paul Cézanne used still lifes in his search for ways to show solidity. Then the cubists took still lifes apart, viewed them from several directions, and reconstructed them in geometric shapes. Recently, pop artists have used common, ordinary, but popular objects for their subjects.

Artists who paint still lifes are interested in the shapes and colors they see before them. They look carefully at the objects and determine relationships, proportions, and angles so that their pictures have unity, balance, and harmony, whether painted in a realistic manner or not.

1. A still life may be just one object, or it may be made up of several items. Collect a variety of items that appeal to you for a **resource bank for still-life setups.** The following are suggested because of the variety of their shapes, colors, and textures, and because they appeal to most people:

   Fruits and vegetables: Gourds, pumpkins, squash, apples, citrus fruits, grapes, mushrooms, cross sections of oranges or cabbages, eggplants, broccoli, cauliflower, potatoes
   Flowers and plants: Cacti, fresh flowers, twigs, dried plants, silk plants

   Containers: Bottles, jars, jugs, teapots, pitchers, bowls, ceramic items, baskets
   Tools, implements: Spoons, typewriters, hammers, pliers, C-clamps, wrenches, can openers
   Other items: Musical instruments, dolls, toys, gloves, hats, shoes, assorted antiques, feathers, butterflies, bones, shells, driftwood, mounted birds and animals, pieces of candy, ribbons, books
   Backdrops: Butcher paper, felt, fabric (plain, patterned, striped, textured), blankets, shawls, beach towels, sheets
   Lighting: Floor lamp or tripod with strong bulb

2. Hang the backdrop on the wall behind the table, and let it drape over the surface in a smooth or slightly rumpled manner. Backdrops eliminate distracting elements and can provide an interesting pattern for your still-life background. They also help unify the composition.

3. Select several items of differing height and width for your still-life setup. Balance something tall with several items close together. Balance something large with several smaller items. Try several combinations, moving and rearranging until you have a pleasing and unified composition. Strive for a satisfying relationship of proportions. Let some objects stand in front of others. You may want to group and isolate some items. Select objects with a variety of textures and colors.

4. Give some thought to lighting. A floodlight anchored in a tripod or a floor lamp on one side of the still life will cast shadows and create highlights.

5. For making value studies and drawings in which the emphasis is on showing modeling and basic forms, spray with white paint items such as the following: plastic maple syrup jugs, wine bottles, rolling pins, croquet balls, square and rectangular blocks of wood, pinecones, seashells, old cowboy boots, and so on. This eliminates color and helps students to concentrate on drawing, shading, and showing modeling through tonal values.

6. When the class is drawing a single object, such as a turkey feather, pliers, wrench, or car keys, rather than an arrangement of still-life objects, each student should have an object in order to be very close to it. A **magnifying glass** provides a close-up look at details and makes for a larger-than-life composition of such small items as insects, seed pods, and so on. A curved reflecting mirror can provide a pleasingly distorted image that is interesting to draw.

7. After choosing and arranging your materials, find the best viewpoint. Then use your viewfinder to focus on your composition, and orient the viewfinder to the format of your drawing paper. Make several quick thumbnail sketches of the outlines that the shapes as a mass

make, shading in the solid parts. This will help you see the positive and negative shapes, their relation to the background, and their position on the paper. Next, consider the individual shapes of the objects, drawing the contours of each as they overlap one another.

8. Blocking in the main vertical, horizontal, and diagonal lines often helps you get started. Then you can draw in the entire shape of the object or objects and more carefully delineate the roundness and contours. Observe the shapes that cast shadows make. Add details that characterize each object: the delicate gills on a mushroom, the woven texture of a basket. Add any decorative patterns you see in the backdrop. Use hatching, cross-hatching, stippling, and blending to create a modeled form. You might try filling in the background solidly to accent the individual shapes in the still life.

Costumed Models

The figure has long been an important subject matter for artists to draw, paint, and sculpt. In both Western and non-Western cultures, artists have depicted portraits and the full figure. The mother and child have always been a favorite subject. Paintings of royalty recorded the power and dignity of the ruler, with artists often being employed as official court painters. National heroes, as well as gods and goddesses, were frequent subject matter. Families often had their portraits painted to record likenesses. In Japan, artists frequently depicted the figure in interior views of homes.

In the Western world, certain artists are well known for their paintings of people. Rembrandt, for instance, wanted to show more than a likeness when he painted a portrait; he wanted to show the person's character. Modigliani stretched and elongated faces and figures to achieve his distinctive style. Expressionist artists showed strong emotions and feelings in their portraits, while the fauves chose wildly unrealistic colors when they painted people. Cubists distorted the figure and showed it from several viewpoints all at once.

Students need to make careful observations when they are drawing—noting proportions, relationships, angles, and contour lines.

1. Have the model wear several **costume items,** dressing as a character from literature, history, or another country. Costume items may include a hat or bonnet, scarf, cape, skirt, belt, sash, blanket, shawl, beads, crown, helmet, armor, bridal gown, and so on.
2. Add interesting and appropriate **props:** cloth-covered table beside the seated model's chair, saddle, musical instrument, bicycle, large basket, ladder, cane, tennis racquet, fan, lasso, broom, sword, banjo, shovel, flowers, and so on. Consider a fabric backdrop to soften or eliminate distracting elements.

3. Two models may pose together, seated and playing cards at a table, sweeping the floor, playing musical instruments, and so on.
4. Think about the emotional aspects, or the character and personality of the figure. Does he or she look tired, ferocious, humorous, wise, proud, arrogant, humble?
5. Look carefully at the gesture and posture of the pose. Use your viewfinder. Try several different points of view. Find angles and curves. Notice the relationship of the figure to the background. Decide if you will draw the entire figure, or from the waist or shoulders up.

Landscapes, Seascapes, and Cityscapes

Although bits of landscapes appear as backgrounds for portraits as early as the late Middle Ages, European landscape painting as such appeared as late as the seventeenth century in Holland. Critics ridiculed landscapes, calling them meaningless, and landscape painting was not accepted until the nineteenth century. The artist usually made sketches on location and created the final artwork in the studio. By mid-century, a few artists began to feel that they could capture the atmosphere and the effects of light by painting outdoors in front of their subject. These were called the *plein air* or "open-air" painters.

Meanwhile, the Chinese had long practiced landscape painting and considered it their highest expression. To them, human beings were small within the natural order, with nature being a living cosmic spirit. Tradition in China called on people to contemplate nature directly or through paintings as a way of achieving harmony with that cosmic spirit. To understand this difference in attitude, we need to know that Christians during the Middle Ages were seeking to look beyond this world to the next; later, during the Renaissance, the natural world was considered the setting for human actions, with artists examining it closely to paint it more realistically.

Beginning in the fifteenth century, oil paints were used in the Western world. Slow-to-dry oil paints provided artists with a broad range of color and allowed them to blend strokes and achieve three-dimensional illusions. On the other hand, Chinese landscapes were made with ink and showed washes and skillful, distinct brush strokes that evoked natural forms and attempted to convey the essence or inner nature of the scene. The viewer usually has an aerial view, with objects not diminishing in a photographic way. One is drawn into the scene and invited to walk through it. If a figure is seen in a Western landscape, it often dominates; figures in Chinese landscapes are small and a part of the world around them.

Students enjoy using pens, colored pencils, charcoal, conte crayons, and watercolors for on-the-spot sketching of landscapes, and find that frequent use of a sketchbook improves their perceptual and drawing skills.

1. You will need a **drawing board** on which to tape your drawing paper. A viewfinder will help you select your subject and frame your composition in the same manner that a camera does. It will stop your eye from taking in too much from a panoramic view and will help you find a focal point. Start by selecting a subject with fairly shallow space, closing in on the main point of interest.

2. Try shifting your point of view so that the horizon is up high. Then try it down low before you decide which point of view best suits you. A high horizon line allows you ample ground space.

3. Let your eyes follow the lines and shapes that direct your attention to the focal point or points. They may be a road, fence posts, an alley, the side of a building, trees, the edge of a lake or river, and so on. Notice which shapes extend off the edges of the paper.

4. After you have chosen your scene, make quick thumbnail sketches to help you see how your composition looks on paper. Look for dark and light masses. Do any shapes in the foreground stand out against the sky? Will you use them to frame or be a focal point? Notice the direction from which the light is coming and the effect light has on the objects in your composition. Dappled light is different from harsh light. Light at different times of the day casts different lengths of shadows and can contribute to the mood of your artwork.

5. Instead of a viewfinder, use natural framing provided by a window, a hole in a fence, an arched door, a gate, an entry hall, and so on.

■ INTERACTIVE EXTENSIONS

1. Select from the Color Gallery an example that clearly illustrates an aspect of each of the principles of art, and defend the reasons for your choices.

2. Save all your examples from your portfolio of "Producing Artworks" projects that relate to the principles of art, and show them to a student who is not in your class. See if that student can name the art principle you focused on in making each artwork.

3. From magazines and other sources, collect at least two nature photographs that illustrate each principle of art. Mount the photographs on a small poster board or in a loose-leaf notebook, and explain how the principles of art are involved.

4. Make a small poster about the principle of balance. Collect photographs from magazines, travel folders, calendars, and such that demonstrate formal and informal, approximate, and radial balance as seen in nature and in artworks. Add labels and captions, and use the poster to teach students about the principle of balance.

5. Make small posters in the same manner as in number 4 about the other principles of art. Collect photographs of both natural objects and artworks that focus on aspects of each principle of art. Then use these "mini-bulletin boards" to teach students about the principles of art.

Chapter

5

Art Criticism, Art History, and Aesthetics

An **art critic** is a professional person who explains, interprets, and evaluates artworks by writing or speaking about them. An **art historian** searches for information about artworks and about artists of the past and may also write or speak about them. An **aesthetician** is a philosopher who ponders the meaning and nature of art. An artist, of course, creates art, whether a painting, drawing, print, sculpture, building, piece of jewelry, or film.

If an artwork has ever bewildered, frustrated, or excited you, learning to perceive and think in the manner of art critics, art historians, aestheticians, and artists can help. Different questioning strategies challenge us to think about art and to clarify what we believe, what we value, and why.

We can investigate and practice ways of describing, analyzing, and interpreting artworks that will help us evaluate their importance and artistic merit, ways that go beyond taking a quick look, and stating our personal preference ("I like it," "I don't like it"), and moving on to the next painting in a gallery or museum.

When we talk about artworks, we clarify our thoughts. We make a conscious effort to receive the communication sent by the artist. We strive to be in touch with the artist's life. We come to know something of the artist's personality, the culture and time period in which the artwork was created, and for what purpose it was created. Through further explorations in art history, we learn what other artists or artworks may have influenced the artist we are studying, or how our artist may have influenced others. We take a second and then a third look at what we see in front of us and then examine what we feel inside. Seeing, investigating, and

then transforming into words may be a complex and difficult process, but it is ultimately rewarding.

Just looking at artworks is oftentimes not enough. When we search for words to describe and analyze them, we progress from **looking passively** to **seeing with greater discrimination and precision.** We move from being casual, naive viewers to achieving a greater sophistication in our perceptions of and responses to artworks. We share and compare our perceptions and enthusiasms, argue our points, and formulate our judgments because when we *talk* about art, we better understand what we are seeing.

Strategies that help us to understand and appreciate an artwork, rather than to merely state a personal preference, intermingle two important components: **art criticism** and **art history.** When we look at an artwork and think like an art critic, we have the visual information right in front of us. We can describe what we see, analyze it, and react to it. Our personal and unique background, and our experiences and attitudes may influence our interpretation. When we look at an artwork and think like an art historian, we learn about the artwork from external sources. We are on a fact-finding mission to collect available evidence, including opinions of critics and historians. To increase our knowledge in this manner, we examine books and other source materials, listen to lectures, and perhaps question a docent in a museum. Art history helps us understand what people were thinking, valuing, believing, and doing at a given period of time, and offers insights as to why an artist painted in a particular manner and what meaning the art had or has.

Responding to artworks requires a simultaneous blend of both art criticism and art history components. Some artworks are only understood from the fact finding of an art history search, but all artworks can be understood, enjoyed, and cherished on a higher level when we harmonize both strategies. Therefore, art history and art criticism strategies are not sharply distinct; in fact, most conversations with an artwork are blends of both. Art criticism and art history enrich and clarify each other.

The discussion that follows encompasses both art criticism and art history strategies for learning from and about works of art. This information will help us perceive and understand better what we see when we look closely at artworks.

■ DESCRIBING THE ARTWORK

Art Criticism

We describe what we actually see before us. We state what art form we see, whether it is two- or three-dimensional, and whether the artwork is a painting, a drawing, a sculpture, and so on. We decide if it has a **vertical** or **horizontal format** or even a **round shape** (called a **tondo**). We state if it is a landscape, a portrait, an abstract work, a sculpture, a mask, and so on. We state what medium was used (oil paint, watercolor, marble, metal, wood, etc.). We observe and comment on the technical properties; that is, we may describe the manner in which paint was applied (thick, swirling brush strokes or thin washes of color) or the repeated, overlapping marks left by the chisel on a wood surface. We make an inventory of the subject matter, noting the literal details of what we see. We note the pose of the figure, the angle of the head, the facial expression, and perhaps, the viewpoint of the artist.

Art History

We describe the results of our fact-finding mission, stating the actual size of the original artwork if we are studying a reproduction of a smaller size. We relate where the artwork is located now and where it was originally meant to be housed—perhaps in a cathedral, a castle, or in the home of a wealthy seventeenth-century Dutch merchant. We tell the name of the artwork and the time and place in which it was created. We give the name of the artist and his or her birth and death dates. We know how to correctly pronounce the artist's name. We consider biographical information that is pertinent to the artwork's creation. We may tell why the artwork was made—whether it is based on some historical event, was created to inspire religious thought or to record how someone looked, or is the product of the artist's imagination. We might need to offer sociological considerations to help us reap deeper understandings and ascertain what

the artwork tells us about the culture and time in which it was produced. The subject matter of Diego Rivera's Frescoes in the Detroit Institute of Arts (see colorplate 23 in the Color Gallery) was the automotive industry in the 1930s and combined Rivera's love of industrial design with his philosophical views about the industry's positive and negative contributions to society. Biographical research makes us aware of Picasso's early years in Paris, when his poverty marked his works. His haunting "blue period" from these years often depicts sad images of lonely, outcast people.

References to **iconography** (image writing) and **iconology** (image study) that we find in source materials identify specific images in artworks with symbolic content and meaning. For instance, in Christian art, a saint may be depicted by an object **(attribute)** that helps the viewer identify the saint. The evangelist John the Baptist is identified with a cross made from reeds, while a winged ox symbolizes Luke, the patron saint of painters. It helps to know that artists used a lighted candle to symbolize the shortness of life and ivy to symbolize eternal life, and that in Christian art, a dandelion stands for grief. To understand the complexities of a culture other than our own, we need to study the different symbols used and their meanings. Iconology helps us learn through literary and philosophical material the cultural attitudes and changes that give meaning and content to the artwork.

Consider the following questions when *describing* the artwork:

What is the subject matter (if any), and what is happening?
How large is the original, and where is it now?
Who was the artist, and when was artwork created? What is the name of the artwork? What is the medium?
What is at the top, bottom, and sides of the artwork?
If figures/portraits are seen, how much is shown, and what is the stance? Is the view three-quarter, profile, or frontal? What is the facial expression?
What is in the foreground, middle ground, background?
How did the artist show the time of day in the landscape?
Where is the horizon?
Do we see diagonal lines and shapes?
Does the artwork show deep space?
Are the contours strong and definite?
Are the edges of the object shown with an outline, or are they separated by color, texture, or value differences?
How do the lines differ? Are they the same or different widths?
How does the tool relate to the surface of the paper (or canvas or wood or plaster)? (A pencil drawing on smooth paper is different from a pencil drawing on coarse, rough paper. Bits of rough paper show

through when crayons or oil pastels are rubbed over it.)

Does the color imitate natural color?

What is the light source? What is its direction?

How are the figures depicted in relation to the landscape: dwarfed by it, infused with it?

Three-dimensional artworks (sculpture/crafts/architecture): Does the artwork have a utilitarian function?

What is the effect of surface quality (highly polished wood grain, chisel marks, etc.)?

Is there a base, and what purpose beyond support does it serve?

■ ANALYZING THE ARTWORK

Art Criticism

Art analysis involves separating the whole artwork into its parts. We **identify the elements of art** and note how they were used in **ordering and controlling the principles of art.** In a **formal analysis** of an artwork, we look at the elements and principles of art that have given the painting, sculpture, or piece of architecture its **form** as well as its **content, meaning,** and **expression.** (In this context, the term *formal* is not the opposite of "informal" or "casual.") Formal analysis goes beyond description by seeking to show *how* the composition works.

The elements and principles of art have many possible relationships. An orderly system of looking at these relationships can help us determine how an artwork is put together. The charts at the end of each section on the principles of art (see Chapter 4) are helpful in this regard. Across the top of each chart are listed the elements of art. A principle of art is listed on the left. We can select any element, connect it with the principle, and then ask ourselves how this element is used. For instance, we may ask, are the colors in the painting balanced formally or informally? Has the artist used different thicknesses and kinds of lines to add variety to the artwork? How are the shapes distributed to create a feeling of movement? How does the simulation of texture create emphasis?

Art History

We compare and contrast the artwork with other works (by the same artist or by other artists) to determine its style and to discover what is unique and especially important about the work. **Comparing and contrasting** two or three artworks is an effective technique that helps us identify similarities and differences in ways that artists have used the elements and principles of art. By looking back and forth to find resemblances, differences, or things the two works have in common, we discover items we may have missed in a cursory glance at only one artwork.

Consider the following questions when *analyzing* the artwork:

How is unity achieved?

How did the artist vary the color (shape, line, texture)?

Is there an illusion of movement?

From looking at several paintings in which artists used perspective, what can we infer about diminishing sizes?

Are the proportions realistic, or are they exaggerated for expressive purposes?

What is the emphasis of the composition? (The arrangements of the parts are sometimes easy to see; at other times, a closer look is warranted.)

How did the artist use dark and light contrast?

Do you know of another artist who used balance in the same way this artist did?

Do any circular, spiraling, or triangular elements lead our eyes through the composition?

Do the lines denote movement and energy?

Could your eyes "take a walk" into the distance seen in the artwork, or is the space shallow and flat?

Why do you think the artist used these colors?

Does the effect of light make strong contrasts, with some parts brightly lit while other areas are in darkness?

Is the artwork unified by gradations and a balance of light and dark?

What do repetition and pattern contribute to the artwork?

How do the positive and negative spaces relate?

■ INTERPRETING THE ARTWORK

Just as two artists look at the same tree and render it in two entirely different manners, we can each look carefully and respond with different feelings to the content of the same artwork. We may be amused, soothed, uplifted, or repelled. We may sometimes ask ourselves questions we cannot answer. In endeavoring to interpret and understand an artwork, art critics, aestheticians, and art historians frequently find problems that they, at least for the moment, are unable to solve. Remember that we are enlarging and extending not only our knowledge about artworks, but our feelings as well. We may respond by feeling that the mood of the artwork is poetic or playful, joyous or sad. It may make us feel annoyed or hostile. It may remind us of a happy or frightening experience from long ago. It may be a narrative painting that causes us to wonder and imagine beyond the actual subject matter that we see. We may feel uplifted by a religious artwork or inspired by a patriotic one. An artwork that focuses on propaganda may sway our opinions. We may enjoy an artwork for the gesture and movement of its realistic subject matter, or we may delight in its exquisite colors, lines, and shapes alone. We may find that an art-work touches the world of fantasy and dreams and makes us ponder and ask questions that are hard to answer.

Some questions dealing with aesthetics that help us interpret artworks are: Why do I feel as I do about this artwork? Why do I find the seascape (or portrait or abstraction) fascinating (or boring)? How did the artist use the medium and technique, and arrange the elements and principles of art to evoke this response in me?

Art Criticism

We respond to the artwork emotionally and try to understand the how and why of our reaction. We interpret with more than our eyes. Our memories, emotions, and values are brought into play as we endeavor to give coherence to our perceptions. We ponder on what is in the work that evokes our feelings and sets the mood of the work—perhaps its colors, shapes, textures, or proportions. Perhaps the subject matter itself or the technical properties of the medium arouse our feelings. We look for evidence within the work of art that supports our opinions.

Art History

We respond to the artwork by knowing how the artist's time and place and such significant events as a war or oppression were influential. We respond more fully if we know the artist's reason for creating the artwork—whether to inspire religious fervor, to record the demeanor of royalty, or to explore new ways of seeing. The artwork may reach us more eloquently if we know significant factors in the artist's life and personality. In viewing some artworks, our study of art history will greatly help our understanding of what we see and are interpreting. For instance, many artists have depicted biblical events by painting the central characters dressed in clothing and in the environment of the artist's time. In the seventeenth century, Rembrandt sought to show the human ministry of the Christian religion in this manner, and identifying the images in these artworks in their symbolic context is important. It is helpful to remember that in reading art history, we sometimes find conflicting statements about the importance or interpretation of a particular painting or school of art.

If we recognize and interpret symbols—that is, pictorial elements that stand for something—we are less likely to misinterpret what we see. Art history books can do much to enlighten us in this respect, because although the symbols had common meanings in the time and culture in which they originally appeared, those meanings may be lost to us today. Even gestures in paintings may have specific meanings, and if we know them, the artwork is richer for us. Hands open and raised to shoulder level in early Christian

art represents a prayerful attitude. A finger placed before the mouth in Persian art means surprise. Color also often has symbolic meanings that vary from culture to culture. Red in China stands for happiness; in ancient Egypt, it stood for evil. Renaissance depictions of Mary's robe are always blue, but in India, blue is the color of the Hindu god Krishna.

Consider the following questions when *interpreting* the artwork:

Is the person's personality, character, or mood revealed?
Why do you think the artist placed the horizon up high (or down low)?
If we see symmetrical or approximate balance, does this give a quiet, rigid, or monumental effect?
If we see asymmetrical balance, what makes us feel that visual balance was achieved?
If the lines and shapes are mostly vertical, what feeling does this give us?
If the lines and shapes are mostly horizontal, does this make us feel peaceful and quiet?
Is the use of deep space exaggerated and expressive?
Does the light seem natural, or theatrical and dramatic?
Does the light focus on certain symbolic areas?
Is the environment frightening, inviting, or depressing?
Does color have a symbolic, realistic, or decorative effect?
Does the artwork reflect an aristocratic lifestyle or a simple, domestic one?
Are symbols used? (Playing cards, for example, may symbolize idleness.)
What in the artist's personal life may have influenced the artwork? What events at the time the artwork was created may have had an impact on the artist's feelings and ideas?

■ JUDGING THE ARTWORK
Art Criticism

We may sometimes wonder if we are making a "correct" or "good" judgment, or if a critic was "on target" in an evaluation of an artwork or an exhibit. How can we decide if an artwork has artistic merit? Do we consider tradition? Do we consider expression and creativity? Is it a matter of personal taste? Does the work mean anything to *you?* If you like it, is it good art? If someone else hates it, does that change your opinion? Can you defend your judgment? Our responses to art are subjective and vary in intensity. You may feel strongly positive or negative about an artwork that makes no impression one way or the other on another person.

When we say, "I don't know anything about art, but I know what I like, and I don't like *that*," we are most likely saying that what we are seeing is unfamiliar to us or that we

Figure 5.1   Winslow Homer, *Breezing Up (A Fair Wind),* **1876. Oil on canvas, 24⅛ × 38⅛ in.**
Gift of the W. L. and May T. Mellon Foundation, 1997 Board of Trustees, National Gallery of Art, Washington.
Homer excelled in showing realistic seascapes in which people faced the forces of nature.

do not understand what we are seeing. Hitler collected and displayed artworks that he described as "degenerate" from a number of artists of his day. Today, we look on these expressive artists as leaders in new ways to paint. What can we do to prepare ourselves to find meaning in an artwork that heretofore we have dismissed or condemned? We may need to research the artwork's context, history, and symbols, and the artist's idea in creating the work.

How, then, do we decide if an artwork is "successful" and has "artistic merit"? Personal preference alone is not an objective standard, of course, but are any standards objective? If not, how can we use them as guidelines for evaluating an artwork's artistic merit? Art changes over the years and differs from culture to culture. For example, if we use beauty as a measure, we may find that others disagree on just what beauty is and that the definition of beauty changes from culture to culture and from century to century. If we judge an artwork on its success or value in conveying an important message, we need to remember that some artistic ideas have no message as such. For example, Islamic art used abstract designs to enrich and embellish functional objects. If we use the criterion of originality alone, we are valuing artists whose highly creative ideas inspired artists who followed. However, we need to consider that some cultures have traditions with well-established rules that do not cherish originality. If we judge an artwork on its realism, we have a problem in that different cultures see imitation in different ways. Furthermore, an artist may have had a very different idea to convey than representing nature as he or she perceived it.

Perhaps we can give some consideration to the following in evaluating an artwork's merit: Does the artwork seem to have an idea, feeling, or concept within it that is indicative of the artist or culture that produced it? Is the composition planned, and does it possess unity? Do all the parts, details, and materials harmonize with the idea behind it? Was the artwork created with skill?

In evaluating paintings and sculptures, we need to determine what **style of art** is emphasized. In a **realistic** work, the subject looks like what we see in nature. In an **expressive** work, our feelings are strongly evoked. In an **abstract** work, a thoughtful arrangement of shapes, colors, and textures is the goal, not a realistic image. In a **fantasy** or **surrealistic** work, the artist delves into the fanciful unreal worlds of dreams, imagination, and the subconscious.

Being familiar with the four styles of art and their **inherent qualities** can help us evaluate an artwork's artistic merit. The inherent qualities of each style are summarized in the following list:

1. **Representationalism or realism:** In these artworks, the emphasis is on the realistic presentation of the subject matter. The people, objects, or landscape look very real and may be considered an imitation of nature. (In the Color Gallery, see colorplates 22 and 27 by Bierstadt and da Vinci, respectively. Can you identify any other artworks that fall mostly in this category?)
2. **Abstraction or formalism:** In these artworks, the emphasis is on the organization of the elements and principles of art. The artist is more interested in lines,

Figure 5.2   John Marin, *Phippsburg, Maine,* **1932. Watercolor, 19⅞ × 15¼ in.**
The Metropolitan Museum of Art, New York. Alfred Stieglitz Collection, 1949. (49.70.145)
Slashes and splashes of paint in dark and light tones make for an abstract landscape in Marin's
lively watercolor.

Figure 5.3   Paul Gauguin, *Self-Portrait,* **ca. 1890. Oil on
canvas, 18³⁄₁₆ × 15 in.**
*© 1997 The Detroit Institute of Arts. Gift of Robert H.
Tannahill.*
Moody, thoughtful, and piercing, Gauguin's eyes and pose give us
clues to his turbulent life, during which he created many
expressionistic artworks both in France and the South Seas.

shapes, and colors (the formal design) than in objects,
people, or landscapes. (In the Color Gallery, see colorplates 26 and 31 by Kandinsky and Lawrence, respectively. Can you identify any other artworks that fall
mostly in this category?)

3. **Expressionism or emotionalism:** In these artworks,
   the emphasis is on the intense feeling, mood, or idea
   related to the visual image, rather than on the realistic
   depiction of people, objects, or landscapes. (In the
   Color Gallery, see colorplates 11 and 21 by van Gogh
   and Marc, respectively. Can you identify any other artworks that fall mostly in this category?)

**Figure 5.4   René Magritte, *La lunette d'approche*, 1963.
Oil on canvas, 69⁵⁄₁₆ × 45¼ in.**
*The Menil Collection, Houston. (Hickey and Robertson,
photographer). © 1997 C. Herscovici, Brussels/Artists Rights
Society/(ARS), New York.*
Magritte used highly realistic images in a dreamlike manner to
create surrealistic artworks.

**Figure 5.5   Hans Hofmann, *Exuberance*, 1955. Oil on canvas.
50 × 40 in.**
*Albright-Knox Art Gallery, Buffalo, N.Y. Gift of Seymour
H. Knox, 1969.*
Hofmann was an abstract expressionist who combined colors,
shapes, and lines in strong, bold compositions.

4. **Surrealism or fantasy:** In these artworks, the emphasis is on the imagination and the world of the subconscious. The artist often depicts objects in a realistic manner but makes unusual connections and relationships. (In the Color Gallery, see colorplates 16 and 33 by Dali and Chagall, respectively. Can you find any other artworks that fall mostly in this category?)

We may look at any piece of artwork and reflect on the artist's **principal intent.** Was he or she trying to show us exactly what the person or place looked like (representationalism/realism)? Was the artist more interested in the abstract elements of lines, shapes, and colors than in showing us exactly what the scene or person looked like (abstraction/formalism)? We may decide that the artist was extremely successful and innovative in the handling of one or more of the elements and principles of art. Was the artist more involved in expressing an emotion or feeling (expressionism/emotionalism)? Sometimes, we are in awe of the emotional impact or mood of an artwork, or the artwork's message uplifts and inspires us. Was the artist dedicated to showing us an imaginary dreamworld—a world of fantasy and of the subconscious (fantasy/surrealism)?

Many artworks do not clearly fall into only one of the previous categories; they may be weighted in one direction and have overlapping emphases. We can then look at an artwork and use the inherent qualities as a basis for judgment. For example, Grant Wood's *American Gothic* (colorplate 18 in the Color Gallery) shows us a realistic-looking man and woman standing in front of a farmhouse. Each detail is noted and painted precisely. In addition, Wood planned his composition carefully, echoing several different shapes and lines, drawing our eyes to a focal point, and creating a pleasing arrangement of the shapes and colors. His use of the formal qualities has resulted in a unified and harmonious composition. Another area to consider is the expression or emotion felt. We cannot help but gaze directly back at the farmer and "read" his character, and then glance at the woman's face and wonder what she is thinking. Thus, a strong emotion is included here. We see no fantasy or dreamworld, so we cannot judge the painting on that basis. We would give it a high evaluation

Figure 5.6   Frank LaPena, *Flower Dance Spirit,* 1981.
Native American symbols speak to the viewer and tell of Native
American cultural beliefs in this formally balanced abstract
composition.
Courtesy Patty and Chris Gibson.

in the first three qualities but would place it in *realism* as
a work of art.

Let's use these styles or inherent qualities of art to
evaluate Kandinsky's *Painting No. 198* (colorplate 26 in
the Color Gallery). We are unable to evaluate the painting
on its realistic qualities, since it is highly abstract, to the
point of being nonobjective. However, if we contemplate
the painting's expressive qualities, we find much to respond to. And its formal qualities are reflected in the
rhythm, harmony, and balance that Kandinsky achieved in
his arrangement of colors, lines, and shapes. Kandinsky
used two terms often associated with music to title his
paintings—*improvisations* and *compositions,* the latter
being more carefully planned and structured than the
former.

Can you find an artwork in the Color Gallery whose
qualities could be judged in the category of fantasy as well

as any other of the three styles of art? Can you locate one
that could be judged solely in one category and no other?

You may want to compare the inherent qualities of one
artwork with those of another artwork with a similar theme
or that was made in another time or culture. Your friends
may not always agree with your judgments and choices.
However, remember that you are evaluating the artwork on
many points that go beyond stating your personal preference. Try making your judgment based on the inherent
qualities in each of the four styles of art.

Art History

We thoughtfully evaluate the factors related to the artwork's importance and its place in the history of art, arriv-
ing at objective conclusions. We comment on the artwork's
influence on other artists or, perhaps, on what artworks
were forerunners of the piece we are viewing.

Consider the following questions when *judging* the
artwork:

Would you recognize this person in real life?
Is the landscape recognizable as a specific place?
For what purpose was the artwork made?
Is the artwork more realistic or more abstract?
Is the artwork mostly concerned with dreams and
    imagination?
Was the artist primarily interested in expressing a strong
    emotion?
Was the artist mostly concerned with formal aspects of
    arranging lines, shapes, and colors?
In which style of art would you categorize the artwork?
What is the artwork's artistic merit within this style of
    art?
How did this artwork influence other artists?
How do the medium and technique contribute to (or
    distract from) the overall effect?
If this artist had lived another hundred years, how do
    you think his or her style might have changed?
Do you think the artist will be remembered and highly
    regarded a century from now? Why?
How do you think the painting would make you feel if
    the artist had used all warm colors instead of cool
    colors?
Is the surface quality of the objects dominant, or is the
    volume and form of the objects more important?
What does the artist's degree of skill in handling the
    medium contribute to the artistic merit of the work?

■ AESTHETICS

Recently, the visual arts curriculum in U.S. schools has
been broadening to include more than the traditional art

production base. The National Art Education Association, as mentioned in the Introduction to this book, lists three other areas of study besides art production; the second in the list is aesthetics. Art educators feel that aesthetic considerations provide a firmer and more comprehensive base for the student engaging in making art, and also that the contemplative thought that relates to aesthetics leads to a fuller and more complete understanding of artworks.

Just what is aesthetics? The word *aesthetics* is a derivation of the Greek word *aisthetikos,* which has to do with sensory perceptions. Indeed, when we place *an* in front of it, we have the word *anesthetic,* which refers to putting the senses to sleep. Therefore, we shall begin with the premise that aesthetics must have something to do with awakening and vitalizing the senses in one way or another.

By definition, **aesthetics** is a branch of philosophy that deals with the nature of art and, as such, is concerned with questions and thoughtful reflections about the meaning and purpose of artistic processes and products, concepts that help us better understand what we see and encounter. When we think, converse, and form questions on aesthetic concerns, we try to evaluate, define, and clarify different cognitive and emotional responses to artworks. Such aesthetic questions cause us to take a fresh look at some of our long-held opinions and ask us to withhold judgments until we have done some critical thinking and some careful studying to learn all we can about what we see. The deeper we delve into the issue of aesthetics, the more we find that the questions we ask, or that others ask us, cannot be answered with a simple yes or no. Often, we find that understanding aesthetics involves being able to accept answers that are neither right nor wrong and to tolerate several points of view. And we often wind up with one question leading us to yet another question.

What is art? What is an artist? How is an art object different from another object? Have you ever consulted a dictionary for a definition of art? Did the dictionary give you a clear understanding of what art is and one with which you could agree? Perhaps not. First, if we can agree that an art object is an object that human beings make and that originates in someone's mind and imagination, we have a working base, a starting point. However "beautiful" a sunset or an autumn tree, they are natural phenomena, not works of art. We use "art" words to describe the colors, lines, and shapes that we see in these natural objects, and in so doing, we find parallels between art and nature. So, what is a work of art, and how is it different from other things? How does a painting of sunflowers by van Gogh differ from the actual sunflowers? The difference is that van Gogh was inspired by the visual information before him and interpreted it in his own unique way to make the painting.

Art, then, is a visible expression of perceptions, feelings, ideas, and values. It is based on human perceptions, and we recognize and understand it through our senses. A wide range of objects can be considered works of art, but all will have distinctive or valued qualities and meanings that individuals or particular cultures accept and preserve. Works of art can make us think about ideas, people, places, events, and spiritual matters, and can make us feel and understand things in the world more deeply than we would otherwise. Some cultures have no word for art since everything the people in those cultures make, wear, and use—even the dwellings in which they live—are artifacts with significant symbolic content, skillful workmanship, and artistic style.

This, then, brings us to the word *beauty,* which usually comes up in any discussion of the word *art.* Can you define beauty? Perhaps we can generally agree that beauty stimulates pleasurable visual and tactile responses in the visual arts. But standards for beauty change through the centuries and from country to country, and the concept of beauty varies from individual to individual, validating the old cliché of beauty "being in the eye of the beholder." This is the position that the relativist or pluralist takes. For example, when we see Picasso's *Guernica* (see fig. 6.29), with its angular, hard-edged shapes, its crisp tones of black and white, its wrenching, agonizing, twisted forms that symbolize dying people and wounded horses, we feel strongly the message that the artist wished to convey: the horror of the Nazi bombing of a small Spanish town. We probably do not describe this painting as "beautiful" in the usual sense of the word, yet it is a highly revered work of "art." The relativist point of view might note that the military personnel who instigated and implemented the bombing mission might have called the artwork "beautiful" in that *their* dreadful, deadly goal was accomplished.

The **relativist** or **pluralist** position, then, holds that there are multiple artistic traditions, all involving different and distinct aesthetic systems, as well as a great variety of artistic productions.[1] Therefore, it behooves teachers to be aware of the multiple artistic traditions and aesthetic values of world cultures to assist students in finding meaning and artistic merit in the many art products produced in these global cultures.

Objectivists, on the other hand, beginning with the classical Greeks and Renaissance scholars, use criteria regarding beauty, including harmony, balance, and such, and they state that actual beauty is *within* the artwork itself.

Ellen Dissanayake takes the **ethological,** or bioevolutionary, approach in relating art to human nature.[2] This ethological view argues that art contributes something essential to the person who makes art or to the person who views it—not simply in that art brings "pleasure" but that it benefits the person's biological fitness. Dissanayake looks at art from the 4-million year perspective of human biosocial evolution and believes that the aesthetic experience cannot be properly understood apart from the psychobiology of sense, feeling, and cognition. She feels that it is wrong to think that "being cultural exempts us from biological imperatives. . . . We use cultures—the elements of our cultures, like tools and language and the arts—to get what we need, biologically, as well as what we are taught to think we need."[3] She feels that "art" has been falsely set apart from life in today's modern and postmodern societies, and that this emphasis on efficiency and acquisition has forced us to devalue or ignore the aesthetic part of our nature. She feels that the arts as we know them define the universal human practice of "making special" certain objects, sounds, movements, occasions, and places. Her view is that modern society—predominantly urban, industrial, and literate—is so disengaged from nature that we have lost sight of the biosocial purposes of making art. She states that "social systems that disdain or discount beauty, form, mystery, meaning, value, and quality—whether in art or in life—are depriving their members of human requirements as fundamental as those for food, warmth, and shelter."[4]

A statement from the National Art Education Association (NAEA) in 1991 regarding the preservation of freedom of expression in the arts declared that individuals have the right to accept or reject any work of art for themselves personally, but do not have the right to suppress works of art to which they may object or those artists with whom they do not agree. The NAEA further declared that it is the duty of the art educator to provide students with a diversity of art experiences and to enable students to think critically. It endorsed the concept of allowing the student:

> to choose from widely conflicting images, opinions, and ideologies. While some works of art may indeed be banal and trivial, and some works may be repugnant and unacceptable to some individuals, the art educator should insist upon the right of every individual to freely express and create in his or her own way and to experience, accept, or reject any particular work of art.[5]

Aesthetic Points to Ponder

1. Is all art beautiful? Can art be ugly? Find an artwork in a magazine or book that you could describe as "beautiful." Then find another artwork that you would describe as "not beautiful." Then try to interpret each artist's message or each painting's meaning. Which artwork was more successful?

2. Must all art contain a message or have a meaningful concept behind it? Can art be an object that exists for its own sake? Can art have practical and functional uses?

3. If you like an object, is it art? If you do not like it, could it still be considered art? What part does popularity play in art?

4. How would a person who lived during the Italian Renaissance define art differently than a twentieth-century artist or a member of a tribe in Africa or Australia?

5. What is the most important art form? Art theme? Art subject? Are landscapes as important as portraits?

6. Should art only please the artists and the culturally elite, or should it touch a wider viewing audience? Does an artist have social responsibilities? Should artists be able to explain verbally the meanings of their works?

7. Is art the same thing as freedom? Is all art creative? Is anything creative art? Can an artist work in today's society with no restraints? Is creativity the same as doing whatever you want? Is all self-expression art?

8. Does our culture value the aesthetic experience? Why or why not? What is an aesthetic experience? What parts of our being are involved in an aesthetic experience: emotional, sensory, intellectual, social, creative, kinesthetic?

9. If a person claims to be an artist, is that person an artist? How do great artists and mediocre artists differ? Can a child be an artist?

10. If an object is in an art museum, does that make the object a work of art? How do museum curators and directors decide what objects to display?

11. Is an artwork forgery a work of art?

12. When you view an artwork for the first time, can you have an aesthetic experience without knowing anything about the artwork's history, or about the culture and/or artist from which the artwork sprang? Would learning more about the artwork increase your aesthetic experience?

13. Should art that is on public display be censored? If your answer is yes, what criteria should be used, and who should make these decisions? If your answer is no, what reasons can you give for your viewpoint? Should public funds be used to buy artworks for public buildings? Why or why not? Who should make these decisions?

14. Do artists have any obligations to society? Does society have any obligations to artists?

15. Will an artwork that was considered "beautiful" several hundred years ago still be considered beautiful today?

16. Is knowing what the artist intended to create necessary for us to relate to the artwork, or can we connect with a piece of art by what we see before us?

17. People have paid millions of dollars to buy works by Monet, van Gogh, and Picasso. Who decides how much an artwork is worth? Does a higher amount of money paid for a painting make it a "better" artwork than one that brought in less money?

18. Suppose you visited a museum and felt that you had a legitimate aesthetic experience when you looked at a particular painting. Later, you learned that the painting was a copy of the original, placed there while the original was on loan. Was your aesthetic experience any less because you were looking at a copy?

19. Recently, a zoo in a large city gave paper, paint, and brushes to an elephant who obligingly swung its trunk, making marks on the paper. The zoo framed and sold the products that the elephant had made as "art." What do you think about this?

■ RESPONDING TO ARTWORKS

Conversations with an Artwork

Asking and answering questions about an artwork is a strategy that involves more than expressing our random feelings about an artwork and stating our personal preferences—preferences that are often based on subject matter or on how realistic an artwork is. Actress Jodie Foster once stated that she loves to be interviewed because it makes her know what she thinks. Of course, the interviewer must ask appropriate questions to obtain this result.

The following inquiries are examples of the kinds of questions that we can ask ourselves to get started in the seemingly complex process of describing, analyzing, interpreting, and judging art. They help us know what we think about an artwork. They ultimately help us understand and evaluate an artwork. They are instrumental in "demystifying" the artist's production without destroying the "magical" qualities inherent in its creation. These questions are based on the use of critical-thinking skills, as explained in Benjamin Bloom's *Taxonomy of Educational Objectives in the Cognitive Domain.*[6]

Bloom's taxonomy outlines levels of critical-thinking skills that can be used in both understanding artworks and in producing our own artworks. These include:

1. **Knowledge,** in which students recall terminology, artwork titles, dates, and such; recognize, name, identify, label, define, examine, show, and collect information.
2. **Comprehension,** in which students explain, describe, translate, interpret, and summarize collected information.

3. **Application,** in which students go beyond the concept or principle that they have learned and use that principle in a new, imaginative, or hypothetical situation. Here they can think creatively, make preferences, and project ideas. They can experiment, predict, imagine, and hypothesize as they attempt to solve problems.
4. **Analysis,** in which students make connections and establish relationships, categorize, compare and infer, classify and arrange, and organize and group information.
5. **Synthesis,** in which students design, plan, combine, construct, and produce.
6. **Evaluation,** in which students critically examine their own artworks or those of others as they learn to criticize, judge, appraise, and make decisions.

To enable students' to grow in these six areas of critical thinking, we may consider questions in the following categories:

RECALLING

Naming: What is the title of this painting?
Listing: What do you see at the top, bottom, and sides of the painting?
Describing: What are the figures in the boat doing?
Matching: Which picture goes with the word *sad?*
Defining: What is meant by "cool" colors?
Observing: What is the woman wearing on her head?
Identifying: Which building is the lightest value of blue?
Counting: How many apples are in the still life?
Completing: This type of artwork is called (sculpture, landscape painting, portrait painting, and so on).

PROCESSING

Comparing: How is this mask like (unlike) that mask?
Explaining: Why did the artist place the horizon so high (so low)?
Inferring: From looking at these paintings, what can we infer about space and diminishing sizes?
Sequencing: Arrange the paintings in order, from those with the brightest and most intense colors to those with the dullest colors.
Classifying: Which sculptures of figures are most realistic? abstract? expressive?
Explaining cause and effect: How did the artist use repetition and pattern to emphasize the face?
Contrasting: How does the texture on the helmet differ from the fur collar?
Making analogies: Can you think of another artist (or culture) who produced art similar to this one?

APPLICATION

Forecasting: If this artist had lived fifty years longer, how do you think his or her style might have changed?

Predicting: Which artist, in this group of six, do you think will be best remembered for his or her technique in a hundred years?

Judging: Which painting do you think shows the most artistic merit?

Imagining: How do you imagine this artist would have painted a horse? Would he have used the same style and technique as he used in painting this landscape?

Applying: How would *you* paint a cubist picture of a penguin?

Hypothesizing: How do you think this sculpture would have looked if the artist had painted it with bright colors?

An Oral Presentation of an Artwork

A short oral presentation of an artwork can help you organize and clarify your thoughts and perceptions. Select an artwork from the Color Gallery, and use art criticism and art history strategies to help you describe, analyze, interpret, and judge it. Read about the artist in reference books to help you with aspects of art history. Then make a five-minute presentation of the artwork to your classmates. The following is an example of how a university student responded to Vincent van Gogh's *Starry Night* (colorplate 11 in the Color Gallery).

This oil painting was made by Vincent van Gogh in 1889, one year before he died. The size of the original is 29 by 36¼ inches. It hangs in the Museum of Modern Art in New York. It is a nighttime landscape that is done in the thick, swirling brush strokes that are characteristic of this artist. We see the sky taking up most of the picture space. The sky is filled with the circular, rolling, spiraling lines and shapes that represent the stars and moon. In the foreground, we see a sleeping village with the tall, dark, triangular shape of a cypress tree reaching upward on the left. Blue and yellow are the dominant colors. Since daytime scenes are far more prevalent as subjects for landscapes, we find a certain fascination in seeing a landscape at night.

Born in Holland in 1853, Vincent, as he signed his artworks and liked to be called, was a sensitive, lonely man whose behavior often alienated people. He always wanted to help people but failed at being a minister, a missionary, and at working for art dealers. Only the last ten years of his life were devoted to art. During that time, he sold only one painting, and that was for eighty dollars. He worked at painting with a fierce intensity, all the while conveying his thoughts and feelings in correspondence with his brother Theo, who supported him financially and emotionally.

Perhaps we see Vincent's longing for a family and a home life in the peaceful village in the middle ground, with its church spire pointing upward and catching our attention. We observe his feverish brush strokes in this painting and can see how he may have even squeezed the paint directly on the canvas, rather than placing it on his palette first. This created thick layers of paint that add an actual texture to the artwork. We can almost visualize Vincent working on this

painting as he stood in the field at night, candles blazing on his palette and around the brim of his hat to help him see.

The round, circular shapes of the stars are repeated a number of times in the dark blue sky in a random pattern with the sizes varied. Our eyes follow the movement of the rolling circles and spirals in the skies. The dark cypress in the foreground tends to stabilize the turbulence. The lightest part of the picture is the haloed crescent moon on the right. It is balanced by the deep green cypress tree on the left, a shape that reminds us of a flame writhing upward as if it were trying to reach the heavens. The gently rolling hills in the background behind the village seem restful and quiet, and tend to lead our eyes to the cypress. We see a great variety of dark and light tones of both blue and yellow used throughout the picture. These were two of Vincent's favorite colors; he believed that yellow stood for love, warmth and friendship. The limited number of colors gives unity to the painting, as do the uniform, thick, swirling brush strokes.

We feel peaceful when we look at the sleeping village with its lights glowing in the windows, even though the busy skies are alive with the restless energy of the stars. We feel uplifted, perhaps even somewhat protected, when our eyes are carried rhythmically upward by the dark form of the tree. We remember summer evenings and looking up at the clear skies and seeing stars that were especially bright. Although Vincent has painted the stars larger and more vibrant than we are accustomed to seeing them without the benefit of telescopes, he has conveyed his deep feelings. He once stated he wanted people to understand that he felt deeply and tenderly. This expressive work of art succeeds in touching our emotions and making us see night skies with perhaps a greater clarity than we would have without Vincent's special vision.

■ TALKING WITH CHILDREN ABOUT AN ARTWORK

Children like to look at artworks and respond to them. When artwork reproductions are placed before them, or when they visit a museum and study original artworks, dialogue can broaden their perceptions. When they describe, analyze, interpret, and make aesthetic judgments about an artwork, they learn a new vocabulary, and repeated encounters with a variety of artworks increase their skills in responding.

Large reproductions (often called study prints or posters), slides, books, and postcards of great artworks are available from supply houses and museums and are relatively inexpensive. Calendars with large, first-rate reproductions of the works of famous artists are readily available. This accessibility is an advancement from the past, when color reproductions were costly and limited in number. Nothing can take the place of seeing original artworks; however, the difficulty of visiting distant and foreign museums is an obvious deterrent for many people.

Using reproductions has certain educational advantages. When you visit a museum, you may see, for instance, one or two works by Winslow Homer. With reproductions, students can compare five or six of his artworks. Or the teacher can select five or six artworks by other artists that deal with the same theme. Students can then compare works that illustrate the four styles of art and discuss how each artist used the elements and principles of art to affect the mood and meaning of his or her artwork.

Large reproductions have advantages over slides and overhead transparencies in elementary classrooms. Reproductions can be viewed in multiples in lighted rooms and left for extended periods of time for students to view. When large reproductions are used in the classroom, children should be seated close to the work being described and analyzed, and they need to know that the work is a reproduction, not the original.

The following dialogue suggests the sort of remarks and teacher responses that could direct students' thinking to a greater understanding of the artwork *Sunday Afternoon on the Island of La Grande Jatte* by Georges Seurat (see color-plate 12 in the Color Gallery):

T: Tell me what you see.

S: A lot of people.

T: Where are they?

S: On the grass. Maybe a park or something because I see some water, too. And I see a border, sort of like a frame painted all around the outside edge.

T: What are the people doing?

S: Just standing there or sitting. Oh, maybe walking. I see a lady with a little girl like she's walking toward me. They are really dressed up for a day in the park. They look like real people, but their clothes look like they're from an old-fashioned movie.

T: Yes, that's how people dressed at the time the artist Georges Seurat painted this artwork, a little over one hundred years ago. Which people are the closest to us?

S: That man and woman on the right.

T: You're right. The artist made them larger than any other figures and placed them lower on the canvas. That makes them seem closer to us. Which other figures seem close to us?

S: Those three on the left that are sitting on the grass. They are looking out toward the water. Maybe there is a sailboat race or something going on. Looks like the black dog is eating their lunch scraps.

T: Those figures are in the foreground, too. Can you see how the artist, Georges Seurat, has painted a shaded area here? What else do you see in the foreground?

S: Oh, I see a little monkey and a little dog running toward the black dog.

T: Let's take a little walk with our eyes back into the distance and find some more figures. How are they like the figures in the foreground?

S: Well, they are dressed like them. They're looking out at the water, most of them anyway, and I see some more parasols. Most of the people seem real quiet. I don't think it looks like a noisy place. Maybe you could hear some quiet sort of music playing if you were there. Oh, I do see one little girl running.

T: Let's have several of you stand and sit in the same positions of the figures in the painting. Look carefully at the painting before you take a position. *(Time-out for this activity.)*

T: Now let's look at the picture again and measure the figures you see in the middle ground. *(Hold a ruler or string upright to measure the heights of the couple on the right, then the central figure with the little girl, and then a figure in the background.)* Seurat painted the figures that he wanted us to see as farthest away the smallest. When artists do this, we say they have used diminishing sizes to show deep space. He also placed them higher up from the bottom of the canvas. They are also lighter in color value. Can you see any other ways he made the figures seem farther away from us?

S: We can't see any stripes or ribbons or anything on their clothes.

T: Right, he made the details and textures less sharp and clear. Let's look and see how many places Seurat used curving lines and shapes. *(Let a student use a pointer to do this.)*

S: The skirts, the parasols and hats, and even the tails on the animals. Oh, yes, the sailboat.

T: I'm glad you noticed that white, curving sail in the background. It is very much like part of the parasol. I think you may have noticed it because it was white, in contrast to the darker blue of the water. Can you find other places in the composition where the artist repeated white? This tends to add unity to the picture and lead our eyes around and throughout the complex organization. He has painted a shadow shape for almost each figure, and that adds unity, too. Describe the colors you see. Are they the same as you would see in nature?

S: Well, I see a lot of green, I guess, but I see light greens, sort of a yellow-green, and some blue-greens. Quite a bit of blue, too. Then I see that reddish-orange color on the clothing and the parasol in the middle. They're probably the same colors the artist saw.

T: Good. Red and green are complementary colors on the color wheel. They are opposites and contrast

strongly with each other. Let's talk about the surface quality of the painting. Do you see it as being smooth or what?

S: It looks, well, kind of grainy when I think of the way most other paintings look, like the one by Gauguin we saw a few days ago.

T: *Grainy* is a good word because Seurat invented a new way to put the paint on his canvas; he called it pointillism. He applied the paint with many tiny dots, one color next to another color, so that when he was done and you, the viewer, stepped away from the artwork, your eyes would mix the colors together. If a lot of white dots are applied with only a few blue dots, your eyes see a light blue.

S: That must have taken him a long time. How large is that painting in the original?

T: It is about 8 by 10 feet in size!

S: Wow! Did he make very many paintings during his life?

T: Only about sixty because he died in 1891, when he was only thirty-one, of a throat infection. He was working with another artist named Signac, who carried on the experiments with pointillism. Look at the way Seurat arranged the people and trees. It all seems very casual and lifelike, yet he was very careful to create a feel of visual balance. We call the kind of symmetry he used informal. One side is not exactly like the other side. The two large figures in rather dark clothing on the right tend to balance the three seated figures and the dog on the left. Can you find other things that balance each other?

S: (*Students use pointer.*)

T: What do you see as the center of emphasis in this painting? What leads your eye to it?

S: I see the lady in the center, the one with the little girl in the white dress. I think it's because she is in the center and is the only one facing us. Then, too, her red parasol contrasts with the green foliage of the trees above her.

S: I don't agree. My attention goes to the couple on the right. They're the largest figures. Their clothing is dark, and the line of the parasol and cane kind of point to them.

T: Do you like looking at this painting?

S: Yes. There are so many things to see. My eyes keep moving back and forth, imagining what the people were saying. It looks like a warm day. It is almost like a photo, but then again, the people all look like they aren't moving—like they're posing and still as statues. Most of the shapes and lines are vertical, the tree trunks and the people. Maybe that's why it looks quiet and peaceful.

S: And l like the new way Seurat painted, that pointillism. It's neat. Could we try making a picture like that
. . . only not 8 by 10 feet!

Strategies for Bringing Artworks to Life in the Classroom

1. Tap young children on the shoulder with a "magic paintbrush" to enable them to have "magic eyes" that see things in a picture. Also use the brush as a pointer to direct students' attention to a diagonal line, a geometric shape, converging lines of perspective, and so on. Use the brush to demonstrate how artists create brush strokes. Try other pointers, such as long feathers when discussing birds, glitter wands when discussing kings and queens, a twig for discussing trees, and so on. (*To make a "magic paintbrush," cover the long handle of a paintbrush with white glue and glitter dust. To make a "super brush," attach a long, tapered dowel to the ferrule of a regular brush.*)

2. A pair of **artist eyeglasses** may give very young or somewhat shy children the confidence to describe the special colors, shapes, or subject matter they see. Children can take turns wearing the glasses while they make comments.

3. Use a **hand puppet** to initiate a conversation about a painting.

4. Have children respond to questions by taking turns talking into a **pretend microphone.**

5. Have several **scraps of textured materials** (satin, lace, burlap, wood, etc.) to use in discussing the simulated textures in artworks. Also, show students a real object (a mango, beads, feather) that is in one of the paintings that they see. Tell the children to watch for the textures or for one of the objects.

6. You may want to **dress in special clothing** and **use props** that are appropriate to the artworks being discussed. For instance, a clown's costume for a circus painting by Seurat, a cowboy hat and saddle for a Remington or Russell painting.

7. **Cut out several openings** in a piece of **butcher paper.** Then cover a reproduction with the paper so that small details can be seen through the openings. Let students guess what the rest of the picture might be. Have them use crayons to try completing the picture on the butcher paper.

8. Use a clear piece of **vinyl** the same size as a reproduction. Then use a broad-point, black, water-based marking pen (Vis-a-vis) to convey certain points. For example, draw around all the round shapes, the contour lines, the perspective lines, all the places where the

artist used red, the distorted shapes, and so on. Wipe the vinyl clean with a damp paper towel, and use again.

9. Have students look quietly at a picture for a minute or so, and then ask them to **make up a good title** for it. This calls for description and interpretation. The children should tell why they chose a particular name. Or tell the children the **name of the picture,** and then have them explain why they think the artist gave it that title. If you are showing several artworks, write the **names of all the pictures** on the chalkboard. Let students guess which title goes with which reproduction.

10. Ask children to **imitate a pose, movement,** or **facial expression** that they see in one of the pictures. Have several students imitate a **group position.** Have other students guess which picture each pose is imitating.

11. Ask students to enter a painting and **take a walk with their eyes,** telling what path their eyes follow and what lines, shapes, and colors direct them. This analysis helps children find a focal point and understand how the artist organized the composition.

12. Take turns using **one word** or **a short phrase** to describe an artwork. For example, start with "curving shapes." The next student repeats the first word or phrase and adds another, such as "Curving shapes and bright colors," and so on.

13. Have students write or discuss what they think a person in a figure painting would write in his or her **journal** or **diary** that night. This calls for interpretive responses.

14. Let one student **interview** a person in a picture, and have another student stand behind the reproduction and answer questions. This calls for interpretive responses.

15. Ask individual students to **pretend to be the artist.** (You might bring along a small artist smock, hat, and palette for role-playing.) Ask the students to imagine preparing to paint the picture. Where did they go to paint the picture? Who posed for the picture? What did they want to succeed in doing? What would they change, add, or "erase," or would they leave the picture just as it is? Ask them what they, as the artist, probably did first when they made the picture. This activity involves reconstructing skills and helps students to think like an artist.

16. **Celebrate the birthday of an artist.** Have students make folded paper hats from newspapers or a large piece of butcher paper. They should then decorate the hats in the manner of that artist. Use cut paper, felt pens, crayons, scrap materials, and so on. Use symbols and motifs to represent the artist's style.

17. Students **imagine the artist alive today.** Discuss where the students would take the artist and what conversations they would have with the artist over the course of one day. What questions would they ask? What would they like to show the artist in today's America? How do they think the artist would react? What would they most like to tell the artist?

18. Two students **imagine a conversation** that might occur if two artists could meet and talk to each other today. Would the artists argue? On what would they agree? Would they be surprised at anything? What themes would they paint about in today's world?

19. Play **tic-tac-toe** on the chalkboard. Divide the class into two teams. Ask questions at the end of a presentation about an artist or painting. Let teams take turns answering and placing an "X" or "O" for each correct response.

20. Use a set of **"Art Cards"** (descriptive phrases related to the elements and principles of art, technical qualities, emotional interpretation, and styles of art). Select appropriate Art Cards, and distribute two or three to each student at the end of a discussion about several reproductions. Place a **numbered envelope** beside each reproduction. Tell students to place each of their Arts Cards in the envelope for the reproduction that they feel is most appropriate. Collect all the envelopes and select one, reading aloud all of the terms on the Art Cards inside. Have students guess which print the cards are describing.

21. Select some landscapes, seascapes, and cityscapes, and ask students to write a travel journal based on an imaginary trip to these places. Ask students to describe what they saw, what they did there, how they traveled there, and so on.

22. Have students write short Japanese poems—**cinquains** (sĭn' cānz), **haikus** (hī' kuz), and **tankas** (tahng' kahz)—about artworks they have discussed. Model this activity first by writing a poem on the chalkboard as students suggest lines. Groups of students can work together to write a poem, with each group choosing a different painting. The lines should express their response to what they see, feel, and know about the selected painting. Two examples of cinquains that were written about famous paintings follow:

Sinbad the Sailor by **Paul Klee**

Sinbad
Traveling sailor
Spearing, thrusting, killing
Fierce monsters from the ocean's depths
Seaman.

Turn Him Loose, Bill, by **Frederic Remington**

Cowboy
Bucking bronco
Pounding hoofs, flying mane.

Hardy, husky, stalwart, brawny
Tough guy.

Ciquains have the following format:

Line 1 (two syllables): State the subject with one word (usually a noun).
Line 2 (four syllables): Describe the subject with two words (often a noun and an adjective, or two adjectives).
Line 3 (six syllables): Describe the subject's action with three words (often three verbs).
Line 4 (eight syllables): Express an emotion about the subject with four words.
Line 5 (two syllables): Restate the subject with another single word, reflecting what you have already said (usually a noun).

Haikus, a form of Japanese poetry, use only seventeen syllables and three lines to create a word picture and mood. Students should use the following format to express their responses to what they see, feel, and know about a painting:

Line 1: Five syllables
Line 2: Seven syllables
Line 3: Five syllables

The following examples of haiku are based on famous paintings:

Bedroom at Arles by **Vincent van Gogh**

See van Gogh's bedroom
Blue walls, two chairs and table
Gone now, dear Vincent.

Acrobat on a Ball by **Pablo Picasso**

Balanced acrobat
Teeters on ball, sandy beach
Steady now, sway, stop.

A tanka is another Japanese short poem. It is made up of five lines in the following format:

Line 1: Five syllables
Line 2: Seven syllables
Line 3: Five syllables
Line 4: Seven syllables
Line 5: Seven syllables

An example of a tanka follows:

Surprised! Storm in the Forest by **Henri Rousseau**

White lightning flashes
Winds blow through the trees and grass
The tiger crouches
See the storm in the forest!
Henri Rousseau, were you there?

When the de Young Museum in San Francisco featured works by Claude Monet, Emily dressed as the fictional character in the children's book *Linnea in Monet's Garden* and, along with her Linnea doll, made her first museum visit.

■ ART MUSEUMS, GALLERIES, AND ART IN PUBLIC PLACES

Museums house many of the world's great artworks, even those that were created long before museums, were built. Many artworks from the distant past were commissioned and created to serve purposes other than hanging in a museum. For instance, in the Western world, religious pieces were made for a largely illiterate populace to teach them Bible stories and to inspire them. These works were displayed in places of worship. Royalty hired court painters to record their likenesses, and these works hung in palaces.

Today, museums have special exhibits that bring together groups of major artworks from many different museums and private collections. Such exhibits may feature the lifetime accomplishments of a single artist or focus on a number of artworks created during the same time period.

Frequent visits to museums can be a lifetime source of enjoyment. Most of us live reasonably close to a major museum, and many people travel in America and abroad, where wonderful museums await.

Entering a museum for the first time, especially a large one, may seem bewildering, so check the maps and guides available at the front desk. These printed materials will help you know what kinds of works to expect and in which rooms they can be found. During some museum visits, you may want to gain an overview of what is there, taking a look at the major galleries and rooms, and gathering quick impressions of the collections. You probably will not be able to take more than a quick glance at each artwork on such a visit, but when you see one that you find especially appealing, linger and enjoy the experience. You will probably finish your visit remembering several magnificent artworks and planning when you will return for another look. Look for what appeals to you and build on it, but keep your eyes open, and find something you are attracted to that you never liked before. Go at your own pace. Occasionally, relax for a while on a seat in a gallery, or find the gallery cafe for a snack. After several hours, you will probably leave with a satisfying feeling of exhaustion and saturation.

The labels posted next to artworks tell the title of the work, the artist, and the medium used. Other pertinent data may include the date the museum acquired the work, the date the artwork was created, and the name of the artwork's present owners if it is on loan from another museum or a private collection.

Another way to plan your visit to a museum is to focus on a specific gallery or collection. Most museums do not arrange their permanent collection of artworks in chronological order, but instead group them geographically or by schools of art. Thus, you will find in separate sections artworks from Egypt, Greece, or perhaps, the Renaissance. In addition to permanent collections, most museums have a gallery or two for changing exhibits; the museum calendar or program will tell you "what's on" at the time you are there. Some popular "blockbuster" shows may even require purchasing tickets in advance.

On a more leisurely museum visit, you can use the following approaches in responding to an artwork that particularly appeals to you:

1. Stand before an artwork, and study all its parts (art elements); then close your eyes and see if you can reconstruct it. If your visual memory is faulty, open your eyes and reexamine the parts more carefully. Then close your eyes and try again. This technique makes you look more carefully at the artwork, really seeing and remembering it.

2. Hold a viewfinder before an artwork that particularly strikes your senses. Frame a significant detail, and focus on that part. Try to find a painting-within-a-painting in this manner, using your viewfinder to locate within the painting's boundaries an area that particularly appeals to you and has a center of interest and an arrangement with comfortable informal balance. Then make a small sketch of what you see through the viewfinder. You will be taking home your personalized selection of your artwork.

3. Sketch the entire artwork. Artists and art students have always trained themselves by drawing from artworks. A student working at an easel, copying from a masterpiece in a museum, is a frequent sight. Even if you do not feel that you are copying it skillfully, your pen or pencil acts as a magnifying glass, focusing your attention on wonderful things that you probably would not see otherwise.

4. Select three works of a similar theme but from three diverse cultures. Choose works in a museum or reproduced in books, or select three figurative works from the Color Gallery, such as:

Vaudeville by Jacob Lawrence (African-American male) (colorplate 31)
Sanzo by Yoshio Taylor (Japanese-American male) (colorplate 25)
Green Violinist by Marc Chagall (Russian Jewish male) (colorplate 33)
Women and Dog by Marisol (Venezuelan female, living in USA/Europe) (colorplate 17)
Flower Dance Spirit by Frank La Pena (Native-American male) (colorplate 24)
The Bath by Mary Cassatt (American female) (colorplate 32)
Girl before a Mirror by Pablo Picasso (Spanish male) (colorplate 29)
Prince Riding an Elephant by Khemkaran (Indian male) (colorplate 20)
We, the People by Armando Alvarez (Mexican-American male) (colorplate 34)

a. Did tradition and history influence the creation of any of these artworks? How?

b. Do any of these works show social, religious, or economic values?

c. In what way has society influenced each artwork?

d. How would each work have been different if created by another culture, in another time period, or in another style?

e. What style of art does each artwork represent?

f.   What cultural or artistic standards are seen in each piece?

g.   For what purpose was each piece created?

Visit the museum bookshop, either before you enter the galleries or afterward. By stopping there first, you will discover by looking at the postcards, reproductions, slides, books, and catalogs, which artworks the museum considers extraordinary enough to have reproduced. This might guide you as to what artworks you do not want to miss or those works you did not know were there. Purchasing these museum-shop reproductions allows you to take your visual memories home in a tangible way. Noted art historian Kenneth Clark has his own fine collection of original artworks in his home, but he also keeps postcard reproductions on his mantelpiece of works that currently fit his mood. If you read a museum catalog after you have seen the exhibit, your knowledge about the artworks and the artists will be enhanced.

You may visit a museum alone or with a friend or group. Each arrangement has advantages. If you are with a friend, you will each be discovering things and sharing what you see. Being alone probably allows you to have a closer relationship with an individual artwork. Have you ever stood before a fine portrait by a seventeenth-century Dutch master and had the almost eerie feeling that the eyes of the person, long since dead, are gazing directly at you alone down through the centuries? Or perhaps you just let the pure visual impact of Kandinsky's vibrant colors drench you in a silent form of communication. Or have you sensed the eternal quality of Egyptian artifacts, or the lonely isolation of an Edward Hopper cityscape?

An audioguide can provide you with an individually guided and sequenced look at an exhibit. Through your personal set of earphones, you are told which artwork to focus on and then are provided with interesting information. You can turn off the tape cassette at any time and linger longer before a particular piece of art or in front of one that has caught your eye but that was not included in the tape's monologue.

Group tours in a museum give visitors the opportunity to have the expert guidance of a trained guide called a **docent.** Such knowledgeable museum lecturers can point out aspects of an artwork that the first-time viewer might miss and pass along pertinent historical information about the artist and time period that gives the trip a special in-depth quality.

If you plan to take a group of children on a museum field trip, make arrangements with the museum ahead of time. The museum may send you a set of slides and written information to use in preparing the children for their visit. Upon your arrival, the museum will provide you with a museum docent who is trained in talking with children. In these situations, do not expect to see everything in one visit; rather, expect to focus on only one exhibit and especially on several works of art. Young viewers need to understand that they may only "touch the artwork with their eyes," since the artworks are very valuable and can be damaged by touching. Many museums provide studio space for children to go to after seeing an exhibit to try their hand at working with a particular medium. In addition, museums often give students worksheets that enable them to go on a guided "treasure hunt," searching for specific things in specific paintings. A visit to the museum shop can give young viewers an opportunity to begin their own small-scale private art collection by purchasing postcard reproductions of the favorite artworks they have just seen.

Not to be overlooked as artwork is the museum itself. Many museums are spectacular pieces of architecture, and some are set in dazzling gardens and grounds that demand our attention. You will usually find outdoor sculpture to admire on the museum grounds. Notice the stately, classical columns of the Metropolitan Museum in New York; be absorbed with the buildings that were once homes and are now museums, such as the Isabella Stewart Gardner Museum in Boston and the Frick in New York. Newer museums, such as the Guggenheim in New York, the Hirshhorn in Washington, D.C., and the Los Angeles County Museum, show styles of contemporary architects and reflect the times. Contrast the new east wing of the National Gallery of Art in Washington, D.C., with the older part of the museum.

Some of the world's major museums have produced museum tour videos. For instance, videos of the New York Metropolitan Museum, the Louvre in Paris, and the National Gallery of Art in Washington, D.C. show some of the finest works in the museums and at the same time offer a glimpse of the museums themselves. In addition, a number of museums are on the Internet and have produced interactive CD-Roms.

Many cities today have policies whereby a percentage of building costs for public and corporate architecture must be designated for the installation of interior or exterior artworks, including sculptures in and near the site, murals, wall hangings, fountains, memorials, and such. Local arts councils can supply visitors with lists of where to find these artworks. Arts councils often schedule "art walks" so that both students and adults can take a guided tour to view these installations.

■ ASSESSING YOUR OWN ARTWORK

Responding to our own artwork in a manner that requires us to examine what we have done by describing, analyzing, interpreting, and evaluating can help us identify where our artwork is successful and where we might wish to improve our skills. By writing a critique of our own process and product, we become more consciously aware of what we have accomplished and where our skills need to be enhanced.

After you complete one of the "Producing Artworks" lessons that follow each of the sections on the elements and principles of art in Chapters 3 and 4, evaluate your progress by using the format that follows. It gives specific steps to guide you, along with a variety of vocabulary terms and phrases to help you thoughtfully critique your own artwork. Use this outline to help you write a one- or two-page critique. First, describe what you actually see in the way of subject matter and technical properties, and then analyze how you used the elements and principles of art. Then reflect on the mood or emotion that you have expressed, and try to relate the meaning of your artwork to the four styles of art. Finally, try to describe the best parts of your composition, as well as ways you think you could improve your artwork.

1. **Describing what I see in my artwork:** medium used; size of the work; technical properties (thick brush strokes, thin washes of color, etc.); type of artwork (landscape painting, still life, figure drawing, portrait, relief print, sculpture, etc.); subject matter (animals, figures, buildings, etc.)

2. **Analyzing the elements of art**
   a. *Colors—What kinds did I use:* primary, secondary, intermediate, complementary, tints, shades, neutrals, warm, cool, bright, intense, dull, dark, light, glowing, soft, harmonious, flat, modeled, monochromatic, sad, happy, expressive, decorative, clashing, high-keyed, low-keyed, representational, realistic, symbolic, imaginative
   b. *Lines—What kinds did I use:* straight, horizontal, vertical, diagonal, curving, smooth, broken, fuzzy, blurred, spiraling, jagged, thick, wide, thin, sharp, graceful, contour, bold, long, short, thick to thin, continuous, meandering, sketchy, hatched, angular, nervous, energetic, delicate, strong, gesture, implied, actual, zigzag, outline, firm, hypnotic, tense, parallel, rough, branching, confusing, stable, stiff, dignified, calligraphic, perspective, realistic, abstract, decorative, graduated, converging
   c. *Shapes/Forms—What kinds did I use:* angular, circular, geometric, free- form, soft-edged, hard-edged, large, small, organic, graduated, repeated, outlined, natural, expressive, threatening, irregular, positive, negative, light, heavy, silhouette, decorative, symbolic, realistic
   d. *Textures—What kinds did I use:* rough, smooth, shiny, soft, metallic, fuzzy, feathery, bumpy, simulated, visual, actual, real, slick, grainy, fluffy, matte, inviting, impasto
   e. *Space—What kind do I see:* deep, overlapping, flat, shallow, distant/lighter, distant/smaller, distant/less detail, distant/higher, negative, perspective, realistic
   f. *Value—What kind did I use:* very dark, medium dark, light, graduated, dramatic, expressive, blended, hatched, crosshatched, stippled, modeled, distance, shadows, shading

3. **Analyzing the principles of art**
   a. *Balance—What kind did I use:* formal or symmetrical, approximate, informal or asymmetrical, radial, uncomfortable, casual, calm, comfortable, achieved by _____
   b. *Emphasis—What is the center of interest, and how did I achieve it:* dominant, subordinate, less important, location, convergence, isolation, contrast, triangular, center, off-center, focal point, eyes, face, unusual or surprising subject matter, directional, eye-leading pointers, texture, lighting
   c. *Proportion—What relationships did I emphasize:* bright to dull, large to small, dark to light, rough to smooth, realistic, distorted, exaggerated, unrealistic
   d. *Movement—What kind did I use:* actual, simulated, illusion, stiff, frozen, static, swinging, sweeping, optical, shifting, mechanical, flowing, random, progressive, regular, alternating, circular, dizzy, diagonal, downward, upward, triangular, animated, realistic, powerful, rhythmical
   e. *Rhythm, Repetition, and Pattern—What kinds did I use:* decorative, motif/module, lines, shapes, colors, graduated, monotonous, dull, lively, realistic, flowing, surface enhancement, revealing form, structural, regular, irregular, random, intriguing, optical, simulating texture
   f. *Variety—What kind did I use:* color, line, shape, texture, value, size, contrast, placement, monotonous, dull, chaotic
   g. *Unity—Does my artwork seem complete and harmonious:* yes, no, somewhat, limitations of each element, harmony among elements, harmony between subject matter and style, overlapping, clustering, interlocking, repetition and variation of colors/shapes/lines

4. **Interpreting the mood or emotion of my artwork:** poetic, playful, humorous, vigorous, peaceful, joyous, sad, religious, narrative, propaganda, energetic, warm, loving, angry, recording a likeness, inspirational, restless, quiet, frightening, dreamlike, charming, mysterious, puzzling

5. **Describing the purpose and/or meaning of my artwork**
   a. *Realism/representationalism:* My artwork is mostly concerned with representing what I saw.
   b. *Expressionism/emotionalism:* My artwork is mostly concerned with telling about a feeling, idea, or emotion.

Responding to Artworks— in a Nutshell

Art Criticism and Art History

DESCRIPTION: *Art Criticism*

What do you see: subject matter, details, placement of objects, pose of figures. Is it a landscape, still life, portrait? Is it a drawing, etching, painting, sculpture? What was the viewpoint of the artist? Note the technical properties of the medium used. ***Identify the elements of art.***

DESCRIPTION: *Art History*

What is the name of the artist and artwork? When and where was it created? Where it is now? What is the artist's birth/death dates? What is the correct pronunciation of the artist's name? What is the size of the original artwork? Do you know pertinent biographical information about the artist?

Aesthetic Qualities/Styles of Art (These may overlap)
1. *Realism:* Artist was interested in representing real subject matter that reminds us of what we see in the natural world.
2. *Abstraction/Formalism:* Artist was interested in effective visual organization of elements and principles of art. Style may range from nonobjective (no objects) to recognizable images and subject matter.
3. *Expressionism/Emotionalism:* Artist was interested in vivid communication of moods, feelings, messages, and ideas. This was often accomplished by unrealistic colors and distortion and exaggeration of shapes.
4. *Fantasy/Surrealism:* Artist was interested in the communication of dreams, of the subconscious, of fantasy, and of images from the imagination. Images are often quite real but are seen in unusual and startling relationships.

ANALYSIS: *Art Criticism*

How is the artwork organized? ***Observe how the artist used the principles of art to arrange the elements of art,*** thereby giving the artwork its form, meaning, and expression. Formal analysis seeks to discover *how* the composition works as it does.

JUDGMENT: *Art Criticism*

Degree of artistic merit in an artwork is decided in relation to the aesthetic qualities found in the four styles of art. We evaluate a realistic work on the basis of its success as a representational artwork, an abstract work on the basis of its success as an abstract artwork, and so on. We state that the "artwork is successful because . . ." and understand that judgment in art criticism is different from stating personal preference.

JUDGMENT: *Art History*

This involves evaluation of the factors related to the artwork's importance and its place in art history. We consider the artist's stylistic or technical innovations, compositional originality, new subjects or variations of meanings for previously depicted subjects, influence on other artists, and recognition during lifetime.

ANALYSIS: *Art History*

We compare and contrast the artwork with other works (by the same artist or other artists) to determine its style and what is unique and important about it. We identify similarities and differences in ways that the artist used the elements and principles of art.

INTERPRETATION: *Art Criticism*

What **feelings, emotions, and moods** are evoked? Response is personal and individual. We consider our own memories, values, and experiences. What in the subject matter or in the formal and technical properties caused our response? Mood and meaning communicated may evoke responses that are happy, frightening, patriotic, hostile, tragic, pleasant, humorous, religious, and so on.

INTERPRETATION: *Art History*

How was the artist influenced by world events? We consider symbolic content. We note the artwork's historical context and meaning. We ask why the artist created it and for what audience. What was the artist's personality like, and how did this influence his or her artwork? What artists or artworks influenced this artist's work?

c. *Abstraction/formalism:* My artwork is mostly concerned with colors, lines, shapes, textures, and values rather than subject matter.

d. *Surrealism/fantasy:* My artwork is mostly concerned with imagination, dreams, and the subconscious.

6. Evaluating the artwork

a. The best parts of the composition in my artwork are in the way I used _____. (Describe your use of *two* of the art elements and *two* of the art principles.)

b. The composition could be improved by changing _____. (Describe an art element and an art principle that could be improved.)

c. The thing I like best about the way I used the art material is _____.

d. I was especially creative in the way I _____.

e. My artwork shows a feeling of (happiness, sadness, humor, etc.) because of _____.

f. This artwork could be compared/contrasted to another artwork: _____.

The following is an example written by a university student who used the outline as a guide for responding to her own artwork:

My artwork is a watercolor painting. I used thick paper and watercolor paints. Some of the brush strokes are thin washes, as in the sky, while others are very thick, as in the stream. The objects depicted are trees, clouds, rocks, and a stream. It is a landscape painting showing a mountainside with tall trees and shrubbery, and a stream flowing through it.

When starting the artwork, I used a thin black marker to outline the objects. I used curvy, meandering lines for the clouds and stream. The trees were made of sketchy, hatched lines. All the colors I used were cool colors—shades and tints of blue or green. The green trees next to the bright blue stream express a happy and fresh feeling. The trees have sharp or jagged edges. Some of the branches are repeated shapes. The clouds and stream take a free-form shape. The water has a shiny texture that I created with dark and light blobs of blue. The clouds are billowy, and the sky is slick light blue. The greatest changes of value are found in the trees. Some of the trees are a bright green, while others have a more avocado tone. The river, by being smaller near the upper part and growing larger in the lower part, creates deep space; the trees show depth by overlapping, and this makes them look thick and dense.

The trees forming large shapes on the right side are balanced informally by some greenery and the descending stream on the left. Variety is shown by differences in the greens of the trees and in the thickness and thinness of blue in the stream. A flowing movement is seen in the water, and the thin brush strokes in the sky also show cloud movement. The first thing I see in my artwork is the group of trees; they are most dominant because they are the largest mass of color and are centered in the composition.

The proportion of the stream to the rocks is of a realistic scale. My artwork seems complete and harmonious.

I was mostly representing a landscape, working with L-frames and a detail of a photograph. The best parts of my artwork are in the way I used texture and color: The texture of the stream was accomplished by applying wet-on-wet washes; the variety of green tones in the trees was obtained by blending various intensities of green. I could improve my artwork with the use of less outline details on the clouds. I could also improve the rocks by my handling of wet-on-dry color washes and layering of colors. I used my imagination with my changes in brush strokes for the clouds and the trees. My artwork shows a mood of relaxation, peacefulness, and tranquility, and gives the feeling that no person has ever set foot on the hillside.

◼ INTERACTIVE EXTENSIONS

1. You are the chair of the Acquisitions Committee at a major museum. Your committee has just voted to use an endowment fund to purchase one of the artworks in the Color Gallery. You are being interviewed on a local radio talk show and must justify your committee's decision. Choose a classmate to be the talk-show host who will ask you questions regarding the controversy surrounding the acquisition. Be prepared to respond to the host's questions (questions that you supply him or her with ahead of time) and those of call-in listeners (your classmates). Practice ahead of time with your talk-show host.

2. Select a classmate to play the role of a friend who has just been notified of his or her inheritance: He or she must choose between two artworks from an aunt's estate (two artworks in the Color Gallery). Your friend asks your advice as to which artwork to choose.

3. You own a prestigious art gallery in San Francisco and have a wealthy foreign client who wishes to purchase an American artwork. Base your interview with your client on why he or she should purchase a particular painting. Choose a classmate to play the role of the client, and brief him or her on appropriate questions and remarks.

4. Make a presentation of two paintings to the class. Select paintings that are very different from each other *or* present two works by the same artist. Use the description, analysis, interpretation, and judgment strategies, asking art criticism questions of the class and giving appropriate art history information.

5. Newspapers and some national newsmagazines contain reviews of current art exhibits. Select one, make a copy of it, and find statements in which the critic described, analyzed, interpreted, and judged the works. Use one color to highlight art criticism statements and another color for art history statements.

6. **Group Activities:**
   a. Each of the students chooses a reproduction in the Color Gallery and studies the artist and artwork. They then write each of eight true facts and two false statements about the artwork on separate note cards. The cards are numbered on the reverse side and put in an envelope, with the student's name written inside the envelope flap. Students trade envelopes, try to identify the two false cards, and then consult with the writer to check answers.
   b. (four students) Each student is an art agent presenting an artwork to a Museum Acquisition Committee (the rest of the class). The price of each artwork is the same, and the museum budget will only allow the museum to purchase one artwork. The first student will be "selling" a realistic artwork; the second, an abstract; the third, an expressive; and the fourth, a fantasy-surrealistic artwork. Each presentation should be based on the artwork's artistic merit and historical significance. Students should use the strategies of description, analysis, interpretation, and judgment to support their comments with evidence seen within the artwork and with what students can find in reference books. Then the Museum Acquisition Committee votes on which artwork to purchase.
   c. (three students) Plan a presentation to a Museum Acquisition Committee. The museum has been given an endowment and is planning to purchase a prestigious and well-known artwork. The committee will vote on which painting to purchase according to the presentations.
7. Select an artwork from the Color Gallery, and ask an elementary child to look at it with you. Ask the child questions that involve describing, analyzing, interpreting, and judging the artwork, as detailed in this chapter.
8. To more directly understand how a child responds to artworks, refer to recent studies about how children understand art, such as the book *How We Understand Art* by Michael J. Parsons (Cambridge University Press, 1987). Use Parson's model to do your own research with children. Compare your results with those of Parsons.

9. Investigate some other ways to become involved in art criticism, such as "A Phenomenological Methodology for Art Criticism" by E. Louis Lankford (*Studies in Art Education* 25 (1984): 151–58) or "An Art Criticism Questioning Strategy within the Framework of Bloom's Taxonomy" by Karen A. Hamblen (*Studies in Art Education* 26 (1984): 41–50). Compare and contrast these with the art criticism in this chapter.
10. Visit an art museum, and then prepare a "treasure hunt" (study sheet) that elementary children could use on a museum field trip. Think of specific questions that would guide the children in seeking out visual information and that would help make their visit to the museum memorable and meaningful. Include games drawings, fill-in-the-blank questions, or missing spot activities (draw a portion from a painting and ask the children to find its source). Include some activities or questions that focus on looking at the museum as a structure in itself.
11. Collect postcards and inexpensive reproductions of artworks. Then read Chapter 3 in *Early Childhood Art* by Barbara Herberholz and Lee Hanson (Dubuque, Iowa: Brown and Benchmark, 1995), and make several art games as described. Your game may focus on aspects of the elements and principles of art or on artists, artworks, and art history.
12. Read at least three "Looking and Learning" sections in *School Arts* magazine. Then select either an artwork from the Color Gallery or a famous artwork in an art book, and write your own version of "Looking and Learning." Use the same format of: Looking Carefully, Comparing, Key Concepts, Resources, Biography, and Suggested Activities. Or read three "Clip and Save" articles in *Arts and Activities* magazine, and use the same format to write a similar version, using artworks found in a local museum, on CD-Rom, on the Internet, or in library books that feature museum collections.
13. Select several of the eighteen Gallery Games cards that follow, and conduct the activities described with a group of elementary students as you present three or more art reproductions. Emphasize description, analysis, interpretation, and judgment.

Gallery Games

You are a television reporter. You saw these paintings being unloaded at the museum for an upcoming exhibit.

Describe them in such a way that your viewers will want to go see the exhibit.

Gallery Games

You have just purchased these paintings at an art auction. They are stored in the basement of your hotel. At 2 A.M. the hotel catches fire. You only have time to save ONE of the paintings.

Which one will you save and why? Give three reasons for your choice.

Gallery Games

You were your aunt's favorite niece/nephew. Her will states that you may choose one painting from her art collection.

Before you can claim the painting, you must first give three good reasons for your choice.

Which painting will you choose and why?

Gallery Games

Show a painting to your friends, and ask them to memorize it visually. Make up three questions, and then remove the painting from sight and see if your friends can answer the questions correctly.

Ask about subject matter, location of details, colors, shapes, patterns, focal point, mood or feelings evoked, and so on.

Gallery Games

I would like (or not like) to be a person in this painting because . . .

Write a page in his/her diary.

OR

I would like (or not like) to take a walk in this landscape because . . .

Gallery Games

Write the letters of an artist's name vertically on paper or chalkboard. Choose one or two friends, and make up a word or a short phrase about the painting or about the artist that begins with each of the letters in the artist's name.

(Example)
D - ancers on diagonal
E - mphasized movement
G - raceful ballerinas
A - dmired Japanese prints
S - culpted dancers and horses

Gallery Games

You have saved your money and can buy a painting for your mom or dad's birthday.

Which painting will you choose? Give three good reasons for your choice.

Gallery Games

Choose two friends, and compose a haiku about a painting. In this form of Japanese poetry, three lines create a word picture and mood.

(Example)
Bedroom at Arles by *Vincent van Gogh*
See Van Gogh's bedroom
Blue walls, two chairs and table
Gone now, dear Vincent

Line 1: five syllables _____
Line 2: seven syllables _____
Line 3: five syllables _____

Gallery Games

Dear _____ (husband/wife/parent/friend):

I just finished posing for the artist _____. My portrait is done at last! I want to tell you about my experience and about the painting.

OR

Dear _____ (husband/wife/parent/friend):

Ah, the life of an artist is _____! I had some difficult problems today, and I had some wonderful things happen. Let me tell you. . . .

Gallery Games

You found a painting in the garage. Should you sell it or keep it? Is it an important artwork?

Call a museum curator and describe it.

Choose a friend who has not seen the painting to be the curator. The curator will ask questions to clarify your description. Describe the subject matter, colors, shapes, lines, focal point, mood, brush work, and so on.

Gallery Games

You are the artist _____.

Today you finished a painting for a client. He/she wants you to change something before he/she will pay you for it.

Tell him/her why you painted it that way and why you do not want to change your artwork.

Gallery Games

Find the focal point in a painting. Sketch the lines and shapes that lead your eye to the focal point.

Gallery Games

Choose two paintings, and tell three ways that they are alike and three ways that they are different.

Use any of these six ways for your comparisons:

- Subject matter, theme, idea
- Elements of art—color, line, shape/form, texture, value, space
- Principles of art—balance, emphasis, proportion, movement, repetition and pattern, variety and unity
- Mood, feeling, emotion
- Technical properties (manner in which paint was applied)
- Style of art—realism, expressionism, formalism/abstraction, fantasy

---

Gallery Games

Make up a story about a painting. This could be a beginning:

A very _____ thing happened today. As _____ was getting ready to _____, a (large, small, scary, funny sad) _____ walked past. So _____

Gallery Games

Choose a friend, and pretend you each own an art gallery. You each want to sell one of the paintings in your gallery to a very rich client.

Make a sales pitch by giving three reasons why the client should purchase the painting from your gallery.

Gallery Games

Choose a friend, and before you show him/her the painting, describe it. Have your friend draw what you are describing—subject matter, figure placement, colors, shapes, focal point, details.

Gallery Games

You are a guard in a museum. You dozed off one day while on the job, and when you awakened, one of the paintings had been stolen.

Quick! Call the police and describe the painting so the police officers can identify it.

Gallery Games

The artist _____ is your aunt/uncle. Your mom and dad have told you that you may go for a visit to his/her art studio.

Write a letter to your uncle/aunt and tell him/her what questions you will want to ask when you are there.

Chapter

6

....

A Narrative Time Line of World Art
Looking at Western
and Non-Western Artworks

*T*his brief **chronological** guide noting the major periods and styles of art and important artists begins with the earliest achievements of humankind and moves through the centuries to artworks created in modern times. *This chapter is a reference only, a point of departure for locating more in-depth information in both visual and written materials.* Numerous books, videos, and other resources go beyond the scope possible within this book.

Though artistic achievements of the Western world— that is, Europe and the United States—receive much attention, students should also be aware of the non-Western

Figure 6.1   Bull, detail of ceiling painting, ca. 12,000 B.C. From the Caves of Lascaux near Montignac, France, 18 ft. long.
Courtesy of French Government Tourist Office.

world's rich history of remarkable artistic accomplishments. Today's culturally diverse population needs to be acquainted with popular art forms, as well as with those of **folk artists** around the world. The importance of the **traditional arts** of Mexico, Japan, China, India, Islam, Africa, Australia, Latin America, and other regions must not be overlooked. A study of **ethnic art forms** from around the world can help us gain insights into our own backgrounds as well as the heritage of other cultural groups. In addition, students need to develop a sensitivity to the art forms that surround us and enhance the quality of our lives—shopping center and mall designs; highway, park, and home landscaping; container, utensil, and packaging designs; jewelry; furniture; clothing; cars; magazines; photographs; advertisements; and films and video.

■ WHEN ART BEGAN

Discoveries in fairly recent years, the first being in 1875, have revealed humans' earliest attempts in **prehistoric times** to visually represent their ideas and feelings. Cave paintings in France and Spain, as well as in North America, show the human form represented as a stick figure, although careful attention is given to the details of the animals shown. The first paintings from these hunting economies were done about thirty thousand years ago in the Old Stone Age. They are found on the roof of the Altimira cave in Spain. Other caves in Spain, as well as some in France, have revealed marvelously painted animals.

The people who made these wondrous depictions of bison, deer, boars, and elephants, as well as symbolic figures of themselves engaged in the hunt, probably did not call their works "art." These early artworks were likely efforts to control the enormous, fierce creatures upon which these people depended for meat and furs. These Stone Age hunters had only the crudest weapons. How such lifelike images, many depicting animals in motion, could have been created in the dark underground caves is difficult to understand. Perhaps the artists were initially inspired to make these images when they observed the bulging contours of the stone interiors of their caves; when they traced a few lines of the creatures, they may have imagined they saw a more tangible form. These early paintings often show arrows and spears pointing at the animals. Early artists used natural colors—pigments they found in different earths, charcoal, and such—and mixed them with fat, blood, egg, or plant juice. They made brushes of animal fur, feathers, moss, and leaves.

Prehistoric humans also fashioned simple stone and bone tools for utilitarian purposes. Even in these earliest implements, we recognize humans' special need to embellish and make beautiful practical objects. During these prehistoric times, both human and animal figures were carved from horns, stones, and other materials. The famous *Venus of Willendorf,* with her broad hips and breasts, represented fertility and was probably called upon to ensure the survival of the tribe.

■ ARTWORKS IN ANCIENT TIMES

Art of the earliest times—the ancient world—gives us some idea about how people lived and what they valued and believed. We know from artworks that from about 30,000 to 2500 B.C., people lived in groups, had a language, made and wore clothing, lived in dwellings, and had distinguishing ways of decorating their containers, utensils, and homes. When people learned to use such metals as bronze and copper, about 3000 or 4000 B.C., civilization as we know it began. People abandoned caves and built shelters. They grew food and raised domestic animals. They invented reading and writing for keeping records and for exchanging information over distances. People lived in larger communities, even cities. Ancient art reached through several cultures, some contemporary with each other. Many of these ancient peoples lived near the Mediterranean Sea and Middle East Asia,

Figure 6.2   Cheops pyramid and sphinx. Giza, Egypt.
Historical Pictures Collection/Stock Montage, Inc.

extending as far as China and Japan. They all left magnificent artistic achievements.

By about 3000 B.C., the four major civilizations had developed in Egypt, China, India, and Mesopotamia. One of the best known of these early civilizations appeared about 3500 B.C. in **Egypt.** The Nile River made the Egyptians prosperous, and the surrounding deserts and the Mediterranean protected the inhabitants. Egyptian civilization, with its art and architecture suggesting stability and permanence, changed little for more than three thousand years, making it not only one of the earliest but the most long-lived civilization in history. Most of what we know of ancient Egypt comes from the tombs of royal families. The Egyptians believed that life on earth, at least for the nobility, continued after death. Thus, the bodies of the nobility were preserved as mummies and the tombs painted with scenes of the pleasures of daily life. The size and exactness of the pyramids are amazing. One pyramid is made up of more than two million blocks of stone, each stone weighing more than 2½ tons. The modern world was fascinated when the untouched tomb of Tutankhamen, brimming with remarkably rich artworks, was discovered in 1922.

Egyptian art is divided into three major kingdoms: the **Old Kingdom,** the **Middle Kingdom,** and the **Empire.** The **pyramids of Giza** are examples of the powerful architectural accomplishments of the first period, a time when Egyptians believed that existence on earth was preparatory to life hereafter. The **pharaohs** represented deity figures on earth, and the tombs they built contained stone sculptures, pottery, jewelry, and useful objects they would need in the afterlife. The Egyptians believed that spirits of their gods dwelt in certain animals and birds, such as the cat and the hawk, and they worshiped these images. An Egyptian pharaoh is often shown in the form of an animal, or at least with some features of an animal. For example, the sphinx has a human head and the body of a lion. The Egyptians often depicted a beetle or **scarab** pushing the sun across the sky in the manner of a dung beetle pushing its egg in front of it. The magical powers of the scarab in a piece of jewelry placed in Tutankhamen's tomb was thought to protect the dead pharaoh.

Elaborate temples built in honor of the ruling emperors characterized the art of the Middle Kingdom and the Empire. The artist, architect, and builders worked together in constructing these edifices, making decorative colonnades, walled surfaces, furniture, and implements. The Egyptians began using the post-and-lintel system in constructing their temples. Sculptural forms were often part of a building's structural support. Also attributed to this splendid age are magnificent examples of metalwork, furniture, pottery, and glassware. The most famous of these temples were uncovered at **Luxor** and **Karnak.** Some of the memorable artworks from Egypt include a bejeweled sculpture portrait of

Figure 6.3   Portrait head of Queen Nefertiti, ca. 1370 B.C., New Kingdom, eighteenth dynasty. Painted limestone, ht. 20 in. *State Museums of West Berlin.*

Queen Nefertiti wearing an ornate headdress (see fig. 6.3) and the coffin cover for King Tutankhamen, dating to 1340 B.C. and made of gold and semiprecious stones. **Hieroglyphs** (picture writing) on the walls of tombs and on scrolls contain figures and objects that represent words or sounds. Architecture and sculpture were the major art forms, with some paintings surviving today on tomb walls. The typical Egyptian stance for figures shows a profile view of the head, arms, and legs, and frontal views of the body and eyes. Important people were painted larger than slaves and servants.

During this time, Mesopotamia (the land between the Tigris and Euphrates Rivers; now called Iraq) was occupied by the **Sumerians,** the **Babylonians,** the **Assyrians,** and the **Persians.** Mesopotamia was a melting pot of different cultures, each passing on its religious beliefs, customs, knowledge, and skills. The land was flat, and the people built shrines on top of manufactured mountains, where they placed offerings to the gods whose forces they believed controlled the universe. They also placed images of the rulers and priests who they believed could ask the gods for mercy and favors.

In this "land between the rivers" in the valley watered by the Tigris and Euphrates, the Sumerians recorded accounts of how they believed their world began, stories with which ancient Hebrew writers were almost surely familiar when they wrote parts of the Old Testament. The Sumerians developed a **cuneiform system** of writing and also developed the world's first legal codes. Mesopotamia lacked wood and stone in any quantity; thus, the Sumerians used mostly sun-dried clay bricks to build temples and palaces replete with relief sculpture, metalwork, and frescoed murals. They seemed to be more concerned with the here and now than with an afterlife. These accomplished builders explored the possibilities of the archway in their architectural constructions. They made glazed tiles for wall decorations. Their most notable achievement in palace construction was a colorful tower called a **ziggurat.** For the most part, Sumerian art tells us about a vigorous artistic society.

The main accomplishments of Assyrian art date from 1000 to 600 B.C. and are seen in the architecturally magnificent palaces that house many fine sculptures and wall paintings. The Assyrians carved gods and animals on walls to protect the king. Statues were worshiped as gods throughout the ancient world. The militant, warlike nature of the people was reflected in their art, with scenes of battles, wounded animals, and monsters found in both sculpture and wall paintings. Assyrian art shows traces of Sumerian art, but on a much grander scale. Unlike the stiff, stylized approach seen in the art of the Egyptians, the Assyrians expressed life with vigor and brusqueness. The Assyrians destroyed and rebuilt Babylon; its luxury under King Nebuchadnezzar was legendary, and the **Hanging Gardens** became one of the **Seven Wonders of the World.** The walls of the city boasted glazed bricks depicting huge reliefs of fierce lions.

The **Minoans** on the island of Crete and the **Mycenaeans,** who lived on the nearby Greek mainland, developed civilizations between 2000 and 3000 B.C. that were quite different from those of Egypt and Mesopotamia. These two groups were fishermen, seafarers, traders, and pirates. The ruling classes lived in fine palaces and villas complete with bathrooms and walls covered with bright paintings. Though they built no temples, the Minoans and Mycenaeans worshiped a mother goddess and sacrificed bulls to her. A double axe and the horns of a bull are symbols that often marked their shrines. Bull leaping was a popular sport that both young men and women practiced. A famous wall painting from Crete, dated 1500 B.C., shows an acrobat grasping the bull's horns while another athlete somersaults over the bull's back. Women played an important part in Minoan religious ceremonies. A well-known terracotta figure shows an elaborately dressed, bare-breasted woman holding a snake in each of her upraised hands. The Mycenaeans built massive stone walls to protect their cities and in time conquered the Minoans and absorbed a good deal of their culture. Disaster came about 1100 B.C. in the form of earthquakes, fires, and invading by armies from the north. The glories of these lands are remembered in **Homer's** epic poems.

Another ancient civilization was that of **Persia,** with its exciting examples of woven and ceramic ware that can be traced as far back as 5000 B.C. Persian rugs continue to delight and fascinate individuals around the world even today.

Another culture—the **Mayas**—some fifteen hundred years before Columbus sailed to the New World—the **Mayas**—in Central America flourished. The Mayas developed a writing system and a refined and notable architecture; they also made spectacular achievements in the world of mathematics and astronomy. Though they lacked metal, wheels, or beasts of burden, they built towering temples and developed agriculture. Most Mayan art is related to the gods they believed controlled the sun, rain, wind, water, and such. Corn was the basis of their life, and every stage of the crop's growth was marked with religious ceremonies. The corn god was the most revered of the deities, and many statues of him were placed in tombs and temples. When the Mayan civilization declined, the **Aztecs** of Mexico and the **Incas** of Peru came into dominance, the latter being in control until Spanish conquerors brought horses and cannons and took over Incan lands in the sixteenth century.

■ CLASSICAL ARTWORKS

The art of the ancient **Greeks** and **Romans** is called **classical art.** The art of Greece began to flower around 600 B.C. Today, we can still find traces of marvelous Greek architecture and sculpture. The Greeks built marble temples with vividly colored details like nothing ever seen before to honor both gods and goddesses. The well-known **Parthenon,** built in the fifth century B.C. under the leadership of the statesman Pericles, was sacred to Athena and stands on the **Acropolis,** a hill overlooking Athens (see figs. 6.4 and 6.5). Although painting was supposedly one of the Greeks' most important arts, it has been all but lost to us. Their ceramic wares with painted depictions tell us much of their way of life. Greek art influenced the entire world, and the Romans borrowed it almost entirely. During the Middle Ages, both the Romanesque and Gothic cathedrals drew upon the Greek influence. In our cities today, we find many public buildings, banks, and architectural landmarks, such as the Lincoln Memorial, that this ancient civilization influenced. Numerous examples of either **Doric, Ionic,** or **Corinthian** columns on buildings are found in cities all over the world.

Figure 6.4 Nashville, Tennessee's, Parthenon, the only full-scale replica of the original in existence.
Photo courtesy of Metro Nashville Board of Parks and Recreation.

Figure 6.5 Parthenon, ca. 447–32 B.C. Acropolis, Athens.
Photo: Barbara Herberholz.

Figure 6.6   Exekias, *Achilles Slays the Amazon Penthesileia,*
ca. 540 B.C. Black-figured neck amphora, ht. 16⅓ in.
Reproduced by courtesy of the Trustees of the British Museum.

Figure 6.7   *Procession,* detail of *Ara Pacis,* ca. 10 B.C. Frieze,
63 in. wide.
© *Alinari/Art Resource, N.Y.*

About 600 B.C., Greece emerged into a new era that
marks the birth of Western civilization and art. The people
no longer worshiped animal gods but fashioned gods in
their own image who had the traits of humans, both bad and
good, and could be understood in human terms. A marble
statue (originally painted with bright colors) of a youth,
Kouros, was made early in the development of Greek
sculpture, 525 B.C., before anatomy was clearly understood.
Greek artists studied anatomy and learned how muscles and
bones control the body positions. Their sculptures seem
like perfect living beings because of the Greeks' belief in
ideal proportions. This lifelike art in classical Greece was
accompanied by the belief that spirits could inhabit images.
Classical sculptors were not interested in expressing emotions in the faces of their figures because they believed that
idealized mortals were almost divine and did not indulge in
ordinary passions. Two of the most famous sculptures are
Winged Victory (the goddess Aphrodite) and the *Venus de
Milo,* both made late in the classical period and showing
lifelike figures of perfect beauty. Some of the names of

Greek sculptors are known to us, the most influential being
Phidias, Myron, Praxiteles, Polyclitus, and Lysippus. Nude
males competed in the **Olympic Games,** held every four
years in honor of the gods, with the victors being celebrated
in sculpture and painting.

At about the time Greece was reaching its most glorious period, the **Etruscans,** with their fierce warriors and
skilled metalworkers, came into power in Italy, north of the
Greek colonies. They worshiped a number of different gods
and placed in tombs everything they deemed necessary in
the afterlife. We know that music and dance were important
to these peoples from the paintings on tomb walls. The
rulers wore purple robes as symbols of office and laid out
their cities on a gridiron plan, as did the Romans who followed them.

The Etruscan city-state of **Rome** was organized in
753 B.C. According to legend, the abandoned twins Romulus
and Remus were suckled by a she-wolf; when they were
grown, they founded the city of Rome at the place where a
shepherd had found them. A famous bronze sculpture com-
memorates this legend. Etruscan rulers were overthrown
about 400 B.C., and the **Roman Republic** was established.
Within a few centuries, the Romans, with their talent for
government and their desire to conquer, expanded into the
largest empire ever known in the world. They borrowed
ideas from all the peoples they had conquered; however, they
replaced the ideal image that Greek sculptors used with a realism that showed every sagging muscle and wrinkle. They
were great engineers, constructing roads, waterways, and

Figure 6.8 *Lady Antonia*, **36 B.C. Marble, ht. 27 in.**
Reproduced by courtesy of the Trustees of the British Museum.

Figure 6.9   Colosseum, Rome (aerial view).
© *Robert C. Lamm*

■ ARTWORKS IN MEDIEVAL TIMES

Medieval art comes from the **Middle Ages,** a period between ancient and modern times—that is, the thousand years between the fall of Rome in the fifth century A.D. and the beginning of the Renaissance in the fifteenth century A.D. Economic and social conditions were such during the Middle Ages that people had to devote full time to survival. The church was the binding source of artistic inspiration and achievement. Its power was felt in law, science, economics, literature, and the Crusades (military expeditions that sought to reclaim the Holy Land from the Muslims).

Until A.D. 313, Christians were a persecuted sect in the Roman world, but when the emperor **Constantine** was converted, Christianity became the official religion of the Roman Empire. Constantine moved his court from Rome to the town of Byzantium, which was renamed Constantinople. Here, the distinctive **Byzantine** style of art developed. **Mosaics** rich with decorative patterns showed figures with long faces and strange gestures. Paintings were flat and decorative, with figures representing saints and holy people, as well as the emperor and empress, depicted in frozen, rigid positions. These images are called **icons,** and in the eighth century, people called **iconoclasts** (image breakers) disapproved of them and destroyed all they could find. Such artists as **Cimabue** and **Duccio** worked with the stiff, formal patterns and flat backgrounds typical of the Byzantines. The flat handling of paint and the decorative style may have been influenced in part by a desire to discard the paganistic influences of Greece and Rome, where realism and humans had been considered of utmost importance.

In the fifth century A.D., barbarians over ran the Roman Empire in the West, and for a while, learning continued only in the monasteries. Because the printing press had not yet been invented, and most people could not read anyway, the church used art to instruct and inspire the people.

public baths. Their engineers were the first to use the **arch** and **concrete** in constructions, and imperial Rome had many **triumphal arches** that were built to celebrate victories. Enormous crowds filled the amphitheaters, such as the **Colosseum** in Rome, to see chariot races and gladiators (see fig. 6.9). On the interior walls of villas and houses of the aristocracy were paintings of landscapes, still lifes, animals, and religious and historical subjects. The best known of these survive in the cities of **Herculaneum** and **Pompeii** because volcanic ashes covered these towns in A.D. 79, thereby preserving them for centuries.

Cultures in the East and West were unaware of each other's existence until the middle of the first century B.C. At this time, Roman armies, in pursuit of a Parthian army, suffered a major defeat, but had their first introduction to the Far East when they saw silk flags and banners. Silk trade developed, causing a ready market in Rome; the route that caravans traveled was called the Silk Road. The East kept the silk-making process a secret for many years. Imperial Rome gradually lost its power over a large part of the Western world after several hundred years of peace, and by the fifth century, the Middle Ages began.

Figure 6.10 *Notre Dame la Grande,* **eleventh century. Poitiers, France.**

Monks kept the glow of culture alive with their **illuminated manuscripts** of sacred and scholarly texts. They worked in rooms called *scriptoriums,* copying the Bible in Latin by hand on fine parchment called **vellum** (animal skin). Decorations and pictures in the margins and for initial letters were called illuminations. **Gold leaf** beaten so thin that you could see through it, and sometimes with a pattern pressed into it, was attached to these paintings and illuminated manuscripts. The **Book of Kells,** made in Ireland about A.D. 800, is a beautiful example of this art form.

In the sixth century, Pope Gregory declared that paintings were useful for teaching people about the Bible. Altar pictures painted on three panels were called **triptychs.** Brightly painted sculptures and colorful stained-glass windows also were used to inform and inspire people. **Giotto's** innovative painting techniques, on both altarpieces and frescoes on church walls, foreshadowed the coming Renaissance.

In A.D. 800, the pope crowned the French king **Charlemagne** as the first Holy Roman Emperor. Charlemagne hoped to restore his Christian homeland to the glory and grandeur of the past, so he imported scholars and artists. To guide them in their work, he brought in manuscripts and works of art from the ancient world. In the latter part of the medieval years, skilled metalworkers made **suits of armor** for knights to wear in combat or in tournaments; other craftspersons wove **tapestries** filled with symbols and stories to hang on the cold stone walls of castles and churches (see fig. 4.26).

Romanesque architecture, in vogue from the ninth to the twelfth centuries, is characterized by churches built of heavy masonry and having dark interiors and rounded arches. Romanesque churches in Europe are massive and to the people of the time suggested the strength and power of the Catholic Church.

Toward the end of the Middle Ages, especially in the twelfth century, the old feudal systems began to deteriorate, and towns began to grow and become centers of learning, with the church providing strong leadership. A style of architecture known as **Gothic** developed, particularly in France, and spread rapidly through much of Europe. (The term *gothic* has its roots in the Italian Renaissance, when it was used disparagingly to describe a style of architecture so barbaric that only the fifth-century invaders of Rome, the Goths, could have been responsible for its use. Gradually, *gothic* lost its derogatory connotation.) Between A.D. 1175 and 1275, eighty cathedrals and nearly five hundred large churches were built in France alone. These splendid **cathedrals**—with their pointed arches, flying buttresses, sculptured images, mosaics, stained-glass windows, and lofty spires that rose higher than any structures ever had before—appeared lighter and more graceful than Romanesque architecture and fit the needs of a deeply religious society. The marvelous French **Cathedral of Chartres** housed eight thousand images in sculpture and stained glass.

Another notable artwork from this period is the **Bayeux Tapestry,** an embroidered pictorial account of the Norman conquest of England in A.D. 1066. Many women stitched the hundreds of figures on the 230-foot-long fabric background of this tapestry.

As the Middle Ages neared its end, the lords who constantly engaged in war between the city-states were intent on ensuring that future generations would remember their glorious battles. **Paolo Uccello** (1397–1475) was the master of these military paintings. He painted an enormous work recalling a Florentine victory in 1456 for Cosimo de'Medici.

■ ARTWORKS IN THE FOURTEENTH TO SEVENTEENTH CENTURIES

Renaissance and Baroque Art

The **Renaissance,** which means *rebirth,* took place between A.D. 1300 and 1600 and stands as one of the greatest periods of artistic development that the world has ever known. Classical art and the ideas of ancient Greece and Rome were rediscovered during this golden age, and artists ceased making the flat, decorative, symbolic images that prevailed during the Gothic days. Portraits were often painted in profile, like the heads by Italian artists seen on Greek and Roman coins. The Italians sought to revive the glorification of the independence and nobility of humans.

Figure 6.11   *Cathedral at Amiens,* **ca. 1225.**
© *Scala/Art Resource.*

Even though they continued to paint religious subjects, they emphasized the lives of human beings and their accomplishments on earth. Two of the most notable artistic developments of this period include the discovery of **perspective** (how to create the illusion of depth on a flat surface) and **chiaroscuro** (shading from light to dark to show modeled forms). Artists practiced ways of showing objects as they appear to our eyes. They studied anatomy to learn how the body works and nature so that their artworks would be more lifelike.

Renaissance artists made many drawings before producing a painting or fresco, and it was at this time that the use of silverpoint, pen, chalk, and charcoal became popular. During the sixteenth century, numerous drawings were done with a wash technique or with a reed pen, while Chinese artists pursued brush drawings. Seventeenth-century Western artists used the pencil extensively.

Earlier, in the thirteenth century, Florentine painter **Cimabue** (ca. 1240–ca. 1302) had begun changing some of the old Byzantine methods by making figures express a

Figure 6.12   Giotto, *Lamentation,* 1305–6. Fresco, 7 ft. 7 in. × 7 ft. 9 in. Arena Chapel, Padua, Italy.
© *Alinari/Art Resource.*

feeling of movement in their gestures and faces and by adding a sense of three-dimensionality to his artworks. He retained the gold background and patternlike arrangements of figures and objects. It remained for the great artist and architect **Giotto** (ca. 1266–1337) to break away from the Byzantine tradition and lay the foundation for the Renaissance. In his scenes of the lives of Christ and Mary, he showed real emotions, naturalism, and human warmth (see fig. 6.12). He shaded the figures and put deep shadows in their clothing. He painted with **egg tempera,** a medium that uses an egg as the binding agent for powdered pigment and that was perfected by the fourteenth-century Florentines. (Egg tempera was the dominant medium for painting until oil paints almost completely replaced it in the sixteenth century.) People had been accustomed to dark colors in the Byzantine panels, and the clearness and brightness of Giotto's works gave the impression of soft daylight on a scene and paved the way for later artists.

Active commerce gave Italy money to sponsor art on a magnificent scale. Both painters and sculptors created lifelike portraits of recognizable individuals. No longer were artists considered little more than capable workers, as they were during the Middle Ages. **Master artists,** who belonged to **guilds,** took on youths as **apprentices** in their workshops. Church officials, the nobility and ruling classes, and wealthy merchants **commissioned** most artworks. The most important patrons of the arts were the **Medici family** of Florence.

Noted artists of the **Italian Renaissance** included the sculptor **Donatello** (ca. 1386–1466). His *David* was the first life-size, bronze, freestanding nude since ancient days. It combined classicism with realism. **Masaccio** (1401–1428) revolutionized painting in his short lifetime. In *The Tribute Money,* a famous **fresco,** he placed solid, modeled figures in a landscape that had great depth. (Fresco, in which pigment is applied to wet plaster, was a popular medium during the Renaissance. Large murals painted in this manner could be viewed from any angle without glare. They also were washable. Assistants helped the artist, since the work was done in sections and

Figure 6.13   Leonardo da Vinci, *The Last Supper,* ca. 1495–98. Mural, oil and tempera on plaster, 14 ft. 5 in. × 28 ft. *Refectory of Sta. Maria della Grazie, Milan. © Alinari/Art Resource.*

had to be completed while the plaster was still wet.) Masaccio is believed to have learned perspective from **Filippo Brunelleschi** (ca. 1377–1446), a great Florentine sculptor and architect. **Lorenzo Ghiberti's** (1378–1455) bronze designs for the massive doors of the Baptistery in Florence won a landmark competition and assured him a place in history.

Sassetta's (ca. 1392–1450) delightful paintings are small, narrative, and reminiscent of medieval book illustrations. The paintings of **Fra Angelico** (ca. 1387–1455), a priest, were made in the traditional manner of the early Renaissance, with decorative patterns and lesser concern for perspective. By the mid-fifteenth century, **Andrea del Verrocchio** (1435–1488) was producing innovative and important sculptures, paintings, and metalworks in his studio and attracting many young artists, among them **Leonardo da Vinci. Andrea Mantegna** (1431–1506) used perspective and foreshortening in a daring and startling manner. *Primavera* and the famous *Birth of Venus,* with their flowing, rhythmic lines, are examples of **Sandro Botticelli's** (ca. 1444–1510) masterpieces.

With the Italian **High Renaissance** came such artists as **Leonardo da Vinci** (1452–1519), often called the greatest genius who ever lived (see colorplate 27 in the Color Gallery). He made scientific studies and invented all kinds of machines, such as submarines and helicopters, that were only realized hundreds of years later. Only a few of his pictures remain, partly because he liked to experiment with

different materials and try different ways of painting, rather than using the traditional media, which were more lasting and durable. He painted *The Last Supper* at the end of the fifteenth century (see fig. 6.13). Da Vinci perfected a distinguishing way of showing lights and darks called **sfumato,** which means smoky or misty. His *Mona Lisa* is probably the most famous painting ever made.

The influence of the Italian Renaissance spread throughout Europe, with artists from northern Europe coming to Italy to learn and then returning to their homelands. The center of art and culture moved from Florence to Rome during the sixteenth century. The popes saw to it that artists worked to glorify the city with their paintings and sculpture. **Michelangelo** (1475–1564) took four years to paint 342 figures from the Bible on the ceiling of the **Sistine Chapel.** Regarding himself primarily as a sculptor (see fig. 6.14), he at first refused to accept the pope's assignment. He developed a monumental style of painting solid, three-dimensional figures.

Another artist of great importance was **Raphael** (1483–1520). A popular young painter who died at age thirty-seven from overwork, Raphael was known as the painter of "sweet Madonnas." He also painted murals in the Vatican. **Bellini** (ca. 1430–1516) was one of the first Italian painters to use oil on canvas. Artists from Flanders had visited Bellini's city, and from them he learned of Flemish experiments with oil paint and with painting on canvas rather than wood panels. **Giorgione** (ca. 1478–1510) and **Titian**

Figure 6.14 Michelangelo, *Pietà*, 1498–1500. Marble, 68½ in. *St. Peter's, Rome.* © *Alinari/ Art Resource.*

(ca. 1488–1576), the most famous of all Venetian painters, were students in Bellini's workshop. Mastering the oil-on-canvas technique, Titian painted with warm, rich colors, sacrificing details for the sweeping effect of the entire painting. His rich colors were built up with layers of contrasting glazes. He enjoyed the esteem of popes and princes, and helped make full-length portraits fashionable. Giorgione, one of the first artists to paint small pictures for private collectors, died at age thirty-two. He integrated figures and landscapes to create moods filled with a poetic reverie. He greatly influenced Venetian painting, especially that of young Titian.

For sixteenth-century women to have careers in art or otherwise was unusual, but **Sofonisba Anguissola** (ca. 1532–1625) became the first well-known woman artist. She and her five sisters came from a wealthy Italian family and were well educated. Anguissola not only painted self-portraits but also created a new kind of picture that showed people in scenes of everyday life. She was invited to paint for King Philip in Spain. Two other women who achieved success as artists during this time were **Lavina Fontana** (1552–1614) and **Artemisia Gentileschi** (1593–1652). Fontana's father taught her to paint, and she became the first woman to make paintings for large public places. The pope invited her to Rome to paint religious works. Many fashionable people had her paint their portraits because she was so skilled in showing their fine clothing and jewelry. Many believe that Gentileschi was the greatest Italian female artist. She often depicted powerful and courageous women from ancient myths, the Bible, or history. Some of her artworks were more than 6 feet high.

Veronese (1528–1588) made paintings that used cool, clear colors and showed many figures, richly dressed in silk, velvet, lace, and jewels. He arranged the figures in large compositions with elegant backgrounds of classical antiquity, nature, or Venetian interiors. His sumptuous style set the standards for eighteenth-century Venetian decoration.

Jean Fouquet (ca. 1420–ca. 1477) was a French court painter. His portraits were monumental in construction, full and rounded in contour, and well composed, ranking him among the first Renaissance painters north of the Alps and making him the founder of a French tradition that was to be developed in the sixteenth century.

The last great sixteenth-century Venetian artist was **Tintoretto** (1518–1594). His works anticipated the coming baroque style. He worked directly on his canvases without making sketches or underpaintings first. He even distorted and exaggerated shapes for the sake of the composition and the drama of the scene.

Much of what we know about these Renaissance artists comes from the writings of **Vasari** (1511–1574), an artist himself who gathered his information by traveling all over Italy. His first work was published in 1550, and an enlarged edition followed in 1568.

The **Late Renaissance** dates from about A.D. 1530 to 1600. The art of the High Renaissance was thought to be so perfect that young artists found it difficult to improve on the past. So some of them broke Renaissance rules and distorted the figures and spaces in their compositions; the results were dramatic, and the style was called **mannerism.** **Parmigianino** (1503–1540) achieved this effect in his *Madonna of the Long Neck.* Other mannerists attracted attention by exaggerating the proportions of the human figure and showing their subjects in unusual postures.

A mannerist painter known as **El Greco** ("the Greek") (1541–1614) came to Venice from Crete to study art. He later moved to Spain, where the Byzantine art he had seen in Crete and the masterpieces of the Italian Renaissance blended with the grimness of Spanish art to influence his work. He made many realistic yet mystical religious works, as well as portraits of the aristocracy. His elongated figures became easily recognizable as the work of El Greco (see fig. 3.9). Typical of these is *The Burial of the Count Orgaz.* His dramatic *View of Toledo* shows a moody storm raging over the city.

The Renaissance also took place in northern Europe—in Flanders (now part of northern France and Belgium) and in Germany in the fifteenth century. Here, artists made paintings filled with details and jewel-like colors. Italian

Figure 6.15   Pieter Brueghel, the Elder, *The Wedding Dance,* **ca. 1566. Oil on panel, 47 × 62 in.**
© 1997 The Detroit Institute of Arts. City of Detroit Purchase.

ideas spread there later. Ghent and Bruges were centers for the wool and weaving trades, and many people—merchants and aristocrats—had money to spend on paintings.

Flemish artist **Jan van Eyck,** who died in 1441, is generally credited with developing a new oil-painting technique. He started a trend in realism that depicted details with a minute precision that was to be typical of Flemish painters for many years. This came about because oil paints, a mixture of dry pigments, oil, and sometimes varnish, lengthened the drying time and let artists work at a more leisurely pace. Van Eyck produced an enormous altarpiece for the cathedral in Ghent, Belgium. Many Flemish artists used the techniques of Renaissance Italian painters; others continued with the Flemish tradition of genre scenes from everyday life. **Hieronymus Bosch** (ca. 1450–1516) had a vivid imagination and invented weird, grotesque creatures in his works. **Pieter Brueghel the Elder** (ca. 1530–1569) worked in the Flemish manner but used perspective and other Renaissance techniques in his depictions of stout, rustic peasants at work or enjoying life (see fig. 6.15). His two sons—**Jan Brueghel** (1568–1625) and **Pieter Brueghel the Younger** (ca. 1564–ca. 1638)—also became artists, taught by their grandmother after he died when the boys were very young.

Rogier Van der Weyden (ca. 1399–1464), an influential early Flemish painter, worked in an extremely natural manner, using warm colors and subtle tonalities in emotional presentations of religious scenes. **Lucas Cranach** (1472–1553) is remembered for his late Gothic mythological scenes and landscapes with figures, the latter showing precise technique and details of German clothing and landscapes. His paintings are quite small, decorative, and jewel-like.

In the sixteenth century, the Reformation split Europe into Protestant and Catholic countries, and many Protestants felt that religious art was a form of idol worship. So without the patronage of the church, artists in northern Europe turned to nonreligious subjects, such as landscapes, still lifes, portraits for wealthy merchants, and scenes of everyday life.

Important German painters of the sixteenth century were **Albrecht Dürer** (ca. 1471–1528) and **Hans Holbein the Younger** (ca. 1497–1543), whose father was also an artist. Dürer has been called the northern Leonardo because he was a learned man in many fields and had traveled to Italy (see fig. 3.25). He is said to have been vain and handsome, and he painted many self-portraits. He was one of the first great engravers. **Holbein,** well known internationally, made many portraits, especially in England, where he painted members of the royal household of King Henry VIII as well as designed jewelry, hall decorations, and costumes for pageants (see fig. 6.16).

Figure 6.16   Hans Holbein the Younger, *Edward VI as a Child,* **probably 1538. Oil on panel, 22⅜ × 17⅜ in.**
Andrew W. Mellon Collection, © 1997 Board of Trustees, National Gallery of Art, Washington.

Figure 6.17   Facade of the Cathedral de Compostela in Galicia, Spain, 1667–1750.
Photo courtesy of the National Tourist Office of Spain.

The seventeenth century is generally known as the **baroque** period in art. (The word is thought to be derived from the Portuguese *barroco,* meaning "an irregularly shaped pearl." The baroque period is also believed to have been named after the founder of the style, Federigo Barocci [1528–1612]. The term *baroque* was first used abusively to describe grotesque objects.) Baroque art was well suited to large-scale pictures found in churches and palaces. Ceilings were often painted with people, horses, and chariots that, when viewed from below, appeared to be floating in the air, an effect called **illusionism.**

Baroque was the dominant style of art in Europe from about 1550 to 1700. It is characterized by dynamic, often violent movement, flamboyant emotion, unusual curving compositions, swirling figures, dramatic lighting, and exaggerated gestures. Elaborate and ornate scrolls, curves, and other symmetrical ornamentation also are typical.

Baroque art began in Rome and extended from Italy to the Catholic countries of Europe—Flanders, Holland, France, and Spain. **Caravaggio** (1573–1619) used strong contrasts of light and dark to make exciting portrayals of

people. The classical landscapes of French artist **Claude Lorrain** (1600–1685) show hills, plains, and the ruins of Rome with tiny figures of people. Another notable artist was **Peter Paul Rubens** (1577–1649), the greatest of baroque painters (see fig. 6.18). Rubens was also an international diplomat with boundless energy. His works were in such demand that he developed a "factory" of helpers. **Anthony van Dyck** (1599–1641) ranks as one of the greatest of all portrait painters.

Another well-known artist of the seventeenth century was **Diego Velázquez** (1599–1660), one of the greatest of all Spanish painters (see fig. 6.19). He was a court painter to King Philip IV of Spain, and he used rich, harmonious colors. His remarkable brushwork created illusions of rich fabrics and flesh. Later, French impressionists admired the manner in which Valázquez made small, roughly textured brush strokes that showed the play of light on a surface.

During the seventeenth century, Holland became a wealthy, powerful, independent Protestant country. While Catholic countries had fostered and utilized art as a part of worship in their churches, the Protestants did not approve

Figure 6.18   Sir Peter Paul Rubens, *The Assumption of the Virgin,* **ca. 1626. Oil on panel, 49⅜ × 37⅛ in.**
Samuel H. Kress Collection, © 1997 Board of Trustees, National Gallery of Art, Washington.

Figure 6.19   Diego Velázquez, *Maids of Honor (Las Meninas),* **1656. Oil on canvas, 10 ft. 5 in. × 9 ft.**
Prado Museum, Madrid. © Alinari/Art Resource.

of religious paintings, and the churches were very plain. However, prosperous merchants, bankers, and other citizens wanted, and could easily afford, art for their homes. They frequently had their portraits painted, singly or in groups. Since Holland was a farming country, domestic animals and landscapes were popular subjects for painters, as were genre paintings that showed the interiors of tidy, comfortable Dutch homes. Some artists specialized in still lifes showing fresh flowers, food, and dishes. A great deal of Holland's wealth came from sea trade, so pictures of ships and the sea were also popular.

Frans Hals (ca. 1580–1666) has been called the first great painter of the seventeenth-century Dutch school. His portraits, with their quick, flashing brush strokes, almost seem to be spontaneous snapshots showing exuberant people with dancing eyes, happy laughter, and joyful gestures. Although fewer than forty of **Jan Vermeer's** (1632–1675) artworks remain, his handling of light influenced nineteenth-century impressionists. He painted humble scenes of daily

life, mostly showing one or more people in cheerful, sunlit rooms filled with household objects. Vermeer was also an art dealer who bought pictures from artists and sold them for a profit.

Pieter de Hooch (1629–1688) was an important genre painter who usually depicted interiors of Dutch homes that showed rooms and receding rooms with a precise perspective. His colors were softly warm and the scenes quiet in atmosphere.

Several women achieved measurable success at this time in northern Europe, the most famous probably being **Judith Leyster** (1609–1660). She expertly painted still lifes, genre scenes, and portraits in her native Holland (see fig. 4.6). She married an artist but kept her maiden name, signing her works with her initials J. L. and a star that stood for her last name "Lodestar." For many years, some of her works were believed to have been created by artist Frans Hals. While in her twenties, she became the only female member of the Harlem painters' guild. In Germany, **Maria Sibylla Merian** (1647–1717) combined art and science by creating paintings and writing books about insects and plant life. She even traveled to South America with one of her daughters and lived in a jungle so she could paint flowers, birds, and insects. **Rachel Ruysch** (1664–1750) became interested in flowers and insects after watching her father, who was an anatomy and botany professor. She and her husband were invited to be court painters for a German ruler. She made many beautiful paintings of fruit and flowers.

French artist **George de la Tour** (1593–1652) is noted for his night scenes that are dramatically lit by candles and torches. The scenes show primarily religious subjects, seen in quiet moods.

One of the most remarkable artists of all time was Dutch painter, **Rembrandt van Rijn** (1606–1669), whose amazing talents captured human emotions in ways never seen before (see fig. 3.22). His many self-portraits chronicle the happy and sad times of his long life. He built up a painting with many layers of color and dramatically lit important areas. One of his first important commissions was a group portrait called *The Anatomy Lesson of Dr. Tulp.* His best-known work is another enormous group portrait called *The Night Watch,* in which he painted the figures in an informal group. He also painted Bible stories and scenes from ancient history.

■ ARTWORKS IN THE EIGHTEENTH AND NINETEENTH CENTURIES

Called the **Age of Enlightenment** or the **Age of Reason,** the eighteenth century was a time when people found happiness and freedom through the exercise of reason in all matters. Authority was fearlessly questioned, and long-held conventions that had governed lives were discarded. Political and social revolutions took place. The American Revolution of 1776 was followed by the French Revolution of 1789. Napoleon's victories and defeats brought about world-shaking developments. People in Mexico and other Latin American countries were also striving for greater freedom. The Industrial Revolution was changing lives.

Leadership in art now changed from Italy to France. Societies were formed to sponsor painting exhibits, some sites later becoming public galleries. Rich connoisseurs built private collections. Academies were founded in European capitals and held exhibits and taught students how to paint according to strict rules. The monumental grandeur of baroque art lingered into the early part of the eighteenth century before it gave way to more informal styles. Fewer palaces and more modest homes were built, and in turn, the smaller rooms needed smaller paintings. Subject matter became more varied, with French artists picturing carefree court life, while other artists emphasized life among the common folk.

The gentry in England had artists portray the quiet life of their country homes. The first great English artist, **William Hogarth** (1697–1764), painted the seamier side of society. The British liked to visit Italy, so Italian artists painted views of their native country to sell to British tourists. Well-to-do colonists in America wanted portraits of themselves painted.

Figure 6.20   Jean-Honoré Fragonard, *The Bathers,* 1772–75. Oil on canvas, 25¼ × 31½ in. *Louvre. Réunion des Musées Nationaux, Paris.*

A style called **rococo**—characterized by free and graceful movement, playful lines, rich colors, ornamentation, and decorative grace—superseded the formal grandeur of baroque. Rococo began in France, and its extravagant, decorative scrolls and rock and plant motifs soon spread to all the fine and decorative arts.

Jean-Honoré Fragonard (1732–1806), one of the greatest of the rococo artists, painted myths, gallantry, and landscapes (see fig. 6.20). His works appealed to the high-living upper classes in France, and he was one of the first French artists to sell his works directly from his studio, rather than from a public exhibit.

Francois Boucher (1703–1770) moved almost exclusively in the world of the French court. He decorated royal architecture and became the most popular painter of his day, with his influence extending not only to painting but also to interior decoration, tapestries, and porcelain. Boucher painted historical and mythological works, portraits, and pastoral scenes, for which he is most famous.

Flemish-born **Antoine Watteau** (1684–1721) was a great rococo artist and a court painter to King Louis XV. He was one of the first to break away from the grandeur of baroque, but his career was cut short when he died of tuberculosis at age thirty-seven.

The first artist to explore the special uses of chalk to and make pastel portraits popular was **Rosalba Carriera** (1675–1757). When a French art collector invited her to leave Venice and come to Paris, Carriera introduced pastel portraits to France and was invited to become a member of the French Royal Academy of Painting. Only the best artists were asked to join the academies, where they could study and exhibit. Carriera was also a member of the academy in Rome.

Jean-Baptiste-Siméon Chardin (1699–1779) painted still lifes and pictures of ordinary people doing their domestic routines or enjoying simple pleasures. His goal was to show goodness and truth in everyday life.

Elisabeth Vigée-Lebrun (1755–1842) made portraits of most of Europe's royalty, including Marie Antoinette, the queen of France. She painted more than nine hundred portraits during her long life and is remembered as one of the best portrait painters of the late eighteenth and early nineteenth centuries (see fig. 4.11). Her fame allowed her to be one of the only three women invited into the French Royal Academy of Painting. Another famous female artist during this time was Angelica Kauffman (1741–1807). Though born in Switzerland, Kauffman traveled as a young girl to Austria and Italy with her artist father. Later, she created many historical scenes and helped introduce neoclassicism. At this time, it was thought that only men could paint historical artworks, but Kauffman refused to accept this idea. She also painted many portraits of royalty, became wealthy, and was one of the founders of the British Royal Academy of Painting.

Popular Venetian artist Canaletto (1697–1768) was the leading view-painter of the eighteenth century. He was a prolific painter, and his panoramic views of cities, canals, churches, bridges, and palaces included much photographic detail.

Francisco Goya (1746–1828) was the official court painter of the king of Spain. He continued to paint even after he lost his hearing in midlife. Napoleon's invasion, with its mercilessly cruel killings, changed Goya's artworks, however, which began to show profound disillusionment with human beings (see fig. 6.21).

During the eighteenth century, excavations in Pompeii, Italy, revealed works of art that stimulated a new interest in the classical works of the ancient world. Called neoclassical, this style of art strongly contrasted with rococo. Its interior design and architecture seem plain and simple when compared with rococo. Artists chose classical subjects and painted in the style they thought the ancient Romans would have used. The most illustrious neoclassical painter was Frenchman Jacques-Louis David (1748–1825). Napoleon, who saw himself in the role of a great empire builder in the tradition of ancient Rome, commissioned David to so portray him, thus sparking a revival of the heroic grandeur of the classical past. David's historical painting *The Oath of the Horatii* created a sensation when first exhibited. It tells a story of self-sacrifice for the higher good. It shows young men swearing to their father to fight to the death, while grief-stricken young women are positioned on the right. Instead of the two states engaging in battle, the three young men will fight three brothers of the opposition.

William Hogarth (1697–1764), one of the most original and influential of British artists, was the son of a schoolmaster who, during the boy's youth, was imprisoned

Figure 6.21   Francisco de Goya, *Y No Hay Remedio (And There Is No Remedy),* from *Los Desastres de la Guerra,* 1814. Etching.
The Metropolitan Museum of Art. Purchase. Rogers Fund and Jacob H. Schiff Bequest, 1922 [22.60.25(15)].

for debt, an experience that marked Hogarth's later art production. He is best remembered for making a series of storytelling pictures and a series of engravings in which he ridiculed the outlandish behavior of Britain's upper classes. He was perhaps the first artist to use his art for social criticism and to direct his work to a large, unsophisticated public. He was also an excellent portrait painter.

Another English artist, Thomas Gainsborough (1727–1788), was both a landscapist and portraitist, often placing his figures in light, feathery landscapes. In *Blue Boy,* he showed his profound appreciation and understanding of van Dyck and Rubens. His work contrasts with the ideals of his great rival, Sir Joshua Reynolds (1723–1792), who was influenced by Venetian and Flemish baroque painters. Reynolds's paintings are composed harmoniously and are completely unified, never being merely pretty or sentimental. Reynolds sought to raise the standing of art and artists. He often dressed up his subjects as characters from myths and ancient history.

During the first half of the nineteenth century, three important art styles were prominent. The first, neoclassicism, was a reaction to the baroque and rococo styles of art, rejecting traditional subject matter and looking to the classical art of ancient Greece and Rome and to the Renaissance for inspiration.

The second art style, the romantic movement, rejected the rigid and orderly conventions of the classical school and was a freer style of art in which the artist depicted historical and literary scenes of dramatic action, melodrama, and heightened emotion. Romanticists thought that showing feelings and emotions was more important than anything. They chose strong colors and dramatic effects, and were inspired by the concept of liberty and anything dramatic, heroic, exciting, exotic, or mysterious. **Théodore Géricault** (1791–1824) is generally credited with creating the romantic style. He emulated the exuberant works of Rubens and showed much spontaneity in his drawing and painting. His *Raft of the Medusa,* which tells of a frigate that sank in 1818, killing many people, was painted when he was twenty-seven and made him famous. Géricault influenced **Eugène Delacroix** (1798–1863), whose numerous artworks showing horses testify to his ability to portray dynamic action.

A favorite theme of the romantic painters was showing the power and grandeur of nature—lofty mountains, strong storms, and rough seas, with human beings pictured as small and defenseless. English painter **Joseph M. W. Turner** (1775–1851) tried to give the viewer a feeling of being present at a scene, rather than showing how it actually looked. He used watercolors as well as oils.

English landscapist **John Constable** (1776–1837) painted directly from nature to produce realistic views of the countryside. His works influenced the **Barbizon school** of landscapists, a group of artists who were a part of the romantic movement that lasted from about 1820 to 1850. Working near the village of Barbizon in France, they sketched out-of-doors and completed their artworks in their studios.

The third major style of art during the first half of the nineteenth century was **realism.** About 1850, artists began to show the commonplace without disguising the harsh realities that industrial progress had left untouched, such as peasants working in the fields. Realists found suitable subjects all around them. They observed and painted peasants and the working classes, whose lives were difficult and unromantic.

Eugene Boudin's (1824–1898) paintings are light and tender in quality, fresh in color and in the portrayal of light and reflections on people and landscapes. He painted luminous skies and gave peaceful impressions of a pleasant landscape. Such artists as Corot, Courbet, Sisley, Manet, and Monet admired Boudin's work.

Jean-Francois Millet (1814–1875) called himself the "peasant of peasants." He devoted himself to scenes of rural life (see fig. 6.22). **Honoré Daumier** (1808–1879) was widely known for his political cartoons and today is considered one of the foremost French painters of his century. He was a confirmed realist, but to stress the true character of his subjects, he resorted to distortion. **Gustave Courbet** (1819–1877) was the foremost proponent of realism, and his emphatic rejection of idealization, painting the world as he saw it, even its unpleasant and harsh sides, immensely influenced modern art. He sometimes applied his

Figure 6.22 Jean-Francois Millet, *The Sower,* 1814–75. **Oil on canvas, 40 × 32½ in.**
Gift of Quincy Adams Shaw through Quincy A. Shaw Jr. and Mrs. Marian Shaw Haughton. Courtesy Museum of Fine Arts, Boston.

paints with a palette knife and worked with only a few somber colors. The landscapes of **Jean-Baptiste-Camille Corot** (1796–1875) reflect his love of nature. His early luminous paintings from nature greatly influenced future landscapists and placed him among the more original artists of the nineteenth century.

French artist **Rosa Bonheur** (1822–1899) was one of the most popular artists of the nineteenth century. A doll in her likeness was even created for little girls. She loved painting animals and did it so well that royalty all over Europe gave her medals for her work (see fig. 4.15).

American Artworks

During the eighteenth and nineteenth centuries, art served a variety of purposes in fast-growing America. Sir Joshua Reynolds's teaching of the importance of historical painting greatly influenced American artist **Benjamin West** (1738–1820). West, one of the early neoclassicists, trained briefly in Philadelphia and then left in 1760 to study in Rome. Three years later, he settled in London, where his studio soon became a gathering place for American students abroad. His painting of *Penn's Treaty with the Indians* shows figures dressed in the clothing of their day, rather than in the Roman togas fashionable with the neoclassicists.

John Singleton Copley (1738–1815) was one of the greatest eighteenth-century American artists. He was largely self-taught and made excellent likenesses of his countrymen, including a portrait of Paul Revere in his work clothes and holding a silver teapot he was making. **Gilbert Stuart** (1755–1828) is famous for his portraits of George Washington, one of which appears on the one-dollar bill. **Charles Willson Peale** (1741–1827) was one of several family members, both male and female, who were artists. His niece, **Sarah Miriam Peale** (1800–1885) was the first American woman to support herself with the money she earned painting.

The most extraordinary American painter was a Pennsylvania Quaker named **Edward Hicks** (1780–1849). Trained as a coach-and-sign painter, Hicks is most famous for his religious works, especially the approximately seventy variations on the theme of a kingdom in which animals and people live peaceably together (see fig. 3.18). Incidentally, the figures in Benjamin West's painting of William Penn signing a peace treaty with the Indians and Richard Westall's engraving were prototypes and inspiration for Hicks's artworks.

Albert Ryder's (1847–1917) almost mystical scenes of the ocean, with their strange, often yellowish, lighting, were painted in a manner that paralleled the romantic style. **George Inness's** (1825–1894) early work was influenced by the Hudson River School, but later, after contact with the Barbizon School, he abandoned precise detail for a broader style, using glowing light and indistinctly massed forms that gave a mystical view of nature.

American artists **William Michael Harnett** (1848–1892) and **John Frederick Peto** (1854–1907) carried realism to the point that the objects they painted seemed like real objects rather than painted images (see fig. 3.16). This kind of art is called **trompe l'oeil,** meaning "to trick the eye."

John James Audubon (1784–1851) pictured the birds of America in their natural habitats in a highly realistic and beautiful way. At nearly the same time, **George Catlin** (1796–1872) left his law practice to devote his life to the portrayal of Native Americans (see fig. 3.15). **George Caleb Bingham** (1811–1879) painted Missouri River genre scenes, showing male figures as they talked, relaxed, danced, made music, fished, or played cards (see fig. 6.23).

Jacksonian democracy created a new pride in the American wilderness. The **Hudson River School** was an unorganized group of artists who were the first to depict the newly perceived grandeur and beauty of America. The best of these was probably **Thomas Cole** (1801–1848), who

Figure 6.23   George Caleb Bingham, *Fur Traders Descending the Missouri,* **1845. Oil on canvas, 29 × 36½ in.**
The Metropolitan Museum of Art, Morris K. Jesup Fund, 1933 (33.61).

first traveled along the Hudson River in 1825 to sketch the Catskills. He later walked through the Adirondacks, the White Mountains, and the old Northwest Territory to make his artworks. His view of the countryside was highly emotional and patriotic. One of his followers was **Asher Brown Durand** (1796–1886), whose landscapes show the engraver's close attention to detail and are remarkably true to the American scene. **Frederic Church** (1826–1900), the only student of Thomas Cole, made large and spectacular landscapes.

In the latter part of the nineteenth century, **Nathaniel Currier** (1813–1888) and **James Ives** (1824–1895) formed a partnership to produce inexpensive lithographs that recorded nineteenth-century life in America. More than four thousand **Currier and Ives prints** by various artists were issued, and they depicted steamboats, trains, landscapes, newsworthy events, and life on the frontier.

Other American artists focused their efforts on other aspects of the American frontier. **Albert Bierstadt** (1830–1902) made grandiose interpretations of the American landscape, most notably the Rocky Mountains and further west (see colorplate 22 in the Color Gallery). **Frederic Remington** (1861–1909), foreseeing an end to the "Wild West," painted cowboys and Native Americans amid scenic grandeur (see fig. 4.5). Likewise, **Charles Russell** (1865–1926) spent years as a trapper and cowboy, drawing and painting the frontier life he saw around him for amusement in idle moments (see fig. 6.24). He was surprised when his works began to sell, and when he married, his insightful wife persuaded him to settle down to art. **William R. Leigh** (1866–1955) roamed the vast American countryside on horseback, sketching as he went and painting the vanishing West until he died.

Figure 6.24   Cast sculpture showing the western theme typical of Charles Russell's work.
Collection of the authors.

Figure 6.25   James McNeill Whistler, *Arrangement in Gray and Black, No. 1,* **ca. 1877. Oil on canvas, 57 × 64½ in.**
The Louvre, Paris. Réunion des Musées Nationaux, Paris.

American **James A. M. Whistler** (1834–1903) lived and worked abroad. He was a socialite, a celebrated wit, and the first American artist to belittle the importance of subject matter, claiming art was for art's sake. He stressed formal, decorative patterns, calling his famous painting of his mother *Arrangement in Gray and Black* (see fig. 6.25). His younger American contemporary, **John Singer Sargent** (1856–1925), also spent much of his life abroad, painting portraits of fashionable people. When he painted for his own pleasure, he created dazzling watercolors.

Winslow Homer (1836–1910) is probably best known for his paintings of the sea (see fig. 5.1). He lived on the rugged Maine coast and worked in both oils and watercolors. He began his career as a lithographer, and later, he recorded scenes of the Civil War for *Harper's Weekly*. He also painted many genre scenes of childhood.

Thomas Eakins (1844–1916) paid unblinking attention to facts when he painted, recording honestly and precisely the reality he saw and remarking at the beauty of the wrinkles in an old woman's skin. His interest in anatomy is reflected in his celebrated work *The Gross Clinic*. Philadelphia-born impressionist artist **Cecilia Beaux** (1863–1942) had a vibrant, fluent style, using whites, yellows, and lavenders against a strong black. She married Eakins in 1884.

African Americans have made artistic contributions since **Joshua Johnson** (1765–1830) made his family portraits, which have a charming modern appeal (see fig. 6.26). Some of his works are in the National Gallery of Art in Washington, D. C., but descendants of the original families

Figure 6.26   Joshua Johnson, *The Westwood Children,* **ca. 1807. Canvas, 41⅛ × 46 in.**
Gift of Edgar William and Bernice Chrysler Garbisch. © 1997 Board of Trustees, National Gallery of Art, Washington.

that owned them retain most of them. **Henry Q. Tanner** (1859–1937) was a student of Thomas Eakins and was the first African-American artist to achieve an international reputation when he was elected to the French Royal Academy of Painting. Working in the Hudson River School, **Robert S. Duncanson** (1817–1872) was recognized in his own time as an outstanding landscape painter whose works were romantic and mystical.

Edward Mitchell Bannister (1828–1901) became known in artistic circles in both Boston, Massachusetts, and Providence, Rhode Island. He felt compelled to be an artist after reading in a newspaper that while "the Negro may harbor an appreciation of art, he is unable to produce it." Only a handful of his paintings depicted blacks, with most of his works being landscapes in the Hudson River School tradition. Bannister won a gold medal at the Philadelphia Centennial Exposition. Also winning an award at the Philadelphia Exposition was **Edmonia Lewis** (1843–1909), whose marble sculptures in the neoclassical style reflected her feelings against racial prejudice and slavery. Her father was an African American, and her mother was a Chippewa Indian. She was the first African American to become known throughout the world as a sculptor.

Impressionism and Postimpressionism

During the 1860s, a group of painters with several common bonds came together in Paris. They were more interested in showing atmospheric effects by the way they used light and color than they were in their subject matter. Because they were mainly interested in light, they insisted on painting in the open air. Because black is rarely seen in nature, they painted shadows made of other dark colors. They worked on scientific color theories. They developed a style of laying tiny brush strokes side by side and often in contrasting colors. The viewer's eyes blended the colors from a distance. The effect was that of showing people and landscapes shimmering in sunlight and dazzling colors.

These artists also shared the common struggle for a number of years of trying to win critical and public acceptance. When **Claude Monet** (1840–1926) exhibited a seascape named *Impression: Sunrise,* an art critic derisively called the group of artists "impressionists," and the artists adopted the name for themselves. When these artists were rejected from showing their works in the prestigious **Salons** (the official exhibitions of the **French Royal Academy of Painting**), they joined together and sponsored eight of their own shows.

Early on, **Edouard Manet** (1832–1883) shocked people with his colorful contrasts and unusual techniques. He inspired younger artists who worked in the impressionist style. When one of Manet's paintings was first exhibited, a man tried to slash it with his cane.

Figure 6.27   Claude Monet, *On the Seine at Bennecourt (Au bord de l'eau, Bennecourt),* 1868. Oil on canvas, 31⅞ × 39½ in. Mr. and Mrs. Potter Palmer Collection #1927.427. © The Art Institute of Chicago. All rights reserved.

Figure 6.28   Camille Pissarro, *Boulevard des Italiens, Morning Sunlight,* 1897. Oil on canvas, 28⅞ × 36¼ in. Chester Dale Collection, © 1997 Board of Trustees, National Gallery of Art, Washington.

Claude Monet painted about forty pictures of the facade of the Rouen Cathedral under many different lighting conditions. He worked rapidly, seizing a particular moment by not mixing different colors on his palette before applying them to his canvas. His rapidly applied strokes of pure colors allowed the eye to blend them. Monet also painted the water lilies and the gardens in his home in Giverny many times.

Camille Pissarro (1830–1903) studied with Corot before meeting Monet in 1859. Pissarro was a kindly father figure who helped younger artists and introduced them to his friends (see fig. 6.28).

Edgar Degas (1834–1917), who was fascinated with motion, specialized in painting ballet dancers and horses. He preferred to paint indoor scenes and even had a wooden horse in his studio to serve as a model. He was interested in a new invention—a portable camera—that could capture unposed action and take pictures from unusual angles. He worked closely with **Mary Cassatt** (1845–1926), an American artist born into a wealthy Pittsburgh family. Cassatt lived and worked in Paris, and is especially known for her portraits of women and children (see fig. 4.9 and colorplate 32 in the Color Gallery). She helped the impressionists gain acceptance in America because she urged her wealthy friends to purchase their works.

Pierre-Auguste Renoir (1841–1919) worked in his youth at a porcelain factory. He is well known for his shimmering effects of light and for his pictures of young women and little girls (see colorplate 28 in the Color Gallery). **Alfred Sisley** (1839–1899) spent most of his life in France, painting landscapes with a delicate sensitivity and careful composition. He remained faithful to impressionism throughout his life, but in addition to recording atmospheric changes in light, he captured the movement of foliage, the shimmer of water, and the textures of cloudy skies. **Berthe Morisot** (1841–1895) was the first woman to join the impressionists, and she persuaded her brother-in-law, Edouard Manet, to take up **plein air** painting (painting outdoors). She shared the impressionists' love of iridescent light but did not use their short, broken brush strokes. Instead, she developed a fragile, feathery technique.

The **postimpressionists** were artists who became dissatisfied with impressionism. They had other visions they wished to explore and express. One of the first postimpressionists was **Paul Cézanne** (1839–1906). He felt that the flicker and shimmer of light on object surfaces did not describe the solidity of natural forms (see colorplate 13 in the Color Gallery). Cézanne felt that everything in nature was basically a cone, cylinder, or cube, and he worked hard to apply his brush strokes in a manner that conveyed this idea of solid forms. (Pablo Picasso and Georges Braque later pursued Cézanne's method of building up simple geometric forms in a style known as **cubism.**) Cézanne liked to paint still lifes because they did not move, as people who modeled for him did, and he could concentrate on the basic forms. He also made many paintings of a favorite landscape, Mont Sainte-Victoire.

Vincent van Gogh (1853–1890), though awakened to the brighter colors that impressionists used when he first came to Paris from Holland, soon reacted against the realism of the impressionists. He put strongly contrasting colors such as blue and yellow next to each other to express his intense feelings more vividly (see figs. 3.3 and 3.13, and colorplate 11 in the Color Gallery). Van Gogh spent time in the south of France, producing landscapes, flowers, and portraits. His swirling brush strokes easily identify his works. His short, ten-year career as an artist ended tragically when he shot himself at age thirty-seven.

Van Gogh was a friend of another artist, **Paul Gauguin** (1848–1903). Gauguin gave up his family and a successful career as a stockbroker in Paris to become a full-time painter (see fig. 5.3). Most of his time as an artist was spent in the South Seas, where he smoothly applied brilliant, arbitrary colors to large, flat areas separated by dark lines. He liked to paint exotic subjects, such as native women set in tropical surroundings ("drawing from nature by dreaming in her presence").

Georges Seurat (1859–1891) was a superb draftsman who invented a new method of painting called **pointillism.** Seurat had studied the science of color and knew that if he painted many tiny dots close to each other, they would mix in the viewer's eye (see colorplate 12 in the Color Gallery). **Paul Signac** (1863–1935) also worked in this manner.

Henri de Toulouse-Lautrec (1864–1901) observed and drew the life in music halls, theaters, circuses, and cabarets of Paris (see fig. 3.4). Born into a wealthy, noble family, he had a normal torso but stunted legs due to childhood accidents. He excelled not only in painting and drawing but also in lithography, making posters that advertised music hall performances.

Until he retired in 1885, **Henri Rousseau** (1844–1910) worked as an official in a Parisian tollhouse and hence is often known as "Le Douanier" (customs official). He is usually categorized as **primitive** or **naive,** since he never had any formal art training. He never waivered in his belief in the grandeur of the contribution he would make to French art. Ridiculed by the public and critics, Rousseau was acclaimed by a number of his artist peers, and his work continues to receive delighted responses from surrealists, pop artists, and the public today. His exotic jungle fantasies were based on sketches he made in the botanical gardens and zoo of Paris (see fig. 4.21). He had a superb intuitive sense of design and detailed pattern.

■ ARTWORKS IN THE TWENTIETH CENTURY

Diversity, rapid change, and all kinds of "isms" mark the artworks of the twentieth century. Classifying artists into these "ism" compartments can be confusing because artists do not always fit neatly into a style, and if they do, they may not continue in that mode for their entire career. Endeavoring to understand and enjoy each artwork in its own right is best. However, an overview of some of the leading schools of art, identifying some of the twentieth-century mainstream artists, can clarify the overlapping and dynamic trends and movements that took place and are still occurring both in America and abroad.

Figure 6.29   Pablo Picasso, *Guernica,* 1937. Oil on canvas, 25 ft. 5¾ in. × 11 ft. 5½ in.
Alinari/Art Resource, N.Y. © 1997 Estate of Pablo Picasso/Artists Rights Society (ARS), New York.

Artists have always been cognizant of the social and cultural events around them. They also are influenced by artists who preceded them and by their contemporaries. In turn, they influence other artists' works. This is especially true in the twentieth century.

Painting

Very early in the twentieth century, many artists stopped depicting recognizable objects and began using colors, lines, and shapes to express their ideas and feelings, a kind of art often called **abstract.** One important style that grew out of postimpressionism was **expressionism.** These artists used violent colors and distortions, and exaggerated the shapes of the things they painted.

Cubism was born at the beginning of the twentieth century, sparked by **Pablo Picasso** (1880–1973) and **Georges Braque** (1882–1963). Their compositions no longer just represented natural objects but created new shapes and forms, showing different planes and viewpoints all at once. Picasso created in many different styles and in a variety of media during his long, productive life (see figure 6.29 and colorplate 29 in the Color Gallery). Born in Spain, he spent most of his life in France. His early works fall into his "Blue period," which his "Rose period" soon replaced. He is probably the most influential artist of the twentieth century. Braque, in addition to working with Picasso on cubism, added unrelated elements to his work, a technique known as **collage.** He often mixed sand with his paints and

had a distinct palette of colors that utilized blacks, grays, dull greens, and browns. The cubist works of **Juan Gris** (1887–1927) emphasized constructive rhythms and abstract components, as opposed to the more intuitive methods of visual analysis that Braque and Picasso used.

The Eight   At the beginning of the twentieth century, wealthy Americans had a taste only for traditional, unexperimental European paintings. As a result of this attitude and to protest their lack of recognition in the United States, a group of American painters organized themselves into **The Eight.** They endeavored to create a distinctly American art form. Led by artist and teacher **Robert Henri** (1865–1929), The Eight included **Maurice Prendergast** (1859–1924), **Arthur Davies** (1862–1928), **George Luks** (1867–1933), **William Glackens** (1870–1938), **Ernest Lawson** (1873–1939), **John Sloan** (1871–1952) (see fig. 6.30), and **George Bellows** (1882–1925). All but Davies sought to interpret city life and human conditions in American cities. Their subject matter was backyards, slums, saloons, harbors, alleys, professional fighters, and the like. Art critics, the public, and traditional artists rejected and scorned The Eight, who were soon nicknamed the **Ashcan School.** Nevertheless, they established an important American genre movement. The independent spirit of The Eight spread after 1908 and culminated in the opening of the **Armory Show** in New York in 1913. The Armory Show has been called the starting point of modern American art.

Figure 6.30   John Sloan, *The City from Greenwich Village*, 1922. Oil on canvas, 26 × 33¾ in.
Gift of Helen Farr Sloan, © 1997 Board of Trustees, National Gallery of Art, Washington.

Figure 6.31   Horace Pippin, *Victorian Interior*, 1945. Oil on canvas, 30 × 24¼ in.
The Metropolitan Museum of Art, New York. Arthur H. Hearn Fund, 1958 (58–26).

About thirty thousand people saw the Armory Show. Approximately a third of the works shown were foreign; they were included to point out the evolution of modern art. This section included works by Delacroix, Corot, Courbet, Goya, Ingres, and a number of the impressionists and postimpressionists.

Some of the works shocked the public. For instance, **Marcel Duchamp's** (1887–1968) *Nude Descending a Staircase* (see fig. 4.14) created such a furor that a frenzied mob threatened to destroy it. In this artwork, Duchamp depicted a female form in a manner that suggested rapid motion, as seen in multiple-exposure photography. One critic likened it to an explosion in a shingle factory. The press endorsed the public's hostile attitude toward the exhibit; nevertheless, the exhibit was a huge success, stirring up curiosity as it traveled to the Chicago Art Institute and Boston. The exhibit managed to find a few supporters and became the subject of somewhat penitent comments from its critics after it closed. From this time on, modern art found a larger audience in the United States.

Alfred Stieglitz (1864–1946) was a brilliant avant-garde leader in the early twentieth century. He was a photographer who had run galleries in New York that had advanced American and European work since 1905. He had arranged the first exhibitions of Matisse (1908) and Picasso (1911) in his Gallery 291.

American Painters   At this time, a number of modern artists emerged in America. **Maurice Prendergast** (1859–1924) was one of the American painters who helped organize the Armory Show. Painting in oils and watercolors, he applied paint in small spots of bright color in a manner similar to the impressionists. A critic derided his work as "spotty canvases" and "artistic tommyrot." His later success was considerable, and Prendergast felt vindicated, remarking that he was "glad they've found out I'm not crazy." **Edward Hopper** (1882–1967) showed the lonely desolation of empty streets and isolated people, and of lighthouses and seacoasts, in his starkly realistic scenes in which light provided a dramatic element. One of the most original of the avant-garde was **Marsden Hartley** (1877–1943), who was influenced by the bold, bright colors of the German **Blue Riders.** His usual theme was the rugged coastline and mountainous terrain of New England, but he also painted patterned, textured abstractions in an almost mosaic manner, showing militarism and flags. **Arthur Dove** (1880–1946) combined an advanced degree of abstraction with mystical images of natural forms. **John Marin** (1870–1953) often represented the rugged coast of Maine and the towers of Manhattan in his spontaneous watercolors marked with slashing brush strokes. In the 1920s, **Charles Demuth** (1883–1935) developed colorful abstractions that showed a strong geometric structure. Italian-born American painter **Joseph Stella** (1877–1946) painted a dynamic series of kaleidoscopic views of the Brooklyn Bridge, and his artworks often had mechanical and city themes.

African-American Painters   A number of African-American artists were born near the turn of the nineteenth century. **Horace Pippin** (1888–1946) taught himself to paint, but unlike his French counterpart Henri Rousseau, was acclaimed in his own lifetime (see fig. 6.31). **Hale Woodruff's** (1900–1980) most famous work is a three-panel series showing a slave revolt on a Spanish ship in

1839, with the slaves being returned to their homeland by John Quincy Adams and other abolitionists. **Richmond Barthe** (1901–1989) was a prolific sculptor who made portraits of famous actors and racial allegories. His award-winning work pays homage to the realist tradition. **Lois Maillol Jones** (1905–) painted cityscapes in the spirit of Cézanne and designed textiles. Many of **Malvin Cray Johnson's** (1896–1934) paintings feature figures posed as if for a photograph, with the backgrounds filled with objects and symbols related to Johnson's African heritage. **William H. Johnson** (1901–1970) struggled with relating his African roots and his European training. His work first show his early years in South Carolina, then city life in Harlem, then the training camps of World War II, and finally, scenes of civic concerns. **Archibald Motley Jr.** (1891–1980) was primarily a genre painter of modern black life and was one of the first African Americans to have a one-man exhibit in the United States. His paintings were often derived from African-American culture and had intensely colored surfaces and images culled from urban sources.

Sargent Johnson (1888–1967) was a pioneering black modernist who received praise for his wood, cast stone, and ceramic sculpture. **Alma Thomas** (1891–1978) became a full-fledged artist after teaching in the public schools in Washington, D.C. Many major museums show her work, which was characterized by the application of flat colors in homogeneous strokes. **Palmer Hayden** (1893–1973) was the first recipient of the Harmon Foundation's Gold Medal for distinguished achievements by an African American in the fine-arts field. His series of works about American folk hero John Henry combines narrative elements with expressionist painting techniques. **Allan Crite** (1910–) has been called an "artist reporter" for re-creating small but important details of life in the predominantly African-American Roxbury neighborhood in Boston.

The **Harlem Renaissance** was a vigorous and vital movement in the 1920s and 1930s. At this time, many black artists focused on their African heritage and expressed pride in their ancestral roots. **Charles Alston** (1907–1977) headed up the influential Harlem Art Workshop in the mid-1920s, which spawned Jacob Lawrence and a number of other artists. Throughout life, Alston balanced two roles as art educator and painter. **Jacob Lawrence** (1917–) emerged after the Great Depression as an important artist (see colorplate 31 in the Color Gallery). Self-taught, he developed a style that combined decorative flat colors and incorporated strong, socially oriented themes from black ghetto life. Lawrence used strong, silhouetted patterns and narrative subject matter to depict African-American history in America. **Romare Bearden** (1914–1988) used painting and collage techniques to express themes related to African-American life in the rural South and the urban North. He incorporated cubist principles and showed the influence of African sculpture. **Hughie**

Lee-Smith (1915–) had parents who encouraged his artistic production. His paintings of aging neighborhoods where old buildings stand isolated and empty often convey a sense of desolation and alienation (see fig. 4.7). **Walter H. Williams** (1920–) studied at home and abroad before becoming artist-in-residence at Fisk University in Nashville. Though he grew up in Brooklyn, many of his paintings and prints draw on his childhood memories of sights and sounds of nature.

Like Hale Woodruff and Jacob Lawrence, **Charles White** (1918–1979) worked during the Great Depression for the WPA (Works Progress Administration) Art Project. He was a strong social critic, working in the style of Mexican muralists Rivera and Siqueiros. **Elizabeth Catlett** (1915–) was active in the civil rights movement and has produced work concerned with social needs.

African-American artist **Norma Morgan** (1928–) is noted for her "magic-realist" etchings and copper engravings. Los-Angeles-born **Betye Saar** (1929–), influenced by African-American folk culture and myths, uses many found and earth-oriented materials, such as leather, wood, straw, and cloth, for her assemblage constructions and imaginative tableaux. **Faith Ringgold** (1930–) was born in Harlem and reflects on her African-American heritage by painting and creating artworks that often combine needlepoint, braided ribbon, beads, and soft sculpture. In the late 1960s, she began to upset mass-market images to "liberate all the Aunt Jemimas and Uncle Toms." A leading member of a movement called **Blackstream, Benny Andrews** (1930–) makes powerful works that attack American junk culture and show that African-American artists are creating art as uniquely American as jazz. **Hilda Robinson** (1928–) received her degree from the University of California at Berkeley after having three daughters. She selects subjects "in her mind's eye and seeks expression rather than representation of what people are."

Mexican Painters   Several important **Mexican artists** made significant contributions during the twentieth century. **Diego Rivera** (1886–1957), after spending a number of years abroad, returned to Mexico in 1921 and studied the traditions of Mexican folk art. He then experimented with Italian fresco techniques, painting overwhelming murals that sang of the triumph of work and the destruction of poverty and oppression (see fig. 4.31 and colorplate 23 in the Color Gallery). **José Clemente Orozco** (1883–1949) created savage caricatures dealing with the Mexican Revolution. **David Siqueiros** (1896–1974) was the most politically active Mexican artist, being imprisoned at one point and fighting in the Spanish Civil War. He exploited folklore and surrealistic and symbolic effects. He also used photographs and new techniques such as airbrushing. **Rufino Tamayo's** (1899–1991) best works are his easel paintings in which he blended European styles with Mexican folklore.

Frida Kahlo (1910–1954) was born in Mexico; her father was an immigrant German Jew and her mother a native of Mexico. She nearly died at age fifteen in a streetcar accident and spent her life in constant pain. She painted many expressive and soul-searching self-portraits. She was married to Diego Rivera.

European Painters **Futurism** was an Italian art movement that began in 1909. One of its key artists was **Umberto Boccioni** (1882–1916). The futurists wanted to incorporate the dynamism of speed, motion, and modern technology into art. **Giacomo Balla** (1871–1958) captured the comic movements of a little dog on a leash in a manner that reminds us of stop-frame photography.

In Germany in 1919, architect **Walter Gropius** founded the **Bauhaus**—a school of architecture, design, and craftsmanship. Its goal was to reunite all forms of artistic efforts—sculpture, painting, and the applied and decorative arts—and to reintegrate them into architecture. It introduced a new concept of art based on the craftwork inspired by the memory of the old craftsmen's guilds. Before the Nazis closed the Bauhaus in 1933, it had exerted an enormous and lasting influence. Its teachers included Kandinsky, Klee, Feininger, Moholy-Nagy, Albers, and others.

In 1905–6, a small band of young architecture students in Dresden formed a group called **Die Brücke** to create a modern artistic community. They were fired with an aggressive zeal about the social role of art. The expressive distortions and simplifications of primitive art excited them. Their works were often angular, harsh, and crowded with details in which they created psychological tensions. Important founders of this movement were **Ernst Ludwig Kirchner** (1880–1938), **Karl Schmidt-Rottluff** (1884–1976), **Max Pechstein** (1881–1955), and **Emil Nolde** (1867–1956).

Other artists working during this time included **Suzanne Valadon** (1865–1938), who became a painter after an accident while working as a circus acrobat. She used strong lines and bright, contrasting colors in her paintings of landscapes and still lifes. **Maurice Utrillo** (1883–1955) was Valadon's son. She brought him painting materials and postcards of city scenes while he was being treated for alcoholism at age eighteen, so he took up painting. He is known for his street scenes, many of which show thick brush strokes and white tones (see fig. 3.21).

Édouard Vuillard (1868–1940) is known for harmonious, decorative, and quietly domestic scenes, in which patterns, objects, walls, and people blend in soft, subdued colors. **Pierre Bonnard** (1867–1947) joined the Nabis (Hebrew word, meaning "prophets") in 1891. The Nabis felt that a painting should not be an imitation of reality but a parallel to nature, stressing subjective, sometimes mystical, perceptions. Bonnard's works are known for their fresh colors and his delight with ordinary objects and events. **Lyonel**

Feininger (1871–1956) painted in a distinctly personal style that is both cubist and architectural in derivation. His buildings, cityscapes, and seascapes are constructed of translucent, overlapping, geometrical planes.

Wassily Kandinsky (1866–1944) was one of the most important artists of the early twentieth century. After giving up a law career in his native Russia, he moved to Germany and turned to art. He soon became a leader of a group called the **Blue Horseman** or **Blue Riders (Der Blaue Reiter)**. The name was taken from a picture by Kandinsky. These artists believed that art should be as abstract as music, that it should have a variety of forms in which artists manifested an "inner desire" with complete freedom from the constraints and conventions of the "fine" art of Europe. Before long, Kandinsky abandoned representation totally, using bright colors and free brushwork (see colorplate 26 in the Color Gallery). He became known as the "father of abstract art." Other leading figures in the Blue Riders were **Franz Marc** (1880–1916), who showed animal life in broad, abstract planes and brilliant colors that bore no relation to nature (see colorplate 21 in the Color Gallery). **August Macke** (1887–1914) was also a founder of the group but was killed in World War I. **Alexei van Jawlensky** (1864–1941), although never formally a member, was close to the aims of Der Blaue Reiter.

Germany came to be the natural home for expressionism. **Ernst Barlach** (1870–1938) made prints and sculpture that showed the range of emotions from despair to ecstasy. His friend **Käthe Kollwitz** (1867–1945) was sympathetic to the poor and oppressed in her lithographs and sculpture, as was Barlach; however, Kollwitz's personal art often showed sad and suffering women (her only son was killed in World War I and her grandson in World War II). The independent spirit of German artist **Max Beckmann** (1884–1950) is manifested in the stark, heavily outlined, massive figures of his paintings and in his numerous self-portraits.

Norwegian artist **Edvard Munch's** (1863–1944) artworks, many almost like recurrent nightmares, are expressive images dealing with his feelings toward death, since the deaths of his mother and older sister profoundly affected his youth (see fig. 3.2). He made paintings, woodcuts, and lithographs.

Henri Matisse (1869–1954) led the **fauves (wild beasts)**, artists who used distorted forms and violent, unrealistic colors for people's faces and figures (see fig. 4.20). Later, Matisse made many paintings whose rich, decorative patterns suggest the Persian carpets that influenced him. He is also famous for his cut-paper collages. Others associated with the fauves include **Georges Rouault** (1871–1958), who later turned from bright to more somber colors. His apprenticeship in a stained-glass shop in his youth may have inspired his use of dark outlines to separate areas of color (see fig. 3.7). As a devout Catholic,

Rouault frequently chose religious subjects. **Raoul Dufy** (1877–1953) arrived at his characteristically spontaneous style around 1910. His oils and watercolors of racetracks, fashionable resorts, landscapes, and flowers showed bright colors and calligraphic brush strokes.

Maurice de Vlaminck (1876–1958) was an energetic giant of a man whose early works were painted in brilliant orange, red, and blue. He experimented with cubism and showed a preference for pure whites and deep blues. After 1915, he began painting strong, stormy landscapes, overcast skies, and lonely villages in a turbulent style. **André Derain** (1880–1954) began as a fauve and was principally concerned with line and color—especially pinks, blues, and violets. He later concentrated more on form and structure, and experimented with cubism, impressionism, and the styles of van Gogh, Gauguin, and Cézanne.

Amedeo Modigliani (1884–1920) was born in Italy but spent most of his short life in Paris. African sculpture, as well as the works of Cézanne and Picasso, inspired the distorted and elongated forms in Modigliani's painting and sculpture (see fig. 4.12). Dutch artist **Piet Mondrian** (1872–1944) carried the idea of using geometric shapes to the extent of using only straight lines and the three primary colors. **Fernand Léger** (1881–1955) developed a style of reducing people and objects to machinelike forms. He celebrated modern technological culture with heroic scale and popular imagery. His works usually have bright colors and definitive black outlines.

The paintings of **Paul Klee** (1879–1940) are filled with signs and symbols that give flight to our imagination. Klee endeavored to capture the spontaneous gaiety of children's art. Another highly imaginative artist, Russian-born **Marc Chagall** (1887–1985) recalled the folktales and imagery of his native village in his fanciful and colorful artworks (see colorplate 33 in the Color Gallery). He is not only remembered as a painter but also as a designer of book illustrations, stage sets, and stained-glass windows.

First appearing in 1915 and losing its impetus by 1923, **dadaism** (French for "hobbyhorse," a name picked at random from a dictionary) symbolized a movement that was deliberately antirational and anti-art. Dadaism first occurred in Zurich and then spread to New York. The original antimilitary protest developed into a complete rejection of the "falseness and hypocrisy" of culture's established values.

Surrealism   In the 1920s, a few artists began painting in a manner called **surrealism.** Their subjects seemed quite realistic, but the combinations of objects and details were unlikely, unusual, sometimes even nonsensical, evoking a subconscious, dreamlike world. **Odilon Redon** (1840–1916) was a precursor of surrealism in painting and in the exploration of the symbols of the subconscious. His works show delicate colors and haunting, mysterious expressions that balance between the real and the unreal.

René Magritte (1898–1967), a Belgian painter, juxtaposed natural objects and those of human origin with scrupulous precision (see fig. 5.4). He often created an effect of disturbing ambiguity. **Salvador Dali** (1904–1989), a flamboyant Spanish surrealist, had an eccentric lifestyle and created a body of paintings in a meticulous style that almost appears three-dimensional (see colorplate 16 in the Color Gallery). He also created jewelry, ceramics, and sculpture. **Giorgio de Chirico** (1888–1978) painted a solitary figure or statue, often in conjunction with a train or lighthouse, in empty Italian cityscapes (see fig. 3.24). Surrealists recognized him as a forerunner of their movement. Spanish painter **Joan Miró** (1893–1983) was a versatile and original artist whose brightly colored, amoeba-like shapes and organic, linear creatures floated and wriggled, defying the laws of gravity. The works of Dutch artist **Maurits C. Escher** (1898–1972) often abound in bizarre metamorphoses and optical illusions that blend elements of surrealism with mathematics.

Ben Shahn (1898–1969) was a social realist artist working with paintings, prints, photography, and calligraphy. He came to New York from Lithuania in 1906. Written words and comments are sometimes included with his images in a delicate, spiky, linear manner.

Georgia O'Keeffe's (1887–1986) style peaked during her years in New Mexico. She frequently painted enormous close-ups of flowers and bones, as well as the vast landscape of the Southwest (see fig. 3.12 and colorplate 30 in the Color Gallery). She was born in Wisconsin and was married to photographer and art dealer **Alfred Stieglitz.**

American artist **Stuart Davis** (1894–1964) used bright, clear colors, simplified forms, and hard edges in his artworks. After 1940, his works were quite abstract and often had zany titles and fragments of letters and words.

Regionalists   During the Great Depression in the 1930s, **Grant Wood** (1892–1942) (see fig.4.23 and colorplate 18 in the Color Gallery) and **Thomas Hart Benton** (1889–1975) painted realistic scenes of life in the Midwest and became known as **regionalists.** Their works celebrate life in small towns and rural America. **Charles Burchfield** (1893–1967), also a painter of midwestern landscapes, based his early, rather mystical works on childhood emotions and memories of the world of nature. During the 1920s and 1930s, he painted more realistic depictions of American landscapes. After 1943, Burchfield's works showed a Nordic mysticism in jagged shapes that created a menacing element. The paintings of **Philip Evergood** (1901–1973) depicted the hunger, social discrimination, unemployment, and political oppression of the Great Depression, placing Evergood in the ranks of the social realists. He worked in the Federal Public Works Project.

Post-World-War-II Painters   After World War II, the United States became the world center of painting, with artists searching for originality and freedom of expression. The two main forerunners of **abstract expressionism** were Armenian-born **Arshile Gorky** (1905–1948) and German-born **Hans Hofmann** (1880–1966). Both immigrated to America. Gorky's fluid forms coagulate and merge to show a personal surrealism verging on abstract expressionism. By 1942, Gorky's free calligraphic brushwork often had no figurative reference. Hofmann's forceful outbursts of color reflected his belief that paintings should be made with feeling, not with knowing (see fig. 5.5). In 1934, Hofmann established highly influential schools in New York and in Provincetown, Massachusetts, where he taught a number of students who became prominent in the 1950s. Most notable of these was **Helen Frankenthaler** (1928–), who often uses washes of color, pouring the thinned paint directly onto unprimed canvases. Her abstract artworks contain no recognizable objects; instead, they glow with color and movement. Frankenthaler married and later divorced **Robert Motherwell** (1915–), a pioneer in abstract expressionism.

Willem de Kooning (1904–) came to New York from Holland when he was twenty-three. His energetic brush strokes and the vitality of his paintings influenced a number of artists. After 1950, he produced a series of female figures with distorted bodies and grimacing faces. He usually worked in a vigorous style, using broad, slashing brush strokes. Russian-born American artist **Mark Rothko** (1903–1970) was another leader of abstract expressionism. He is best known for his canvases that show large, horizontal bars of thinned pigments.

Swiss-born **Sophie Taeuber-Arp** (1889–1943) and her husband, French artist **Jean Arp** (1887–1966), influenced each other's artworks, sometimes designing works together. Sophie made some of her husband's paintings into woven tapestries. She used pure and simple geometric shapes painted with glowing colors. Jean is famous primarily for his abstract sculpture.

Jackson Pollock (1912–1956) was a leading member of the New York school of abstract expressionism. He is best remembered for his later work, known as **action painting.** This technique called for placing the canvas on the floor and pouring and splashing paint across the surface from all four sides to create an allover texture of lines and splatters. Pollock was fascinated by Mayan glyphs and intrigued with Navajo sand painting because of the way it is painted in large movements on the ground. **Mark Tobey's** (1890–1978) work paralleled the abstract expressionist movement, but he was highly influenced by Japanese Zen philosophy and painting. His works show a kind of calligraphic, spontaneous brushwork called "white writing."

The Western world in the 1950s was shocked and dazzled by the abstract expressionists working in New York. The scale of their paintings, the artists' unorthodox behavior, and the general aura of the movement often diverted attention from other trends. In the 1960s, a group of U.S.

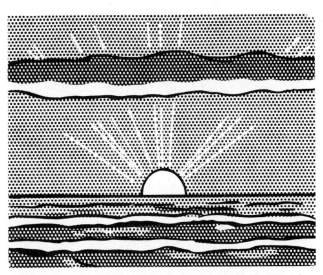

Figure 6.32   Roy Lichtenstein, *Landscape,* **1964. Pencil and touche on paper, 16⅞ × 21¼ in.**
San Francisco Museum of Modern Art. Gift of John Berggruen.

artists rebelled against abstract expressionism and began depicting in their artworks images of commonplace things, such as dartboards, lightbulbs, flags, comic strips, and pies and cakes. Some important **pop artists** were **Andy Warhol** (1930–1987) (see fig. 2.24), **Wayne Thiebaud** (1920–), **Jasper Johns** (1930–), **Roy Lichtenstein** (1923–) (see fig. 6.32), **Claes Oldenburg** (1929–), and **Robert Rauschenberg** (1925–).

In the mid-1960s, **op art** emerged. This type of abstract art exploits the optical effects of pattern. Hard-edged, black-and-white or colored compositions seem to vibrate and change shape as we look at them. **Victor Vasarely** (1908–), born in Hungary, is known as the "father of op art" (see fig. 6.33). British artist **Bridget Riley's** (1930–) closely packed, curving parallel lines create a strong impact on our eyes (see fig. 4.18).

Josef Albers (1888–1976) began teaching in America when the Nazis closed the Bauhaus in 1933. He was as concerned with the applied arts as with the fine arts and was responsible for one of the first laminated wood chairs. His nonobjective paintings were highly structured in their use of color.

Frank Stella (1936–) began as an abstract expressionist but experimented in a number of ways. His works became more systematic and rigorously formal; some of them are as large as 10 feet high and 20 feet long.

Andrew Wyeth (1917–), son of illustrator **Newell Convers Wyeth** (1882–1944), has spent his life painting the landscape and neighbors near his home in Pennsylvania. He uses watercolor and drybrush and has perfected the technique of egg tempera. Wyeth achieves a stark, highly realistic effect that often has a strange, eerie quality of loneliness.

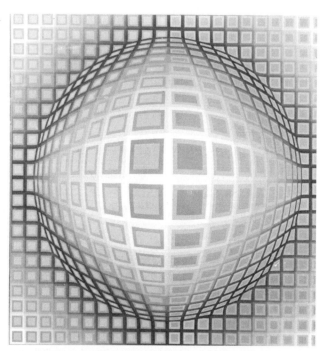

Figure 6.33 Victor Vasarely, *Vega-Nor,* 1955. Oil on canvas, 78¾ × 78¾ in.
Albright-Knox Art Gallery, Buffalo, New York. Gift of Seymour H. Knox, 1955. © 1997 Artists Rights Society (ARS), New York/ ADAGP, Paris.

British-born **David Hockney** (1937–) in Los Angeles and not only paints but makes enormous "joiners," photo collages of numerous single shots.

Fritz Scholder (1937–) is part Native American. His expressionistic paintings and lithographs speak of the Native American in today's society.

Anna Mary Robertson (Grandma Moses) (1860–1961), a celebrated primitive or naive painter, began to paint at age sixty and had her first one-woman show in New York in 1940. She painted in minute detail the scenes and events from the countryside that she remembered.

Photography

Photography, being communication, is a personal statement of an artist, and good photographs have recognizable styles in the same manner that paintings do. Photographs may reveal the nature and character of their subjects, while being carefully composed and sensitively designed. **L. J. M. Daguerre** (1787–1851) announced in 1838 the invention that bears his name (daguerreotype), and photography entered the public domain. Several important names in the field of American photography follow.

Mathew Brady (1823–1896), in showing the carnage of the battlefield in his Civil War photographs, presented the world for the first time with such images. He took many

Figure 6.34 Dorothea Lange, *Migrant Mother,* 1936. Gelatin-silver print, Nipomo, Calif., 12½ × 9⅝ in.
The Museum of Modern Art, New York. Purchase. Copy Print © 1997 The Museum of Modern Art, New York.

photographs of Abraham Lincoln that showed Lincoln's strength, dignity, and nobility.

Alfred Stieglitz (1864–1946), after buying his first camera for seven dollars and fifty cents, became dedicated to photography and to his New York gallery (where he displayed the work of other artists, including that of his wife, Georgia O'Keeffe). **Edward Weston** (1886–1958) gained worldwide recognition from his romantic, soft-focus pictures. He then adopted "straight photography" and focused on close-ups of peppers, roots, shells, and other objects. **Ansel Adams's** (1902–1984) landscapes of western America show fine details, a full range of tonal values, and great depth of field.

Berenice Abbott (1898–1991) captured the personality of her subjects in a number of fine portraits. She spent ten years photographing New York's architecture, transportation, and people. **Margaret Bourke-White** (1904–1971) photographed industry and cities, as well as natural disasters and World War II. **Dorothea Lange** (1895–1965) made sensitive pictures of the Dust Bowl victims of the 1930s as they migrated to California to seek work (see fig. 6.34). Her photographs helped bring these people federal assistance. Other notable photographers were **Imogene Cunningham** (1883–1976), **Man Ray** (1890–1976), and **Paul Strand** (1890–1976). **Gordon Parks** (1912–) depicted African-American life, including a famous portrait of Malcolm X.

Architecture

The invention of the elevator and the development of steel for structural skeletons were major breakthroughs in architecture. **Louis Sullivan** (1856–1924) was a turn-of-the-century American pioneer whose work led to the evolution of the skyscraper. Sullivan observed that "form follows function" and led architects in rethinking their designs from the inside out. **Le Corbusier** (1887–1965) solved urban design problems with steel columns and reinforced slab constructions. In Europe, a new international architecture that rejected decorative ornamentation and traditional materials evolved between 1910 and 1930. **Walter Gropius** (1883–1969) used these principles in designing the Bauhaus in Germany, a building that shows the interior and exterior simultaneously in opaque and transparent overlapping planes. Between 1956 and 1958, **Mies van der Rohe** (1886–1969) and **Philip Johnson** (1906–) designed and built the elegant, austere Seagram Building in New York, with vertical lines emphasizing the feeling of height and providing a strong pattern.

Frank Lloyd Wright (1869–1959), one of the most influential American architects, designed bold and elegant homes and public buildings, often harmonizing his meticulous attention to design detail with nature and the surrounding site. **Buckminster Fuller** (1895–1983) was a forward-thinking inventor, architect, and structural engineer. Polyhedroms found in nature inspired Fuller's development of the **geodesic dome.**

Sculpture

The twentieth century has also seen important and significant developments in sculpture. **August Rodin** (1840–1917) is called the "father of modern sculpture." Despite bad critical reactions to his first works, he began to win recognition and was commissioned to make a bronze door for a Paris museum. Though the door was never completed, some of his later works, such as *The Thinker,* were based on figures planned for the door. He constantly experimented with new techniques and ideas. He made sculptures of hands alone; sometimes, he carved part of a body from a stone and left much of the block uncut and unpolished. **Constantin Brancusi** (1876–1957), born in Romania, explored an ovoid theme throughout his life, abstracting into stone or metal the essence of physical life-forms. American sculptor **Alexander Calder** (1898–1976), with his engineering background, created incredible animated toys before he became widely known for his freestanding metal **stabiles** and his **mobiles** with moving elements (see fig. 4.19).

English sculptor **Henry Moore** (1898–1986) carved and cast enormous, reclining and seated figures, often using the theme of mother and child. Such natural forms as driftwood, polished stones, and shells, as well as archaic Mexican sculpture, influenced Moore. In 1929, he began piercing holes through solid masses in his works to create negative spaces. He liked his works to be displayed outdoors. Also from England, **Barbara Hepworth** (1903–1975) moved from biomorphic to geometric forms, exploring the inter-play of voids and solid masses, and reducing her forms to simple shapes with subtle finishes.

Marino Marini (1901–1980) of Italy depicted the same theme—a horse and rider—many times. His figures often show a primitive roughness, as if they had recently been excavated. **David Smith** (1906–1965) is known for his cubiform elements of stainless steel—polished, abraded, and arranged at odd angles. Displayed monumentally against the sky, his sculptures command extraordinary authority. **Alberto Giacometti** (1901–1966), a Swiss sculptor, cast sticklike figures of varying scale, often placing them in dramatic groups (see fig. 6.35).

Louise Nevelson (1899–1988), an American of Russian Jewish origin, made sculptures composed of found objects, usually wood, arranged in boxes or shelves and occupying a wall taller than the spectator. The assembled sculpture was sprayed in white, black, or gold, which unified the objects and reduced the shadows. American **Duane Hanson** (1925–) is well known for his life-size figures of fiberglass resin. The figures are realistic to the smallest detail, are dressed in real garments, and often hold real props (see colorplate 15 in the Color Gallery). As a child, **Marisol** (1930–) often traveled to Venezuela and New York with her wealthy French parents. Her brightly painted sculptures of boxy figures are made of wood plaster and found objects, and they satirize contemporary customs and manners (see colorplate 17 in the Color Gallery). **Judy Chicago** (1939–), though trained as a painter, gained enormous recognition with her large, collaborative projects that show feminist content. *The Dinner Party* tells women's history through thirty-nine place settings arranged on a triangular table, each dedicated to a great woman in the past (see fig. 6.36). Chicago has also written books and made films.

Minimalism and Postmodern Art

In the early twentieth century, cubism was born and was later followed by all sorts of innovative art that gradually came to be described as **modern art.** Soon, young artists

Figure 6.36   Judy Chicago, *The Dinner Party—Judy Chicago,* **1979. Mixed, 47 ft. per side.**
© Judy Chicago, 1979. Photo by Donald Woodman.

Figure 6.35   Alberto Giacometti, *Man Pointing,* **1947. Bronze, 70½ in. x 40¾ × 16⅜ in.**
The Museum of Modern Art, New York. Gift of Mrs. John D. Rockefeller 3rd. Photograph © 1997 The Museum of Modern Art, New York. © Artists Rights Society (ARS), New York/ ADAGP, Paris.

began challenging the status quo of modern art. A group of artists began creating works called **minimalism**—art that reduces visual images to basic, simple geometric shapes and forms, eliminating all expressive content. All but the essence of a shape allows viewers pure meditative responses. Works are often large and use industrial fabrication materials and techniques.

Beginning in the mid-1960s, **postmodern art,** meaning "after modernism," began. Postmodern artworks are mostly reactions to modern art, especially to minimalism and pop art. The images are often excessively ornamental. Postmodern art often uses images, techniques, and ideas

Figure 6.37   Renzo Piano and Richard Rogers, *Centre National d'Art et de Culture Georges Pompidou, Paris,* **1971–77.**
Photo by Barbara Herberholz.
An example of postmodern architecture.

from history, in contrast to modern artists, who strove to discard the past and aimed at individual innovations. While modern artists concentrated on creating a special style, postmodernists may change styles and media frequently. Included in postmodernism are conceptual art, earthworks, photorealism, and neoexpressionism.

Figure 6.38   Maru Hoeber, *Momentary Fleets,* **1982.**
This was a temporary (six-week) site-specific sculpture installed in the Sacramento River for Sculpture Sacramento, a competition that focused on the creation of public art. It consisted of fourteen 6 to 9 ft. origami boats folded from 40 ft. squares of water-resistant paper.
Photo by Maru Hoeber.

■ AFRICAN ART

The enormous continent of Africa is three times the size of the United States. Its geography features forests, deserts, grassy savannas, and highlands. Its tribal people live as nomads or in small farming villages. Each of the many African tribes and kingdoms has its own customs, religion, and language, and each has its own special art. African art varies from realistic to abstract, depending on its function, the particular tribal culture, and the individual artist. Africa's largest art-producing tribe in terms of both quantity and forms is the **Yoruba** (see fig. 6.39).

Art, rather than being a separate entity in Africa, is an integral part of the harmonious blend of the tribe's spiritual and social life. Much African art has been made for social and religious ceremonies—ceremonies to ensure good harvests, to protect the tribe, to honor ancestors, to ensure fertility, to cope with natural forces, and to instruct and motivate daily life. Art objects relate to the spiritual realm; transmit the laws, moral codes, and history of each tribe to its young; and facilitate communication between the people and the world of the supernatural. They also indicate their owners, wealth and status. The objects made serve a vital purpose while also beautifying the environment. Some of the art objects are not made to be permanent but are used for an occasion and then discarded.

Tribes are modeled on an enlarged family, with the family being the basic unit. The leader or chief represents authority and embodies the tribe's power and wealth. The chiefs and councils of elders and subchiefs try to preserve tribal customs, with many rituals to promote fertility and to appease the unknown that might bring death, disease, and

Figure 6.39   *Yoruba Headdress,* nineteenth to twentieth century, Nigeria. Wood, paint, nails; ht. 15¹⁵⁄₁₆ in.
The Metropolitan Museum of Art. The Michael C. Rockefeller Memorial Collection. Bequest of Nelson A. Rockefeller, 1979 (1979.206.192).

disaster. Ritual acts of purity are intended to cleanse an individual of evil forces, strengthen the life force, and restore order after disruption. A priest or medicine man usually supervises rituals. Many ceremonies are directed toward ancestors, who are part of the tribe's power and who may mediate between the natural world and the supernatural. A type of ritual sculpture common to most African groups is a fetish. **Fetishes** are endowed with special powers for particular purposes, perhaps to ward off evil spirits or to attract good ones.

While recent Western art generally has tended to represent a particular artist's expression and his or her view of the world and of society, African art fulfills tribal needs, being used for specific purposes on special occasions. European art often represents nature and makes narrative references; African tribal art relies on formal, direct sculptural qualities, such as exaggerated proportions and emphasized

Figure 6.40   Nimba Mask, Baga tribe of Guinea. Wood, ht. 46½ in.
The Metropolitan Museum of Art. The Michael C. Rockefeller Memorial Collection. Bequest of Nelson A. Rockefeller, 1979 (1979.206.17).

Figure 6.41   Antelope headpiece, nineteenth to twentieth century, Bamana tribe, Mali. Wood, ht. 35⅗ in.
The Metropolitan Museum of Art. The Michael C. Rockefeller Memorial Collection. Gift of Nelson A. Rockefeller, 1964 (1978.412.435).

heads, eyes, mouths, navels, and genitals, to express or embody its power. Mouths and curving horns of an animal may suggest food and survival as well as signify the animal's power.

The wearing of masks and headdresses during ceremonies is believed to ensure that the dancer will be possessed by the spirit or force being portrayed. Tribes place great importance on the ability of these masks to influence the spirit world (see fig. 4.13). Three types of masks are (1) the **face mask,** worn to hide the identity of the person wearing it); (2) the **helmet** (or shoulder mask)—a large,

carved mask that rests on the wearer's shoulders and sometimes weighs 75 pounds and makes the wearer appear 8 feet tall; and (3) the headpiece or **headdress** (worn like a cap). Mask wearers are entirely costumed while performing with dance and music. Masks are used for major community life events and the life cycle of birth, puberty, marriage, and death. Decorated instruments—drums, harps, ladles, and staffs—are also used in rituals. Deities called **orishas,** along with myths, societies, and cults, require a great variety of masks. Masks can also be a mark of authority, with an actual officer or magistrate wearing a police officer's or

Figure 6.42 *Stool with Caryatid,* nineteenth century, Luba tribe, Zaire. Wood, glass beads; ht. 23¼ in. *Boltin Picture Library.*

a judge's mask. Masks have been carved for special functions, rituals, initiation ceremonies, funerals, and agricultural rites. They are designed to give the wearer courage, to frighten the enemy, and to fight evil forces. Some masks are worn for entertainment.

African masks are extremely notable in their impact and form. Picasso and Braque were inspired by these masks as they developed cubism, as was Modigliani when he painted and sculpted his elongated and distorted portraits.

In addition to masks, sculptures of the human figure are dominant African art forms, although animals may lend features and characteristics of special powers. Sculpted figures are usually tranquil, static, and frontal. Monumental in form, if not in size, they are usually made of a single piece of wood with planes that emphasize contrasting shadows. Figures may be divided into abstract pole types (**Sudanese**) and naturalistic rounded types (**Guinea Coast** and **Congo**). Some sculptures honor past tribal members and the dead.

These works are quite abstract, showing amazing creativity and imagination. The sculptures are believed to hold the spirits and energies of the people they honor, since the sculptures do not show how people actually looked. Ancestor figures are not themselves worshiped; rather, they are intermediaries, and many ceremonies are directed toward ancestors. **Reliquaries,** or grave figures, are sculptural forms placed above containers holding the bones of ancestors.

Much of African sculpture is made of wood, often a single log, with a natural oil finish that not only brings out the beauty of the grain but also is believed to enrich the magical power of the carving. Finished carvings are often ornamented with paint, beads, seeds, and fibers. Many carvings were created in the nineteenth and twentieth centuries. Most of what we see today was created during the last hundred years, since climatic conditions did not favor earlier preservation, but these works help us understand the art created by past generations.

White African sculpture shows much variety, it is characteristically well crafted, aesthetically rich, highly abstract, and expressive, and generally shows little regard for realism.

In Mali, the village people of **Dogon** carve stools, jars, bowls, doors, and figures in both human and animal forms that blend geometric and organic shapes. The sculptural design of their houses and granaries, with their organic relationship to the natural contours of hillsides, inspired contemporary city planners.

The aristocratic **Ife** in **Nigeria** peaked between the twelfth and fourteenth centuries. Here, bronze sculptures were made by the lost-wax method of casting, a skill probably learned in Egypt. To the south of Ife was the **Benin** kingdom, where outstanding cast bronze sculptures were created between the sixteenth and nineteenth centuries. The casting technique may have been learned from the Ife in southwestern Nigeria, which was the seat of the Yoruba kingdom from the eleventh until the seventeenth century. Both Benin and Ife sculptures may have roots in the **Nok** culture in present-day northern Nigeria, with pieces of Nok sculpture being dated between the fifth century B.C. and the second century A.D. Both Ife and Benin figure sculptures show much decorative repetition and are quite lifelike, although some are stylized and show distorted proportions.

Many African tribes carve ivory and make objects of clay. Goldsmithing occurs on the Guinea Coast. Weaving is done on simple horizontal or vertical looms, often in narrow bands. Figures may be woven in or stamped on later.

African traditions began to change when trading, Christianity, and Western education were introduced. Cities began to grow, and modern technology created a separation between art and life. Contemporary art objects currently are being created more for their individual aesthetic appeal than for the traditional reasons of the past.

Figure 6.44   Zhu Da, two sheets from an album of ten paintings, Ch'ing dynasty, seventeenth century. Ink on paper, ht. 10⅟₁₆ in.
Courtesy of Freer Gallery of Art, Smithsonian Institution, Washington, D.C. (55.21–B,H.).

Figure 6.43   *Areogun,* 1900–1910, African, Nigeria, Yoruba tribe, Village of Osi. EPA Society mask, wood with polychrome painted decoration, ht. 49½ in.
The Toledo Museum of Art. Purchased with funds from the Libbey Endowment, Gift of Edward Drummond Libbey.

■ CHINESE ART

With four times the population of the United States and a history that is twenty times longer, China has a cultural heritage as old as India's. Chinese art has influenced the art of Japan, Southeast Asia, Korea, and parts of Indonesia.

In early China, the highest forms of expression were calligraphy, painting, and poetry. Students practiced calligraphy for years before becoming painters. By meditating and contemplating nature, the artist was able to translate natural forms with skillful strokes of the brush. Many artists believed in Tao or "The Way," which enabled them to harmonize with nature. They used black ink on white paper or silk, which symbolized the Taoist idea of duality. Also guiding the artist in making landscape paintings were the cosmological principles of **yin** and **yang,** meaning the synthesis of two opposite forces.

Landscape paintings expressed many religious philosophies—the discipline and order of Confucius, the natural and romantic harmony of Tao, and the spiritual and metaphysical insights of Buddhism. The intense colors of Western artists were not available to early Chinese painters; instead, they used black and gray ink, earth colors, and mineral pigments. Of special concern to Chinese artists were trees and mountains, with artists endeavoring to capture their essence or nature. Predominantly horizontal and flat shapes were often stacked vertically to create a feeling of depth.

Skilled use of the brush has long dominated Chinese painting. Fifteen centuries ago, **Hsieh Ho** established a manifesto of six guiding principles that have unified Chinese artists' work ever since: (1) The work must be imbued with life and spirit; (2) the brush must be handled with vigor, giving inner strength to each line; (3) one must be truthful in depicting objects; (4) color should be as it appears in nature; (5) one must attend to harmony in composition and arrangement of the picture; and (6) one should endlessly copy and transcribe masters of the past. Chinese artists spent many years practicing quick, precise strokes, working to show the spirit and the form of the subject through simple, fluid lines that expressed movement, energy, and emotion. Artists were scholars and also used brushes to write.

Over the centuries, Chinese painting styles changed. The artists used three basic formats: (1) The **album leaf** was part of a sequential book that combined calligraphy, poetry, and painting; (2) the **hanging scroll** was vertical in format and stored in a roll (a scroll is a long roll of silk, parchment, or paper; the viewer starts at the bottom and moves the eyes upward); (3) the **handscroll** had a beginning, development, and an end and varied in length from 12 inches to 40 feet. Viewers of a handscroll meditated on each portion of the scene as it unrolled from right to left. Artist and owners added red seal stamps and sometimes wrote poetic thoughts in vertical rows of calligraphy.

After the eleventh century, an increased interest in landscape painting in which ink and watercolors were brushed on silk and paper showed that artists felt that strong colors did not reflect nature's colors and detracted from the brushwork. Line was all important, rather than the light and shadow of Western artists. Colors were softly blended, and if figures were present, they were infused in the surroundings. Buildings, boats, and people were tiny in comparison to the landscape. The Chinese saw the physical universe—earth and sky—as a unit; they believed that the earth was covered with heaven's canopy and that the stars controlled peoples' destiny.

The belief that people should live together peacefully and should respect their elders was reflected in the earliest Chinese paintings, which showed many images of people. After Buddhism came to China, however, Chinese art changed and instead emphasized Buddhist concepts of nature and meditation. Artists focused on a single idea or object so that they could realize the beauty of the idea or object while capturing its mood. The result was fewer people in paintings.

In their gardens, the Chinese used rocks and water as symbols and arranged trees and plant life symbolic of their beliefs concerning the body and the universe. Lords and kings could afford animals in their gardens to symbolize their wealth and power. By 300 B.C. however, gardens began to represent spiritual peace and served as places to worship in the Taoist and Buddhist traditions.

An outline of **Chinese dynasties** and the artworks representative of each dynasty follows. (A dynasty refers to a succession of rulers who were members of the same family.)

Prehistoric (ca. 5000–1700 B.C.)

Tools and weapons made from stone and jade with polished and decorated surfaces are representative of the New Stone Age. Pottery was made to store grain, with painted pieces also being buried in tombs for use in the afterworld. The thin, fragile pots made later were used in rituals.

Shang Dynasty (1700–1111 B.C.)

When they died, Shang rulers were provided with useful and ceremonial objects, as well as chariots, horses, servants, and family members. Bronze ritual vessels for wine or food were cast with inscriptions that told of the occasion of the vessel's creation. These objects were skillfully crafted and sometimes resembled suits of armor. During the Shang and Chou dynasties, many bronze tools, animal forms, vessels, and weapons were produced, all showing a variety of shapes and decoration. Typical is the hollow-legged tripod *Li-Ting* in figure 4.25, which is an example of the piece-mold process rather than the lost-wax method.

Chou (1111–221 B.C.)

In 1111 B.C., Chou people came from the west as conquerors, and images were substituted for live animals and people in the royal tombs. Objects made of jade were used in burials and were thought to be indestructible. Confucianism (ca. 550–478 B.C.) began. Confucius advocated respect for nature and also humility and patience. He advised that people not withdraw from society but take an active role in it. His thinking focused on human relations and the consequences of one's acts, emphasizing mutual responsibility as the basis of ethics and intellectual life. His Golden Rule predated that of Jesus by five hundred years. Taoism (ca. 604 B.C.) emphasized the relationship of human beings to the universe and being in harmony with nature, a principle that is deeply planted in Chinese minds to this day.

Ch'In (221–207 B.C.)

King Cheng, the first emperor of China, was a vicious tyrant who buried scholars alive and burned the *Classical Texts*. However, he united China, saving it from the internal conflicts of the Warring States (475–221 B.C.). He began the construction of the Great Wall as protection from invaders in the north. King Cheng's tomb, which was only recently discovered, was a huge complex of underground palaces and pavilions that contained seventy-five hundred life-size soldiers and horses made of baked clay, using the slab and coil technique.

Modern Period: Han Dynasty (206 B.C.–A.D. 220)

The modern period occurred at the same time as the Roman Empire. Buddhism was introduced from India, and the arts flourished under this new religious spirit. China's borders expanded north to Korea, south to Vietnam, and west to Afghanistan. Silk production increased tremendously, with trade routes reaching Rome and allowing contact with other cultures. Derived from observing the repetition of the seasons, the Chinese idea of duality—*yin* (darkness, dampness, softness, passiveness) and *yang* (brightness, dryness, hardness, action)—greatly influenced art.

The legends of Confucius and Taoism provided much of the material for the early art of the Han dynasty. The number of chambers in tombs increased, so that the tombs looked much like the Han houses of the living. Elaborate murals on the walls showed narrative storytelling scenes. Bronze mirrors with polished fronts and low-relief designs on the reverse sides were placed in tombs to bring the dead person into ultimate harmony. Technology improved, giving much vitality to art. Rubbings over carved reliefs became popular. Artisans carved elaborate designs in objects after hundreds of coats of lacquer had been applied. When the Han dynasty collapsed, China fell into chaos until the T'ang dynasty came to power about four hundred years later.

Six Dynasties and Northern Wei (A.D. 221–618)

For three hundred years, China had many short-lived dynasties in the south. The Tartars (non-Chinese people) founded the Wei dynasty in the north. They adopted Chinese customs and Buddhism. Ninety percent of the people of northern China had adopted Buddhism by A.D. 400. Enormous Buddhas, relief carvings, and paintings represented a mix of Indian, central Asian, and Chinese cultures. Monasteries and Buddhist temple complexes were established. Monks carved the famous Colossal Buddha into stone cliffs in the Gobi Desert, and other Buddhas were carved in caves and dwellings, the caves being used as way stations by travelers on the Silk Road. The temple complexes consisted of buildings arranged across a central axis within a walled compound. One of the buildings was a **pagoda,** a tower made up of several stories, which was the Chinese version of the Indian stupa. Another building housed the sculptures of the main deities. Small figures made of gilt bronze were objects of dedication and used in temples, shrines, and homes.

T'ang Dynasty (A.D. 618–907)

The T'ang dynasty became the largest and most powerful civilization in the world. Fine arts and decorative arts—goldware, textiles, and glass—flourished. Thousands of household articles and human figures have been recovered from T'ang tombs. During this time, Chinese sculpture, expressing the new vigor of the Buddhist faith, flourished, although non-Buddhist art, with its lively ceramic horses and riders that represented the warriors who kept order at home and safeguarded the borders, perhaps tells more of T'ang's vigor. The horse has always been a popular image in Chinese art, and many stone carvings, clay modelings, and cast bronze horses were made at this time. A decorative style of landscape painting ("blue and green") and figure painting reached a high point. In the late T'ang period, poetic monochromatic landscapes painted in ink on silk appeared. Prints were carved from woodcut blocks and printed on large presses. Tea drinking became popular, necessitating the production of decorative ceramic ware. Porcelain, a hard, white, nonporous, translucent ceramic was developed at this time, eight hundred years before it was produced in Europe.

Sung Dynasty (A.D. 960–1127 [Northern]; A.D. 1128–1279 [Southern])

The powerful Sung dynasty is famous for its scrolls, which were often 50 feet long, and its classical examples of porcelain, each identified by the name of the village that produced it. Although landscapes were painted during the T'ang, the best examples were produced during the Sung dynasty. These works, with their deep, mystical space and airy landscapes, showed a reverence for nature combined with Confucian philosophy and the serenity of Buddha. Monumental landscape paintings, usually with a large mountain, were typical of Northern Sung, while Southern Sung paintings showed a sense of calm, peace, and humans' unity with nature (see fig. 6.45). These scrolls were viewed in private, not displayed on museum walls as they are in the West. Also of high quality were the woven and embroidered silks and tapestries, along with lacquerware, carved jades, hardstones, and ivory carvings.

Yuan Dynasty (ca. A.D. 1280–1368)

During the Yuan dynasty, cities grew, and silk and ceramic items were exported to other countries. The miserable situation

of foreign domination brought a change of status for artists, and this period is one of individuality and inventiveness. Paintings were more assertive, with some artists discarding ink washes and substituting dry brush lines. Pottery became heavier, while the shapes became sturdier. Overglaze enamels and underglaze designs were introduced.

Ming Dynasty (A.D. 1368–1644)

Porcelain reached a high point during the Ming dynasty. Some painters produced in the conservative traditional manner, and others worked as individualistic scholar-gentlemen, basing their style on various sources. The **Imperial Palace** (Forbidden City) was established at this time.

Ch'ing Dynasty (A.D. 1644–1911)

The Ch'ing dynasty emphasized intricate patterns, bright colors, and technical perfection in ceramics. Thousands of workers produced ceramics for export to Europe. **Courtyard gardens,** through which people could walk in covered corridors while looking out lattice windows, became popular. Painting and calligraphy flourished.

The People's Republic of China (A.D. 1949–Present)

China's art since 1949 has reflected the social and political life of the new government. Many posters have been produced, their themes related to political and popular heroes, defense, women-centered issues, minorities, and political propaganda. Images are representational, as there is no place for pure abstraction.

Figure 6.45   Attributed to Mu Qi, *Swallow and Lotus,* **Chinese, Southern Sung dynasty, mid-thirteenth century. Hanging scroll, ink on silk, 91.8 × 47 cm.** © *The Cleveland Museum of Art, 1997, Purchase from the J. H. Wade Fund 1981.34.*

Figure 6.46   Wu Zhen, *Poetic Feeling in a Thatched Pavilion,* **Chinese, Yuan dynasty, 1280–1354. Hand scroll, ink on paper, 23.8 × 99.4 cm.** © *The Cleveland Museum of Art, 1997. Leonard C. Hanna Jr. Fund 1963.259.*

Figure 6.47   Kung Hsien, two details of *Landscapes in the Manner of Tung Yuan,* Ch'ing dynasty, late seventeenth century. Handscroll, ink on paper, ht. 10½ in., full length 31 ft. 10 in. Top is Section 2; bottom is Section 6. *The Nelson-Atkins Museum of Art, Kansas City, Missouri. (Purchase: Nelson Trust) 48-44.*

■ INDIAN ART

Present-day India, only half the size of the United States, has a larger population than North and South America combined. As far back as 3000 B.C., a Neolithic culture existed in the Indus Valley, in what is now Pakistan. It had large cities, paved streets, fortifications, and blocks of houses and public buildings. Excavations have located pottery, carved seals, and sculptures of small female figures, attesting to a mother-goddess cult. Small **seals,** used to sign legal documents and contracts, were carved in reverse and contain animal designs replete with anatomical detail; the human form is more abstract and simplified.

To understand the art of India, we need to understand something of this country's two leading religions—Hinduism and Buddhism—which have shaped India's art during the last twenty-five hundred years. **Hinduism** incorporated earlier native beliefs and art traditions, with Hindu artists dealing with stories and legends about the major gods. Tribes from the north invaded India about 2000 B.C. and introduced the **Vedas,** hymns similar to the ancient Greek myths or the Old Testament poems. These became the **Upanishads,** marking the beginnings of Hinduism, the world's oldest religion. Much of Indian art is based on Hinduism, which began about 700 B.C. It has many gods and is

rich in images. Not having a single leader, Hinduism is a collection of the beliefs and ideas of many peoples and various cultures. **Reincarnation** (rebirth in another form) and **karma** (reward or punishment based on behavior in a previous life) are two strong Hindu beliefs. Hinduism is based on an identity of humans with nature. Hindus believe that people can learn about the universe through worship. The Hindu's goal is to find the true nature of the self in light of the only real Existence, or Brahma, with all people on a cycle of reincarnation until they finally become one with Brahma.

Cast metal Indian sculptures are filled with symbolic meaning, depicting Hindu gods and expressing the creative force of the universe. Indian art has many animal forms, especially **Ganesha,** an elephant that symbolizes prosperity for his worshipers. Many early pieces of Indian art reflect the Hindu concept of reincarnation, as well as myths about Brahma, the creator; Vishnu, the preserver; and Shiva, the destroyer.

Many gods represent different aspects of nature. Especially important are **Vishnu,** the preserver of the world; **Krisha,** believed to be an incarnation of Vishnu; and **Indra** a god of war with many arms that symbolize his inner energy. **Shiva** is a puzzling Hindu god and symbolizes creativity as well as the myth of death. The hand that points to

Figure 6.48 Nataraja: *Shiva As King of Dance,* **South India, Chola period, Bronze sculpture, eleventh century. ht. 111.5 cm** © *The Cleveland Museum of Art, 1997. Purchase from the J. H. Wade Fund, 1930.331.*

Figure 6.49 *Seated Buddha,* **India, Gandhara region, Kushar period, Gray schist sculpture, first half of third century** A.D. **100 × 29.5 cm.** © *The Cleveland Museum of Art, 1997. Leonard C. Hanna, Jr., Fund 1961.418.*

the foot shows that the dance represents life; the fourth hand assures us that all is well and that death/life, or creativity and change, are part of our lives. Shiva is the god who destroys creation as old age destroys youth. Shiva is depicted as god of dance, god of bounty and of wrath, god of destruction and fertility. Many Shivas were made during the eleventh century.

Hindu gods have certain characteristics: Shiva has three eyes; Brahma has four faces; many gods have four arms. These attributes symbolize extraordinary knowledge and power.

Hindu architects cut great temples directly into solid "living" rock formations in the belief that rock was the matrix that contained the potential of all forms.

While Hinduism is rooted in prehistoric times, Buddhism emerged from it about 500 B.C. Siddhartha Gautama, the Enlightened One who established Buddhism, was born the son of a rich nobleman about five hundred years before Christ. Until the gods arranged for him to see four signs depicting old age, illness, death, and hunger, he was kept from seeing any suffering. He preached a life of withdrawal from earthly individuality, one in which the goal was **nirvana,** the ultimate release from rebirth and entry into oneness with the universe. In early artworks, Buddha is represented symbolically, rather than as a human form, by the

lotus, the **wheel,** the **bodhi tree,** the **footprint,** or the **stupa.** The first images of Buddha in human form appeared during the Kushan dynasty (ca. A.D. 50–320). Occupations by Alexander the Great's Greek legions had brought contact with Greek and Roman civilizations, and the style of the early sculptures of Buddha showed this influence. These early sculptures show Buddha seated cross-legged (lotus position) and include a third eye on the forehead, long earlobes, and a hand motion. The third eye looks within. A bump on top of the head symbolizes enlightenment and wisdom. Long earlobes indicate the weight of heavy jewelry and tell that Buddha was once a prince. Sculptures of Buddha are still and static, focusing on peace, contemplation, and meditation.

Indian paintings are seen in temple murals, manuscript pages with miniature illustrations, and palm-leaf paintings. These paintings show a love of the ideal. Buildings often are not painted in proportion to figures, since the events shown were considered more important. Perspective is often tilted, and shadows are lacking.

Indian architects built **stupas,** beehive-shaped domed buildings that evolved from burial mounds, early on to honor Buddha and other important leaders. These burial mounds contain relics of Buddha's body and are pilgrimage sites for his followers. Stupas indicate Buddha's royalty and have four gates covered with relief sculpture (depicting Buddha's previous lives), through which believers enter and then walk around the dome while meditating and reading Buddhist teachings carved on the walls. The stupa, with its parts determined by rigid rules of magical proportions, is a cosmic symbol that is a small replica of the universe.

Buddhism and Hinduism have shared the same architectural styles. At **Khajuraho,** a number of sacred Hindu, Buddhist, and some Jainist (Jainist is a branch of Hinduism) temples were built around the eleventh century, yet all have similarities. With conical domes and elaborately carved surfaces, the impressive Hindu temple dedicated to Shiva as Mahadeva, Lord of Lords, reminds us of a group of beehives. Sanctuaries and halls are found within its walls. Most of the ancient temples employ post-and-lintel construction; that is, the walls, or columns or posts, support a heavy masonry ceiling.

The Gupta dynasty (A.D. 320–600) is called the golden age of Buddhist art. Artists began depicting Buddha with a bony protuberance on the top of his head, wheels on his palms and soles, webbed fingers, elongated ears, and a third eye. Wall paintings show detailed views of courtly elegance. Crowns, necklaces, bracelets, and patterned cloth show intricate designs and craftsmanship.

Hinduism revived in the latter part of the Gupta dynasty, and during the Pallava dynasty (A.D. 500–750), sculptured temples with numerous deities were carved from rounded outcroppings of granite. High-relief sculptures show episodes in the lives of the more than three thousand Hindu deities that represent symbols, aspects, or attributes. The greatest of all the rock temples was carved around A.D.750 to 900 and is in western India at Ellura. It features a sanctuary, shrines, and enormous life-size elephants. During the Chola dynasty (ca. A.D. 907–1053), cast bronze sculptures achieved a high quality of excellence.

Muslims from Afghanistan arrived in northern India during the eighth century. Most of the area was united under Mogul leaders by 1526. Muslims brought with them aspects of Persian culture that were changed somewhat by Indian concepts. Court painters copied European paintings and began using shading and showing depth. They depicted romances, epics, and historical events. In the Mogul's attempt to eliminate imagery, many Hindu and

Buddhist temples were destroyed and replaced with palaces with formal gardens and mosques. These were made of marble and set with precious stones and mosaics. Painting studios were closed, and the weaving of gold cloth was banned during the declining years of the Mogul culture.

Southern India escaped Mogul domination. During the Nayak dynasty (ca. A.D. 1550–1743), long, covered galleries were added to the existing temples. Enclosed by high stone walls and topped with towers, the temples featured many carved and painted Hindu deities.

During the Rajput dynasty (A.D.1500–1800), a local literature developed that focused on love stories and heroes. Various illustration styles developed in different regions; some were quite colorful and highly patterned. Rajput paintings lacked perspective, illusions of depth, and shading.

Fabric arts are important in India and include fine embroidery pieces, woven items, printed fabric, and fabric decorated by the batik process. Decorations are often intricate with overall patterns and borders. **Batik,** a wax-resist technique used for decorating fabrics, has reached a high degree of excellence in India. Designs are applied with melted wax, a dye is applied, and the wax is removed

The British East India Company, and later the English Crown, developed trade during the nineteenth century. India became independent in 1947, with Pakistan being partitioned as a Muslim state. Many buildings in present-day India reflect British influence, but the art of India still depicts its religion principally in the traditional styles that are hundreds of years old.

■ ISLAMIC ART

About A.D. 600, a new religion that was to become one of the world's largest took shape about 2,000 miles east of India in the city of Mecca. Followers of Islam are called Muslims. Within a hundred years, the Islamic religion spread westward from Arabia (now Iran) to Spain and east to India. The Arabian prophet **Muhammed,** a merchant who, in A.D. 613, started preaching a faith that centered on one god called **Allah,** founded the Islamic religion. Muhammed incorporated his beliefs in the **Koran.** The calligraphy (beautiful writing) in this book is alive with flowing letters, circular gold decorations, and arabesques. (**Arabesques** are decorative, flat, abstract designs of plant life done in swirling geometric patterns.) Muhammed eliminated slavery, gambling, and wine, and taught that people were accountable for their deeds, reaping punishment in the afterlife. The five **Pillars of Islam** are faith, prayer, alms-giving, fasting, and a once-in-a-lifetime pilgrimage to Mecca.

Since Muslims believed that death in battle for their faith promised them entry to Paradise, Islam spread by force. New conquests were commemorated by the

Figure 6.50 *Sita in the Garden of Lanka* from the *Ramayana, Epic of Valmiki,* ca. 1720, India, Pahari, Guler School. Gold and color painted on paper, 55.5 × 79 cm. © *The Cleveland Museum of Art, 1997. Gift of George P. Bickford 1966.143.*

construction of a **mosque,** a Muslim house of worship that must be oriented toward Mecca. Each mosque has a wall with niches called **mihrabs,** a staired pulpit, and at least one tower, called a **minaret,** from which the faithful are called to prayer five times a day.

Early Muslim teachings did not allow depictions of animals or humans, and these images are only seen in art about everyday life or about the court. Thus, arabesques and other geometric designs are used to decorate tiles, rugs, miniature paintings, and many craft objects. Rich calligraphy, Persian rugs, elaborate compositions, and highly decorative and stylized landscapes are typical of Islamic art. Islamic artists strongly desired to fill all spaces with patterned motifs. Since the representation of nature and even the human form is forbidden, Islamic art is rich in abstract symbolism. Persian carpets serve as prayer rugs, floor coverings, blankets, cushions, and saddle bags. They are often designed in a medallion pattern of rich colors, incorporating abstract flowers and animals.

Islamic architectural works have achieved a high degree of beauty. Mosques are covered with mosaics and filigree in geometric designs on the carved walls and on stained-glass windows. Designs for these geometric patterns are called **tessellations,** meaning that the repeated shapes fit together perfectly.

The first Moors landed in Spain in A.D. 711, and the last left in 1492. In 1248, when they controlled much of Spain, they built a famous palace, worship place, and citadel—the **Alhambra**—using the characteristic filigree and tile on the many walls, ceilings, and arches. During the 800s, Spain had some three hundred Muslim mosques. The architecture is slightly ethereal, with sequences of arches, spindly columns, and pierced stone screens. The white marble Taj Mahal in India, built in 1632 in memory of a Muslim ruler's wife, is a well-known, elegant structure with its fine filigree, beautiful gardens, and reflecting pools.

During the fifteenth to the seventeenth centuries, Persian **miniatures** were at their height. Due to the restriction on depicting the human figure, these miniatures were highly decorative and were hidden in books. Rules, mostly from China, required that artists use no shading and no perspective, with the views being from slightly above and with the horizon at the top and all the figures the same size. Different scenes are sometimes within one composition. Landscapes and architecture may be seen in the backgrounds. Colors are decorative rather than realistic, and variations in proportion often show a servant smaller than his master. Because of rules established by Islamic laws, faces show no emotion, even though a scene might be romantic or violent, because this might disturb the desired peaceful effect. The unifying use of tiny patterns to fill in the background tends to create a lack of deep space. For the paints, finely ground minerals were sifted through silk before being mixed with a binder. Silk and linen paper was polished with a crystal egg or mother-of-pearl.

■ JAPANESE ART

Throughout history, Japanese artists have selectively assimilated external cultural influences, especially from China, and creatively absorbed and transformed these influences into unique Japanese art forms. The name *Japan* comes from Chinese characters that mean "Land of the Rising Sun." Japan has had many fiercely proud rulers who saw in art a means to political ends, as well as objects of beauty for beauty's sake.

Shintoism and **Buddhism** are Japan's two basic religions. Shintoism grew from a primitive form of ancestor worship and emphasizes reverence for family, race, and the rulers as the direct descendants of the gods. Buddhism was introduced in the sixth century from Korea.

The great theme of Japanese art has been the combination of human beings and nature and natural materials. Japan's wood buildings harmonize with natural settings. Both architecture and sculpture tend to be on an intimate human scale and show skilled craftsmanship. Inside the small Japanese houses of wood, paper, and fiber is often found a singular flower arrangement or a painting whose subjects reflect their love of nature. Early Japanese art served religious beliefs, but the art of the last three hundred years increasingly shows the secular interests of many different classes of people.

Japanese art tends to be less formal and more expressive, concrete, particular, narrative, decorative, and public than Chinese art. In both countries, painting is closely related to writing, and calligraphy is considered a fine art. Chinese and Japanese paintings do not use Western ideas of perspective and shading, leaning toward linear rather than modeled form, using asymmetrical balance, and treating space as an active rather than a negative element. Japanese paintings often tell stories, and tend to be more detailed and decorative than Chinese painting. Artists paint scrolls and screens with calligraphic brush strokes and use perspective to give the illusion of space. Japanese ceramics are well designed and skillfully crafted.

The vigorous and decorative Japanese landscape paintings strongly contrast with the subtle brush-and-ink landscapes of the Chinese. Japanese artists often applied colors in a flat manner in conjunction with a gold or silver background. The Japanese also were more interested than the Chinese in showing figures in storytelling situations. Although both countries made hanging scrolls, the Japanese hanging scrolls show more angular brushwork and a hard-edge technique. A

Figure 6.51   Katsushika Hokusai, *Fuji in Clear Weather*, 1831–33. Japanese, Ukiyoye School, 1760–1849. Color woodblock print, 25.5 × 37.5 cm.
© The Cleveland Museum of Art, 1997. Bequest of Edward L. Whittemore 1930.189.

tilted perspective in Japanese painting tends to give a bird's-eye view of buildings without roofs or walls. Around the eleventh century, screen paintings appeared and were used to brighten the interiors of homes and temples.

Zen, a religious sect focused on meditation, inspired the tea ceremony. Other notable Japanese art forms include flower arranging and garden design. Japanese **dry gardens** emphasize texture and pattern. Garden artists may use a large stone to symbolize an island and then rake sand in beautiful patterns to represent the waves of the sea. Bronze, wood, and dry lacquer show Buddhist influence. Some sculpture is decorated with inlaid stone, gilded, or painted. Dramas and dances call for the creation of unique masks. The architectural design of Japanese homes features modular walls and sliding screens. Huge castles, shrines, and palaces exemplify typical Japanese styles.

Japanese woodblock prints (**ukiyo-e,** meaning pictures of the "floating world") captured scenes from everyday life. As early as the eighth century, these multiple prints were used to create inexpensive religious images and to illustrate books. During the Edo period (A.D. 1615–1868), the Japanese made many of these affordable prints. A prosperous merchant class and changes in lifestyles produced the art of ukiyo-e. Games, theaters, festivals, love, fashion, music, dancing, and hairstyles were all subject matter for these artists. Though the school of ukiyo-e began with painting, thousands of these woodblock prints were produced for mass consumption and reflected rapid changes in tastes and styles. These popular pictures have been called "magnificent scraps of paper" and "poor man's art" because common folk could afford them. Japanese woodcut prints, especially those by Hiroshige, Hokusai, Harunobu, and

Utamaro, are known worldwide. In the early days, professional wood carvers translated the artist's drawing. Hokusai was the only artist who could do his own carving. When trade with Europe opened in the nineteenth century, these artists learned of paintings that were done by single artists and began to make the entire print themselves. In turn, many Western artists—Cassatt, Gauguin, van Gogh, Matisse, and Monet, for instance—were intrigued and influenced by Japanese woodblock prints, with their emphasis on linear elements, the flat use of color, the bird's-eye view, and space not used merely as background but as a part of the design.

Utamaro (1753–1806) created a standard of sensuality and worldliness in his female subjects, using expressive lines and a plain background. **Hokusai** (1760–1849), born in Edo, the capital of Japan, was adopted by an important artisan family because he was a younger son. As an apprentice to a mirror maker, he learned engraving and later applied his skills to cutting woodblocks. He tried his hand at a number of occupations and had more than fifty different names during his life. He became Hokusai when he was forty-six. Most of the work for which he is famous was done after he was seventy years old. Hokusai experimented with Western motifs and techniques and led and created a renewal of interest in the Japanese landscape. In later years, he signed his works "Old Man Mad about Drawing." He died at age eighty-nine. **Hiroshige's** (1797–1858) landscapes were more realistic than Hokusai's, and he often depicted seasons and changes in weather.

Important periods in the history of Japanese art follow.

Archaic Period (Pre-Buddha) Jomon Culture (5000–200 B.C. [in the South])

Clay pottery with incised or cord-impressed designs (4000–250 B.C.) are the earliest art objects from Japan. These were found at pit dwellings of the Neolithic hunter-gatherers called Jomon. Also found were small clay or stone figures, decorated bracelets, earrings, and blades of bone, ivory, and horn. Pottery figures with animal and human features guarded grave sites.

(Pre-Buddha) Yayoi Culture (200 B.C.–A.D. 300 [in the South])

Rice cultivation began, and wheel-thrown pots with smooth surfaces were made. The Yayoi culture is best known for its blades, mirrors, and swords, and for its bronze ceremonial bells decorated with representations or abstractions of daily and ceremonial scenes. It also had pottery grave guardians (horses, warriors, and swords) that were more sophisticated than those of the Jomon culture.

(Pre-Buddha) Kofan (Old Mound) (A.D. 300–ca. 650)

People of the Kofan culture built enormous, mounded tombs surrounded by moats for emperors and clan leaders. The tombs were elaborately equipped with fired clay miniatures of people, animals, and houses. Clay figures were placed around the mound as "guards." Jewels, iron weapons, and bronze mirrors were found in some tomb interiors. A new equestrian and military culture is seen in later artifacts. Asian cultural influences came to Japan.

Japanese reverence for nature is the basis of Shinto, the Way of the Gods. Shinto is the oldest practiced religion in Japan. Ancestors and Kami (gods in nature) are honored with prayers and gifts. Because Shintoists do not focus on an afterlife, ceremonies relate to such aspects of life as harvests, peace, and health. The wooden gate or entrance to Shinto shrines is made of two pillars holding an inverted arch, reminiscent of a pagoda roof. With the frame as a symbol for the sky, the structure's horizontal bar stands for the earth. The Sun Goddess lives in a bronze mirror in the main buildings of the Great Shrine at Ise, the ancestral shrine of the imperial family and the most sacred Shinto shrine in Japan.

Asuke (A.D. 555–710)

The Japanese eagerly adopted Buddhism in 552 when a Korean king sent Buddhist scriptures, a bronze Buddha, and lavish gifts to the Japanese court. Buddhists believe that humans are at one with nature. Buddhism brought to Japan a sophisticated and complex religious doctrine, complete with cultural traditions and developed art forms. **Prince Shotoku** (A.D. 592–622) was instrumental in the spread of Buddhism, importing Chinese artistic, literary, philosophical, and political forms. Large temple complexes built for ceremonies incorporated pagodas (towers several stories high, with roofs curving upward at the corners, that contained relics of Buddha). Mainly built of wood with tile roofs, these temples were different in design from their counterpart, the Indian stupa. Painted or gold-leafed wood was the favored sculptural material. Since Buddhism originated in India, many of the images show Hindu influences. Early sculptures were modeled of clay, and some were carved in wood and cast in bronze. When new emperors came into power, they would have a new Buddha cast, each ruler trying to have his Buddha made larger than any before to demonstrate the emperor's important position.

Nara (A.D. 710–794)

The capital was moved to Heian in 784, and a golden age began, with Japan adopting much of Chinese culture at this time. The dominant clan, the Fujiwaras, surrounded the court with artists who created lacquered wooden carvings and high-quality painted scrolls. Painting and sculpture adapted Chinese Buddhist themes. The T'ang style predominated in Buddhist architecture, painting, and sculpture. Large, lifelike sculptures were produced in dry lacquer and bronze, along with unfired clay sculptures, which originated in India. Most buildings were made of wood, which fire, weather, and wars easily destroyed. Buildings were often rebuilt and changed, the architecture never being completely static. Roofs were massive, elaborate, and supported by huge pillars. Most walls, interior and exterior, were moving panels that could be rearranged. Gardens contained many views, landscapes, and visual surprises, and provided artistic and spiritual balance, expressing themes based on philosophies of beauty or the meaning of life. Gardens had several elements: rocks, which represented islands, mountains, and so on; water, which stood for the continuity of life and the sea, and also provided for the musical sound of waterfalls; and shrubbery, which was shaped and trimmed as a piece of sculpture. Love of nature was seen indoors in the form of **bonsai** (dwarf trees) and **ike bano** (floral arrangements).

Heian (A.D. 794–1185)

When the Fujiwara clan gained control of the throne and moved the capital to the city of Heian, a native Japanese artistic style began to replace the heavily influenced Chinese technique. Early sculptures were carved from solid wood and left unpainted so as not to impair the wood's fragrance. The Japanese court ended diplomatic missions to China in 894, with the result that the Japanese began creating more of their own artworks—paintings of the numerous deities of new religious sects. The Pure Land sect favored light and graceful architecture to contain their seated Buddhas and his attendants. Temple complexes contained peaceful gardens, ponds, and large sculptures. Late Heian (Fujiwara, A.D. 897–1185) was marked by luxurious pomp and elegant court life. Illustrated novels on handscrolls had the text presented in calligraphy, which was considered as important an art form as the pictures. This style in Japanese art is thought of as the first pure example of Japanese art. Decorated screens for dividing rooms were another art form. In 1185, civil war ended what is called the golden age, ushering in political upheaval for 430 years.

Kamakura (A.D. 1185–1333)

Zen, a Buddhist sect introduced from China, spread during the Kamakura period. It was marked by strong self-discipline and meditation, and was attuned to the active and violent samurai; the warrior class supported it. Zen advocated

Figure 6.52 *Guardian Figure,* **Kamakura period, 1183–1333, Japanese, Shiga Prefecture. Wood, ht. 168.5 cm.**
© *The Cleveland Museum of Art, 1997. Leonard C. Hanna, Jr., Fund 1972.159.*

intuitive and emotional responses to life situations. It emphasized the Buddha-nature in humans and nature. Continuous warfare destroyed Buddhist temples, but a new military government later restored them. A new, vigorous, realistic style of art began, leading to portraits of warriors, priests, and common citizens. Sculptured temple guardians, lifelike in anatomy and color, and some possessing glass eyes, were vividly real to frighten evil spirits. The *Guardian Figure* (see fig. 6.52), with its feeling of ferocity, energy, and movement, is typical of this period. **Ukiyo-e,** depicting scenes of Japanese life, was a new art style that emerged with the arrival of peace. Zen monks introduced new art forms, including scroll painting **(makimono).** These were elaborate depictions of warriors' exploits and daily lives, and were painted with bright colors and bold pattern. Art became more realistic, more colorful, and less religious. Sculpture, under Zen influence, declined. The harmony between works of human origin and natural objects influenced the design of homes, gardens, and temples.

Ashikaga (A.D. 1336–1573)

With a weak central government, the Ashikaga period (also known as the Muramachi period) was a time of violent social unrest and upheaval. Zen thinkers developed the starkly beautiful dry or rock gardens, using bright and dark rocks and carefully raked sand or pebbles to symbolize waves, the sea, ships, and islands. They carefully arranged elements in these remarkable artistic abstractions to create an illusion of movement. The first Europeans (Dutch and Portugese) arrived and set up trading posts, and Christian missionaries began efforts to convert the people. The Japanese grew suspicious of these foreigners, thereby planting the seeds of Japan's fear of the outside world.

Momoyama (A.D. 1573–1615)

In 1573, the emperor expelled the military shogun and also destroyed monasteries and killed monks to break the political power of the Buddhists. Daimyo, the emperor's successor, brought together the great families, enabling Japan to have one rule after 250 years of disunity. Art was revitalized. Narrative and portrait painting flourished. The art of ink brush painting (**sumi**) was introduced, and puppet theater became popular. Daimyo built palace-fortresses, surrounded by moats and reflecting the grandeur and wealth of their masters, which soon became the new cultural centers. Official residences had brilliantly painted screens and sliding doors, while private homes had a subdued style with small teahouses. The tea ceremony, a graceful and beautiful ritual, reflected the subtle relationships of human beings to ritual and nature. The ceramics industry responded by creating many styles of pottery to meet the need, among them "Raku ware" and "Shino ware." In 1592, Korean potters introduced Chinese porcelain. The Japanese Kakiemon ware showed a greater freedom of design. The capital shifted to Edo, the future Tokyo, after 1650. A prosperous society was united and strong. Traders were expelled, and Japanese Christians were strenuously persecuted, with thousands being killed. Foreign books and technical knowledge were outlawed. Japan was almost entirely cut off from the outside world.

Tokugawa (Edo) (A.D. 1615–1868)

The Tokugawa (Edo) period was named for a village that became Tokyo. At this time, Japan's isolation provided peaceful stability (see colorplate 19 in Color Gallery). Home design emphasized being surrounded by nature. Refined tea ceremonies provided time for contemplation and

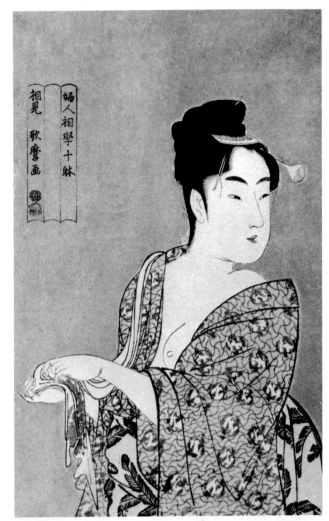

Figure 6.53   Kitagawa Utamaro, *Uwaki, Noso, Half-Length Portrait*, Japanese, 1753–1806, Edo period. Color woodblock print, 36.2 × 25.4 cm.
© *The Cleveland Museum of Art, 1997. Bequest of Edward L. Whittemore 1930.218.*

relaxation, with an emphasis on simplicity and humility. Japan's isolation radically changed in 1854, when Commodore Perry's war fleet appeared and forced the shogun to open Japanese ports to the West. A growing, wealthy middle class demanded artworks for their homes, and such masters as Hokusai, Hiroshige, Utamaro, and Harunobu created inexpensive and easily reproduced woodblock prints. They originally portrayed actors and courtesans, but soon began depicting all subjects. Utamaro introduced large head portraits of generalized beauties, focusing on the elements of shape and color (see fig. 6.53). The energetic and imaginative Hokusai, with his thirty-six views of Mount Fuji, and the popular Hiroshige, with his poetic depictions of the country's weather and seasons, were two great landscape

Figure 6.54 Soga Shokahu, *Orchid Pavilion Gathering*, **Edo period, 1730–81, Japanese. Hanging scroll, ink on silk, 122.5 × 55.5 cm.**
© *The Cleveland Museum of Art, 1997, Purchase from the J. H. Wade Fund, 1979.53.*

artists of the early nineteenth century. These late ukiyo-e prints of Japanese subjects show the influence of Western perspective and shading while symbolizing Japanese reverence for country and nature.

Meiji (A.D. 1868–1912)

The shogunate was discredited, and power was restored to the throne. This was the beginning of a period of rapid industrialization that quickly elevated Japan to a position of world power.

Taisho (A.D. 1912–1926); Showa (A.D. 1926–present)

Contacts with the outside world during the late nineteenth century brought an increased interest in realistic art and the use of Western themes and techniques. Trade with Europe created a demand for woodblock prints, textiles, metalwork, painted fans, screens, inlaid lacquer, and metalwork. Ideas from Europe and America replaced the isolationist policies of the Tokugawa military overlordship. The Nihonga style developed as a synthesis of East and West, old and new. Japan's contemporary art forms show this harmonious relationship in a reverence for nature and beauty. During this time, the appeal of **ukiyo-e** (or "floating world" paintings), a popular art form since the early 1500s, increased in the form of woodblock prints, many showing Kabuki actors, courtesans, and such.

■ MEXICAN ART

Four cultural groups developed in ancient Mexico and Central America: the Olmec, West Mexican, Mayan, and Aztec. The **Olmec** culture, located in the swampy lowlands along the eastern coast, has been called the "mother culture" of Mexico because of its influence on all later civilizations. The Olmec lived about three thousand years ago and are best remembered for their gigantic sculptured human heads that were used for religious ceremonies (see fig. 6.55). Sculptures of Olmec gods had both animal and human elements—for instance, half-human, half-jaguar figures.

The next oldest culture was the **West Mexican,** centered in Colima. West Mexicans made small clay sculptures of dogs, called effigies, that were believed to have special powers in serving the dead.

Another group, the **Mayas,** began to dominate the region called Teotihuacan in the central highlands north of today's Mexico City. They flourished from 300 B.C. to A.D. 800, which is approximately the same period as the Han and T'ang dynasties in China. Mayan nature worship centered around Tlaloc, god of rain, and Quetzalcoatl, a feathered serpent. The Mayas built enormous, complex pyramids for their rituals.

Figure 6.55   Olmec head.
Museo de Antropolgia, Universidad Veracruzana, Jalapa Region, Vera Cruz, Mexico.

By A.D. 800, the great Mayan culture covered the Yucatan peninsula and areas in present-day Belize, Guatemala, and Honduras. The Mayas built cities with huge temples and pyramids, some of them 175 feet high. They were advanced in both architecture and mathematics, having the most accurate calendar of any culture anywhere. Their shamans governed and also were mediums between the natural and spiritual worlds. The ancient Mayan city of Tikal, which occupied 50 square miles, was discovered in the late nineteenth century. Archaeologists believe that about fifty-five thousand people lived there. The relief carvings on monuments and buildings were complex and geometric, depicting human, animal, and plant forms.

The warlike and religious **Aztec** civilization represents the largest culture of ancient Mexico and Central America. Emerging between A.D. 1200 and 1325, the Aztec people followed the command of their god to leave their settled homes and begin anew wherever they saw an eagle perched on a cactus. And so they founded Tenochtitlan in 1325 on a swampy island that became the center of their great empire that spread over central and southern Mexico. This was the 25-square-mile city that Cortez and his Spanish soldiers conquered in 1519, what is today Mexico City. Enormous sculptures were carved for ceremonies for the sixteen

hundred gods and goddesses in the Aztec religion. The Aztecs practiced human sacrifice because they believed that their sun god had died to create man and required repayment with human blood. Their intricately designed calendar stones, some 12 feet in diameter and weighing up to 24 tons, depicted signs for the twenty days of the Aztec months.

Mask-making is highly developed in Mexico because masks have been used in rituals and ceremonies to "transform" the wearer into a particular god and to give him or her the power of the animal or god that the mask symbolizes. In ancient Mexico, warriors wore masks depicting fierce jaguars and birds of prey to frighten their enemies. The earliest masks were made of clay, stone, and wood, and were decorated with gold, turquoise, jade, and other precious materials. The tradition of mask-making continues in Mexico today and shows a blending of Christian symbols with ancient ones. Often, mask-making skills are passed within families from one generation to the next. Masks combine creativity and imagination with traditional symbolism. Some masks combine two faces. Though wood is a popular mask-making material, many other materials are also used.

Following the Mexican Revolution of 1910, the Minister of Education implemented the idea of using murals as a way to teach the history of Mexico to large numbers of people who otherwise had little or no access to education. Mexico's famous muralists—Diego Rivera (see colorplate 23 in the Color Gallery), José Clemente Orozco, and David Alfaro Siqueiros—were influenced by both pre-Columbian and colonial murals and by European muralists and fresco-painting techniques. They painted large artworks designed to tell the history and proud traditions of the native people and to arouse in them feelings of pride and desires for agrarian reform.

Throughout the centuries and up to the present day, traditional arts and crafts, usually referred to as "folk art," have flourished in Mexico. Made for functional, social, personal, and religious purposes, the containers, masks, clothing, jewelry, and such have a distinct and colorful character (see fig. 4.2). Different regions tend to specialize in specific styles and media. Paintings, prints, and posters from contemporary artists are rich in variety and form, and tell us much about the political and social lives, customs, religions, and values of Mexico's peoples.

Mexico's most famous woman artist is **Frida Kahlo** (1910–1954). Her many strongly autobiographical self-portraits reflect the lifelong pain that she suffered after a bus accident when she was fifteen. These portraits are frontal poses and often surrealistic. Kahlo was married to Diego Rivera.

Today, Chicano artists, especially in California and Chicago, continue the tradition of creating large, boldly expressive murals. (*Chicano* refers to first-generation persons born in the United States of Mexican heritage.) In the

Figure 6.56   Frog mask, Oaxaca, Mexico,
Collection of the authors.

spread out over the continental United States. *Tradition* is the manner in which a group of people views and uses its past, a past that has been passed on in oral accounts and visual images. Tradition, then, becomes those things that members of the culture both remember and emphasize. Some traditions may include elements of the past that are chosen to meet the needs of the present, needs such as identity, security, or well-being. This definition of tradition implies that change is an integral part of the cultural group and influences how the group adapts to its surroundings.

Before the arrival of European settlers, more than three hundred tribes lived in what is now the United States and Canada, but they kept no written records. Diversity among the tribes was great, with many different languages being spoken. Although the cultures varied greatly from each other, they had many things in common. Two were a reverence for nature and the belief in many supernatural beings governing all aspects of life. Native-Americans have always revered the forces of nature. They hunted, fished, gathered food, or farmed, so they needed the full cooperation of nature to survive. Rain and rich soil ensured good crops. Plenty of fish, deer, or buffalo provided sufficient food and skins for clothing and shelter. A drought or other natural disaster could mean starvation. Another commonality of Native Americans is that their art was and is practical as well as aesthetic. It includes everyday functional and utilitarian objects, as well as those created for religious or ceremonial purposes.

Native Americans have created many beautiful objects from local natural materials, such as wood, animal skins, bones, grasses, seashells, and clay. They decorate these objects with different designs and symbols that have special meaning for their particular tribes. The artworks of Native Americans provide visual information about tribe beliefs, customs, rituals, and way of life. The various art forms and craft objects that Native Americans make are as diverse as the tribes. Native American art is usually grouped in the following cultural/geographic categories: the Eastern Woodlands, the Southwest, the Eskimos, the Plains, the Pacific Northwest, and California.

The **Eastern Woodlands** comprises a large geographical region wherein dwelled hunters, fishermen, farmers, and fighters. Some tribes were nomadic. The Iroquois, in particular, were fascinating, being a confederated nation of six tribes that formed the largest cultural group of Native Americans. One of the interesting aspects of Iroquois religious practice was the False Face Society. Believing that spirits cause sickness, the Iroquois sought to overcome these evildoers through dance rituals involving various carved masks. The twisted and distorted features in these masks were meant to frighten away the evil spirits. In addition to these masks, which were carved directly from tree trunks, the Iroquois also braided masks from corn husks.

Trees also gave the tribes shafts for spears and arrows, and bark for house walls, boxes, trays, canoes, cradle

United States today, artists **Gilbert S. Lujan** (nicknamed "Magu"), **Carmen Lomas Garza,** and many others are making cultural connections in their art production of traditional Mexican folk art—**retablos, santos, carretas, diablito figures,** and **papel picado.**

Posters were very important during the early consciousness-raising period of the Chicano art movement. Just as Chicano murals served to give pride to Chicano people, who previously had no idea of the indigenous civilization to which they were connected as offspring of Mexican parents, the Chicano posters announced rallies and meetings that dealt with Chicano issues and cultural events. Like the muralists, the poster artists had Mexican antecedents who had used inexpensive means to make multiple images available to large numbers of people. Chief among the Mexican graphic artists who influenced Chicano poster art was **José Guadelupe Posada.** Well-known contemporary poster artists working in the United States today are **Rupert Garcia** and **Malaquias Montoya.**

■ TRIBAL ART OF THE UNITED STATES AND CANADA

Tribal art of the United States and Canada includes the traditions, language, and art of hundreds of different groups

Figure 6.57   Hand-coiled Southwestern Pueblo terra-cotta pot shows bird and flower motif.
Collection of the authors.

boards, snowshoes, and toboggans. Clothing of caribou, moose, and hare hides was decorated with moose-hair and porcupine-quill embroidery. Sometimes, the tribes also painted straight and curved lines on clothing. Other notable art objects from this region include the beadwork of the Huron and Ojibways and the quilled birchbark of the Micmac.

Twenty to thirty thousand years ago, early peoples are believed to have crossed the Bering Sea and settled in the **Southwest.** They learned to use the abundant clay to fashion beautiful coiled pots about A.D. 400 through trade with Mexico (see fig. 6.57). They hunted and farmed and left rock paintings (pictographs) and carvings (petroglyphs) that they believed would help them capture an animal's spirit. In the Southwest, pueblos were functional and innovative and were the first apartment houses. They were several stories high and made of adobe bricks to help keep out the cold of winter and the heat of summer. The Pueblo people were peaceful farmers and fought only when the Apache and Navajo attacked.

The tribes in the Southwest used a variety of dance masks. The Hopi people made small, carved wooden figures called kachinas to represent hundreds of different kachina spirits—supernatural beings that oversee religious and social activities. The kachinas were used to teach the children about the different spirits. The Navajos developed sand paintings for religious ceremonies, and many of the designs were secret; only the artist and the medicine man were allowed to see them. Later on, after the Spaniards had

introduced sheep, the Navajos borrowed weaving techniques from the Pueblos and began to create rugs, which were traded to white settlers and tourists (see fig. 3.14). The Navajos are also well known for fashioning silver and turquoise jewelry, another skill learned from the early Spaniards.

For thousands of years, the **Eskimos** of Canada and Alaska have survived their cruel environment. Recently, they have become especially well known for their prints and for their carvings from bone, ivory, and stone of the birds and animals native to the northlands. Before the Eskimos began to sell their products, their artwork was used mostly to decorate tools and other objects, such as harpoon heads, knives, needle cases, goggles, wooden bowls, and such. Wooden masks were made for religious ceremonies and represented spirits of both animals and people (see fig. 6.58). In general, masks that realistically showed humans or animals were worn during secular dances, whereas the more abstract and stylized masks had religious significance. Masks were based on visions seen by shamans, but often were fashioned by carvers working under the direction of the medicine man. Only the shaman who had seen the vision knew the mask's precise meaning, but others had a general idea of its significance, since each mask represented the spirit of the creature it depicted.

Lack of trees made it necessary for Eskimos to use driftwood or, more recently, lumber purchased at a trading post to build kayaks. A kayak may have no piece of wood more than 1 foot long in its framework. Animal bones were sometimes used in place of wood in the kayaks. The rest of the world has imitated the design of Eskimo kayaks. This has also been the case with Eskimo clothing, such as the fur parka, which is both functional and attractive.

The nomadic **Plains Indians,** made up of such tribes as the Arapaho, Cheyenne, Comanche, Crow, and Sioux, roamed from the Mississippi River to the Rocky Mountains. After obtaining horses and rifles from European explorers, they became excellent buffalo hunters. Today, many Americans live in a "throwaway" society in which many items go to waste, but the Plains people were more environmentally sound. The buffalo was used for food, shelter, moccasins, leggings, tepees, clothing, and shields. Designs painted on shields were believed to have magical powers and were the real means of protection. Buffalo hides were used as robes, which husbands and wives made together. The painting of these hides was a major development among Native Americans. The men painted the figures of warriors and horses, since only those who participated in these activities were allowed to paint representations of them. The women worked with nonrepresentational, geometric shapes. They also made items for personal adornment, such as head gear and necklaces, using feathers, hair, bones, horns, and claws. The Plains Indians are also known for their cradle boards, which they used to carry their young.

Figure 6.58   Eskimo Kuskokwim River mask, Alaska. Wood, ht. 36½ in. The mask represents Negakfok, the Cold Weather Spirit.
Courtesy of The National Museum of the American Indian/Smithsonian Institution (#29613).

Another outstanding craft of the Plains Indians was quill embroidery, which is done nowhere else in the world. Porcupine quills take dyes well. They are softened with water and then flattened, and have a smooth, glossy surface somewhat like straw. Abstract and floral patterns prevail. Beadwork began on the Plains about 1800, but only after very small beads became available about 1850 did the craft progress rapidly. Pipes were carved from catlinite (named after American artist George Catlin, who sent samples east from Minnesota for testing) or pipestone and used for many

purposes, some in ceremonies or private rites but many for pleasure alone.

Northwest Coast tribes, such as the Haida, Kwakitl, and Tlingit, lived along the Pacific coast from California to Alaska. Although they farmed, hunted, and gathered food, they mainly depended on ocean salmon for food. They used cedar planks to build gable-roofed houses. Wood was abundant and was used for canoes, which were needed for fishing and for travel. The clan's totems, or supernatural animal beings, were carved and often painted with stylized designs on tall totem poles that stood in front of homes as a sign of prestige. These totems were the center of the culture (see fig. 6.59). People also entered houses through totem poles, especially on ceremonial occasions. A doorway for this purpose was carved in the base of the pole. These skilled carvers also decorated their canoes and made rattles, dishes, and masks, using stylized designs of figures and animals. Masks worn in the Northwest Coast tribes were believed to transform the wearer into chief of the undersea world. Religious rituals centered around the supernatural beings governing the sea and its inhabitants.

Handsome blankets were woven for the chiefs of a subtribe of Tlingit Indians called Chilkats. Male artists provided the designs, and the women did the actual weaving, using mountain goat wool and shredded cedar bark. Designs were based on family crests, inherited through the family clans.

The **California Indians** produced some of the finest and most beautiful baskets in the world. They used three basic methods: plaiting, twining, and coiling. Tribes in northern California used twining; these baskets were flexible and decorated with an overlay of fern stems and yellow bear grass. Central California tribes used both twining and coiling. Southern tribes used fine coiling with bundles of grass for fibers, lashed with rushes, grass, or wood splints. Indian women competed to see who could make the smallest basket; examples of these must be viewed with a magnifying glass! Chumash Indians of the Santa Barbara area produced sturdy canoes and created stone vessels, including large, thin-walled pots, and mortars with pestles and dippers. Their shell work included beads and pendants, often decorated with inlay, and finely carved bowls made from abalone.

In the 1880s, legislation known as the Indian Act was passed. It was based on the assumption that Native Americans were morally and culturally inferior to white people. Native Americans were required to register with government agencies, which then limited where Native Americans could live and work. Children were sent away to special schools, where they were forbidden to use their Native American language and customs. By the time they finished school, they found it difficult to fit into either Native American or white society. Certain Native American customs,

Figure 6.59   Totem pole, Haida, British Columbia.
Museum of Anthropology no. A50034, The University of British Columbia, Vancouver, Canada.

such as the Northwest potlatch ceremonies, were outlawed. Some groups held them secretly but risked imprisonment if caught. By the time these laws were repealed in 1951, Native American culture and identity had been seriously damaged. Today, many Native American artists are working to keep their history and traditions alive.

Traditional designs and motifs seen on Native American craft objects depict animals, figures, plants, and geometric shapes in a symbolic, stylized manner. Many Native Americans today, however, have chosen to take a new direction in their paintings and are using realistic styles in their portraits and landscapes, incorporating and infusing traditional symbols and themes from their rich cultural heritage.

Native Americans in the United States were introduced to poster and oil paints at the Indian Schools that the federal government established to train them to produce sellable art. As late as the 1970s, the Indian School in Santa Fe, New Mexico, stressed painting as an art form, in addition to pottery, sculpture, jewelry making, and weaving. One of the leading teachers there, Fritz Scholder, inspired many successful contemporary Native American painters.

Figure 6.60   Gina Gray, *Plains Warrior*, 1991, Pawhuska, Okla. 17 × 22 in.
From the collection of the artist.

■ INTERACTIVE EXTENSIONS REGARDING WESTERN ART

1. On a long piece of paper, make a chronological time line of important periods of Western art, leading artists/artworks, characteristics of the period/style, and concurrent events in science, math, music, drama, politics, and literature.
2. Study your art history time line from activity 1, and reflect on how art affected or was affected by the events of its time.
3. How did World War II affect art in the United States? Research and report on the major influences on art and the leading artists at this time.
4. From your time line in activity 1, select two periods and report on who supported the artists and how artworks reflect that sponsorship. Illustrate your report with slides or Xerox copies of artworks.
5. After researching the life and works of a particular artist, pretend to be that artist, and write a letter to a young relative, inviting her or him to spend a week with you. Tell your relative about the kind of artworks you do, how you do them, and why you think he or she would enjoy getting acquainted with you.
6. Because you are a famous artist, you are to be interviewed on the "Today" show, where you will discuss three or four of your artworks. Choose another student to serve as the interviewer, and supply this person with appropriate questions so that you can respond in a manner that will help the audience understand your work. In impersonating the artist, you can wear an appropriate costume and use props.
7. Find a quotation by an artist in a reference book. Use the quotation to make a small poster. Use calligraphy and illustrations in the manner of that artist. Design a border, and make an illuminated initial to begin the quotation.
8. Make a painting or drawing in the manner of one of the artists in the Color Gallery. However, choose subject matter that the artist never tried. For instance, paint a penguin in the manner of Picasso. Paint a butterfly the way Renoir might have painted it.
9. Make a crossword puzzle about one of the artists and his or her artwork in the Color Gallery.
10. Select an artwork with two or three large figures. Use the grid system to enlarge it on a large, heavy piece of foam board. Paint it with tempera. Then cut out the face areas, and let students peek through the openings to have their pictures taken
11. Write a front page for a newspaper that might have appeared in the lifetime of an artist or of several artists who lived at the same period of time. Record news about the artists, as well as events that were happening at that time.
12. Make a book in which you write questions and answers about a particular artist, a poem you wrote about the artist, a short biography, and so on. Include postcard reproductions of the artist's works.
13. You and another student are artists visiting a Parisian cafe. Agree and disagree on your choices of subject matter and themes, your styles of art, your differences in techniques and paint application. Compare your working habits, childhood experiences, different personalities. Consider when and where you each lived and how this affected your work. Show three or four of your paintings that are typical of your oeuvre. Use them to tell what you were attempting to do and whether or not you feel you accomplished it. Why do you think you will be famous in one hundred years?

■ INTERACTIVE EXTENSIONS REGARDING NON-WESTERN ART

1. Visit a natural history, anthropology, or art museum that has art objects from tribal and world cultures. Compare objects made from wood, clay, or fiber from two diverse groups. Or compare containers, clothing, body ornaments, masks, sculptures, paintings, and so on from two or more different groups. Think about why the objects were made, the construction techniques, the decorative effects, and the symbolism used.
2. In a museum or in library books, find two pieces of ceremonial art, and report on their cultural contexts. Tell about the values, ideas, expressive content, and symbolism that the objects transmit to the viewer. Find out when objects were made and if such objects are still being made and used by that cultural group.
3. In library books, find and make copies of four different objects from four different cultures that depict the human form (or animal forms), and compare differences and similarities, if any, from one culture to another. Is one more abstract? Does one show distortion, exaggeration of body parts or features? Does one show an extensive use of pattern and decorative elements? Do any show action? Which ones show a figure engaged in specific activities?
4. Attend a different culture's local festival or religious ceremony. Observe what art objects are important parts of the ritual. What symbolism is contained within the art objects? Are music and dance used, and if so, how are they integrated in the ceremony? How long has this particular festival or ceremony taken place? Has it been modified since it was brought to America from its original venue?
5. In library books, compare the shapes and forms used by African mask makers with the shapes and forms in temple carvings in India.

6. Find a picture of an art object from another culture, and tell why you think a museum should purchase it and make it available to future generations.

7. As early as A.D. 770, Japanese artists were making woodblock prints. Look in art books to find how other countries have used woodblock prints. Discover other ways of making prints in other cultures.

8. Find pictures of Greek temples and/or temples in Mexico or India. How are they different?

9. Find pictures of Spanish architecture, and note how it is indebted to Moorish art.

10. Find an example from the Book of Kells, and compare its calligraphy and illustrations with Islamic manuscripts.

11. Demonstrate an art form from another culture, and explain it in its appropriate context. For example, demonstrate how to make a Japanese dry garden, using a tray filled with fine sand, several small rocks, and a comb for raking patterns in the sand. Explain the cultural content and context of dry gardens.

12. Select a book that contains photographs of artworks from a culture with which you are unfamiliar. Choose one picture, and without reading any of the text, write a paragraph in which you endeavor to describe and interpret what you see. Then read to discover how and why the object was created, how it was used, and what symbolism is seen in it. Finally, write another paragraph about what you see and feel about the work.

13. Research and make a time line of the traditional arts of one of the following: China, Japan, India, Africa, or Native Americans.

14. Research and report on world cultures and how their religious beliefs influenced their visual images. How are some of the changes reflected in religious architecture? Explain.

15. Compare and contrast Mayan and Aztec pyramids, religions, calendars, and writing systems.

16. Compare and contrast Mexican, Chinese, and Japanese pottery, dolls, and costumes.

Pronunciation Guide

Angelico, Fra—An JAY lee koh, Frah
Anguissola, Sofanisba—Ahn GWEES so la, So fah NISS bah

Balla, Giacomo—BAHL la, JAH koh moh
Barlach, Ernst, BAHR lahk, Airnst
Bellini, Giovanni—Bel LEE nee, Joh VAH nee
Bierstadt, Albert—BEER tstaht, AL bert
Boccioni, Umberto—Boh CHO nee, Oom BER toh
Bonheur, Rosa—Bahn uhr, ROS ah
Bonnard, Pierre—Bo NAHR, Pee EHR
Bosch, Hieronymus—BOSH, Heer AHN ni mus
Botticelli, Sandro—Bot ti CHEL lee, SAN droh
Boucher, François—Boo SHAY, Fran SWAH
Boudin, Eugene—Boo DINH, Uh ZHEN
Brancusi, Constantin—BRAHN koo see, KAHN stuhn teen
Braque, Georges—BRAHK, Zhorzh
Brueghel, Pieter—BROY gel, Peter
Brunelleschi, Filippo—Brew nell LESS kay, Fee LIP po

Canaletto—Kah nah LET toh
Caravaggio, Michelangelo—Kah rah VA joh, Mee kel AHN jay lo
Carriera, Rosalba—Car ree AYE rah, Rose AHL bah
Cassatt, Mary—Cah SAT
Cézanne, Paul—Say ZAHN
Chagall, Marc—Shah GAHL
Chardin, Jean-Baptiste—Shar DAN, Zhahn Bap TEEST
Cimabue—Tshee ma BOO aye
Copley, John Singleton—COP lee
Corot, Jean—Caw ROH, Zhahn
Courbet, Gustave—Koor BAY, Goos TAHV
Cranach, Lucas—KRAN uck

Dali, Salvador—DAH lee, SAHL van dore
Daumier, Honoré—Dohm YAY, Oh noh RAY
David, Jacques-Louis—Dah VEED, Zhahk Loo EE
de Chirico, Giorgio—de KEY ree co, JOHR jyo
Degas, Edgar—Duh GAH, ed GAHR
de Hooch, Pieter—dee HOKE, Peter
de Kooning, Willem—duh KOE ning, VILL em

Delacroix, Eugène—Duh lah KWAH, Uh ZHEN
De La Tour, Georges—Duh lah TOOR, Zhorzh
Demuth, Charles—Duh MOOTH
Derain, André—Duh RAN, ON dray
Diebenkorn, Richard—DEE ben korn
Donatello—Dah na TELL lo
Duccio—DO tshee yo
Duchamp, Marcel—Doo SHAHM, Mahr SELL
Dufy, Raoul—Dew FEE, Rah OOL
Dürer, Albrecht—DUHR er, AL brekt

Eakins, Thomas—A kinz
El Greco—El GREH coh
Escher, M. C.—ESH uhr

Feininger, Lyonel—FINE in gurr
Fouquet, Jean—Foo KAY, Zhahn
Fragonard, Jean-Honoré—Frah goh NAHR, Zhahn Oh noh RAY
Frankenthaler, Helen—Frank en TALL er

Gauguin, Paul—Goh GINH
Gentileschi, Artemisia—Djen tee LESS kay, Ar tay ME zee a
Géricault, Théodore—ZHAY re koh, TAY oh dor
Ghiberti, Lorenzo—Ghee BAIR tee, low RENT soh
Ghirlandaio, Domenico—Geer lahn DAH yoh, Doh MAY nee koh
Giacometti, Alberto—Jah ko MET tee, Ahl BAIR toh
Giorgione, Giorgio—Johr JOY nay, Johr joh
Giotto di Bondone—JOHT toh, dee Bohn DOH nay
Gorky, Arshile—GOR kee, ARSH shul
Goya, Francisco—GAW Yuh, Fran SIS coe
Gris, Juan—GREES, Wahn
Gropius, Walter—GRO pih us, Wall tur
Grunëwald, Mathis—GREWN vahlt, MAH tis

Hals, Frans—HALLS, Frahnss
Hofmann, Hans—HOHF mahn, Hahns
Hogarth, William—HOE garth
Hokusai—Hohk SY
Holbein, Hans—HOHL bine, Hahns

181

Ingres, Jean—INH gr, Zhahn
Inness, George—IN us

Jawlensky, Alexei von—Yah VLENS key, Ah LEX

Kandinsky, Wassily—Kan DIN skee, VAH see l'yee
Kirchner, Ernst Ludwig—KEERKH ner, Airnst LOOT vik
Klee, Paul—Clay
Kokoschka, Oskar—Koh KOSH kah
Kollwitz, Käthe—KAHL wits, Kate uh

Laurencin, Marie—Loh rahn sinh
Le Corbusier—Luh Core boo zee ay
Léger, Fernand—Lay ZHAY, Fair NON
Le Nain, Antoine and Louis—Luh NINH, Ahn TWAHN, Loo EE
Leonardo da Vinci—Lay oh NAR doh da VIN chee
Leyster, Judith—LIE ster
Lichtenstein, Roy—LICK ten steen
Lipchitz, Jacques—LIP sheets, Zhahk
Lippi, Fra Filippo—LEEP pee, Frah Fill LEEP poh
Lorrain, Claude—Luh RAN Klohd

Macke, August—MACK uh
Maes, Nicolaes—MASS, NIK o lay
Magritte, René—Muh Greet Ruh NAE
Maillol, Aristide—MY yoh, AH ris teed
Manet, Edouard—Man AY, Eh doo arh
Mantegna, Andrea—Man tay nya, Ahn DRAY ah
Marin, John—MARE uhn
Marini, Marino—Mah REE nee, Mah REE noh
Marisol—Mah ree SOHL
Masaccio—Mah SAH chyo
Matisse, Henri—Mah TEES, On REE
Medici—MED uh chee
Merian, Maria Sibylla—MARE e uhn, MAH REE ah Suh BEE La
Metsys, Quentin—MET sis, Kwen ten
Michelangelo Buonarroti—My kel AHN jay loe, Bwoh nah ROE tee
Mies van der Rohe, Ludwig—MEES vahn dair ROH-eh, Loot vik
Millet, Jean-François—MEH yah, Zhahn Fran SWAH
Miró, Joan—Mee ROH, Ho AHN
Modigliani, Amedeo—Mo DEE lee ah nee, Ah meh DAY oh
Mondrian, Piet—MOHN dree ahn, PEET
Monet, Claude—MO nay, Klohd
Morisot, Berthe—Moh ree ZOH, Bairt
Munch, Edvard—MOONK ED var
Muybridge, Eadweard—MY brij, ED wurd

Nolde, Emil—NOHL duh, AY muhl

Oldenburg, Claes—OLE den berk, Clays
Orozco, José Clemente—Oh ROHS coe, Ho SAY Kleh MEN tay

Parmigianino—Par me dji ah KNEE no
Pechstein, Max—PEX stine
Peto, John Frederick—PEE toh

Picasso, Pablo—Pea CAH so, Pahb lo
Pissarro, Camille—Pee SAH roh, Ka MEE
Poussin, Nicolas—Poo SINH, NEE koh lahs

Raphael—RAHF ay el
Rauschenberg, Robert—ROW shen berg
Redon, Odilon—Ruh DAWN, Oh dee YON
Rembrandt van Rijn—REM brant van Ryne
Renoir, Pierre-Auguste—Ren WAHR, Pee EHR oh GOOST
Rivera, Diego—Ree VAY rah, Dee AY goh
Rodin, François-Auguste—Roh DAN, Frahn swah oh GOOST
Rouault, Georges—Roo Oh, Zhorzh
Rousseau, Henri—Roo SO, On REE
Rubens, Peter Paul—ROO benz
Ruysch, Rachel—RO iss, RAH shell

Saarinen, Eero—SAHR uh nen, EER oh
Sassetta—SAHS SAY tah
Schmidt-Rottluff, Karl—Shmeedt ROHT loof, Kahrl
Scholder, Fritz—SHOWL duhr
Seurat, Georges—Suh RAH, Zhorzh
Shahn, Ben—Shawn
Signac, Paul—SEEN yahk
Siqueiros, David—See key AIR ohz
Sisley, Alfred—SEES ley
Stieglitz, Alfred—STEEG lits

Tamayo, Rufino—Tah MAH yoh, Roo fee noh
Thiebaud, Wayne—TEE bo
Tintoretto, Jacopo—Teen toh RET toh, Jah KOH poh
Titian—TISH yan
Toulouse-Lautrec, Henri de—Too LOOZ Lah TREK, On REE duh

Uccello, Paolo—Oo TCHEHL loh, POH loh
Utrillo, Maurice—Oo TREE oh

van der Weyden, Rogier—van duh VIE den, ROW jay
van Dyck—van DIKE
van Eyck, Jan—van IKE, Yahn
van Gogh, Vincent—van GO
Vasari—Va SAHR ee
Vaserely, Victor—Vah zuh RAY Lee
Velázquez, Diego—Vay LAS kes, DEE AYE goh
Vermeer, Jan—ver MAIR, Yahn
Veronese, Paolo—Ver oh NEES, POH loh
Verrocchio, Andrea del—Ver ROK kyoh, Ahn DRAY ah
Vigée-Lebrun, Elizabeth—VEE zhaye lub run, Ale EE za bet
Vlaminck, Maurice de—Vlah MANK
Vuillard, Édouard—VWEE yahr, Ay Doo ARH

Warhol, Andy—WOHR hohl
Watteau, Antoine—Wah TOH, Ahn TWAN

Art Forms: Two- and Three-Dimensional

Artworks are either two-dimensional or three-dimensional. Two-dimensional objects have height and width. Three-dimensional objects have height, width, and depth.

■ TWO-DIMENSIONAL ARTWORKS

1. **Drawings** are made by moving an implement that leaves a mark across the flat surface of a material, usually paper. The following are some of the mainstream drawing media:
   a. Charcoal—available in vine, compressed, and pencil form
   b. Colored chalk—for use on paper, not chalkboards
   c. Conte crayons—available in black, brown, and sienna
   d. Ink—used with pen or brush
   e. Oil pastels—similar to crayons but softer, more opaque and more intense in color; may be blended
   f. Pastels—similar to chalk but finer and available in a wider range of colors
   g. Pens of all sizes and colors
   h. Pencils, black, from hard (H) to soft (B); colored
   i. Wax crayons

2. **Paintings** depend more on color than do drawings and usually are executed on paper or canvas. *Pigment* is a finely ground powder that is used to give color to paint. The *binder* is the liquid that holds the pigment together and causes it to stick to the painting surface. The *solvent* is the material used to thin or remove the paint. Paint media include:
   a. Acrylics—quick-drying synthetic paint that was introduced during the 1950s; applied thinly or heavily in the manner of oil paint; solvent is water.
   b. Egg tempera—pigment is mixed with egg and water and applied to gessoed wood panels; applied in layers; very durable; in use before oil paints were invented.
   c. Encaustic—pigment is mixed with melted wax; ancient technique.
   d. Fresco—done with watercolors on moist plaster walls for murals.
   e. Gouache (pronounced "gwash")—opaque watercolor.
   f. Oil paint—pigment ground into linseed oil for the binder; turpentine is the solvent; colors may be blended on palette or directly on canvas; slow to dry. (The paint tube was invented in the nineteenth century, allowing artists to take their canvases outdoors and to paint directly from nature, rather than from memory and from sketches.)
   g. Tempera—used in schools; dries quickly; opaque; inexpensive and water soluble; generally used with stiff flat or round bristle brushes.
   h. Watercolor—transparent; used with soft brushes; available in trays or tubes; binder is gum arabic.

3. **Prints** are original artworks made in multiples. The Chinese developed printmaking two thousand years ago. As early as A.D. 770, the Japanese were making woodblock prints. Prints are made on paper or fabric from the inked image of a prepared surface. An "artist's proof" is a trial print and is made first. Prints are signed at the bottom: on the right, the artist's name and date; on the left, the numerical order of each print, followed by the total number of prints made. Thus, the seventh print in an edition of twenty-four would be signed 7/24. Print techniques include:

a. Intaglio—reverse or relief prints; image is scratched or etched into the surface, and ink is forced into the grooves; excess ink on the surface is wiped away and the image transferred by applying pressure so that ink appears on the paper; etching is an example of this process.

b. Lithographs—image is applied with a greasy medium on a flat piece of limestone, aluminum, or zinc; when ink is applied, it sticks to the drawing and runs off the treated surface, enabling a print to be made of the image.

c. Relief prints—image is raised from the background, and a special printing ink (oil or water-based) is applied to raised areas; linoleum, woodblock, potato, scratch-foam, card prints, eraser prints, and even fingerprints are examples of this popular printing activity.

d. Serigraphs—silk is stretched on a frame; an image is transferred to the surface with the areas not to be printed blocked out so that the ink may be pressed through the silk onto the paper or fabric with a squeegee.

4. **Collages** are paper, fabric, photographs, string, and various found materials combined to adhere to a surface. Cubists, dadists, and a number of artists during the 1950s and 1960s were the first to make collages.

5. **Calligraphy** is "beautiful writing" that is usually accomplished with the skillful use of a chisel-tipped pen or a brush.

6. **Photography** (both black-and-white and color), **computer art, films,** and **video** are media that are the results of modern technology.

7. **Graphics** refers to designs that artists make for publication and other commercial uses, such as advertisements, logos, letterheads, brochures, wrapping paper, posters, greeting cards, and so on.

■ THREE-DIMENSIONAL ARTWORKS

1. **Sculpture** is freestanding and viewed from all sides. It may be *additive* (in which the artist adds parts as work progresses) or *subtractive* (in which the artist carves or takes parts away as work progresses). *Bas-relief* sculpture is usually mounted on a wall and is meant to be viewed from the front only. Artists work in clay, wood, stone, metal, plaster, wax, glass, plastics, and fibers. Sculpture processes include:

a. Carving—stone or wood or other materials are cut or chipped to create a solid form.

b. Modeling—clay is shaped into a form, usually over an armature.

c. Cast—a form is created; a mold made from the form is then filled with molten metal or other liquid, such as plaster or slip.

d. Assembled—different materials (wood, fabric, wire, cardboard, and so on) are collected and joined together to create a form.

2. **Crafts** are made by hand for a utilitarian function (to wear, to contain things, etc.). They include:

a. Ceramics—clay objects that are fired at a high temperature in a kiln; they may be glazed or left bisque; uses are containers, lamps, and so on.

b. Fibers—may be spun, dyed, woven, batiked, quilted, tie-dyed, printed, stitched; used for clothing, draperies, floor coverings, and so on.

c. Glass—blown by forcing air through a tube into globs of molten glass that are attached at the end of the tube; cut and formed, stained; used for containers, jewelry, lamps, windows; can also be cast.

d. Leather—dyed, imprinted, stitched, shaped; used for clothing, shoes, belts, purses.

e. Metals—pounded, welded, soldered, cast, enameled; used to form bowls and plates and flatware, belt buckles, containers, jewelry.

f. Plastic—cast, cut, adhered; used for containers, furniture, architecture.

g. Wood—carved, painted, glued, pegged; used for furniture, containers, jewelry.

3. **Product design** concerns furniture, appliances, housewares, tools, dishes, clothing, automobiles, and such that are made commercially and mass produced after a product designer working with engineers plans them.

4. **Architecture** concerns spaces where we dwell, worship or meditate, meet, learn, work, and play. Materials, site, climate, intended use, budget, and sometimes cultural tradition determine actual form. *Interiors* are designed to enhance space. *Landscape design* is an important factor. *City planning* is vital to the design and future growth of urban and suburban areas.

5. **Theater design** includes stage design, costuming, and lighting.

Resources for Art Education

Student Textbooks for Elementary Classrooms

Art in Action, Guy Hubbard; Textbooks, Grades 1–8; Harcourt, Brace and Company, 6227 Sea Harbor Dr., Orlando, FL 32821

Discover Art, Laura Chapman; Textbooks, Grades 1–6; Davis Publications, Worcester, MA 01608

Packaged Art Programs for Elementary Classrooms

Alarion Press, P.O. Box 1882, Boulder, CO 80306

Art Image, Grades 1–6, Monique Briere, Art Image Publications, P.O. Box 568, Champlain, NY 12919

Art in Action Enrichment Program, Levels I and II, Barbara Herberholz, Harcourt, Brace and Company, 6227 Sea Harbor Dr., Orlando, FL 32821

Clear: The Skills of Art, Levels I and II, Kay Alexander, 1988, Crystal Productions, Box 2159, Glenview, IL 60025

Spectra Program, Learning to Look and Create, Kay Alexander, 1988, Dale Seymour Publications, 1100 Hamilton Court, Menlo Park, CA; *Take Five: Guided Analysis of 40 Artworks,* 1989, Crystal Productions, Box 2159, Glenview, IL 60025

Reproductions of Artworks

Art in Action Enrichment Programs I & II, Harcourt Brace, Orlando, FL

Austin Reproductions, Inc., 815 Grundy Ave., Holbrook, NY 11741 (sculpture replicas)

Fine Art Distributers/Haystack Publishers, 80 Kettle Creek Rd., Weston, CT 06883

Knowledge Unlimited, Inc., P.O. Box 52, Madison, WI 53701–0052

New York Graphic Society, Ltd., P.O. Box 1469, Greenwich, CT 06482

Shorewood Reproductions, 27 Glen Rd., Sandy Hook, CT 06482

Starry Night Distributors, Inc., 19 North St., Rutland, VT 05701

Universal Color Slide Co., 1221 Main St., Suite 203, Weymouth, MA 02190

University Prints, 21 East St., Winchester, MA 01890

Museum Reproductions (catalogs available)

Metropolitan Museum of Art, Institutional Sales, Special Services Office, Middle Village, NY 11381–0001

Museum of Fine Arts, Boston, P.O. Box 244, Avon, MA 02322–0244

Museum of Modern Art, 11 West 53rd St., New York, NY 10019–5401

National Gallery of Art, Publications Service, 2000 B South Club Drive, Landover, MD 20785

Videos and Computer Software

Alarion Press, Inc., P.O. Box 1882, Boulder, CO 80306

Crizmac Art and Cultural Education Materials, 1641 N. Bentley, Tucson, AZ 85716

Crystal Productions, P.O. Box 2159, Glenview, IL 60025

Dale Seymour, P.O. Box 10888, Palo Alto, CA 94303

Forest Technologies, 514 Market Loop, Suite 103, West Dundee, IL 60118

Great American Artist series (available in art supply catalogs)

Museum without Walls, video series (available in art supply catalogs)

Wilton Programs, Reading and O'Reilly, Box 541, Wilton, CT 06897

Magazines

Art Education, National Art Education Association, 1916 Association Dr., Reston, VA 22091

Arts and Activities, 591 Camino de la Reina, Suite #200, San Diego, CA 92108

Scholastic Art, Scholastic Inc., 902 Sylvan Ave., Box 2001, Englewood Cliffs, NJ 07632 (formerly *Art and Man*)

School Arts, 50 Portland St., Worcester, MA 01608

Art Supply Catalogs

Beckley Cardy, One East First St., Duluth, MN 55802 (800–227–1178)

Dick Blick, Dept. A., Box 1267, Galesburg, IL 61401

Nasco, 901 Janesville Ave., Fort Atkinson, WI 53538; also 1524 Princeton Ave., Modesto, CA 95352 (800–558–9595)

Sax Arts and Crafts, P.O. Box 51710, New Berlin, WI 53151 (800–558–6696)

Triarco Arts and Crafts, 14650 28th Ave. North, Plymouth, MN 55447

R. B. Walter, P.O. Box 920626, Norcross, GA 30092

Children's Books on Art and Artists

ABC Series by Florence C. Mayers (Costumes and Textiles, Los Angeles County Museum; Egyptian Art from the Brooklyn Museum; Museum of Fine Arts Boston; Musical Instruments from the Metropolitan Museum of Art; the Museum of Modern Art; The Alepf-Bet Book from Israel Museum, Jerusalem; A Russian ABC Featuring Masterpieces from the Hermitage).

Activities for Creating Pictures and Poetry by Janis Bunchman and Stephanie Bissell Briggs (Worcester, Mass.: Davis Publishing, 1994).

Alphabet Animals by Charles Sullivan (New York: Rizzoli Publishing, 1991).

The American Eye, Eleven Artists of the Twentieth Century by Jan Greenberg and Sandra Jordon (New York: Delacorte Press, 1995).

Animalphabet from A to Z (New York: Metropolitan Museum of Art).

Annotated Art: The World's Greatest Paintings Explored and Explained by Robert Cumming (New York: Dorling Kindersley, 1995).

The Anti-Coloring Book (series) by Susan Striker (New York: Holt, Rinehart and Winston).

Art for Children (series) by Ernest Raboff (New York: J. B. Lippincott, 1987–1988). *Marc Chagall: Leonardo da Vinci; Albrecht Dürer; Paul Gauguin; Paul Klee; Henri Matisse; Michelangelo; Pablo Picasso; Rembrandt van Rijn; Frederic Remington; Pierre-Auguste Renoir; Henri Rousseau; Henri de Toulouse-Lautrec; (New York: J. B. Lippincott, 1987–1988). Vincent van Gogh; Diego de Silva y Velazquez.*

Art for Children (series) by various authors (New York: Chelsea House, 1994). *Brueghel: The Story of a Clown and a Jug; Chagall; My Sad and Joyous Village; Da Vinci: The Painter Who Spoke with Birds; Degas: The Painted Gesture; Good Day, Mister Gauguin; The Impressionists; Matisse; The Essential Painter; Miró: Earth and Sky; Picasso: A Day in His Studio; The Renaissance; Rousseau: Still Voyages; van Gogh: The Touch of Yellow.*

Art Concept Books (series) by Sharon Lerner (Minneapolis: Lerner, 1974). *Square Is a Shape; Orange Is a Color; Straight Is a Line.*

An Artist Grows Up in Mexico by Leah Brenner (Albuquerque, N.M.: University of New Mexico Press, 1987).

Artistic Trickery, the Tradition of Trompe L'Oeil Art by Michael Capek (Minneapolis: Lerner, 1995).

Artist in Overalls: The Life of Grant Wood by John Duggleby (San Francisco: Chronicle Books, 1994).

Artists by Susan and John Edeen (Palo Alto, Calif.: Dale Seymour Publications, 1988).

The Art Lesson by Tomie de Paola (New York: Putnam and Grosset Book Group, 1989).

The Art Pack by Christopher and Helen Frayling and Ron van der Meer (New York: Knopf, 1993).

Art of _____ (series) by Shirley Glubok (New York: Macmillan, 1988). Colonial America; New American Nation; Old West; Southwest Indians; Northwest Coast Indians; North American Indians; Plains Indians; Spanish in the United States and Puerto Rico; China; India; Japan; Africa; America in the Gilded Age; Photography; Ancient Peru; Ancient Rome; Etruscans; Vikings.

Behind the Scenes (series) by Andrew Pekarick (New York: Hyperion Books for Children, 1992). *Painting Behind the Scenes; Sculpture Behind the Scenes.*

Black Americans of Achievement (series), Gordon Parks, photographer (New York: Chelsea House, 1991).

The Block by Romare Bearden, poems by Langston Hughes (New York: Viking, Metropolitan Museum of Art, 1995).

A Blue Butterfly: A Story about Claude Monet (New York: Doubleday, 1995).

Bonjour, Mr. Satie by Tomie de Paola (New York: Putnam and Grosset, 1991).

Book, Eyewitness Books by Karen Brookfield (New York: Alfred A. Knopf, 1993).

Buffalo Hunt by Russell Freedman (New York: Holiday House, 1988).

Camille and the Sunflowers, a Story about van Gogh by Laurence Ankholt (New York: Barron's, 1995).

C as in Cézanne by Marie Sellier (New York: Peter Bedrick Books, 1995).

Catalphabet (New York: Metropolitan Museum of Art, 1994).

Celebrate America in Poetry and Art (Washington, D.C.: National Museum of American Art).

Celebrating America, A Collection of Poems and Images of the American Spirit, compiled by Laura Whipple, art provided by the Art Institute of Chicago (New York: Philomel Books, 1994).

Children in Art, The Story in a Picture by Robin Richmond (Nashville, Tenn.: Ideals Children's Books, 1992).

A Child's Book of Art, Great Pictures, First Words, Selected by Lucy Micklethwart (New York: Dorling Kindersley, 1993).

A Child's Book of Play in Art, Great Pictures, First Words, selected by Lucy Micklethwait (New York: Dorling Kindersley, 1996).

Color by Ruth Heller (New York: Putnam and Grosset, 1995).

The Color Box, illustrated by Giles Laroche (Boston: Little, Brown, 1992).

Color Dance by Ann Jonas (New York: Greenwillow Books, 1990).

The Color Wizard by Barbara Brenner (New York: Bantam Doubleday Dell, 1989).

Come Look with Me (series) by Gladys S. Blizzard (Charlottesville, Va.: Thomasson-Grant, 1991, 1992). *Enjoying Art with Children; Exploring Landscape Art with Children; Animals in Art.*

Computer Graphics: How It Works, What It Does by Larry Kettelkamp (New York: William Morrow, 1989).

Crocodile's Masterpiece by Max Velihuijs (New York: Farrar, Strauss and Giroux, 1992).

David Macauley (series) (New York: Doubleday). *Cathedral, the Story of Its Construction; Castles; Pyramids.*

Diego by Jeanette Winter, text by Jonah Winter (New York: Alfred A. Knopf, 1991).

Dinner at Magritte's by Michael Garland (New York: Dutton Children's Books, 1995).

Eight Hands Round, a Patchwork Alphabet by Ann W. Paul (New York: Harper Collins, 1991).

Eyewitness Art (series) by various authors (New York: Dorling Kindersley, 1994). *Looking at Paintings; Color; Gauguin; Goya; Impressionism; Manet; Monet; Perspective; Post-Impressionism; The Renaissance; van Gogh; Watercolor.*

Family Pictures, Cuadros de Familia by Carmen Lomas Garza (San Francisco: Children's Book Press, 1990).

Famous Artists (series) by Antony Mason (Hauppauge, N.Y.: Barron's, 1995). *Cézanne; Leonardo da Vinci; Matisse; Michelangelo; Miró; Monet; Picasso; van Gogh.*

Famous Children (series) by Tony Hart (Hauppauge, N.Y.: Barron's, 1993). *Toulouse-Lautrec; Picasso; Leonardo da Vinci.*

First Impressions: Introduction to Art (series) by various authors (New York: Abrams, 1993). *John James Audubon; Mary Cassatt; Marc Chagall; Leonardo da Vinci; Francisco Goya; Michelangelo; Claude Monet, Pablo Picasso; Rembrandt; Andrew Wyeth.*

First Words by Ivan Chermayeff and Jane Clark Chermayeff (New York: Harry N. Abrams, 1990).

A Fish That's a Box by M. M. Estgerman (Arlington, Va.: Great Ocean Publishers, 1991).

A Fishy Color Story: Learning about Colors by Joanne and David Wylie (Chicago: Children's Press, 1983).

A Fishy Shape Story: Learning about Shapes (Chicago: Children's Press, 1984).

Georgia O'Keeffe by Linda Lowery (Minneapolis: Carolrhoda Books, 1996).

Getting to Know the World's Greatest Artists (series) by Mike Venezia. (Chicago: Children's Press, 1990). *Botticelli; Brueghel; Mary Cassatt; Dali; da Vinci; Gauguin; Goya; Edward Hopper; Picasso; Paul Klee; Michelangelo; Monet; Rembrandt; van Gogh.*

The Girl with a Watering Can by Ewa Zadrzynska (New York: Chameleon Books, 1989).

Go In and Out the Window, An Illustrated Songbook for Young People by Claude Marks, music edited by Dan Fox (New York: Henry Holt, in association with the Metropolitan Museum of Art, 1987).

Grandma Moses, Painter of Rural America by Zibby Oneal (New York: Puffin Book, 1986).

Great Painters by Piero Ventura (New York: G. P. Putnam's Sons, 1987).

Hailstones and Halibut Bones by Mary O'Neill (New York: Doubleday, 1989).

Harriet and the Promised Land by Jacob Lawrence (New York: Simon and Schuster, 1993).

Hispanics of Achievement (series) by various authors (New York: Chelsea House). *Diego Rivera; Salvador Dali; Frida Kahlo.*

History of Women Artists for Children by Vivian Epstein (Denver, Colo.: VSE Publishers, 1987).

Houses and Homes by Ann Morris, photos by Ken Heyman (New York: Greenwillow Books, 1992).

How the Animals Got Their Colors by Michael Rosen, illustrated by John Clementson (New York: Harcourt Brace Jovanovich, 1992).

How Artists See (series) by Colleen Carroll (New York: Abbeville Kids). *Animals; People; Weather; Elements; Land; Buildings; Universe.*

How to Draw and Paint People by Angela Gair (Secacus, N.J.: Wellfleet Press, 1991).

How to Show Grown-Ups the Museum by Philip Yenawine (New York: Museum of Modern Art, 1985).

I, Juan de Pareja by Elizabeth Borton de Trevino (Toronto, Canada: Farrar, Straus and Giroux, 1987).

I Know That Building: Discovering Architecture with Activities and Games by Jane D'Alelio (Washington, D.C.: Preservation Press, 1989).

I Live in Music, poem by Ntozake Shange, paintings by Romare Bearden (Welcome Book distributed by Stewart, Tabori and Chang, 1993).

An Illustrated Treasury of Songs, Traditional American Songs, Ballads, Folk Songs, and Nursery Rhymes (New York: Rizzoli, in association with the National Gallery of Art, 1991).

Imaginary Gardens: American Poetry and Art for Young People by Charles Sullivan (New York: Henry N. Abrams, 1989).

Inside the Museum, A Children's Guide to the Metropolitan Museum of Art by Jay Richardson (New York: Abrams, 1993).

Inspirations: Stories about Women Artists by Leslie Sills (Niles, Ill.: Albert Whiteman, 1989).

Introducing the Artist (series) by various authors (Boston: Little, Brown). *Rembrandt; Michelangelo; Picasso.*

I Spy: An Alphabet in Art by Lucy Micklethwait (New York: Greenwillow Books, 1992).

Jacob Lawrence, American Scenes, American Struggles by Nancy Shroyer Howard (Worcester, Mass.: Davis, 1996).

The Joke's on George by Michael O. Tunnell (New York: Tambourine Books, 1993).

The Journey of Diego Rivera by Ernest Goldstein (Minneapolis: Lerner, 1996).

Katie's Picture Show by James Mayhew (New York: Bantam Books, 1989).

Leonardo da Vinci by A. and M. Provensen (New York: Viking Press, 1984).

Leonardo da Vinci by Ibi Lepscky (Woodbury, N.Y.: Barron's Educational Series, 1984).

Lerner (series) by Sharon Lerner (Minneapolis: Lerner, 1970). *The Self-Portrait in Art; Kings and Queens in Art; The Warrior in Art; Farms and Farmers in Art; Portraits in Art; Circus and Fairs in Art.*

Let's Go to the Art Museum by Virginia K. Levy (Pompano Beach, Fla.: Veejay, 1983).

Li'l Sis and Uncle Willie by Gwen Everett (New York: Rizzoli, 1992).

Linnea in Monet's Garden by Christina Bjork, illustrated by Lena Anderson (New York: R & S Books, 1985).

Little Mouse's Painting by Dianne Wolkstein, illustrated by Maryjane Begin (New York: William Morrow, 1992).

Lives of the Artists: Masterpieces, Messes (and What the Neighbors Thought) by Kathleen Krull (New York: Harcourt Brace, 1995).

Look Alive: Behind the Scenes of an Animated Film by Elaine Scott (New York: William Morrow, 1992).

Looking at Paintings by Frances Kennet and Terry Measham (New York: Van Nostrand Reinhold, 1979).

Looking at Paintings (series) by Peggy Roalf (New York: Hyperion Books for Children, 1992). *Cats; Children; Circus; Dancers; Families; Flowers; Horses; Landscapes; Seascapes; Self-Portraits.*

Looking for Vincent by Thea Dubelaar and Ruud Bruijn (New York: Checkerboard Press, 1992).

Marc Chagall, Painter of Dreams by Natalie S. Bober (Philadelphia and New York: Jewish Publication Society, 1991).

Margaret Bourke-White, Photographer by Carolyn Daffron (New York: Chelsea House, 1988).

Matisse from A to Z by Marie Sellier (New York: Peter Bedrick Books, 1995).

Meet Edgar Degas by Anne Newlands (Toronto, Canada: Kids Can Press, 1988).

Meet Matisse from Nelly Munthe (Boston: Little, Brown, 1983).

The Metropolitan Museum of Art Activity Book by Osa Brown (New York: Harry N. Abrams, 1990).

Michelangelo's World by Piero Ventura (Kirkwood, N.Y.: Putnam Publishing, 1989).

Miró for Children by Helene Lamarche (Montreal, Canada: Montreal Museum of Fine Arts, 1986).

Mommy, It's a Renoir! by Aline D. Wolf (Altoona, Pa.: Parent Child Press, 1984).

Mona Lisa: The Secret of the Smile by Letizia Galli (New York: Doubleday, 1996).

Mouse Paint by Ellen Stoll Walsh (New York: Harcourt Brace Jovanovich, 1992).

Move Over, Picasso! A Young Painter's Primer by Ruth Aukerman (New Windsor, Md.: Pat Depke Books, in association with the National Gallery of Art, Washington, D.C., 1994).

Murals—Cave, Cathedral, to Street by Michael Capek (Minneapolis: Lerner, 1995).

My Journey through Art: Create Your Own Masterpieces by Kathryn Cave (Hauppauge, N.Y.: Barron's, in association with the National Gallery of Art, Washington, D.C., 1994).

National Gallery of Art Activity Book, 25 Adventures with Art by Maura A. Clarkin (New York: Harry N. Abrams, in association with the National Gallery of Art, 1994).

N. C. Wyeth's Pilgrims by Robert San Souci (New York: Harry N. Abrams, 1992).

Numbers at Play: A Counting Book by Charles Sullivan (New York: Rizzoli International Publications, 1992).

Optical Illusions in Art or—Discover How Paintings Aren't Always What They Seem To Be by Alexander Sturgis (New York: Sterling, 1995).

Pablo Picasso by Ibi Lepscky, translated by H. R. MacLean (Woodbury, N.Y.: Barron's, 1984).

The Painter's Eye, Learning to Look at Contemporary American Art by Jan Greenberg and Sandra Jordan (New York: Delacorte Press, 1991).

Painting: Great Lives by Shirley Glubok (New York: Charles Scribner's Sons, 1994).

The Patchwork Quilt by Valerie Flournoy (New York: Dial Books for Young Readers, 1985).

The Peaceable Kingdom by E. Zadrzynska (New York: M. M. Art Books, 1995).

Picture This: A First Introduction to Paintings by Felicity Woolf (New York: Doubleday, 1989).

Picture This Century, An Introduction to Twentieth-Century Art by Felicity Woolf (New York: Bantam Doubleday Dell, 1993).

Pish, Posh, Said Hieronymus Bosch by Nancy Willard (New York: Harcourt Brace Jovanovich, 1992).

Portraits of Women Artists for Children (series) by Robyn Montana Turner (Boston: Little, Brown, 1991). *Georgia O'Keeffe; Rosa Bonheur; Mary Cassatt; Frida Kahlo; Faith Ringgold; Dorothea Lange.*

A Potter by Douglas Florian (New York: William Morrow, 1991).

The Princess and the Painter by Jane Johnson (New York: Farrar, Strauss and Giroux, 1995).

The Private World of Tasha Tudor by Tasha Tudor (Boston: Little, Brown, 1992).

The Real Color Book by Barbara and Donald Herberholz (Gold River, Calif.: Barbara and Donald Herberholz, 1905 Studebaker Place, 1985).

Rembrandt's Beret by Johnny Alcorn (New York: William Morrow, 1991).

Rembrandt Takes a Walk by Mark Strand (New York: Clarkson N. Potter, 1987).

Round Buildings, Square Buildings and Buildings That Wiggle Like a Fish by Philip Isaacson (New York: Alfred Knopf, 1990).

Samplers and Samplemakers: An American Schoolgirl Art 1700–1850 by Mary Jane Edmonds (New York: Rizzoli, 1987).

The Seven Ancient Wonders of the World, a Pop-Up Book by Celia King (San Francisco: Chronicle Books, 1990).

The Shapes Game, verse by Paul Rogers, pictures by Sian Tucker (New York: Henry Holt, 1990).

Shapes, Lines, Colors, Stories (series) by Philip Yenawine (New York: Bantam Doubleday Dell, 1991).

A Short Walk around the Pyramids and through the World of Art by Philip Isaccson (New York: Alfred A. Knopf, 1993).

Smudge by Mike Dickinson (New York: Abbeville Press, 1987).

Songs of the Wild West, commentary by Alan Axelrod, arrangements by Dan Fox (New York: Metropolitan Museum of Art, 1991).

Spirals, Curves, Fanshapes and Lines by Tana Hoban (New York: Greenwillow Books, 1992).

Spot a Cat: A Child's Book of Art by Lucy Micklethwait (New York: Dorling Kindersley, 1995).

Spot a Dog: A Child's Book of Art by Lucy Micklethwait (New York: Dorling Kindersley, 1995).

Square, Triangle, Round, Skinny (four books in a box) by Eugenia and Vladimir Radunsky (New York: Henry Holt, 1993).

Starting Home, the Story of Horace Pippin, Painter by Mary E. Lyons (New York: Charles Scribner's Sons, 1993).

Take a Look, an Introduction to the Experience of Art by Rosemary Davidson (New York: Penguin Books, 1993).

Talking to the Sun: An Illustrated Anthology of Poems for Young People, compiled and edited by Pat Cummings (New York: Bradbury Press, 1992).

Talking with Artists, compiled and edited by Pat Cummings (New York: Bradbury Press, 1992).

Tar Beach by Faith Ringgold (New York: Crown, 1991).

Thinking about Colors by Jessica Jenkins (New York: Dutton Children's Books, 1992).

Understanding Modern Art, an Usborne introduction by Monica Bohm-Duchen and Janet Cook (Tulsa, Okla.: EDC Publishing, 1988).

Usborne Story of Painting, Cave Painting to Modern Art by Anthea Peppin (Tulsa, Okla.: Hayes Books, 1980).

Vincent van Gogh by Sergio Bitossi, English adaption by Vincent Buranelli (New York: Silver Burdett, 1987).

Visiting the Art Museum by Laurene K. Brown and Marc Brown (New York: E. P. Dutton, 1986).

A Visit to the Art Galary by Annie Reiner (New York: Simon and Schuster, Green Tiger Press, 1991).

A Weekend with . . . (series) by various authors (New York: Skira/Rizzoli, 1991). *Degas; Leonardo da Vinci: Picasso; Rembrandt; Renoir; Rousseau; Velasquez; Homer.*

What It Feels Like to Be a Building by Forrest Wilson (Washington, D.C.: Preservation Press, 1988).

What Makes a ____ a ____ (series) by Richard Muhlberger (New York: Metropolitan Museum of Art, 1993). *Bruegel; Degas; Monet; Raphael; Rembrandt; van Gogh.*

Who Has Seen the Wind? edited by Kathryn Sky-Peck (New York: Rizzoli, with Museum of Fine Arts, Boston, 1991).

Women Artists by Susan and John Edeen (Palo Alto, Calif.: Dale Seymour Publications, 1988).

The World of Art through the Eyes of Artists (series) by Wendy and Jack Richardon (Chicago: Children's Press, 1991). *Animals; Cities; Entertainers; Families; Natural World; Water.*

Young Discovery Library (series) by Sarah Matthews (Ossining, N.Y.: Young Discovery Library, 1988–1989). *On the Banks of the Pharaoh's Nile; Cathedrals: Stone Upon Stone; Long Ago in a Castle; Living in Ancient Rome; The Story of Paper; Japan: Land of Samurai and Robots; Behind the Wall of China; and more.*

Art from Diverse Cultures

Annie and the Old One by Miska Miles, illustrated by Peter Parnall (Boston: Little, Brown, 1985).

Aztec Indians by Patricia McKissack (Chicago: Children's Press, 1985).

Chancay and the Secret of Fire by Donald Charles (Kirkwood, N.Y.: Putnam and Grosset, 1992).

Children of Promise edited by Charles Sullivan (New York: Harry N. Abrams, 1991).

Children's Atlas of Native Americans (New York: Rand McNally, 1992).

Crafts of Many Cultures by Aurelia Gomez (New York: Scholastic Professional Books, 1992).

Don't Tell Anybody But . . . There Are Anasazi in Canyon de Chelly by Michael Fillerup (Chinle, Ariz.: Navajo Curriculum Development and Production Center, 1990).

Emperor and the Nightingale (book and cassette) by Hans Christian Anderson; read by Glenn Close, music by Mark Isham (Saxonville, Mass.: Rabbit Ears Storybook Classics, 1988).

Flyaway Girl by Ann Grifalconi (Boston: Little, Brown, 1992).

The Folk Art Counting Book by Amy Watson and staff at the Abby Aldrich Rockefeller Folk Art Center (New York: Harry N. Abrams, 1992).

The Girl Who Loved Caterpillars by Jean Merrill (Kirkwood, N.Y.: Putnam and Grosset, 1992).

The Goat in the Rug by Charles L. Blood and Martin Link (New York: Four Wings Press, 1990).

Houses and Homes by Ann Morris, photos by Ken Heyman (New York: Greenwillow Books, 1992).

Indian How Book by Arthur Park (New York: Dover, 1975).

The Kids' Multicultural Art Book by Alexandra M. Terzian (Charlotte, Vt.: Williamson Publishing, 1992).

Land of the Long White Cloud: Maori Myths, Tales and Legends by Kiri Te Kanawa, illustrated by Michael Foreman (Boston: Little, Brown, 1990).

The Legend of the Indian Paintbrush by Tomie de Paola (New York: Putnam and Grosset, 1991).

Liang and the Magic Paintbrush by Demi (New York: Henry Holt, 1980).

The Magic Vase by Fiona French (New York: Oxford University Press, 1991).

Moon Rope Un Lazo a la Luna, written and illustrated by Lois Ehlert, translated into Spanish by Amy Prince (San Diego/New York: Harcourt Brace Jovanovich, 1992).

Navajo ABC, a Dine Alphabet Book by Luci Tapahonso and Eleanor Schick (New York: Simon and Schuster, 1995).

Northern Lullaby by Nancy W. Carlstrom, illustrated by Leo and Diane Dillon (New York: Philomel Books, 1992).

Pancho's Pinata by Stefan Czernecki and Timothy Rhodes (New York: Hyperion Books for Children, 1992).

Papagayo the Mischief Maker, written and illustrated by Gerald McDermott (San Diego/New York: Harcourt Brace Jovanovich, 1992).

Pyramids of Ancient Egypt, Living History Series (New York: Harcourt Brace, 1992.)

Pyramid of the Sun, Pyramid of the Moon by Leonard Fisher (New York: Macmillan, 1988).

Shadow, translated and illustrated by Marcia Brown (New York: Charles Scribner's Sons, 1991).

Shaka, King of the Zulus by Diane Stanley and Peter Vennema, illustrated by Diane Stanley (New York: Morrow Junior Books, 1988).

South, North, East and West, edited by Michael Rosen, introduction by Whoopi Goldberg (Cambridge, Mass.: Candlewick Press, 1992).

Sundiata by David Wisniewski (New York: Clarion Books, 1992).

Sunrise Island, a Story of Japan and Its Arts by C. Alden (New York: Parents' Magazine Press, 1971).

Ten Little Rabbits by Virginia Grossman and Sylvia Long (San Francisco: Chronicle Books, 1991).

Turquoise Boy, a Navajo Legend by Terri Cohlene, illustrated by Charles Reasoner (Mahwah, N.M.: Watermill Press, 1990).

When Clay Sings by Byrd Baylor, illustrated by Tom Bahti (New York: Charles Scribner's Sons, 1987).

Why the Sky Is Far Away, retold by Mary-Joan Gerson, illustrated by C. Golembe (Boston: Little, Brown, 1992).

Zomo the Rabbit, written and illustrated by Gerald McDermott (San Diego/New York: Harcourt Brace Jovanovich, 1992).

Notes and Bibliography

Introduction

1. E. D. Hirsch, *The Schools We Need* (New York: Doubleday, 1996).
2. *Quality Art Education, Goal for Schools: An Interpretation* (Reston, Va.: National Art Education Association, 1986).
3. *The Journal of Aesthetic Education* 21 (1987): 151–59.
4. Elliot W. Eisner, *The Role of Discipline-Based Art Education in America's Schools* (Los Angeles: Getty Center for Education in the Arts), 16–21.

Chapter 1

1. Gina Gray, letter to authors.
2. W. J. Strachan and Bernard Jacobson, *Henry Moore Animals* (New York: Aurum Press, 1983), 13.
3. Marie Mitchell, "Overlapping Traditions," *Crosswinds,* Native American Issue, 4(8): 15.
4. Ibid.
5. Ibid.
6. Ellen H. Johnson, ed., *American Artists on Art from 1940 to 1980* (New York: Harper and Row, 1982), 152–56.
7. Ellen Harkins Wheat, *Jacob Lawrence, American Painter* (Seattle: University of Washington Press, 1982), 41.
8. Cindy Nemser, *Art Talk* (New York: Charles Scribner's Sons, 1975), 179.
9. Diana MacKown, *Dawns and Dusks* (New York: Charles Scribner's Sons, 1976), 168.
10. Johnson, ed., *American Artists on Art from 1940 to 1980,* 90.
11. Dore Ashton and Jack Flam, *Robert Motherwell* (New York: Ashville Press, 1982), 12.
12. *Dear Theo, The Autobiography of Vincent van Gogh,* ed. Irving Stone (Garden City, N.Y.: Doubleday, 1946).
13. Mitchell, "Overlapping Traditions."
14. MacKown, *Dawns and Dusks,* 14.

Chapter 1 Recommended Further Reading

Campbell, David, ed. *Native American Art and Folklore, A Cultural Celebration.* New York/Avenel, N.J.: Crescent Books, 1993.
Grieder, Terence. *Artist and Audience.* Orlando, Fla.: Holt, Rinehart and Winston, 1990.
Hill, Rick, Nancy Marie Mitchel, and Lloyd New. *Creativity Is Our Tradition: Three Decades of Contemporary Indian Art.* Santa Fe, N.M.: Institute of American Indian and Alaskan Native Culture and Arts Development on the Campus of the College of Santa Fe, 1992.

Horowitz, Frederick A. *More Than You See: A Guide to Art.* 2d ed. Orlando, Fla.: Harcourt Brace Jovanovich, 1992.
Lippard, Lucy R. *Mixed Blessings, New Art in a Multicultural America.* New York: Pantheon Books, 1990.
Nagle, Geraldine. *The Arts—World Themes.* Dubuque, Iowa: Brown and Benchmark, 1993.
Robinson, Walter. *Instant Art History from Cave Art to Pop Art.* Columbine, N.Y.: Fawcett, 1995.
Slatkin, Wendy. *Women Artists in History from Antiquity to the 20th Century.* Englewood Cliffs, N.J.: Prentice Hall, 1990.
Steves, Rick, and Gene Openshaw. *Mona Winks, Self-Guided Tours of Europe's Top Museums,* Santa Fe, N.M.: John Muir Publications, 1988.
Steves, Rick, and Gene Openshaw. *Europe 101, History and Art for the Traveler.* 4th ed. Santa Fe, N.M.: John Muir Publications, 1990.
Strickland, Carol, and John Boswell. *The Annotated Mona Lisa: A Crash Course in Art History from Prehistoric to Post-Modern.* Kansas City: Andrews and McMeel, 1992.
Sullivan, Charles, ed. *Children of Promise, African-American Literature and Art for Young People.* New York: Harry N. Abrams, 1991.

Chapter 2

1. Gary L. Gerhart, "Motivational Techniques in the Elementary Art Class," *NAEA Advisory,* Fall 1987.
2. Tom Anderson, "Talking about Art with Children from Theory to Practice," *Art Education,* January 1986.
3. Howard Gardner, "Interview by Ron Brandt," *Educational Leadership,* December 1987/January 1988, 30–34.
4. J. Piaget, *The Construction of Reality in the Child* (New York: Basic Books, 1954).
5. Viktor Lowenfeld and Lambert Brittain, *Creative and Mental Growth,* 8th ed. (New York: Macmillan, 1987).
6. Desmond Morris, *The Illustrated Naked Ape* (New York: Crown Publishers, 1967), 93–96.
7. Ibid.
8. Ibid.
9. Constance K. Kamii and Norma I. Radin, "A Framework for a Preschool Curriculum Based on Some Piagetian Concepts," *Journal of Creative Behavior* I (1967): 314–24.
10. See Mary Sue Foster, "Art Education in Japan, a Textbook-Based Curriculum," *School Arts,* May 1990, for more information about the Japanese art program for elementary school.
11. Rob Barnes, *Teaching Art to Young Children, 4–9* (Boston: Allen and Unwin, 1987).

12. Guy Hubbard, *Art in Action,* Grade 1 (Austin, Texas: Holt, Rinehart and Winston, 1987), 62–63.
13. Laura Chapman, *Discover Art,* Grade 2 (Worcester, Mass.: Davis Publications, 1985), 86–87.
14. J. Naisbitt, *Global Paradox: The Bigger the World Economy, the More Powerful Its Smallest Players* (New York: William Morrow, 1994).
15. W. Keens, "Future Tense/Future Perfect," *Art Education* 44, no. 5 (1991): 22–25.
16. K. Freedman, "Possibilities of Interactive Computer Graphics for Art Instruction: A Summary of Research," *Art Education* 44, no. 3 (1991): 41–48.
17. S. Ambron, "New Visions of Reality: Multimedia and Education," in *Interactive Multimedia: Visions of Multimedia for Developers, Educators, and Information Providers,* eds. Sueann Ambron and Kristina Hooper (Redmond, Wash.: Microsoft Press, 1988).
18. D. C. Gregory, "Art Education Reform and Interactive Integrated Media," *Art Education* 48, no. 3 (1995): 8–17. D. Thornburg, "Campfires in Cyberspace: Primordial Metaphors for Learning in the Twenty-First Century," Keynote Address at meeting of National Art Education Association, Reston, Va., 1995. P. C. Dunn, "Interactive Technology and Art Education," *Translations from Theory to Practice* 6 (Summer 1996)l: 2. P. C. Dunn, "More Power: Integrated Interactive Technology and Art Education," *Art Education* 49, no. 6 (1996): 6–12.
19. H. Gardner, *Frames of Mind: The Theory of Multiple Intelligences* (New York: Basic Books, 1993).
20. E. McCown and A. Malnig, "Collectors Editions," *ComputerLife,* October 1995, 114–21.
21. P. C. Dunn, *The Curriculum Navigator for Art: Elementary School* (interactive computer program) (Palo Alto, Calif.: Addison Wesley/Dale Seymour Publications, 1995).

Chapter 2 Recommended Further Reading

Bartlett, Nancy Lewis. *Children's Arts and Crafts.* Worcester, Mass.: Davis Publications, 1986.
Brookes, Mona. *Drawing with Children.* Los Angeles: Jeremy P. Tarcher, 1986.
Brown, Maurice, and Diana Korzenik. *Art Making and Education, Disciplines in Art Education: Contexts of Understanding.* Urbana, Ill./Chicago: University of Illinois Press, 1993.
Chapman, Laura. *Approaches to Art Education.* New York: Harcourt Brace Jovanovich, 1978.
Clark, Gilbert A., and Enid Zimmerman. *Resources for Educating Artistically Talented Students.* Syracuse, N.Y.: Syracuse University Press, 1987.
Cornia, Ivan, Charles Stubbs, and Nathan Winters. *Art Is Elementary: Teaching Visual Thinking Through Art Concepts.* Layton, Utah: Gibbs Smith, 1983.
Cromer, Jim. *History, Theory and Practice of Art Criticism in Art Education.* Reston, Va.: National Art Education Association, 1990.
Day, Michael, and A. Hurwitz. *Children and Their Art* 6th ed. New York: Harcourt Brace Jovanovich, 1995.
Dorn, Charles M. *Thinking in Art: A Philosophical Approach to Art Education.* Reston, Va.: National Art Education Association, 1994.
Edwards, Betty. *Drawing on the Right Side of the Brain.* Boston: Houghton Mifflin, 1979.
Eisner, E. W. *Educating Artistic Vision.* New York: Macmillan, 1972.
Feldman, Edmund Burke. *Philosophy of Art Education.* Englewood Cliffs, N.J.: Prentice Hall, 1996.
Galbraith, Lynn, ed. *Preservice Art Education: Issues and Practice.* Reston, Va.: National Art Education Association, 1995.
Gardner, Howard. *Art Education and Human Development.* Los Angeles: Getty Center for Education in the Arts, 1990.
Gardner, Howard. *Artful Scribbles: The Significance of Children's Drawings.* New York: Basic Books, 1980.
Henley, David. *Exceptional Children/Exceptional Art: Teaching Art to Special Needs.* Worcester, Mass.: Davis Publications, 1992.
Herberholz, Barbara, and Lee Hanson. *Early Childhood Art.* Dubuque, Iowa: Wm. C. Brown, 1995.

Hucko, Bruce. *Where There Is No Name for Art.* Santa Fe, N.M.: Sar Press, 1996.
Hurwitz, Al. *The Gifted and Talented in Art: A Guide to Program Planning.* Worcester, Mass.: Davis Publications, 1983.
Johnson, A. *Art Education: Elementary.* Reston, Va.: National Art Education Association, 1992.
Kellog, Rhoda. *Analyzing Children's Art.* Palo Alto, Calif.: National Press Books, 1969.
Lahti, N. E. *Plain Talk About Art.* Brooklyn, N.Y.: York Books, 1989.
Lanier, Vincent. *The Visual Arts and the Elementary Child.* New York: Teachers College Press, 1983.
Lankford, F. Louis. *Aesthetics: Issues and Inquiry.* Reston, Va.: National Art Education Association, 1992.
Lansing, K. *Art, Artists, and Art Education.* New York: McGraw-Hill, 1969.
Linderman, Marlene. *Art in the Elementary School: Drawing, Painting, and Creating for the Classroom.* 4th ed. Dubuque, Iowa: Wm. C. Brown, 1990.
Lowenfeld, Viktor, and Lambert Brittain. *Creative and Mental Growth.* 8th ed. New York: Macmillan, 1987.
Parks, Michael E. *The Art Teacher's Desktop Reference.* Englewood Cliffs, N.J.: Prentice Hall, 1994.
Parsons, Michael. *How We Understand Art: A Cognitive Development Account of Aesthetic Experience.* New York: Cambridge University Press, 1987.
Qualley, Charles. *Safety in the Artroom.* Worcester, Mass.: Davis Publications, 1986.
Spandorfer, Merle, Deborah Curtiss, and Jack Snyder. *Making Art Safely.* New York: Van Nostrand Reinhold, 1992.
Szekely, G. *From Play to Art.* Portsmouth, N.H.: Heinemann Education Books, 1991.
Thompson, Christine Marme, ed. *The Visual Arts and Early Childhood Learning.* Reston, Va.: National Art Education Association, 1995.
Topal, Cathy Weisman. *Children, Clay and Sculpture.* Worcester, Mass.: Davis Publications, 1983.
Topal, Cathy Weisman. *Children and Painting.* Worcester, Mass.: Davis Publications, 1992.
Wachowiak, Frank. *Emphasis Art.* 6th ed. New York: Harper and Row, 1997.
Wilson, Brent, Al Hurwitz, and Marjorie Wilson. *Teaching Drawing from Art.* Worcester, Mass.: Davis Publications, 1987.
Young, B., ed. *Art, Culture, and Ethnicity.* Reston, Va.: National Art Education Association, 1990.

Chapter 3

1. Rudolf Arnheim, *Art and Visual Perception; A Psychology of the Creative Eye,* 2d ed. (Berkeley: University of California Press, 1974).
2. Betty Edwards, *Drawing on the Right Side of the Brain* (Los Angeles: J. P. Tarcher): Kimon Nicolades, *The Natural Way to Draw* (Boston: Houghton Mifflin, 1975).
3. Edwards, *Drawing on the Right Side of the Brain.*
4. Ibid.

Chapter 4

1. George L. Thomson, *Rubber Stamps and How to Make Them* (Edinburgh, Scotland: Canongate Publishers). Joni L. Miller and Lowry Thompson, *The Rubber Stamp Album* (New York: Workman Publishing).

Chapter 5

1. Lynn M. Hart, "Aesthestic Pluralism and Multicultural Art Education", *Studies in Art Education* 32 (Spring 1991): 3.
2. Ellen Dissanayake, *What Is Art For?* (Seattle: University of Washington Press, 1990).
3. Ibid.
4. Ibid.

5. NAEA Advisory, "Censorship and the Arts" (Adopted by the National Art Education Association Board of Directors, Motion 17, September 1991).

6. Benjamin Bloom, *Taxonomy of Educational Objectives. Handbook I: Cognitive Domain* (New York: McKay, 1956).

Chapter 5 Recommended Further Reading

Addiss, Stephen, and Mary Erickson. *Art History and Education: Disciplines in Art Education: Contexts of Understanding.* Urbana and Chicago: University of Illinois Press, 1993.

Atkins, Robert. *A Guide to Contemporary Ideas, Movements, and Buzzwords.* New York: Abbeville Press, 1990.

Barrett, Terry. *Criticizing Art: Understanding the Contemporary.* Mountain View, Calif.: Mayfield Publishing, 1994.

Battin, Margaret P., John Fisher, Ronald Moore, and Anita Silvers. *Puzzles about Art, An Aesthetics Casebook.* New York: St. Martins Press, 1989.

Chalmers, F. Graeme. *Celebrating Pluralism: Art, Education, and Cultural Diversity.* Los Angeles, Calif.: J. Paul Getty Institute for the Arts.

Clark, Kenneth. *What Is a Masterpiece?* New York: Thames and Hudson, 1979.

Cromer, Jim. *History, Theory and Practice of Art Criticism in Art Education.* Reston, Va.: National Art Education Association, 1990.

Dickie, George. *Aesthetics: An Introduction.* Indianapolis: Bobbs-Merrill, 1971.

Dickie, George, and Richard Sclafani, eds. *Aesthetics: A Critical Anthology.* New York: St. Martin's Press, 1977.

Dissanayake, Ellen. *What Is Art For?* Seattle: University of Washington Press, 1990.

Dissanayake, Ellen. *Homo Aestheticus.* New York: Free Press, 1992.

Feldman, Edmund Bruke. *Varieties of Visual Experience.* 3d ed. Englewood Cliffs, N.J.: Prentice Hall, 1987.

Finn, David. *How to Visit a Museum.* New York: Harry N. Abrams, 1985.

Frayling, Helen, and Ron Van Der Meer, *The Art Pack.* New York: Alfred A. Knopf, 1992.

Goldstein, Ernest et al. *Understanding and Creating Art.* Books 1 and 2. Dallas, Texas: Garrard, 1986.

Heller, Nancy G. *Women Artists, An Illustrated History.* Rev. ed. New York: Abbeville Press, 1987.

Horowitz, Frederick A. *More Than You See.* 2d ed. New York: Harcourt Brace Jovanovich, 1992.

Hughes, Robert. *Nothing If Not Critical.* New York: Alfred A. Knopf, 1991.

Hughes, Robert. *The Shock of the New.* New York: Alfred A. Knopf, 1981.

Hurwitz, Al, and Michael Day. *Children and Their Art: Methods for the Elementary School.* 5th ed. San Diego: Harcourt Brace Jovanovich, 1991.

John, Arthur F. *Introduction to Art.* New York: Harper Collins Publishers, 1992.

Kampf, Avram. *Chagall to Kitaj: Jewish Experience in Twentieth-Century Art.* Westport, Conn.: Praeger/Greenwood Publishing Group, 1991.

Kissick, John. *Art Context and Criticism.* 2d ed. Dubuque, Iowa: Brown and Benchmark, 1996.

Krathohl, David R., Benjamin S. Bloom, and Bertram B. Masia. "A Condensed Version of the Cognitive Domain of the Taxonomy of Educational Objectives" (Appendix B, pp. 186–93). In *Taxonomy of Educational Objectives: The Classification of Educational Goals, Handbook II: Affective Domain.* New York: David McKay, 1964.

Lankford, E. Louis. *Aesthetics: Issues and Inquiry.* Reston, Va.: National Art Education Association, 1992.

Lanier, Vincent. *The Arts We See: A Simplified Introduction to the Visual Arts.* New York: Teachers College Press, 1982.

Malino, Frederick. *Understanding Paintings: The Elements of Composition.* Englewood Cliffs, N.J.: Prentice Hall, 1980.

Maquet, Jacques, *The Aesthetic Experience: An Anthropologist Looks at the Visual Arts.* New Haven, Conn.: Yale University Press, 1986.

Mittler, Gene A. *Art in Focus.* Mission Hills, Calif.: Glencoe, 1989.

Moore, Ronald, ed. *Aesthetics for Young People.* A cooperative effort among the American Society for Aesthetics, the *Journal of Aesthetic Education,* and the National Art Education Association, 1995.

Munro, Eleanor. *Originals: American Women Artists.* New York: Simon and Schuster, 1979.

Nash, Ann Bachtel. "Teaching Aesthetic Perception in the Elementary School." *Art Education,* Sept. 1985, 6–11.

Osborne, Harold. *The Art of Appreciation.* The Appreciation of the Arts series. New York: Oxford University Press, 1970.

Parsons, Michael J. *How We Understand Art: A Cognitive Developmental Account of Aesthetic Experience.* New York: Cambridge University Press, 1987.

Parsons, Michael J., and H. Gene Blocker. *Aesthetics and Education: Disciplines in Art Education: Contexts of Understanding.* University of Urbana and Chicago: University of Illinois Press, 1993.

Perkins, David N. *The Intelligent Eye: Learning to Think by Looking at Art.* Santa Monica, Calif.: The Getty Center for Education in the Arts, 1994.

Phipps, Richard, and Richard Wink. *Invitation to the Gallery: An Introduction to Art.* Dubuque, Iowa: Wm. C. Brown, 1987.

Ragans, Rosalind. *Art Talk.* Mission Hills, Calif.: Glencoe, 1988.

Rosenberg, Harold. *Art and Other Serious Matters.* Chicago: University of Chicago Press, 1985.

Roskill, Mark. *The Interpretation of Pictures.* Amhearst, Mass.: University of Massachusetts Press, 1989.

Sewell, Darrel, Dewey Mosby, and R. A. Minter. *Henry Ossawa Tanner.* New York: Rizzoli, 1991.

Sheppard, Ann. *Aesthetics: An Introduction to the Philosophy of Art.* Oxford, England: Oxford University Press, 1987.

Sporre, Dennis J. *Perceiving the Arts: An Introduction to the Humanities.* Englewood Cliffs, N.J.: Prentice Hall, 1985.

Sproccati, Sandro, ed. *A Guide to Art.* New York: Harry N. Abrams, 1992.

Staniszewski, Mary Anne. *Believing Is Seeing: Creating the Culture of Art.* New York: Penguin Books, 1995.

Steves, Rick, and Gene Openshaw. *Europe 101.* 4th ed. Santa Fe, N.M.: John Muir, 1990.

Steves, Rick, and Gene Openshaw. *Mona Winks.* Santa Fe, N.M.: John Muir, 1988.

Waterfall, Milde, and Sarah Grusin. "Where's the Me in Museum?" In *Going to Museums with Children.* Arlington, Va.: Vandamere Press, 1989.

Weitz, Morris. "The Role of Theory in Aesthetics." In *Aesthetics and Criticism in Art Education,* edited by Ralph A. Smith. Chicago: Rand McNally, 1966.

Winner, Ellen. *Invented Worlds: The Psychology of the Arts.* Cambridge, Mass.: Harvard University Press, 1982.

Woodford, Susan. *Looking at Pictures: Cambridge Introduction to the History of Art.* Cambridge, Mass.: Cambridge University Press, 1983.

Yenawine, Philip. *How to Look at Modern Art.* New York: Harry N. Abrams, 1991.

Zucker, Paul. *Styles in Paintings, a Comparative Study.* New York: Dove Publications, 1963.

Chapter 6 Recommended Further Reading

Berlo, Janet Catherine, and Lee Ann Wilson. *Arts of Africa, Oceania, and the Americas: Selected Readings.* Englewood Cliffs, N.J.: Prentice Hall, 1993.

Biair, Sheila S., and Jonathan M. Brown. *The Art and Architecture of Islam 1250–1800.* New Haven, Conn.: Yale University Press, 1994.

Brommer, Gerald F. *Discovering Art History.* 3d ed. Worcester, Mass.: Davis Publications, 1996.

Canaday, John. *What Is Art? An Introduction to Painting, Sculpture and Architecture.* New York: Alfred A. Knopf, 1980.

Caruana, Wally. *Aboriginal Art.* World of Art. New York: Thames and Hudson, 1993.

Chadwick, Whitney. *Women, Art and Society.* 2d ed. London: Thames and Hudson, 1996.

Clark, Kenneth. *What Is a Masterpiece?* New York: Thames and Hudson, 1992.

Cooper, J. C. *An Illustrated Encyclopedia of Traditional Symbols.* New York: Thames and Hudson, 1988.

Feldman, Edmund Burke. *The Artist: A Social History* Englewood Cliffs, N.J.: Prentice Hall, 1994.

Feldman, Edmund Burke. *Varieties of Visual Experience.* 3d ed. Englewood Cliffs, N.J.: Prentice Hall, 1992.

Fichner-Rathus, Lois. *Understanding Art.* Englewood Cliffs, N.J.: Prentice Hall, 1994.

Gombrich, E. H. *The Story of Art.* 16th ed. New York: E. P. Dutton, 1995.

Hart, Fredrick. *The History of Art: Painting, Sculpture, and Architecture.* 4th ed. Englewood Cliffs, N.J.: Prentice Hall, Abrams, 1993.

Heller, Nancy G. *Women Artists, An Illustrated History.* New York: Abbeville Press, 1987.

Hobbs, Jack A. *Art in Context.* 4th ed. New York: Harcourt Brace Jovanovich, 1990.

Horowitz, Frederick. *More Than You See: A Guide to Art.* 2d ed. New York: Harcourt Brace Jovanovich College Publishing, 1992.

Janson, H. W. *History of Art for Young People.* New York: Harry N. Abrams, 1992.

Janson, H. W. *History of Art.* 5th ed. New York: Harry N. Abrams, 1995.

Jones, Arthur F. *Introduction to Art.* New York: Harper Collins, 1992.

Lamm, Robert C., and Neal Cross. *The Humanities in Western Culture.* Vols. 1 and 2. Dubuque, Iowa: Wm. C. Brown, 1992.

Lipman, Jean, and Tom Armstrong. *American Folk Painters of Three Centuries.* New York: Arch Cape Press, in association with the Whitney Museum of American Art, 1980.

McCarter, William, and Rita Gilbert. *Living with Art.* New York: Alfred A. Knopf, 1985.

Ocvirk, Otto G. et al. *Art Fundamentals: Theory and Practice.* Dubuque, Iowa: Wm. C. Brown, 1993.

Phipps, Richard, and Richard Wink. *Invitation to the Gallery: An Introduction to Art.* Dubuque, Iowa: Wm. C. Brown, 1987.

Preble, Duane, and Sarah Preble. *Artforms.* 4th ed. New York: Harper and Row, 1993.

Random House Library of Painting and Sculpture. Vols. 1–4. New York: Random House, 1981.

Richardson, John A. *Art: The Way It Is.* 4th ed. Englewood Cliffs, N.J.: Prentice Hall, 1992.

Smithsonian Institution, *National Museum of American Art.* New York: Bullfinch Press, Little Brown, 1996.

Steer, John, and Antony White. *Atlas of Western Art History: Artists, Sites, and Movements from Ancient Greece to the Modern Age.* New York: Facts on File, 1994.

Stokstad, Marilyn. *Art History.* New York: Abrams, 1995.

Strickland, Carol. *The Annotated Mona Lisa.* Kansas City: Universal Press Syndicate, 1992.

Tregear, Mary. *Chinese Art, World of Art.* New York: Oxford University Press, 1980.

Vasari, Giorgio. *The Great Masters.* New York: Park Lane, 1988.

West, Shearer. *The Bullfinch Guide to Art History.* New York: Little Brown, 1996.

Willett, Frank. *African Art: An Introduction.* Rev. ed. New York: Thames and Hudson, 1993.

Index